THE SOCIAL MUSEUM IN THE CARIBBEAN

Sidestone Press

THE SOCIAL MUSEUM IN THE CARIBBEAN

Grassroots Heritage Initiatives and Community Engagement

CSILLA E. ARIESE-VANDEMEULEBROUCKE

Published by Sidestone Press, Leiden
www.sidestone.com

Imprint: Sidestone Press Dissertations

Lay-out & cover design: Sidestone Press
Image cover: *The Social Museum in the Caribbean*, photographs by Csilla Ariese-Vandemeulebroucke and design by Krijn Boom

Printed and bound in Great Britain by
Marston Book Services Ltd, Oxfordshire

ISBN 978-90-8890-592-6 (softcover)
ISBN 978-90-8890-593-3 (hardcover)
ISBN 978-90-8890-594-0 (PDF e-book)

DOI dataset: https://doi.org/10.17026/dans-zfm-yw7s

The research leading to this dissertation received funding from the European Research Council (ERC) under the European Union's Seventh Framework Programme (FP7/2007-2013) / ERC-Synergy project NEXUS1492, grant agreement n° 319209.

The research visits to Jamaica & Grenada (2014) were sponsored by Leiden University Fund/Van Walsem.

Contents

What I find is that you can do almost anything
or go almost anywhere,
if you're not in a hurry.

Paul Theroux
The Happy Isles of Oceania

To all the scientists in my family
For paving the way

1

Introduction

We get so involved in giving voices to people of the past, that we often forget what the people of the present are saying.
Carmen A. Laguer Díaz (2013: 565)

Museums carry an old reputation of being temples of knowledge, storehouses of history. They were commonly known as institutions that are great at caring for the past and delivering educational monologues. For roughly the past half century, museums have worked diligently to reinvent themselves as institutions in the service of the present and its societies. The museum of today aims to collect history *and* contemporary, engage in dialogue rather than monologue, and encourage debate and interactive learning. Contemporary museums wish to embed themselves as dynamic actors within their present-day communities. They do so by placing communities at the heart of their missions and the core of their institutions. In the context of this world and this time, the epitome of the museum is the *social* museum.

This social museum has become the ideal or idealized image of the museum around the world. Yet, its presence is perhaps most suitable and most important in the Caribbean region, an area characterized by widespread cultural, linguistic, ethnic, political, and religious diversity. Defining the Caribbean is difficult, as many parameters can be selected as the basis for a definition. Geologically, it can be characterized as the Caribbean plate or geographically as those islands and countries which are washed by the Caribbean Sea. For this research, based on shared political and cultural ties, a broader definition of the Caribbean was relevant which stretches to include the Bahamas and Turks & Caicos Islands in the Lucayan Archipelago, as well as Belize in Central America, and Venezuela, Guyana, Suriname, and French Guiana in South America.

It is this broad, diverse, yet linked Caribbean which is the setting of this research. "Culturally diverse, the region shares a common pre- and post-colonization history, though nuanced by the peculiar local histories and geographies of the individual countries" (Cummins *et al.* 2013: 7). The individual islands and countries in the Caribbean, as well as their societies, both share commonalities and have their own particularities. While such a diversity might seem challenging to museums wishing to be strong societal actors, in fact it encourages and allows for profoundly social museums to exist in a diversity of types and models which mirror the variety of the communities they are centered around. In the context of the Caribbean, the social museum is a widespread phenomenon and a strong societal actor.

In this fragmented, extended archipelago of the Caribbean, museums are tasked not only to engage with a diversity of communities, but also with finding ways to reconcile conflicted pasts and complex presents. St. Lucian poet Derek Walcott, in his Nobel Lecture, warned fellow Antillean writers not to "make too much of that long groan which underlines the past" (Walcott 1992). Instead, he suggested to weave together layers of both past and present, while ensuring that neither overwhelms the other. His metaphor for how historians, writers, and artists can achieve this, echoes with relevance for museums:

> *Break a vase, and the love that reassembles the fragments is stronger than that love which took its symmetry for granted when it was whole. The glue that fits the pieces is the sealing of its original shape. It is such a love that reassembles our African and Asiatic fragments, the cracked heirlooms whose restoration shows its white scars.*
> Derek Walcott (1992)

It is precisely here where the social museum in the Caribbean situates itself. Museums throughout the region have, are, and will rely on grassroots heritage initiatives and community engagement to write their own reconciliations of past and present. This dissertation aims to explore both *what* museums are doing in this regard – their participatory practices – and *how* they are choosing to work – their community engagement processes.

Couched in the theoretical discourse of the New Museology, this dissertation asks how Caribbean museums are realigning their societal role in relation to contemporary Caribbean communities. The answer is approached from a macro and a micro level, presenting both a broad view of the mosaic of Caribbean museums and offering depth to this image.

The macro level assesses the participatory practices employed by Caribbean museums and is the result of visits to 195 museums throughout the region. This fieldwork consisted primarily of museum visits and discussions with staff, requiring the development of a unique mixed methodology which combines museological and anthropological techniques. By approaching the museum visit as an event, the museums could be studied more holistically and experientially, although there are some limitations due to the temporality of the data. The collected data was visualized through a computer science collaboration, supporting the analysis of different variables. This macro level research resulted in a broad understanding of Caribbean museums and their participatory practices.

The micro level was designed to add depth by investigating the complexities and the dynamics of community engagement processes. To gain this deeper processual understanding, two case studies were conducted with fieldwork consisting of interviews, participant observation, and community surveys. The *Kalinago Barana Autê* in Dominica showcases an ongoing process of collaboration and negotiation between Dominica's government and the Indigenous Kalinago community. The *Bengal to Barbados* exhibition in Barbados marks the beginning of a complex co-curation project between a national museum (*Barbados Museum & Historical Society*) and the heterogeneous, local

East Indian community. By investigating both practices and processes – the macro and micro levels – the dissertation examines how Caribbean museums are actively considering and reconsidering their societal roles.

Museum History

A history of the 'museum' as a concept stretches back to ancient times and its origin cannot be placed in any one part of the globe. Throughout history and all over the world, people have collected items and kept them safe in specific locations, often through the appointment of curators or custodians (Kreps 2011b: 457). As James Clifford noted "accumulating and displaying valuable things is, arguably, a very widespread human activity not limited to any class or cultural group" (Clifford 1997: 217). Within this historical, global phenomenon, the origin of the term 'museum' itself is rooted in Europe in the Renaissance (Findlen 1989). It was the next step in the development of a myriad of types of collections which had been known under various names such as library, theater, studio, gallery, *wunderkammer*, or cabinet (*e.g.* Borromeo [1625] 2010; Felfe 2005; Findlen 1994; Quiccheberg [1565] 2013). Many of these collections were highly private and accessible only to a handful of privileged persons (Findlen 1989). The contents of these collections were incredibly varied, often seamlessly bringing together nature and culture, ordinary and exotic. Gardens, as living collections of flora, easily fit within this concept and the wider quest for scientific knowledge (*e.g.* Masson 1972; Svensson 2017). The Enlightenment influenced the development of the museum towards encompassing a significantly more public role in the late 18th century and throughout the 19th century. In this era, travelling collections became popular, which showcased natural history, ethnographic models, or anatomical specimens to a broader public for their general education and instruction (Podgorny 2013). The late 19th century and early 20th century also saw the rise of the Great Exhibitions, which were massively popular and attracted audiences from all classes. Many of these exhibitions were meant to collect and showcase resources and valuables from around the world – predominantly from colonies – and also, most problematically, included exhibitions of peoples (Corbey 1993). Although aimed to educate visitors, these exhibitions also functioned like markets in which parts of the world were exploited for their natural and human resources and sale was an underlying goal. The vision for these exhibitions was one of bringing order to a colonial experience which was perceived as chaotic (Corbey 1993: 360). This was also the era which saw the birth of the modern museum institution, as a place for the collection and display of objects to a relatively wide public, aiming to educate and civilize (Bennett 1988; 1995). Within this development, the national perspective was dominant – an imbalance still present in the museological discourse today. Designed as places of order and surveillance, museum visitors were supposed to influence each other to civilized behavior and thus the lower classes could be 'improved' (Bennett 1988: 81 & 86). These modern museums were strongly tied to, or rooted in, the Great Exhibitions, often owing (parts of) their collections to these exhibitions, and sometimes even their buildings or raison d'être.

It is within this history that we find the origins of the first museums in the Caribbean (Cummins 1992; Cummins 1998; Cummins 2004; Cummins 2013; Modest 2010; Modest 2012). Many of these early museums and collections were founded by commercial and political leaders, designed for the promotion of local natural resources to new clients and investors. In a sense, collecting practices echoed those of the earliest Caribbean-European encounters, which had resulted in natural resources and people being taken to Europe as proof of the 'discoveries' (Modest 2012). In the 19th century Caribbean, natural-history and geology collections were most commonplace, having been amassed through systematic surveys of islands and countries as part of the colonial enterprise. As mentioned, these types of collections were also stimulated through the Great Exhibitions, which inspired the creation of committees and societies in the Caribbean to provide materials for these exhibitions. A height of activities in this regard was related to the Great Exhibition held in Jamaica in 1891. Rising interest in the fields of anthropology and archaeology further stimulated these early Caribbean collections and museums, which by playing into tropes of socio-cultural evolution 'proved' why colonizers were entitled to the resources of the colonies. In this interplay between imperial expansionism and scientific exploration, Caribbean museums and collections functioned as mirrors to imperial centers (Cummins 2004: 232).

At this same time, there were political leaders who advocated the social improvement of Caribbean populations through educational reform (Cummins 2004: 229). One of these was Lt. Col. Reid who created legislation for the foundation of public libraries with museum displays throughout parts of the British West Indies, beginning in Bermuda in 1839 (Cummins 1992: 34). Reid envisioned that these museums, which would contain collections of natural history and art, would benefit the Caribbean public at large. In practice, the opportunities of the newly emancipated majority populations were limited in terms of time to spend on 'leisure' activities. Even more so, Alissandra Cummins has critically pointed out that "it was the inaccessibility of the European concept of 'museum' to the African cultural sensibility which proved to be the greatest barrier of all" (Cummins 1992: 34). The absence of West Africans from the histories told through these early museums reinforced this estrangement (Cummins 2013: 32).

Some of these early Caribbean museums can still be found in the region today and were included in this study. The *St. Vincent Botanic Gardens: Curator's House* was opened in 1891, although the gardens themselves had already been founded in 1765. *Musée L'Herminier*, whose building still exists although it is now no longer a museum, was opened in 1872, while the *Natural History Museum of Jamaica* and the *Institute of Jamaica* can trace their beginnings to 1879. *Musée Schoelcher* opened its doors in 1887 (see figure 1), and the *National Museum & Art Gallery of Trinidad & Tobago* – then called the *Royal Victoria Institute* – was founded in 1892. Many of these early Caribbean museums were focused heavily on all aspects of natural history, some of which complemented these with art collections. Ultimately, this specific historical development of Caribbean museums supported a legacy of the Caribbean as being predominantly a natural rather than a cultural region. Wayne Modest has argued that this notion has influenced how the image of the Caribbean region was invented and has continued to impact perceptions of the Caribbean and its people as not being 'cultural enough' (Modest 2012).

Following independence, Caribbean museums were left with the colonial legacies of their collections. These collections had been dominated by natural history, and to a lesser extent art and archaeology. The latter had been created as 'salvage

Figure 1: Musée Schoelcher, Guadeloupe, was opened to the public in 1887.

anthropology' – collecting and cataloguing the cultures of rapidly 'disappearing' peoples – effectively limiting them to collections of Amerindian archaeology.

> *While black Africans were of some anthropological interest, blacks from the Caribbean and the United States did not fit into either of the salvageable categories of a dying race or having a culture that was disappearing due to European contact. New World blacks, it was thought, were already tainted by European contact and its civilizing forces and therefore seen to lack practices worthy of cultural significance – and related objects – worthy of anthropological interest.*
> Wayne Modest (2012: 92)

The narrow scope of Caribbean museums, the emphasis on nature over culture, and the lack of virtually any collections relating to the majority populations of the region, became increasingly problematic when "existing museums in the region were co-opted by post-colonial governments to become agents of identity creation" (Farmer 2013: 172). Governmental museums in these newly independent Caribbean states sought to develop new collections and include African histories and heritages into their narratives, evolving into post-colonial institutions and supporting new national identities. An example of this is the creation of museums in restored plantation houses, which thematically discuss histories of slavery, resistance, emancipation, and independence. Moreover, this period also encouraged the development of grassroots heritage initiatives, as "long experience with disinheritance and marginalization amongst ordinary people strengthened communal or personal approaches to history-making" (Cummins 2004: 238). As part of this shift, ephemeral museums took on a unique role of focusing on the present. It is within this history that we find today's social museums in the Caribbean: new or old institutions which are working through community engagement practices and processes to place themselves firmly within their contemporary Caribbean communities.

Previous Research

Community engagement (see *Community Engagement*, page 39), as both a theory and a practice, has been researched extensively within museology. Authors such as Elizabeth Crooke (2007; 2008; 2011a; 2015), Viv Golding & Wayne Modest (2013), Ivan Karp and colleagues (1992), and Sheila Watson (2007), have been instrumental in reflecting on the relevance of community and community engagement for museums. Community engagement has been particularly studied in terms of Indigenous or source communities (Clavir 2002; Cooper & Sandoval 2006; Fuller 1992; Peers & Brown 2003b). Many critical evaluations of community engagement have focused on the benefits and impacts of specific projects, exhibitions, or museums (Fouseki 2010; Fouseki & Smith 2013; Lagerkvist 2006; Perkin 2010; Ronan 2014; Smith 2015). In addition, Nina Simon's (2010) practical publication of her personal experiences with numerous community engagement practices has been hugely influential in guiding museums who wish to develop similar projects. Ultimately, whether theoretical, practical, or critical evaluations, museums in Europe and North America have been overly represented in the museological literature related to community engagement.

Nonetheless, community museums, networks of community museums, and regional museological cooperation have also received significant attention in Central- and South America (*e.g.* Barnes 2008; Burón Díaz 2012; De Carli 2004; Françozo & van Broekhoven 2017; Zea de Uribe 1982).

Within the Caribbean, a number of museum surveys have explored the existence of museums in the region and have presented suggestions for future developments or improvements. These surveys which took a regional perspective were often restricted to a single linguistic area, *e.g.* only the English-speaking Caribbean. The focus for most of these surveys has been on assessing the needs of these museums in order to strategically support their 'development.' 1933 saw the surveying of museums in the British West Indies (Bather & Sheppard 1934), followed by a survey through the Caribbean Conservation Association (Lemieux & Schultz 1973), reports and workshops by CARICOM (Caribbean Community Secretariat 1979; Singleton 1978), an assessment by the Island Resources Foundation (Towle & Tyson 1979), a report for UNESCO (Solomon 1979), and another for the Organisation of the American States (Rivera & Soto Soria 1982). Curator Frances Kay Brinkley published a concise review of museums in the Eastern Caribbean in *Museum*'s edition dedicated to Latin America and the Caribbean (Brinkley 1982). UNESCO also undertook extensive surveys of Caribbean museums (Whiting 1983) and Caribbean monuments and sites (Delatour 1984). Many of these reports stressed the problems encountered by Caribbean museums, a lack of funding or of trained staff, and in general highlighted neglect and deficiencies. The aim of these surveys was to make concrete suggestions or recommendations: *e.g.* the development of a 'mobile museum' in the region, the creation of a travelling conservation laboratory, the foundation of a museums studies program or training, and the establishment of a regional museums association (Cummins 2017; Whiting 1983: 13-16). In 1987, all these recommendations came together in the foundation of the Museums Association of the Caribbean (MAC). Over the years, MAC has provided a number of resources about Caribbean museums which take a very broad view of the region. Its directories of Caribbean museums (separated into the four linguistic areas) were updated several times, most recently and extensively in 2011 (Museums Association of the Caribbean 2011a; 2011b; 2011c; 2011d). These contain 1107 museums,[1] although the information per museum is very basic (its name, address, and contact information). MAC also contacted these museums with a questionnaire for a more detailed survey, which received 110 responses (Sands of Time Consultancy 2011).

Besides these regional surveys, scholarly research into Caribbean museums has been published as well. The work of Alissandra Cummins (1992; 1994; 1998; 2004; 2012; 2013) has been seminal in this regard, focusing on the history of Caribbean museums, predominantly in the English-speaking Caribbean, and their role in the development of identity and meaning-making. The book *Plantation to Nation* (Cummins *et al.* 2013) deserves particular recognition as the first to focus on the growth of Caribbean museums and museology, regardless of nation or language. Several of its articles are referenced throughout this dissertation, particularly in the theoretical chapter. The book

---

1   The Spanish-speaking museums form the majority of this number (832), including all Central American countries from Mexico to Panama, as well as Colombia and Venezuela.

also included several studies of individual museums. Similar studies have been published independently (*e.g.* Collomb & Renard 1982; Inniss 2012; Lee 2015; Ramtahal 2013), as well as articles which have focused on museums in a specific country or island (*e.g.* Callender 2015; Gilette 2000). Regional scholarly literature has focused on diversity (Brookes 2008), or provided more generalized overviews (Maréchal 1998). Without disregarding the importance of the studies, reports, articles, and books referenced above, there has not been any previous research specifically into community engagement from a Caribbean regional perspective. As far as it has been possible to uncover, this work is the first in that regard.

Research Questions and Objectives

This research into Caribbean museums is set within the larger transdisciplinary ERC-Synergy project *NEXUS1492: New World Encounters in a Globalising World*, which investigates the impacts of colonial encounters in the Caribbean. The primary two objectives of NEXUS1492 are: (1) to provide a new perspective on the first encounters between the New World and Old World by focusing on the histories and legacies of the Indigenous Caribbean, and (2) to raise awareness of Caribbean histories and legacies, striving for practical outcomes in future heritage management efforts with implications for local communities, island nations, the pan-Caribbean region, and globally. Within this larger project, the research presented in this PhD dissertation relates to both of these objectives by means of its focus on the topic of Caribbean museums and community engagement. It relates to the first objective of NEXUS1492 by placing the development of Caribbean museums within a wider historical and colonial framework and by analyzing them through the legacy of natural and cultural collecting which started off during these first encounters. It resonates even more strongly with the second NEXUS1492 objective by focusing on the contemporary role of Caribbean museums and how this influences diverse communities. As part of such a large, transdisciplinary research project, collaboration was possible with colleagues from the fields of anthropology, archaeology, computer sciences, education, genetics, geochemistry, heritage studies, network sciences, and physical geography. These collaborations not only helped to advance the questions and methodologies of this study, but also provided opportunities to conduct fieldwork together and enabled the development of joint research projects to support this research or improve its outreach. In addition, the possibility to receive feedback on all stages of the development of this research from such a wide array of specializations was very valuable.

Primarily, this dissertation seeks to answer the question:

> *How are Caribbean museums realigning their societal role in relation to contemporary Caribbean communities?*

It focuses on answering this main question by hypothetically identifying community engagement as the primary approach through which Caribbean museums might achieve such societal repositioning. Following on this hypothesis, it is possible to identify four sub questions. By finding the answers to each of these, the ultimate aim is to identify solutions to the main question as well. The sub questions are:

1. Theoretically, what are participatory practices and what are the intended outcomes of community engagement processes for communities and individuals?
2. What are the characteristics of contemporary Caribbean museums and how are they adopting and adapting participatory practices?
3. How are community engagement processes, including their value and outcomes, perceived by Caribbean communities?
4. How do community engagement practices and processes affect the role of Caribbean museums in relation to Caribbean society?

The research as a whole is placed within the theoretical discourse of the New Museology and is influenced by post-colonial theories and the current discourse on heritage. This theoretical foundation directs the research towards community engagement as the primary focus, which is encapsulated in the first sub question. The main research approach is designed to take place on a macro and a micro level, where the former is well-suited to investigate participatory practices on a regional scale and the latter is appropriate for a deeper understanding of community engagement processes. Thus, the second sub question corresponds to the macro level and is to be answered through a regional survey of Caribbean museums and their participatory practices. The micro level relates to the third sub question, whose focus on the processes and perceptions calls for a case study approach. The case studies revolve around on-going or newly beginning community engagement processes and the perceptions of the participants are the core subject matter. The case studies in Dominica and Barbados were selected in part due to the hypothetically complex dynamics of engagement between minority communities and local government(al institutions). Finally, the macro and micro levels are analyzed together in a detailed discussion. There, in a series of answers and observations, interpretations can be made about how community engagement practices and processes actually affect the role of Caribbean museums.

Outline
To conclude this first, introductory chapter, an outline is presented of the remainder of the dissertation in order to guide the reader. This outline sketches the contents of each chapter and indicates where the reader may find the answers to the separate sub questions.

Chapter 2 presents the theoretical frameworks which lie at the basis of this research project, and roughly aims to answer the first sub question. Couched in the New Museology, the chapter discusses this theory in detail, as well as the development of two related theories: post-colonial theories and the current heritage discourse. It delves into the history of the term 'museum,' identifies a suitable working definition for this research project, and explores a number of museum models. Specific focus is also placed on the definitions of 'community' and 'community engagement' and on the meaning and relevance of these terms in the Caribbean in general and for this research project in particular. The theoretical framework is essential for understanding the methodology developed for this dissertation research.

Chapter 3 follows by describing the methodology of the research as a whole. It begins by considering the research approach and its design into a macro and a micro level. A detailed description of the regional museum survey of 195 museums is provided.

This section discusses the selection of islands and countries, and the museums visited within them. It describes the fieldwork methodology, as well as the computer science collaboration which resulted in the creation of various data visualizations placed throughout this dissertation. Similarly, for the micro level research, that is the two case studies, the selection criteria are discussed along with the fieldwork methodology. The section details how data was collected and what kind of data was collected during the fieldwork sessions. In closing, the chapter reflects on the research ethos, considering the role of the researcher in the field, the presence of possible biases, and notes the code of ethics employed. The chapter thus describes where, how, and what kind of data was collected in the course of this research.

Chapter 4 presents the main findings of the regional museum survey, or the macro level approach, with examples of participatory practices from Caribbean museums. The chapter is structured by participatory practice: each practice is first categorized and followed by multiple practical examples. This extensive collection of Caribbean participatory practices aims to answer the second sub question and provide a broad regional perspective. It is of notable relevance to museum professionals wishing to adopt or adapt participatory practices. In addition, a reading of this chapter benefits from consulting the online accessible Caribbean Museums Database which contains detailed entries of all 195 museums.

Chapters 5 & 6 present the findings of the two case studies, or the micro level approach, by detailing the processes surrounding two community engagement projects which were ongoing at the time of this research. Chapter 5 focuses on the *Kalinago Barana Autê* in Dominica, a museum envisioned and managed by the Indigenous Kalinago community but constructed and owned by Dominica's government. This long-term collaboration process allows for a closer look at how the Kalinago community perceives the value and outcomes of the museum, particularly in light of its ownership model. Chapter 6 concerns the *Bengal to Barbados* exhibition project in Barbados, a co-curation project between the local East Indian community and the *Barbados Museum & Historical Society*. The very beginning of this collaboration provides insight into the development of the exhibition and the process of finding shared goals, especially in the context of a heterogeneous community. Both case studies highlight specific answers to the third sub question. While the cases are particular, they reveal some of the complexities which any community engagement process in the world could encounter.

Chapter 7 is the stage of an extensive discussion of the research as a whole and combines both macro and micro level perspectives. It develops a broad yet detailed image of the community engagement practices and processes in Caribbean museums. It is structured around a series of nine insights, each of which is discussed in detail. The chapter contains interpretations, statements, results, and discussion points, all of which tie back to the final sub question as well as the main research question. It considers the societal role of Caribbean museums by exploring differences such as the museum's location, its type of content, or its ownership. It furthermore discusses community engagement processes in terms of challenges or conditions for success. The chapter sketches a wide diversity of ways in which Caribbean museums, often complementarily to each other, are realigning their societal roles and engaging with contemporary Caribbean communities.

In closing, Chapter 8 provides a short conclusion of the complete dissertation, revealing the image of the social museum in the Caribbean. It ends by indicating a number of possibilities for further research.

As a final note to the reader, while most figures can be found in line with the text within the relevant chapters, the full page visualizations produced in the course of this research are placed as a series immediately before Chapter 7. This facilitates returning to them while reading the discussion. The full image credits for all figures can be found in the list of figures. The appendix contains an index of the names of all museums researched as part of the regional museum survey. It also includes the questionnaires and their collated responses conducted in the course of the two case studies.

2

Theoretical Framework

Rather than only being an institution that provides comment at a safe distance, to be meaningful a museum must actively co-produce with its community, effect change, and forge dynamic connections. It is this active museum that is the antithesis of the disconnected museum of old.
Elizabeth Crooke (2015: 482)

Crooke echoes the main sentiment of the New Museology which developed roughly around the 1970s in direct opposition to what was seen as 'traditional' museology. This older museology had been focused on methodology and practical issues, whereas the New Museology argued that museums needed to revisit their purpose before critically examining their practice (Vergo 1991). As the New Museology has developed, the discussion has shifted strongly to communities and their role within the museum – and, vice versa, the museum's role for communities.

This chapter sketches the theoretical frameworks which form the basis of this research project and dissertation. Both are rooted firmly within the sphere of the New Museology and its current forms. It is this particular theoretical conceptualization of the role of the museum, and the associated ideas of what contemporary museum practices and processes could look like, that lies at the core of the formulated research questions, informed the research approach, as well as influenced the analysis of the results. The main focus of the chapter thus consists of a discussion of the New Museology, its development over the last few decades, and a number of critical reflections. In order to fully understand the theory, its origin is placed within the framework of both historical developments and the emergence of two interrelated concepts: post-colonial theories and the current heritage discourse. Situating ourselves in this contemporary museological mindset requires a (re)definition of the term 'museum,' and a reflection on its meaning as it is currently epitomized by the International Council of Museum's (ICOM) definition. Such a redefinition was also necessary for this research project in order to understand the institution in a broader sense and to develop a definition that was appropriate for fieldwork in the Caribbean. Finally, the concepts of *community* and *community engagement* are presented within the current academic and museological debates. A consideration of these terms is placed within a Caribbean context in order to consider their relevance in the region and their applicability. It is argued that although 'community' remains difficult to define, community engagement is of particular importance for Caribbean museums due to the region's marked diversity.

The chapter thus provides the foundational understanding of community engagement in museums – its participatory practices and its processes – the central topic which this research explored within the context of the Caribbean region (see *Research Questions and Objectives,* page 18). While Crooke refers to this type of institution as the 'active museum,' it is argued here that community engagement in the Caribbean is characterized by the *social* museum.

New Museology

Emerging in the early 1970s, the New Museology began as a movement against the 'old museology' – which had mainly been concerned with museum *methods* and practices – to shift the focus of museology to the *purpose* of museums in the bigger picture (Davis 2008: 397; Scott 2006: 48; Vergo 1991: 1). This shift in focus can be explained by historical developments and pressures from three different arenas. First of all, the geopolitical dismantling of much of the colonial system following the Second World War. Many museums that had been created as a part of colonial/imperialist structures – such as traditional museums of ethnography or museums set up in colonies by colonizers – now had to find a new purpose outside the colonial frame (Sauvage 2010: 100). Secondly, in a number of countries, most notably Australia, Canada, and the USA, Indigenous communities issued challenges to museums to include their heritages within the main narratives (Nicks 2003: 20; Sauvage 2010: 108). It began with Indigenous communities expressing their dismay with and disapproval of the way human remains of their ancestors were treated in museum displays and storages. These criticisms led to repatriation claims or discussions with museums on how such sensitive materials should be treated in the collections. As collaboration continued, Indigenous communities challenged the authority of the curatorial voice in other matters and insisted that their expertise and knowledge be included within other areas of the museum (Davis 2008: 398). Thirdly, the wide spread social movements of the 1960s for civil rights, world peace, and ethnic harmony called for a reevaluation of societal goals overall, which resonated through in museums as well (Davis 2008: 397). It was within the framework of these historical developments that the position of the museum in society came under scrutiny.

To be sure, discussions about the role or purpose of the museum are not exclusively the domain of the New Museology. For instance, when museums became more widely accessible to the public in the beginning of the 19th century – the so-called 'birth' of the modern museum – they were also intended to be in the service of society (Bennett 1995: 92). However, this role was played out by 'civilizing' the middle and lower classes through education, self-surveillance, and by the 'beneficial influences' of the upper classes (Bennett 1988: 86). It was suggested then that museums could provide a more wholesome alternative for those who otherwise squandered their time and wages in pubs. Under the New Museology, the societal role of museums is seen in a different light, but still "echoes nineteenth century notions of museums as instruments for positive social change" (Perkin 2010: 110). As the New Museology theory gathered support and its advocates demanded change, ICOM altered its definition of the museum in 1974 to include the phrase: "*in the service of society*" (Fuller 1992: 329).

The shift towards the New Museology resulted in a different approach to museum practices which continues today (*e.g.* Fleming 2012). Whereas previously the focus had lain heavily on collections and objects, now many museums place people and stories at the heart of their exhibitions. This requires a more emotive style of communication with visitors and a different approach to museum pedagogy. As cultural diversity and human rights have been given higher priority, museum practice has been characterized more by collaborations with minority or excluded communities and less by dominant monocultural narratives. Thus, while the core idea of the New Museology to focus on the societal role of museums is no longer *new*, it has continued to develop in recent years into more activist, participatory, and grassroots practices.

As it is seen now, the museum's purpose should be to work actively towards a variety of societal improvements (Silverman 2010), three of which are noted here in particular. Most commonly, authors point out that museums today should battle social inequality and work towards **social inclusion**.[2] This point is particularly emphasized, as museums are still frequently critiqued for their legacy of exclusion and social elitism (Sandell 2012). Thus, museums today should make an effort to target previously marginalized groups or communities and support the elevation of their position within society (Cummins 1992: 49; Kelly 2006: 8; Sandell 2003: 45). This can be done on three levels: individual (*e.g.* by promoting self-esteem and confidence), community (for instance by social regeneration), or societal (by promoting tolerance and respect, or by challenging stereotypes). Access to the museum should be enhanced for those at risk of being socially excluded (Sandell 2003: 48). However, policies of inclusion are not necessarily unproblematic and a critical caveat is necessary: generally, inclusion can either be achieved on the basis of universalism or by politics of difference (Lagerkvist 2006: 55). Emphasizing universalism and the commonality of all of humanity runs the risk of forcing homogeneity. On the other hand, while politics of difference account for diversity, promoting diversity can be critiqued as being discriminatory. Thus, museums pursuing social inclusion policies must carefully consider the manner in which they do so and try to avoid (accidental) societal exclusion, discrimination, or unwarranted homogenization in the process. Engaging in policies of inclusion requires careful deliberation beforehand and the possibility of conflicts arising must always be taken into account. Furthermore, Anwar Tlili (2008) cautions against measuring social inclusion through visitor numbers alone, as there may be many other barriers to inclusion besides physical access.

The push to work towards greater social inclusion is often mandated through public policies which have direct implications for (governmental) museums (Sandell 1998; Tlili 2008). However, more than merely politically, the desire for inclusivity is also echoed ideologically in the museum discourse and practically as guidance for museum staff. As an example of the former, the foundation of *The International Journal of the Inclusive Museum* in 2008 provided a scholarly platform to discuss how the museum can become more inclusive. At the same time, on the ground, museum staff members are concerned with matters of inclusivity (*e.g.* Cole 2014), although there is still much

---

2   This is distinctly different from the civilizing aim of museums in the nineteenth century. Although the goal was for lower classes to become more civilized and behave 'properly,' there was certainly no desire to remove class differences and to create a more egalitarian society.

work to be done in terms of the representativity of staff. The concepts of the inclusive museum and the social museum are connected and share a number of characteristics but do not overlap wholly. The social museum relates to the societal roles museums are taking on in relation to various communities. However, as will be discussed in greater detail later, this societal realignment is not always or not necessarily inclusionary, but can be focused on other societal aims or even be considered exclusionary towards some.

Secondly, beyond social inclusion, museums should actively engage in **community development**. There are many examples of ways in which museums have attempted to alleviate community problems or provide practical support: promoting education, improving literacy, supporting local economies, encouraging urban regeneration, or assisting local development (*e.g.* Davis 2008: 398; Fuller 1992: 332; Kelly 2006: 4-5). As stated in the opening quote of this chapter, if museums wish to solve community problems, it is crucial that they become agents of change rather than merely passive presenters of the past. For this purpose, heritage can be an exceptionally powerful tool for reshaping the present. One can think of the multiple cases in which, for instance, Indigenous peoples have legally retained rights based on a proof of heritage (through NAGPRA[3] or other legal frameworks). Museums may also support communities by providing a physical and emotional space away from existing problems or challenges. For instance, in the aftermath of hurricanes Irma and Maria in 2017, *Museo de Arte de Ponce* in Puerto Rico reopened with temporary free entry to offer their local community a "tiny piece of normality" and a space for leisure in a time of great challenges (Monahan 2017). Beyond providing a respite from the crisis, several museums on the island engaged in collecting and distributing food and water or functioned as communication hubs and power stations (Stapley-Brown 2017).

A third, oft repeated, societal improvement that museums may work towards is that of **sustainability**. This should be seen on several levels, starting with the sustainability of the museum itself and the local environment (Davis 2008: 398), but furthermore encompassing the sustainability of the communities connected to the museum or even globally. The sustainability of communities is often encouraged through social cohesion which aims to enhance a sense of collective responsibility in order to achieve collective survival (Crooke 2008: 417-418; Perkin 2010: 108). It works by strengthening community members' sense of belonging and, therefore, draws them more tightly to one another. Building social cohesion is often proposed as a way to counter the destructive effects that globalization can have on communities (Nederveen Pieterse 2005). On the other hand, museums can also work towards sustainability of the global environment or humanity by targeting the global community and its collective responsibilities. Sustainability as a focal point or museum mission can also be directed at the preservation of cultures, languages, materials, or skills – indeed any type of tangible or intangible heritage preservation.

Considering the above three purposes, what should a contemporary museum be like according to the New Museology? Again, we can identify three main characteristics: museums should be **arenas for debate**, **self-reflexive,** and **relevant**. The first of these rests on the principle that museums are profoundly political spaces (Onciul 2013: 81). As such, museums cannot shy away from being controversial or discussing difficult

---

3   The Native American Graves Protection and Repatriation Act. Enacted in the USA in 1990.

THE SOCIAL MUSEUM IN THE CARIBBEAN

topics within their exhibitions (Davis 2008: 400; Sauvage 2010: 109). As places of debate, museums do not merely lecture their visitors, but rather engage in dialogue with them. In order to stimulate dialogue, ideas become more important than objects – or, the role of the meaning of objects changes (Gurian 1999) – and, in doing so, museums become places of meaning-making. Another necessity for stimulating dialogue is a shift in authority: museums are no longer the owners of knowledge, transferring this upon the visitors, but rather, visitors and curators each contribute their own expertise to the conversation (Smith & Waterton 2009: 110). This requires frequent negotiation with communities in order to empower them and rework the pre-existing power balance (Sandell 2003: 55). In practice, this has resulted in museum exhibitions that focus more on stories and people rather than on objects, and in presenting these stories as multi-faceted and open for debate and interpretation. Besides giving visitors space to add their voices to the exhibition, the museum becomes an arena for debate also through activities, events, or via online platforms and social media.

The second characteristic, self-reflexivity, requires museums to be critical of their own (*e.g.* racist, imperialist, colonialist) pasts and the origins of their collections, and for museum staff to acknowledge that they are subjective individuals influenced by their own identities, heritages, knowledges, and experiences (Butler 2015; Lidchi 2010: 201; Sauvage 2010: 109). In consequence, it entails a critical stance toward museum practices, especially concerning the representation of non-Western cultures (Varutti 2013: 59). Self-reflexivity requires a constant evaluation of museum practices, processes, and products (McLean 2008: 289). Towards the public, museums should strive to reveal the power present within their exhibitions. Instead of presenting the exhibition as a neutral or objective space, power and authority must be accounted for and put on display (Nederveen Pieterse 2005: 176). A self-reflexive museum is therefore characterized by both self-awareness and self-critique, striving to reveal subjectivity and compensate for inequality.

Finally, a New Museology-inspired museum is characterized by its aim to be highly relevant to its society and communities. As Nina Simon puts it, "relevance is a key that unlocks meaning. It opens doors to experiences that matter to us, surprise us, and bring value into our lives" (Simon 2016: 25). Thus, such a museum works actively for presently living persons, as well as for future generations. For instance, they may make themselves relevant to their communities by acting as a surrogate home and accepting donated objects into their care (Candlin 2016: 115). While this helps to build collections for the future, it also supports contemporary communities by valuing their meaningful objects and promising to care for them. Museums may also work towards being a more relevant institution by lowering their focus from an international or national level to individual or community levels. Alternatively, first voice, pluralist, or multi-vocal approaches can be applied to attract new audiences or to increase relevance by the self-representation of targeted communities (Galla 2008: 10-11; McLean 2008: 289; Sauvage 2010: 109). Naturally, the content matter of the museum is vital in providing relevance.

To recapitulate, the New Museology developed in opposition to the older museological discourse under the influence of political decolonization, challenges from Indigenous communities, and strong social movements. It essentially shifted the focus of museology from museum practices to the purpose of museums. Putting societal needs first, social inclusion, community development, and sustainability have been varyingly put forth as the main objective. In order to achieve this, museums strive to be arenas for debate, self-reflexive, and highly relevant. Over the last few decades, the discourse of the New Museology has become increasingly more activist and participatory as it has firmly placed communities at the heart of all museum work.

As a final point, it is frequently lamented that it is difficult (or even, 'impossible') to measure the values that these new museological approaches aim to increase. For instance, how does one measure an increase in social cohesion or sustainability? The research by Carol Scott (2006; 2009; 2015) has been instrumental in providing ways in which such museum values can be measured and 'success' may be proven to funding bodies or policymakers. However, in practice still too often measurement of the success of a museum relies on statistics related to admission numbers which do not fully reflect the extent to which a social mission is fulfilled. Therefore, a gap often remains between the museum's mission and practical proof of its achievements towards this mission unless new approaches for assessing the societal value of museums are employed. The case studies in Chapters 5 & 6 present some approaches as to how the values of museums and community engagement projects may be assessed from the point of view of participants.

As noted in the introduction to this chapter, the development of the New Museology discourse was influenced by a number of other theories emerging from related or relevant scientific fields. A prominent example of this can be seen in the impact which post-colonial theories had on the origin of the New Museology, as well as the influence they continue to have on its current form. Following the geopolitical decolonization which was gradually set into motion after the Second World War, post-colonial theories developed as a way in which the experiences and effects of colonialism could be critically examined. Initially, the discourse formed within the field of literature studies in the 1960s. It was inspired, among others, by Jacques Derrida, who developed a philosophical exercise, which could be used for literary analysis, known as deconstruction, by which writing may be deconstructed for hidden discourses, such as for (unintentional) colonial stereotypes or imperialist expressions (Derrida [1967] 1976; Gosden 1999: 199). In his seminal book, Edward Said argued that orientalism – that is, a specific and stereotypical dichotomy of East/West – can be perceived within academia as much as in the work of literary writers (Said [1978] 2003: 2). As a result, post-colonial theories were lifted beyond literature and permeated other academic fields, such as anthropology, archaeology, and political science. No longer necessarily focusing on literary deconstruction, but more broadly on all possible effects of colonialism, the theoretical field has been applied to many different topics: *e.g.* slavery, migration, representation, gender, race, resistance, or place (Kreps 2011a: 71).

This effort to critically examine the widespread effects of colonialism has taken some time to develop and its current relevance should not be underemphasized. As Chris Gosden has pointed out: "the independence of colonies did not immediately end the influences of colonialism and make us truly post-colonial in thought and by instinct" (Gosden 1999: 203). In the Caribbean, colonial legacies continue to be palpable. Colonialism has impacted the history of each island and country, resulting in today's geopolitical sub-regions, often identified through the four linguistic areas (Dutch, English, French, and Spanish). Beyond political organization and language, colonialism has deeply and profoundly impacted many aspects of life – in the case of museums, it has impacted the origins of their collections, the scope of their narratives, but possibly also their current curatorial cultures and societal roles. Although the full scope of continued colonial legacies in the Caribbean is far too broad to discuss here, some of its possible effects on museums, as exemplified by differences in museums from the four linguistic – and thus geopolitical – areas, are considered towards the end of this dissertation.

A point of criticism should be recognized here. Post-colonial theories have been extensively explored by prominent scholars from beyond what has been called the Western sphere – *e.g.* Homi Bhabha and Gayatri Chakravorty Spivak. In the post-independence Caribbean, a cohort of historians took on these theories to develop a new historiography and an interpretation of the history of the region from a post-colonial perspective (Farmer 2013: 172). Nonetheless, despite the concern of post-colonial theories with former colonies and revealing Eurocentric biases, some critics have said that the field is "characterized, if not defined, as a specifically Western analytical perspective" (van Dommelen 2010: 105). This critique is important to keep in mind, especially concerning the current state of the field and the continuing globalization of the region. Namely, Kevin Farmer noted that Caribbean museums are at risk due to a "nascent neo-colonial mentality" (Farmer 2013: 176), while others have flagged the exploitation of the region and its cultural heritage for the purposes of tourism as a neo-colonial phenomenon (*e.g.* Williams 2012) – that is, placing power in foreign hands. If political decolonization has not led to a post-colonial but rather a neo-colonial reality, attention is needed to avoid carelessly applying post-colonial theories from a purely Western analytical perspective if one wishes to appropriately unpack colonial biases.

Bearing this in mind, as well as the application of the discourse to a wide array of disciplines, post-colonial studies can be characterized as follows. There is often a strong focus on writing alternative histories, based on the perspectives and perceptions of Indigenous, non-Western, or otherwise marginalized communities (Karp & Lavine 1991). In doing so, people who were previously invisible or only present in the margins of mainstream history are granted a voice, a presence, and an identity. In the post-independence Caribbean, identity construction and nationalism required a shift in focus to the previously suppressed, but often majority, populations. These new histories "sought to combat the issue of the colonial self as inferior, replacing it with a notion of self as superior" (Farmer 2013: 174). Secondly, post-colonial studies are characterized by strong critical (self-)reflection. For anyone working in this manner, this can mean reflecting upon their own identity, culture, or nation, as well as a critical assessment of the discipline within which they are working. Understanding the discourses that shape our work and our way of thinking are advocated as a way to more deeply understand the power relations embedded in the work we create (Kreps 2011a: 72). Certainly, the need to adjust power relations that have been skewed by colonialism is a commonly emphasized aim. It should be clear at this point that the discourses of the New Museology and post-colonial theories share a number of common ideals and approaches.

Post-colonial theories, when applied specifically within the museum, can take on various forms. One example of this is by a critical reflection on the definition of the museum and its biases. Christina Kreps has strongly critiqued the notion "that the museum is a uniquely modern, Western cultural invention [...] to the point of neglecting other cultures' models of museums and curatorial practices" (Kreps 2011b: 457). Her research presents examples of museum models and curatorial practices, primarily from Indigenous communities in Asia and Oceania, and aims to place the concept of museology within a broader, global frame. Within the context of this dissertation, the definition of the museum will be examined in greater detail later in this chapter.

In agreement with her insight, even if the 'museum' is not a colonial concept per se, it does exist within a colonial frame (Sauvage 2010) and specific museums do have profoundly colonial roots. Nonetheless, it would be too simple to just call for the dismissal or destruction of these museums, as Kristine Ronan has effectively shown how Indigenous communities have taken colonial tools, such as museums, and used them to shape their own lives (Ronan 2014: 141). Similarly, Alissandra Cummins has shown how museums in the English-speaking Caribbean have confronted their colonial pasts and realigned their missions to serve new communities (Cummins 1998; 2004). Yet, as Kevin Farmer has pointed out, "in the experiment of nationalism in the Caribbean, the creation of this image of the region as comprising primarily descendants of Africa has seen the marginalization of certain other ethnic groups" (Farmer 2013: 173). Thus, there is certainly a continued need in the region in terms of post-colonial approaches and presenting alternative histories in museums.

Within the post-colonial discourse on museums, the concept of the 'contact zone' has been particularly widely discussed. Originally introduced by linguist Mary Louise Pratt, the contact zone refers to "social spaces where cultures meet, clash, and grapple with each other, often in contexts of highly asymmetrical relations of power, such as colonialism, slavery, or their aftermaths as they are lived out in many parts of the world today" (Pratt 1991: 34). James Clifford linked the concept to museums, presenting a series of case studies of cultural consultation or collaboration processes which he described as contact work (Clifford 1997). Although Clifford stressed the power imbalances inherent in the contact zone, the concept has also been used by museologists in a more optimistic sense, as a dialogical space of equal reciprocity. Robin Boast has argued strongly that Clifford presented a more complicated view, even going so far as to say that the contact zone – in encouraging participation on certain terms, but silencing opposition – can be considered neo-colonialism (Boast 2011: 64). He states: "thus, always, is the contact zone an asymmetric space where the periphery comes to win some small, momentary, and strategic advantage, but where the center ultimately gains" (Boast 2011: 66). In the Caribbean, there are certainly cases in which the (national) museum operates as a contact zone in an asymmetric space. Yet, as Clifford already pointed out, grassroots museums effectively show how communities can use the museum-structure towards their own means, outside of these asymmetric spaces (Clifford 1997: 216-218).

How can museums continue working through post-colonial theories towards the aims of the New Museology? For this, it is helpful to consider Christina Kreps' concept of the *post-colonial museum* which is "fundamentally about inverting power relations and the voice of authority" (Kreps 2011a: 75). This is achieved by combining the methods mentioned above – by writing alternative histories, including multiple perspectives and diverse voices, applying different notions of identity, revealing Eurocentric biases and assumptions in the Western museum concept, and by extending critical reflection to look inwards upon the museum itself and its practices (Kreps 2011a: 72). With varying intensity and results, the process of decolonizing the museum has been occurring around the world. One of the more common practices is a critical examination of the origins of the collections and the acknowledgement of the historical contingencies under which they were acquired. The oft resulting step away from a dependency on objects and collections mirrors developments in the field of heritage studies.

To discuss the characteristics of the current discourse on heritage, it is helpful to begin by contrasting it with the previous discourse, known as the authorized heritage discourse (AHD). Under the AHD, heritage was used as a noun, most commonly to refer to monuments or sites: objects from the past that were physically present in the landscape (Smith & Waterton 2009: 29-30). The values of this heritage were seen as intrinsic (that is, inherently known and unchanging) and experts were in charge of defining what was or was not deemed to be heritage. Special attention was paid to heritage that was considered to be significant for all of humanity (so-called 'universal heritage'). The AHD called for specific ways in which to manage this heritage, such as the perpetual conservation of the qualities or characteristics which contained this intrinsic value.

Under the influences of postmodernism, as well as new notions of identity formation and cultural pluralism, the meaning of heritage has been significantly altered. As K. Anne Pyburn so pointedly put it: "there is no such thing as 'tangible heritage;' a building is not heritage" (Pyburn n.d.: 1). Heritage is now more seen as a verb (a thing one does), rather than something that is (Smith & Waterton 2009: 43 & 49). According to this understanding, heritage is fluid and intangible to a high degree. It is no longer determined or controlled by experts but experienced and created by everyone (Russell 2010). As such, there is space for a plurality of meanings and values rather than one intrinsic value. The terminology used when discussing the new heritage discourse reflects this deep change in meaning. Heritage is *constructed*, it is *invented*, it is *manipulated*, it *alters* with changing circumstances, it is *selective*, and it is *discarded* when no longer needed (Crooke 2008: 423). Most importantly, heritage is a politically charged tool that communities or individuals can put to use towards achieving their own agendas (Smith & Waterton 2009: 75). Perhaps Steven Hoelscher defined heritage most eloquently as "the present-day uses of the past for a wide array of strategic goals" (Hoelscher 2011: 202). As such, heritage is no longer a fixed, unchanging object from the past but rather a fluid and intangible resource or action in the present.

There are clear implications of this heritage discourse for museums, especially when looking at the terminology mentioned above. Laurajane Smith's research in the U.K. has shown that today's museum visitors are not mainly, or not merely, looking for an educational experience. Rather, "the museum visit may be understood analytically as a cultural performance in which people either consciously or unconsciously seek to have their views, sense of self, and social or cultural belonging reinforced" (Smith 2015: 459). In this sense, museums are a space in which heritage is performed, constructed, supported, and changed. Museums are tasked with this role in "the process of 'heritage-making'" (Smith 2015: 459) and visitors expect not only to learn but also to feel.

In this changed discourse, it is clear that an understanding of heritage now relies less on artefacts and more on meanings and the intangible (Waterton *et al.*

2006: 347). In addition, there is room for a plurality of meanings that can reflect alternative values, views, and histories – in line with one of the main trends within post-colonial theories. As such, it strongly advocates inclusivity, not only for deciding which heritage may be important for a specific community but also what to do with it or how to manage it. In championing inclusivity, there is also a strong link between the current heritage discourse and the aims of the New Museology. There is, however, a risk here due to the power inherent in heritage. Communities may seek help from museums in order to achieve certain goals. In these cases, a museum must be sure that they are willing to support this community in achieving those goals, while running the risk of potentially excluding or going against the wishes of other communities. Conflict may be difficult to avoid when a museum decides to support one community's agenda over that of another; decisions will require careful deliberation. In addition, the fluid nature of heritage implies the need to be flexible and changeable for museums or similar cultural institutions. Moreover, the emphasis on the intangible nature of heritage has moved museums towards rethinking their collections and object-centered approaches and to include other cultural elements into their narratives. Alissandra Cummins has argued that especially in the Caribbean, heritage is valued not for its tangible remains but for the "shared, lived, defining (intangible) experiences" (Cummins 2012: 26). Focusing on heritage and its intangible aspects has changed exhibition practices to include more sensory experiences. Certainly, along with knowledge of the developments in post-colonial theories, an understanding of the current discourse on heritage is crucial to grasp the ways in which museums are adjusting what they present to the public and how.

Such a discussion of the theoretical frameworks underlying this research project is crucial, not only because it provides the perspectives from which to understand how the research questions were answered, but indeed also as the reason why specifically *these* questions were asked to begin with. This is the essence of the Foucauldian[4] definition of discourse, namely, that there are specific ways in which we can talk about – or ask questions about – specific topics (Foucault [1969] 1972; Hall 2010: 6). According to Michel Foucault, discourses not only provide a perspective but also imply a certain kind of knowledge and behavior. He explains this through the constant link between power and knowledge in which knowledge and power both infer and create each other (Foucault [1975] 1977; Gosden 1999: 198; Hall 2010: 48-49). That is to say, having a certain kind of knowledge can create power, while on the other hand, having power allows for the creation of knowledge.

One of the key points here is that discourses are historically specific and that they provide a specific framework for a *limited amount of time* (Foucault [1969] 1972; Hall 2010: 46). A change in discourse is called a discursive shift and frequently results in theoretical shifts within academia as well as the development of new methods and practices. Within society these shifts can also be felt, for instance in new political movements. On the other hand, as follows from the power/knowledge concept, political movements or events may also be the *cause of* discursive shifts. The wider discursive shift from colonialism to postmodernism can be seen as underlying the emergence of

---

4   This is distinct from semantic discourse theories which focus on an analysis of conversation (Hall 2010: 44).

the three interrelated theoretical fields: New Museology, post-colonial theories, and the current discourse on heritage.

It is within the framing of those same three theoretical fields that this research was designed, developed, and conducted. To be more precise, given the topic 'museums in the Caribbean,' it was the New Museology discourse which led to the specification of this topic by directing it towards the *societal role* of museums in the Caribbean. Influenced by the way in which the New Museology discourse has developed in recent years to be strongly about communities, the research questions were phrased so as to focus on participatory practices and community engagement processes. Methodologically, it implied focusing the research on museums in the present and contemporary communities, rather than taking on a historical perspective or choosing a collections-based approach. Inspired also by post-colonial theories, the idea of conducting the research entirely through a few case studies was discarded, instead opting to include a region-wide survey in order to allow a greater diversity of museums and communities to be covered and thus to improve the inclusivity of the research project and present multiple narratives and histories. Fieldwork was conducted in line with these discourses by ensuring that the museum visit was seen as a cultural performance which included more than just the building and its objects, but also depended on the staff, other visitors, and the context of the museum. Self-reflexivity was an important method in all phases of research, which will be discussed in more detail towards the end of the next chapter. Both the regional survey and the individual case studies were conducted in a way to provide multi-vocality, and to let the value of community engagement practices and processes be assessed by the community members themselves. Analysis and interpretation of the results was also placed within these discourses, choosing to focus on the societal impact of community engagement, placing emphasis on grassroots museums, or developing hypotheses of differences due to colonial pasts. In summary, all aspects of this research were influenced predominantly by the New Museology and the interrelated developments in post-colonial theories and heritage discourse. This influence ties back to how the very essence of the research, namely the 'museum,' was perceived.

Defining the Museum

The role and rationale of the museum has changed over the centuries and, along with it, so has its definition. In the words of John Whiting: "there are as many definitions of a museum as there are authors on the subject" (Whiting 1983: 1). The history of the origin of the museum was already briefly discussed in the introductory chapter of this dissertation, which allows us at this point to focus on how alterations of the term 'museum' over the last century have led to the current definitions and models. On a global stage, the International Council of Museums (ICOM) has been an influential actor in terms of providing a standard definition that not only defines its 20,000 institutional members across the world, but for instance is also incorporated directly into the national heritage legislation of some countries (Murphy 2004). Thus, the undeniable international influence of the ICOM definition warrants a brief overview of its historical development, followed by some critiques and reflections.

ICOM's first museum definition was adopted in 1946 and encapsulated a view of the museum as being centered on a fairly broad range of collections:

> *The word "museums" includes all collections open to the public, of artistic, technical, scientific, historical or archaeological material, including zoos and botanical gardens, but excluding libraries, except in so far as they maintain permanent exhibition rooms.*
> ICOM (1946: 2.2)

In 1951, ICOM added terminology expressing the need for a museum to be a "permanent establishment" (ICOM 1951: 2), thereby restricting the concept and excluding institutions of a more temporary nature. A decade later, the definition was reworked again, now stating that collections had to consist of "objects of cultural or scientific *significance*" (my emphasis; ICOM 1961: 2.3). Influenced by the development of the New Museology and the reconsideration of the purpose of museums, the definition was significantly altered in 1974[5] by stating that a museum was "in the service of the society and its development," further specifying the museum to be a "non-profit making institution," reintroducing the need for museums to be "open to the public" and dropping the need for significance by simply stating that they contained "material evidence of man and his environment" (ICOM 1974: 2.3). Over the following three decades, this definition of the museum remained unchanged, with the exception of the introduction of gender neutrality, altering "man and his environment" to "people and their environment" in 1989 (ICOM 1989: 2.1). During these decades, it was only the specification following this definition – which validates the inclusion of, among others, archaeological sites, zoos, science centers, nature reserves, and exhibition galleries – that was expanded a number of times. Finally, the most recent amendments to the definition in 2007 have entirely eliminated this list specifying what types of institutions qualify as museums. An even greater change at this time was the incorporation of intangible heritage into the museum definition, which now reads:

> *A museum is a non-profit, permanent institution in the service of society and its development, open to the public, which acquires, conserves, researches, communicates and exhibits the tangible and intangible heritage of humanity and its environment for the purposes of education, study and enjoyment.*
> ICOM (2007: 3.1)

Despite the statement that museums should be 'in the service of society,' the current ICOM definition reflects mostly an old museological discourse on museums and heritage, emphasizing permanence and education, with a focus on collections and objects. As an organization, ICOM has also received criticism for becoming increasingly Eurocentric and for having limited the opportunities for participation for members from *e.g.* the Caribbean and Africa by changing the requirements for national

---

5   UNESCO's *Round Table on the Development of the Role of Museums in the Contemporary World* (Santiago de Chile, 1972) had included ICOM's director and is also seen as a formative moment in drafting the 1974 ICOM definition.

committees. Fiona Candlin has eloquently pointed out the irony that despite the drive for museums to become more inclusive to visitors, many museum associations or organizations adhere to strict rules which limit membership and exclude those museums which are seen as ineligible (Candlin 2016: 11). Indeed, there are a number of points where ICOM's view of the museum does not line up with the New Museology and contemporary museum practices and processes. The definition above is quite different from, for instance, the idea of the museum visit as a cultural performance where views, identities, and a sense of belonging are reinforced (Smith 2015: 459). In addition, much of the focus remains skewed towards national institutions and perspectives, leaving little room for local views or grassroots developments.

Although new revisions to the ICOM definition are being planned, it seems impossible for the reality of museums on the ground and this internationally referenced theoretical definition of the concept to neatly overlap. Museums and museum models have to a greater extent been practically affected by the ideals of the New Museology, while the root of the ICOM definition continues to keep it tethered to an older museology. For this research project, it was therefore necessary to develop a much broader definition of the 'museum,' which was appropriate for contemporary museums and museum models throughout the world, but specifically for those in the Caribbean. This was approached as a 'working definition,' enabling adjustments as needed while fieldwork was being conducted in the region. The approach took the actual visits to museums as a point of departure, resulting in a definition that is rooted predominantly in practice. This broad working definition was: *a museum is a space for tangible or intangible heritage, which provides opportunities for knowledge transfer, and is open to the public.* Taking on this working definition enabled the inclusion of museums which were, for instance, for-profit or non-permanent and did not restrict the definition to certain types of collections or activities. By applying this definition, it was possible to visit a wide range of museums throughout the Caribbean region and to identify a number of museum models from a New Museology perspective. This has enabled the research and its discussion to be drawn away from the 'usual suspects,' such as national museums, into lesser-known – but equally important – terrain. By including living museums, spaces where persons actively embed intangible heritage into tangible sites, it was possible to study World Heritage Sites such as historic city centers (Galla 2005: 105; Galla 2008). This academic and museological rebalancing is much needed: "like curators choosing a series of plastic artefacts from a mass of incongruous items and placing the remainder into storage, […] academics have conceptually de-accessioned or warehoused organizations that do not support 'the desired narrative'" (Candlin 2016: 139).

Revisiting the New Museology and its demand for museums to work towards societal goals, the purposeful design of two museum models can be readily discerned. Originally developed in France in the 1970s, the ecomuseum was a concept that placed community issues at the core of the museum's institutional mission (Davis 2008: 398-400). The concept of the community museum that was developed in the same decade in Mexico, consists of a network of smaller museums that focus on local community outreach, while being supported by a larger national institution (Barnes 2008: 214-215). Both of these museum models can also be found to a greater or lesser degree in the Caribbean. In addition, a number of other museum models were identified which are aligned to the New Museology discourse and community engagement. While none of these museum models fits wholly within the ICOM definition of the museum, they can easily find a place within the abovementioned working definition. The following presents a brief overview of five of these museum models to showcase how the New Museology and this working definition of the museum informed this research project and the selection of museums to include in the study. These five models are: grassroots museums, private museums, micromuseums, ecomuseums, and hybrid museums.

In the course of this research project and particularly the regional museum survey, museums were described based on a number of characteristics. One of these characteristics was the ownership of the museum and contained 5 categories: governmental, grassroots, private, mixed, or unknown (see *Regional Museum Survey*, page 49). **Grassroots museums** are considered to be those which are owned by an individual, community, or non-governmental organization and are not directly incorporated into, or financed by, private enterprise. If not owned by an individual, the grassroots museum of an organization or community is often based on a shared ethnicity, religion, language, cultural heritage, or location. A grassroots museum can be a collection that is publicly on display in a person's home, an institution run through a historic society, or a cultural display in a community gathering place. Most grassroots museums contain collections which are a mix of both tangible and intangible heritages. When objects are present, they are not always 'musealized' in the sense of Marzia Varutti's use of the term (Varutti 2013: 67) – they may still be handled, used, or not be conserved. This certainly does not imply that they do not receive museological care, as items in collections may be catalogued, protected in cases or boxes, and contain labels. Rather, objects may be given more active roles during museum visitation than what has been seen as the norm. Grassroots museums exist throughout the entire Caribbean region, but they are particularly abundant in those places where governmental support to culture and museums may be limited or non-existent. In some places, the grassroots museum may be the only museum, such as the *Heritage Collection Museum* on Anguilla, and its importance and value for both local communities and visitors is unparalleled. A network of community museums, similar to that set up in Mexico, exists in Cuba and in a comparable fashion in Martinique, but is not common throughout the region as a whole. However, in some places national museums have set up outreach museums in communities that are distant from the capital. In Jamaica, for instance, both the *National Museum Jamaica* and the *National Gallery of Jamaica*, located in Kingston, have set up outreach museums in Montego Bay.

Within this study, another category of museum ownership was **private museums**. In contrast to grassroots museums, private museums are directly incorporated into or financed by private enterprise. Although they share many similarities with grassroots museums, this close tie to a corporation tends to influence the mission and scope of the museum. Private museums can be found throughout the region: rum distilleries or cigar factories with exhibitions and tours are quite common, as are money museums in banks. In the Dominican Republic one can find multiple amber museums due to unique occurrence of this natural material on the island. In many of these examples, the mission of the private museum is centered on the associated enterprise and one of the goals is to encourage visitors to develop product awareness and spend money in the

Figure 2: The artworks of Museo Bellapart, Dominican Republic, are accessed through a Honda dealership.

(gift) shop. Certainly these museums also have other goals than only advertisement, but their subjectivity and dependency on the enterprise are evident. At the same time, there are other examples of private museums where the dependency between the enterprise and the museum appears to be purely financial in the other direction. This is the case when individuals have amassed significant wealth through their business and have chosen to invest this into the creation of a collection and a museum. Thus it is possible in the Caribbean to find a contemporary art museum in a Honda dealership (see figure 2) or an Amerindian archaeological museum in a former Coca-Cola factory.

By using the abovementioned wider working definition of 'museum,' this research project was able to place emphasis both on grassroots and private museums alongside governmental museums. This was seen as a necessary research approach, as "museum development cannot afford to turn its back on private initiative, especially when the contribution of the state may be supplemented" (Arjona *et al.* 1982: 80). Following Cummins' observation that Caribbean communities can feel a disinheritance or disassociation from mainstream national narratives (Cummins 2004: 238), these diverse museum models may be more widely appropriate.

Present within both of these two categories of grassroots and private museum ownership, two characteristic museum types warrant attention. The term '**micromuseum**' was coined by Fiona Candin to refer to "small independent single-subject museums" (Candlin 2016: 1). Her study focused on micromuseums in the U.K. and was very strongly centered on museums with a single subject matter, such as the *Bakelite Museum* or the *Vintage Wireless Museum*. Such museums also exist in the Caribbean, for instance the *West Indies Cricket Heritage Centre* in Grenada. Regarding these micromuseums, an interesting characteristic is how they can be at once more public and more private than traditional governmental museums: "whereas it is less public in the sense of being open to audiences than a major institution, the business of the museum – the authorship of the displays, the labour involved, the people who work there, and its financial standing – is much more public" (Candlin 2016: 43). Thus a micromuseum might be less public due to its location within a home, its limited opening hours, or the owner's right to bar a visitor from entering for personal reasons. A visitor's behavior in such a museum might be more like that of a guest. However, at the same time, much of the museum work that often remains hidden 'back stage' in bigger institutions can be openly visible to the visitor. It is not uncommon for the visitor to meet the owner of the museum or to see exhibition development in progress. In the Caribbean, some of these observations of the characteristics of micromuseums also hold true for grassroots or private museums with a broader mix of subject matters, such as the *San Nicolas Community Museum* in Aruba. Dedicated to collecting a mix of local natural history, rural history, or art, these small, independent, multiple-subject museum may also have this distinct quality of being both more public and more private at the same time.

The museum model of the **ecomuseum**, as hinted at above, focuses on a (frequently local) community and the social, cultural, and natural environment it shares (Davis 2008: 398). Although an ecomuseum can be governmentally or privately owned, they are often set up as grassroots initiatives by communities or a collaboration between communities. They usually consist of more than a solitary museum building, for instance by encompassing a landscape or multiple sites and buildings within the community, or by incorporating parks, replica structures, or gardens. Collections may contain largely intangible heritages, such as data from oral history projects, language skills, or traditional crafts. Nancy Fuller has defined ecomuseums as "community learning centers that link the past with the present as a strategy to deal with the future needs of that particular society" (Fuller 1992: 328). These museums are characterized by the importance of their activities and other engagements that extend far beyond the physicality of the ecomuseum itself. Often, an ecomuseum has a double focus, first of all on the preservation and transmission of cultural heritage and secondly on environmental sustainability (de Varine 2006: 227). Both of these goals are linked tightly to the (local) community and its specific, contemporary needs. For instance, an ecomuseum may provide activities that help their community members develop certain skills, which are deemed necessary to function better within their particular (social, cultural, or natural) environment. Therefore, the ecomuseum can be characterized as a community *process* rather than a *product* in itself (Davis 2008: 403; Fuller 1992: 331). This implies that the ecomuseum, once opened, is not 'finished,' but rather ever changing according to the needs of the community. At the same time, once the community feels they have no need for the ecomuseum, it can simply be closed. Collomb & Renard (1982) published a review of the *Ecomusée de Marie-Galante: Habitation Murat* on Marie-Galante, but many other examples of ecomuseums exist throughout the Caribbean (for a more detailed discussion and additional examples, see *Ecomuseums*, page 73).

Finally, a broad definition of the term 'museum' enabled this research to include **hybrid museums**: museums which combine their mission with that of another type of institution or corporation. Hybrid museums can have governmental, grassroots, or private ownership. In the former we may find university museums or military museums. Grassroots hybrid museums may consist of a combination of exhibitions with a religious building, such as a synagogue, temple, mosque, or church. Some examples of hybrid private museums, such as money museums, were already mentioned above, but this category might also include art galleries. In all of these examples, the meaning or mission of the museum is affected due to the additional functions it carries by means of the associated institution, enterprise, or organization. These additional functions might carry restrictions or obligations that are otherwise not common for museums. For instance, one has to be a trained and active member of the Jamaican military in order to work at the *Jamaican Military Museum and Library*. Religious museums may similarly limit their staff to members of their religious community. The focus of the activities of hybrid museums may entail different museum practices as well. For instance, university museums focus strongly on their research activities, being relevant to the student curriculum, and they tend to have larger research or reference collections, while they may not necessarily invest as much effort into their exhibition activities.

In summary, although the international influence of the ICOM definition of the 'museum' cannot be ignored, it poses certain difficulties as it is rooted in an old museology view of the museum and does not practically work well for museums that exist within the framework of the New Museology discourse. Furthermore, the ICOM definition tends to be exclusive, while the New Museology is aimed strongly towards inclusivity. In order to approach this research, a working definition of the term 'museum' was developed, based in practice on museum visitation in the Caribbean. According to this definition, a museum is a space for tangible or intangible heritage, which provides opportunities for knowledge transfer, and is open to the public. This wider definition enabled the identification of various museum models which might otherwise not have fallen within the scope of the research, namely: grassroots museums, private museums, micromuseums, ecomuseums and hybrid museums.

Community Engagement

> *If the idea of 'community' most frequently embraced is something that is 'good',*
> *'safe' and 'comfortable', it is with an acute sense of paradox that we note its emer-*
> *gence out of a distinctly un*comfortable *and challenging context.*
> Laurajane Smith & Emma Waterton (2009: 13-14; original emphasis)

How can museums respond to the changes they are expected to make, based on the New Museology and related to post-colonial theories and the current heritage discourse? How can museums sufficiently expand their social role, so that they are not only working *for* society, but *within* society (Crooke 2008: 418)? In answer to these questions, community engagement is most often proposed as the ideal method for museums to achieve this deeply social role anchored within contemporary discourses (van Broekhoven *et al.* 2010; Simon 2010). Community engagement, including participation, collaboration, consultation, and negotiation, has been extensively discussed within museum studies over the last few decades.[6] However, before we discuss the meanings of these terms, it is necessary to take a step back and begin with a critical evaluation of the concept of 'community.'

A discussion of the use of the term community starts with a contradiction: on the one hand, it is frequently accepted or used without definition and, on the other hand, it is a term that is difficult to define. When left undefined, it tends to act as a buzz word that carries positive – almost utopian – connotations (Smith & Waterton 2009: 13). However, this does not account for the fact that community is *not* inherently good. In fact, communities are as much about inclusion as they are, de facto, about exclusion, meaning that their desires and actions can be conflicted or contested (Smith & Waterton 2009: 93). This is due to the fact that the meaning of the term has changed and no longer refers to 'the public' or 'everyone' (in the sense that 'communal' still refers to common use). How, then, can we attempt to define the concept? At a very basic level, a community is an abstract grouping of people who share a sense of belonging based on a shared characteristic. Such a sense of belonging may be constructed on the basis of locality, common experiences, characteristics such as language, religion, ethnicity, or other cultural markers (Crooke 2008: 416). It should be clear, then, that communities are not fixed entities: instead, they are fluid and can be created or discarded as desired. Like identity, communities are activated depending on the social setting or occasion (Karp 1992: 3-4).

There are a number of myths or stereotypical associations that tend to adhere to the term community. Besides the notion that community is inherently a good thing, these include the assumptions that communities are homogeneous units, that they are necessarily geographically based ('local'), that they have long established roots, or that their characteristics are easily recognizable (Crooke 2011a: 172; Gable 2013: 38; Smith & Waterton 2009: 18). Community is also on occasion mistakenly used synonymously with the term *minority* and placed in opposition to *society* as the mainstream majority. Eric Gable has warned that these misconceptions have influenced "the romance of community among those who work in museums" (Gable 2013: 39). Some of these perceptions may have lingered from previous definitions of community. However, communities are currently understood as heterogeneous, fluid, and they can take on any size. They are *imagined* in the same way that Benedict Anderson describes the nation (Anderson 2006: 6): in most cases, not everyone within a community knows each other personally, so instead their common sense of belonging is imagined. If we now understand identity as consisting of many different facets, some of which are more important at certain moments than others, it is understandable how people can all belong to more than one community at a time and how such membership may be "fleeting, partial, or innate, lifelong, and unshakeable" (Onciul 2013: 81). Considering communities such as the LGBTQ or the online community, it is clear that many of these myths do not reflect the actual nature of communities. As a final point, it must be emphasized again that communities have the "potential to be both beneficial and detrimental" (Onciul 2013: 79). Because communities tend to define themselves in opposition to what they are not, they are exclusive in

---

6   Community involvement approaches have become popular in other areas as well, for instance public archaeology, civic engagement in policy making, community feedback in game development, or urban development planning.

essence. In doing so, depending on their power and ambitions, they can be marginalizing to a greater or lesser extent (Golding 2013: 20).

How has this current understanding of community affected museums in their work? Both in museological theories and practices, *community* has come to either replace or exist in contrast to *the public, audience,* or *visitors* (Crooke 2011a: 170). These latter three terms reflect a perception of people in museums as a largely homogeneous and passive group, consuming museum products, such as exhibitions and events. Visitor demographics usually allow for only a few outwardly visible characteristics to be noted, for instance, age, gender, or a distinction between local and tourist. Of course, these do not begin to account for the multitude of characteristics that may determine an individual's sense of identity or community. In contrast, applying the notion of community allows the museum to look at people as heterogeneous groups of actors within the museum process, *e.g.* youth communities (Ariese-Vandemeulebroucke 2018). This can have two concrete effects on the museum. First of all, it allows for a broader investigation of audiences, so that museums can provide services that are better suited to the specific communities they wish to target. Considering how people "belong to many communities, often simultaneously" (Karp 1992: 12) this is not an easy task. However, it is certainly a worthwhile adjustment museums are making in the face of greater cultural diversity and contemporary notions of complex identities. Secondly, it allows for the involvement of community members throughout the entire museum process – rather than only as recipients of a completed product. Thus, in the broadest sense, *community engagement* is the multitude of ways in which museum staff involve communities in the museum process. Reflecting on the last few decades, Elizabeth Crooke noted that "the sustained interest in the concept of community has had a major impact on museum practice" (Crooke 2015: 481) and that "it is not just a case of museums representing or symbolizing community; now it is museums forging community identity, altering community experiences, and improving community life" (Crooke 2015: 486).

Setting community engagement as an overarching method of involvement, there are many different manners in which this involvement can take place. There are two principal ways to approach community engagement models. First of all, methods can be identified based on the degree to which power is shared between the museum institution/staff and community members. Such a scale was devised for social work by Sherry Arnstein (1969), whose eight step ladder of citizen participation ranged from manipulation (non-participation) to citizen control. Within the sphere of museums, Nina Simon's work has been greatly influential. She proposed four models, ranging from contributory (by which a community contributes to the work of the museum) to hosted (meaning that the museum acts as a host for the work of a community) (Simon 2010: 190-191). For heritage conservation, Amareswar Galla similarly proposed three models, ranging from consultation to community cultural action (Galla 2008: 22). The necessity to look at community engagement from the perspective of power sharing is echoed in critical museological research which supports the need for *negotiation* over *consultation* (*e.g.* Fouseki 2010). Nonetheless, it is important to remember that during any community engagement process the power balance may shift and be different during the various stages of the process, making such typologies and models difficult to apply in practice (Onciul 2013: 82).

Secondly, community engagement can be defined by specific activities – so-called participatory practices – no matter whether the initiative for these activities lies with the museum or the community. The repatriation of objects, which can be seen as one of the reasons for the emergence of the New Museology, is one of these participatory practices (Nederveen Pieterse 2005: 175; Peers & Brown 2003a: 6). Crowdsourcing, defined as "the practice of obtaining information or services by soliciting input from a large number of people, typically via the Internet and often without offering compensation" (Ridge 2013: 436) is another which has gained popularity in recent years. Exhibition co-curation, participatory action research, community consultation groups, participation in interactive displays, community collections management, hosting community activities – there are countless examples of participatory practices.

Considering the wide variety of community engagement methods and participatory practices, it is not surprising that the goals or reasons for applying these methods are also abundant. Community engagement methods and participatory practices are mostly designed to benefit both community members and the museum and its staff, although the type of benefit and its extent might be different for these groups. For museum institutions and staff, reasoning frequently revolves around relevance and purpose: "if the public is not interested in what we are doing, then what are we doing?" (Pyburn 2008: 202). Certainly, being institutions that are open to the public, museums depend greatly on public support (Crooke 2008: 415). This is especially true for museums working deeply from a New Museology perspective, who wish to become stronger social actors and attract different (perhaps previously excluded or neglected) communities (Simon 2016: 51-56). Motivations may be political or democratic, hinging on notions of social inclusion and the decolonization of the museum. However, the need to target new audiences may not only stem from ideals of inclusivity, but it may simply be a demand from governments or funding bodies (Fouseki 2010: 181). Set within a larger academic trend to be pluralistic, interdisciplinary, and reflexive, other forms of knowledge and expertise are welcomed to balance out the museum narrative (Campbell 2008: 310). From the point of view of communities or community members, engagement with the museum is beneficial on various grounds. For the individual, engagement may result in a stronger sense of identity, self-efficacy, confidence, empowerment, or new skills and knowledge (Ohmer 2010: 6). For communities, the goals are usually more long-term, such as solving community problems, adjusting power relationships, increasing communal efficacy, or fostering cross-cultural understanding (Onciul 2013: 94). Most of these goals generally concern community engagement and its inherent benefits, while individual projects would of course also lead to specific benefits, such as the repatriation of a certain collection or the inclusion of a community's voice in a museum exhibition.

Keeping in mind that community is as much about exclusion as it is about inclusion, community engagement can not only be beneficial but may also lead to conflict and contention. First of all, community members and museum staff not only have different reasons for getting involved in community engagement processes, they also desire other outcomes, which may take place on different time scales. For instance, museum staff may be working towards a short term exhibition production deadline, while community members could be seeking long term political influence. If, perhaps due to a lack of transparency, these different desires are not made clear from the outset, disappointment can arise along the way. Conflict can also occur if one of the parties

THE SOCIAL MUSEUM IN THE CARIBBEAN

holds more power throughout the process and only their goals are reached (Clifford 1997). In reviewing community engagement projects, frustration is often apparent with community members who feel that they are not being listened to or that their needs are not being met (*e.g.* Fouseki & Smith 2013: 236-238). In these cases, museums may be accused of tokenistic community engagement (Lagerkvist 2006: 59). Although the fact that both parties have different aims can be a source of friction in itself, many of these problems stem from a lack of transparency and unequal power balances. Especially for community members who already consider themselves to be in a disadvantaged position in society, issues of power can be more sensitive and problems may arise more easily (Lagerkvist 2006: 63). Power inequalities may be perceived from the very beginning, for instance if the museum is the one taking the initiative in the engagement process. By inviting a community in to collaborate, this may already reinstate (perceived) superiority (Varutti 2013: 62). In the worst case, community members may see unequal community engagement as a form of exploitation by the majority and accuse the museum of cultural appropriation or neo-colonialism (Kreps 2011a: 81). For instance, in a critical review of the *National Museum of the American Indian*, USA, two Indigenous scholars characterized the employment of Indigenous staff not as an effort to be inclusive but rather as the creation of "living exhibitions in the persons of the tour guides" (Hilden & Huhndorf; quoted in Ronan 2014: 136).

Another difficulty is the matter of representation. In almost all cases, it is not practically possible to work together with an entire community and all of the museum staff. Thus, community engagement is ultimately based on individual representatives from all participating groups (Onciul 2013: 81). However, museums frequently assume that individual community members can and do represent their whole community. At the same time, community members express the pressure, both from the museum and their own communities, to be proper representatives (Fouseki 2010: 181). The heterogeneity within communities can also make controversy difficult to avoid (Lagerkvist 2006: 54). Still, controversy, if negotiated carefully and handled correctly, may be turned into fruitful opportunities for community engagement (Lagerkvist 2006: 65).

To attempt to avoid some of these problems, a number of conditions or values have been proposed to improve the success of community engagement. The investment of plenty of time is one of these conditions. The real importance of community engagement, it is argued, are the results that can be achieved throughout the whole process, not simply the end product or exhibition (Smith & Waterton 2009: 116). Trust and respect between parties is something that needs time to develop. Time is especially important for the community members, who are generally more interested in long term results and communal benefits, rather than reaching a deadline for the exhibition opening. It is stressed, therefore, to see an exhibition (for instance) as only an intermediate part of the engagement process: a process that begins long before and continues long after the opening event. Parity and equal access are also important conditions. In practice, this might mean that not all of the meetings take place at the museum, but that a location is found where all those involved may feel like equals. Time and sensitivity are also needed to investigate first of all which communities or museums to engage with, how to contact the members of these communities, and how to reach significantly representative participants.

In summary, the concepts of community and community engagement have been defined above. Various community engagement methods were described, based either on their degree of power sharing or on the types of participatory practices involved. Although benefits were noted for all parties involved in community engagement processes, some criticisms, common pitfalls, and risks of conflict were also indicated. The remainder of this chapter will consider community and community engagement in a Caribbean context in order to assess the relevance and applicability of the terms in this particular region.

What better way to place the concept of community in a Caribbean context, than with the words of Jamaican historian Rex Nettleford?

> *The encounter of Africa and Europe on foreign soil and these in turn with the indigenous Native Americans on their long-tenanted estates and all in turn with latter-day arrivants from Asia and the Middle East, has resulted in a culture of texture and diversity held together by a dynamic creativity severally described as creative chaos, stable disequilibrium or cultural pluralism.*
> Rex Nettleford (2003)

Whereas identity construction is complex everywhere, Nettleford argues that identities are even more diverse and fragmented in the Caribbean (Nettleford 2004). When the process of political decolonization was set into motion throughout the Caribbean, national and ethnic identities were the first to enter the debate. Newly independent states struggled to define themselves, often in opposition to their former colonizer, in a condition of great diversity. Jamaica's national motto from 1962 ("out of many, one people") reflects the need to construct unity out of diversity. Within the larger Caribbean region, for instance through organizations such as CARICOM, the construction of a regional Caribbean identity is still on the agenda as one of the main priorities. During its 30th anniversary, Maxine Henry-Wilson urged delegates that "the creation of a Caribbean person or identity cannot be accidental or incidental to our actions and activities" (Henry-Wilson 2003). Considering the diverse ethnicities, languages, religions, and cultures of the people in the region, it has been suggested that such a regional identity could be constructed on the basis of pluralism, rooted in a culture shared by all (Nettleford 2004). This could largely be based on the shared experience of recent or distant migration. As Alissandra Cummins pointed out, "in essence, it is a region where (virtually) everyone came from (virtually) everywhere else, whether voluntarily or by force" (Cummins 2012: 26).

Within Caribbean museums, identity construction has been similarly complex (Farmer 2013). In some places, communities of African descendants have received the strongest representation in recent years, while other communities are underrepresented. Besides ethnicity, Caribbean communities and identities are also diverse in many other facets, such as religion, language, culture, or local history, and this provides enormously varied opportunities for potential engagement with museums. Elsewhere in the world, community engagement practices have been criticized for focusing too much on ethnic communities, which has created an imbalance in the voices that are heard (Mullen Kreamer 1992: 377). The pluralism of the Caribbean, combined with the continuous presence of temporary visitors provides a unique situation for Caribbean museums that wish to apply community engagement methods. Although 'community' remains difficult to define in general, the pluralism and diversity of the Caribbean makes community engagement particularly important for museums in the region. Pushing the concept of community in a wider framework beyond the local/tourist dichotomy, Caribbean museums can work with dynamic, fluid, heterogeneous communities in all aspects of their work.

There are some challenges facing Caribbean museums that wish to pursue community engagement as part of their work. Although not unique to the Caribbean, museums need to struggle to prove their relevance and impact in order to have access to resources and not be the lowest priority in terms of political or financial consideration. Representativity can be a challenge if museum staff insufficiently reflects the local diversity of communities, creating a discrepancy between the museum and its surroundings (Brookes 2008: 2). Perhaps the most severely challenging condition is the legacy of cultural disinheritance – the fact that museums in the colonial era were used as tools of suppression by denying certain communities their heritage (Cummins 1992: 38). Finally, some local and visiting scholars have noted that museum visitation is not a part of Caribbean culture and that local adults rarely enter museums (Brookes 2008: 3; Gilette 2000: 47; Whiting 1983: 73). However, this research has not found this to generally be the case. Although certain museums in the region do attract more visitors and fewer locals, this seems to be the result of museum-specific policies rather than a cultural trend.

Despite the challenges facing Caribbean museums, some of these have created positive opportunities for community engagement. For instance, a lack of governmental support for museums has in many places inspired the creation of grassroots museums (see *Grassroots and Governmental Museums*, page 67). Similarly, limited or colonially biased collections and a lack of staffing can be remedied by the donation of objects or by individuals volunteering as guides or working as staff at the museum. This crowdsourcing of objects and knowledge, along with the donation of time and expertise, and the high occurrence of grassroots museums, reflects some of the participatory practices that are commonly employed in the Caribbean (see *Caribbean Participatory Practices*, page 67). As such, community engagement can take place throughout the entire museum process (from inception to development to execution), rather than only temporarily during the museum visit or for the duration of a specific project. Community engagement in the Caribbean has also resulted in a large amount of multilingual museum products, which literally reflect the voices of multiple communities (Maréchal 1998: 47).

The intended goals of Caribbean community engagement practices are not essentially different from those anywhere else in the world. The main point is that they need to be relevant and inclusive to Caribbean communities. For instance, there has been a lack of local popular support for Eurocentric heritage projects, such as those focusing on European-influenced great houses (Cummins 1992: 42). On the other hand, support has been greater, especially among local adult communities, for museums and collections focused on the recent history of local (rural and urban) traditions (Brookes 2008: 5). For some specific communities, feeling pressured by the homogenizing effect of globalization and a separation from younger generations, the transmission of cultural heritage, skills, and knowledge are the most important intended outcomes. As with community engagement in any museum, relevance remains key.

Facing the particular context of the Caribbean, its colonial histories, and its pluralism of communities, museums in the region have embraced the New Museology and post-colonial theories to adjust their roles in society. By adopting and adapting participatory practices and by investing in community engagement processes, they have become increasingly social museums.

3

Methodological Framework

I treat museum visits as events that include various individuals and spoken exchanges as well as objects, displays, and buildings.
Fiona Candlin (2016: 17)

The museological literature abounds with examples of studies of visitors in museums, as well as guides and toolkits for museum professionals wishing to develop evaluations of their museum, exhibitions, or programs. There is a wealth of methods for those interested in understanding visitors and evaluating their museum experiences, from demographics and focus groups, to heat mapping and personal meaning mapping (Davidson 2015). Visitor studies methods fall short, however, for those community members who may be affected by the museum but who have chosen not to visit the museum. And although some studies have focused on assessing the experiences of (usually external) people involved in museum projects, there is still relatively little emphasis on evaluating the involvement of museum staff. In addition, limited resources exist for those who want to be a museum visitor and conduct a critical museum visit. Such a review is often the domain of museum studies students, who are provided with checklists of museum aspects which they can consider during their visit (*e.g.* for Department of Museum Studies, University of Leicester: Kavanagh 1994). While these checklists are certainly useful, they fragment the museum visit into isolated categories such as building, governing bodies, or displays. In consideration of these limitations, this research project necessitated the development of a unique methodology which borrows and combines approaches from museum studies, visitor studies, and anthropology. A combination of these approaches made it possible to gather data about museums, their staff, and their visitors from museum visits. Additionally, a different combination of methodologies from these fields supported the development of the case studies research, enabling the collection of data related to the perceptions of participants in community engagement processes. Although Fiona Candlin's *Micromuseology* (2016) was not published until after this project's fieldwork was completed, her approach of holistically treating the museum visit as an event is similar to the methodology used in the regional museum survey.

This chapter will describe and critically consider the methodology developed for this research project. Firstly, it will show how I designed an approach aimed to tackle the main research question of this dissertation. This approach identified the main areas that required research, which directed the research to take place on both a macro and a micro level, and thus informed the development of the sub questions. Secondly, the specific methodology for the macro level research is explained in detail. This part of the study was a regional museum survey throughout the greater Caribbean and included visits to 195 museums in 25 different islands or countries. Thirdly, the micro level methodology is introduced, which focused on two particular case studies: the *Kalinago Barana Autê* in Dominica and the *Bengal to Barbados* exhibition project in Barbados. Finally, a section on research ethos is included to familiarize the reader with the general attitudes and philosophies, as well as codes of conduct, which guided fieldwork and all other aspects of this research project.

Research Approach

To consider the overall research approach, let's revisit the main research question (see *Research Questions and Objectives*, page 18): *How are Caribbean museums realigning their societal role in relation to contemporary Caribbean communities?* In order to begin to find an answer to this question, we step back to the theoretical framework of this dissertation and place ourselves again in the mindset of the New Museology. The question is framed with a knowledge of 'museums' and 'communities' as was defined in the previous chapter which allows for a broad definition of the concept of the museum and a fluid, heterogeneous understanding of communities. From this New Museology perspective, community engagement forms the key to answering the research question. How, then, do we reach these answers? Fundamentally, an understanding of museums in the Caribbean is crucial in order to begin to comprehend their societal role and how this may have changed or still be changing. Once this picture has crystallized, a deeper consideration is necessary of how Caribbean museums adopt and apply community engagement. This can be achieved by looking on the one hand at participatory practices – *what* museums are doing to engage with communities, or vice versa – and on the other hand at community engagement processes – *how* such engagement takes place. So, how are Caribbean museums realigning their societal role in relation to contemporary Caribbean communities? By adopting participatory practices and undertaking community engagement processes.

Through this research approach, the answers to the main research question can be identified in terms of either *practices* or *processes*. This separation into either product or procedure led the research design to require two levels: macro and micro. A macro level approach is suitable to collect a broad sample of participatory practices. On the other hand, a micro level approach is appropriate to understand community engagement processes deeply. A very broad but relatively shallow study of participatory practices is thus complemented by a very deep but relatively narrow investigation of community engagement processes. Together, these two levels form a more comprehensive understanding of community engagement in Caribbean museums. To collect data on both levels, different studies were needed with their own methods, requiring a unique mix of museological and anthropological techniques. Developing a suitable mixed methods toolkit was particularly important in order to conduct this combined macro and micro study in the span of a PhD research project.

Macro level research took the form of a regional survey of Caribbean museums and their participatory practices, taking place over the course of multiple fieldwork sessions in 2013-2016. To my knowledge, this was the first Caribbean study of community engagement to include museums from all four linguistic areas. Not only is it a unique study in this regard, but it is also notable for encompassing museums of a wide variety of types of content, and for including grassroots and private museums as well as governmental institutions. As mentioned above, the study was able to include 195 museums in 25 different islands or countries, thereby reflecting the broad diversity of museums which can be found in the region. This macro level research gathered basic information about each museum, but also particularly focused on the participatory practices that were present in each. The next section of this chapter contains a more detailed description of the methodology of this regional survey, including which museums were visited, what data was collected, how this data was collected, and how analysis and interpretation were undertaken.

Micro level research was conducted in the form of two in depth case studies of ongoing community engagement processes. The case study in Dominica consisted of three separate visits (March 2015, July-August 2015, and March 2016), and the case study in Barbados of two (October 2015, and February-March 2016). Each case study consisted of three phases: exploratory visit, main case study research, and presentation of results. The macro level regional survey of Caribbean museums provided the setting for the exploratory visit in both cases, enabling the visitation of the museums in question and offering opportunities to meet with persons involved in the ongoing or developing community engagement process. Upon invitation from these persons, case study research was planned and conducted, in the form of interviews, participant observation, and community surveys. Again in both cases, I presented results of the study to community members for discussion and feedback as a final follow up. A more detailed description of the case study approach is found further on in this chapter, while the methods which were particular to each case can be found in the individual case study chapters.

By defining the research according to this macro and micro level, it was possible to finalize the sub questions. The first of these asks what participatory practices are and what the intended outcomes are of community engagement processes. This question has already been tackled on a theoretical level in Chapter 2. The second question concerns the characteristics of contemporary Caribbean museums and how they adopt participatory practices. This question relates to the macro level approach, and is answered through the regional survey, the results of which are presented in Chapter 4. The third question wonders how Caribbean communities perceive community engagement processes. Naturally, this question is directed at the micro level and is answered by the two case studies, which can be found in Chapters 5 & 6. Finally, the last question relates to how these community engagement practices and processes affect the societal role of Caribbean museums. This complex question is tackled in Chapter 7 in a discussion from multiple angles which provides a series of answers. Finally, a mosaic answer to the main research question is illustrated in Chapter 8.

Regional Museum Survey

The regional museum survey provided the framework for the collection of the macro level research data. Fieldwork was the central component of this data collection, requiring extensive preparation beforehand and detailed data management, analysis, and interpretation afterwards. Fieldwork was conducted throughout almost the entire span of the four year research project, beginning in October 2013 and ending in October 2016. Fieldwork sessions took two different forms: externally-organized visits and self-organized visits. The former were those instances where I was in the Caribbean for a conference or other event, which included scheduled site visits to museums or field trips to heritage sites. In these cases, the selection of museums had been determined by others than myself, thus influencing the sample and sample size. Self-organized visits led to the majority of data collected and as I planned these visits, the included museums were selected based on my criteria. The primary difference between the externally-organized and self-organized visits is thus the selection of museums, while the data collection methods were the same.

The main goal of the regional museum survey was to get a broad impression of museums in the Caribbean and their participatory practices. It was understood that in order to grasp this diversity, it would not suffice to visit only one or two islands. Instead, I determined that it would be necessary to visit at the very least one island or country from each of the four linguistic areas: the Dutch-, English-, French- and Spanish-speaking Caribbean. Besides allowing for a linguistic diversity, the research was designed to include both the Greater and the Lesser Antilles, as well as mainland countries in Central and South America. Due to time constraints and research feasibility, it was not possible to visit every island and country in the Caribbean region. Thus, unfortunately, it was necessary to be selective. The selection of islands and countries was mainly determined based on the parameters above, thus ensuring the inclusion of all linguistic areas and geographic sub-regions. Those islands and countries which were ultimately not included in this research remain valuable areas for future museological research which may expand the image of Caribbean museums developed in this work. Of particular note is Cuba with its Cuban Museum Network which consisted of 328 institutions in 2013 (Linares 2013: 66). Visiting a representative sample of Cuban museums was not feasible in the course of this research project, but the history and evolution of Cuban museums has been thoroughly researched by others such as Marta Arjona Pérez (Arjona *et al.* 1982), José Linares (2013), and Jorge Rolando García Perdigón (2014).

Ultimately, in the course of externally-organized visits, fieldwork was conducted in: Belize, French Guiana, Suriname (2013); Barbados, St. Lucia (2015); and Grand Cayman (2016). These six island or countries correspond to 32 of the museums visited. In the form of self-organized visits, fieldwork took place in: Anguilla, Aruba, Carriacou, Curaçao, Grenada, Jamaica, St. Barthélemy, St. Maarten, St. Martin (2014); Bequia, Dominica, Dominican Republic, Guadeloupe, Marie-Galante, Martinique, Puerto Rico, St. Vincent, Tobago, and Trinidad (2015) (see figure 3). In these 19 islands or countries, 163 museums were visited. An index of all the museums visited can be found in the appendix (see *Index: Caribbean Museums Database*, page 251).

In order to ensure the inclusion of a broad sample of Caribbean museums and their participatory practices, it was equally important to not limit the fieldwork to certain types of museums. This was aided by the development in the field of a broad working definition of museums, namely that a museum is a space for tangible or intangible heritage, which provides opportunities for knowledge transfer, and is open to

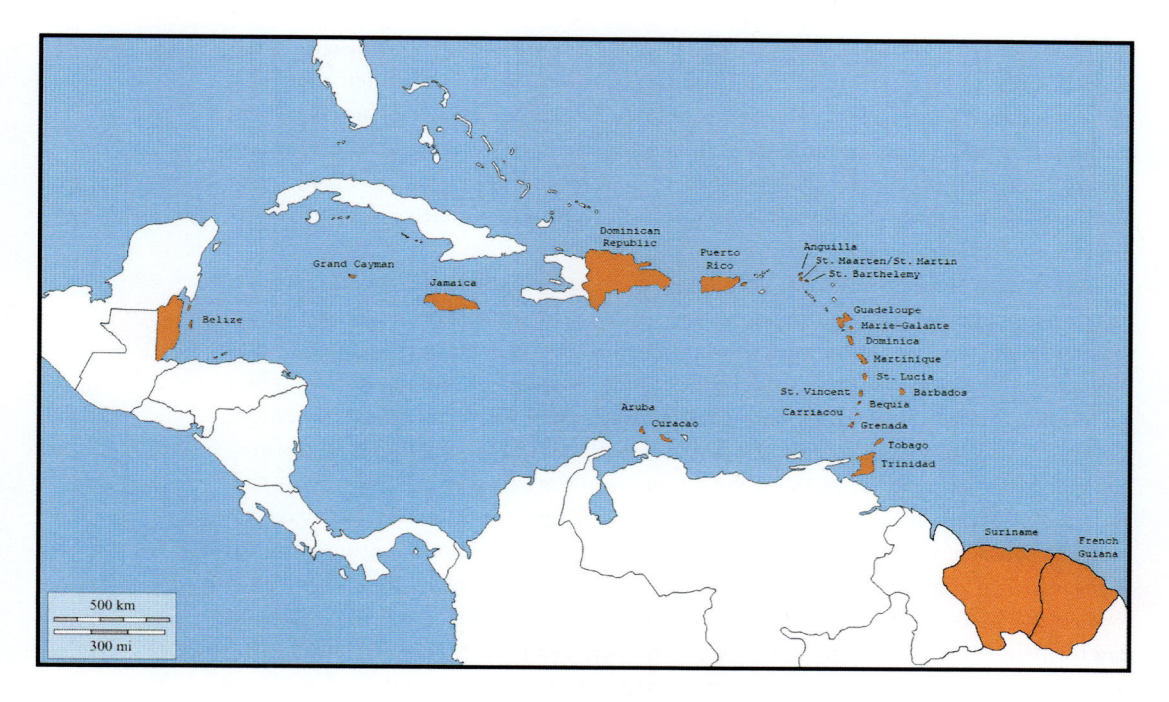

Figure 3: Map of the islands and countries in the Caribbean where fieldwork was conducted.

the public (see *Defining The Museum*, page 33). By applying this definition, it was possible to include museums of all types of content, all sizes, all models of ownership, and regardless of visitation numbers or associated communities. Indeed, in order to be able to gain a broad understanding of participatory practices, the selection of museums was not directed towards any specific types of communities.

To be able to plan fieldwork, the first step was to identify the existing museums in any given place. In this regard, the Museums Association of the Caribbean (MAC) was an unparalleled resource. Its directories of museums in the Caribbean (Museums Association of the Caribbean 2011a; 2011b; 2011c; 2011d) provided a starting point for research, which was complemented by information from well-known travel guide books, online travel reviews, tourism websites, and museum websites. Additionally, the development of a contact network of persons working in or with museums in the region was crucial to verify the existence of museums, to schedule meetings with museum staff, or to plan visits to museums which were temporarily closed to the public due to refurbishment or still under construction. MAC's annual conference, in which I participated every year (2013-2017), was instrumental for developing and maintaining this vital contact network. Finally, while a primary selection of museums to visit was always made before any given fieldwork session – along with a preliminary schedule – this was frequently adjusted in the field as flyers or other information became available.

In the course of these self-organized visits, the selection of museums visited in any island or country differed greatly. Particularly in some of the smaller places, the selection can be considered comprehensive in the sense that all known museums were visited. In other places, especially those where the existence of many museums was known beforehand, the selection was not exhaustive. Ultimately, decisions were made firstly based on the determination to include a wide range of museum types and secondly on practical matters related to the itinerary and scheduled meetings. Time was always set aside to visit a wide range of museums in the capital city, in combination with trips beyond the capital. On the whole, though, the selection cannot be deemed complete. Nonetheless, it does intend to cover a broad spectrum of museum types throughout the region and aims to be representative of the diversity of museums in each island or country.

Preparation for fieldwork was very important, particularly for efficiently navigating through islands and countries so as to visit a broad selection of museums in the available time, while maintaining a thorough fieldwork methodology. To support this, extensive preparation went into understanding the locations of museums, how to best get around, and when museums were expected to be open. For every fieldwork session, a list of possible museums to visit was prepared with contact information and opening hours. This list was used to map out the museums in the island or country and to plan an itinerary. When museums were located closely together, for instance in a city center, multiple could be visited in one day. Other visits required a full day if the museum was very large or if island hopping was required to reach them. Finally, the list and map formed the basis for a draft daily schedule. Sundays proved to be the most difficult day for fieldwork due to museums not being open and public transport often being very limited. Having prepared all this information before entering the field provided possibilities for flexibility and adjustments when needed, for instance when a museum turned out to be incidentally or unexpectedly closed,[7] or when new visits warranted addition to the schedule.

Despite the importance of preparation, there is no substitute for the event of the museum visit. It is never wholly possible to understand the museum from a distance – a researcher must experience the museum, its objects, and participate in exchanges with staff and visitors personally in order to gain a full, holistic understanding. This is particularly necessary so as to grasp how the official images and representations of the museum may differ from reality on the ground. Thus, museum visits were approached not only analytically but also experientially and to some extent subjectively. In this sense, the methodology shared some similarities with that of phenomenology, which in archaeology, for instance, has been employed to use sensory experiences to interpret cultural landscapes (Tilley 1994). For much of the fieldwork sessions, I began the museum visit in the capacity of a regular tourist and the research purpose of the visit was not immediately revealed. This allowed for interactions with staff and visitors to occur as they might with any other visitor to the museum. When permitted, the museum, its surroundings, displays, and labels were extensively photographed, enabling the collection of a visual record of the museum. GPS coordinates of the museum were saved. Usually at the end of the visit, when the museum had been wholly explored and experienced, I would approach museum staff with some questions, making sure to reveal the purpose of these questions for this research. At this point, a business card

---

7   For instance, a museum might be incidentally closed for a staff training (*Museo de San Juan*, Puerto Rico) or due to a power outage (*Liberty Hall*, Jamaica). Unexpected closure might be temporary, due to the owner being on maternity leave (*Sur la Trace des Arawaks*, St. Martin), or permanent (*Musée L'Herminier*, Guadeloupe).

would always be given to enable staff to contact me directly with any questions or to redact any information. On some occasions, these exchanges would expand the regular museum visit, for instance by providing a tour of the museum collections or storage areas. The nature of museum visits was also different in those cases where meetings had already been arranged beforehand with staff. Oftentimes the meeting would frame the following museum visit, which was frequently guided by the staff member.

By approaching the museum visit as an event, data collected in the field consisted primarily of photographs and field notes. As mentioned, photographs were collected whenever possible and permitted of all aspects of the museum. In addition, while in the field, daily field notes were written in order to reflect on the museum visits and all the personal encounters and meetings. Along with leaflets, flyers, and online museum resources, these c. 9500 photographs and field notes (c. 91000 words or 164 pages) formed the core data of the regional museum survey. In order to be able to analyze and interpret this abundance of data, and to discover trends, similarities, and differences, it was decided to develop a database.

The methodology of seeing the museum visit as an event has implications for the temporality of the collected data. Most museums were visited on a single occasion, and the data collected and the corresponding database entries thus reflect a specific moment in time. Even if further information was obtained through flyers, museum websites, or visitors' reviews, the single visit formed the core of the collected data. The reader should note that the database cannot reflect a permanent perspective of museums in the Caribbean, just as it cannot contain a total representation. I am already aware of museums that have been closed since visiting, others which have opened, and yet others which have been altered or damaged. In a region with on the one hand considerable construction and development, particularly under the influence of the tourism industry, and on the other hand significant environmental changes, the museum scene is in constant flux. Hurricanes Irma and Maria were particularly destructive and impacted many museums and collections in their wake in 2017.

At this point, it should be reiterated that fieldwork was supported tremendously by many people who assisted or accompanied me on museum visits, or provided information or access. Members of the Museums Association of the Caribbean and its conference delegates were pivotal in providing information and access to museums, as well as offering feedback on the research in progress. The role of the staff at all museums visited deserves deep appreciation, first and foremost for their museum work, and secondly for their research assistance. Finally, twenty colleagues (from the NEXUS1492 research project, associated HERA-CARIB and NWO Island Networks projects, and affiliated researchers) accompanied me on one or more museum visits, sharing their experiences. Arlene Álvarez and John Angus Martin, in the Dominican Republic and Grenada respectively, provided access to their institutions, introductions to others, and fieldwork collaboration. Particular mention and appreciation is due to Mariana de Campos Françozo who collaborated in multiple fieldwork sessions and thus provided a wealth of additional insights.

As mentioned, a database was designed for the regional museum survey which was filled in following every fieldwork session. The entry form consists of two sections: the first concerning the museum, its exhibitions, and its participatory elements, the second regarding the museum's collection of Amerindian archaeological artefacts. This second section was designed specifically for use by NEXUS1492 colleagues who were working with Amerindian archaeological collections in European museums (Françozo & Strecker 2017). The two sections had been designed so that both these museological studies could use the same database, although with different data and research aims. The use of the same database structure enabled further collaboration in the analysis and visualization of the two datasets (van Garderen 2018). For this study, whenever relevant and applicable, the second section was filled out with data from the regional museum survey. However, most entries only contain information in the first section of the form. The fields in this first section will be discussed shortly and can be viewed in a slightly condensed version of a blank entry form (see figure 4).

The database entry form begins with basic information of the museum for anyone wishing to also visit the museum. Here one can find the name of the museum, visiting address and GPS coordinates, phone number, website, the name of a contact person, and the opening hours. The field for the entry price reflects the standard fee for a non-local adult. The year in which the museum was first opened to the public is included, as well as its current system of ownership. An indication of the size of the museum is made by a rough estimation of how long an average visit to the museum would take, less than half an hour (small), more than an hour (large), or in between (medium). The languages in which museum labels, guided tours, or audio tours are available is also noted. A photograph of the façade of the museum, as well as a photograph of the inside (when permitted) are embedded directly into the form. This first section also contains information regarding the event of the museum visit as experienced by myself: when this took place, which colleagues, if any, accompanied me, and what the status of the museum was when visiting, *e.g.* open, closed temporarily, still under construction, or closed permanently. A longer field is included for comments, which contains a descriptive account of the museum visit, summarizing my field notes.

The database entry form's first section contains two larger fields with checkboxes: one regarding the contents of the museum and its displays (as visible to the public) and one concerning the participatory elements which were present or evidence of which was observable at the time of the museum visit. The meaning of the categories in the 'content' checkboxes is presented briefly (see table 1). Some of these categories overlap in some areas and are not rigidly defined. It should be noted that it does not only cover the content of the museum, but also refers in some cases to its characteristics, for instance the type of building in which it is housed. A definition or explanation of the 'participatory elements' checkboxes can be found in Chapter 4, where each participatory practice is separately presented along with examples from the field.

As mentioned previously, an index of the museums included in the regional museum survey and thus in the Caribbean Museums Database is included in the appendix (see *Index: Caribbean Museums Database*, page 251). The full Caribbean Museums Database, which contains the complete entries of all of these museums, totaling 600 pages, is accessible online as a resource accompanying this dissertation. Although not intended to function as a stand-alone publication, it provides access to the data collected in the course of this research. As such, it is not the intention to expand or alter the database in this format, merely to provide readers with the opportunity to consult the database, much of which could not be fully discussed in the course of this dissertation. The temporality of the data, due to the fieldwork methodology by which most museums' data was collected during a single visit, may have implications for the comprehensiveness and correctness of the data.

Following the completion of the database, and in order to make comparison and analysis of these 195 museums more feasible and useful, the characterization of museums was reconsidered by assessing two of the fields and condensing their categories. Firstly, 'ownership' as originally designed for the database contained seven categories: governmental, grassroots (individual), grassroots (community), NGO, private, mixed public and private, and unknown. This was reduced to five categories: governmental, grassroots, private, mixed ownership, and unknown. This was achieved by simply grouping the museums from the three categories grassroots (individual), grassroots (community), and NGO into one. More difficult was condensing the 'content' categories, as many of these are not necessarily collapsible into a larger category. It was decided to develop a new categorization of seven museum types: archaeology, art, built heritage, history, mixed content, nature/science, and popular culture. Each museum was reviewed in order to determine which category most predominantly characterizes the museum as a whole. Those museums which were characterized similarly strongly by two or more of these types, were designated 'mixed content' museums.

Nonetheless, visualization, analysis, and interpretation remained complex. Thus, a collaboration was developed with NEXUS1492 colleague and computer scientist Mereke van Garderen who is a specialist in information visualization (van Garderen 2018). Firstly, this collaboration aimed to develop a map of museums included in the regional museum survey and Caribbean Museums Database. This was a complex task, as the geographic layout of the region in its characteristic string of islands makes it difficult to represent such a heterogeneous distribution of information without words or symbols overlapping. In order to tackle this challenge, Van Garderen developed a method which is based on an overlap removal algorithm[8] (van Garderen *et al.* 2016; van Garderen *et al.* 2017). This enabled the visualization of the entire dataset, including all the museums on smaller islands, by making sure the symbols for the museums did not overlap, but were still placed in the approximate vicinity of their actual location. To symbolize the museums, Van Garderen designed glyphs which could simultaneously visually represent museums by both type (glyph color) and by ownership (glyph shape). By processing the data and running scripts to generate these maps digitally, it was possible to develop a map showing all the museums, but also to generate maps per museum type or per museum ownership category (see figures 44-49).

Secondly, following on the development of the maps, the collaboration continued with cross tabulations for multiple variables, enabling a visualization of the absolute number of co-occurrences, for instance by museum type and ownership together. These cross tabulations are useful for visualizing how many museums of a certain type are present per island/country, or how many of them are grassroots museums or governmental museums (see figures 53-56). Cross tabulations were also designed to see whether there was any difference in museum types or ownership when museums were grouped according to the four linguistic areas.

Thirdly, the collaboration investigated the participatory practices as they are employed by Caribbean museums. A cross tabulation of participatory practices

---

8   To be more exact, a minimum-displacement overlap removal with orthogonal ordering constraints.

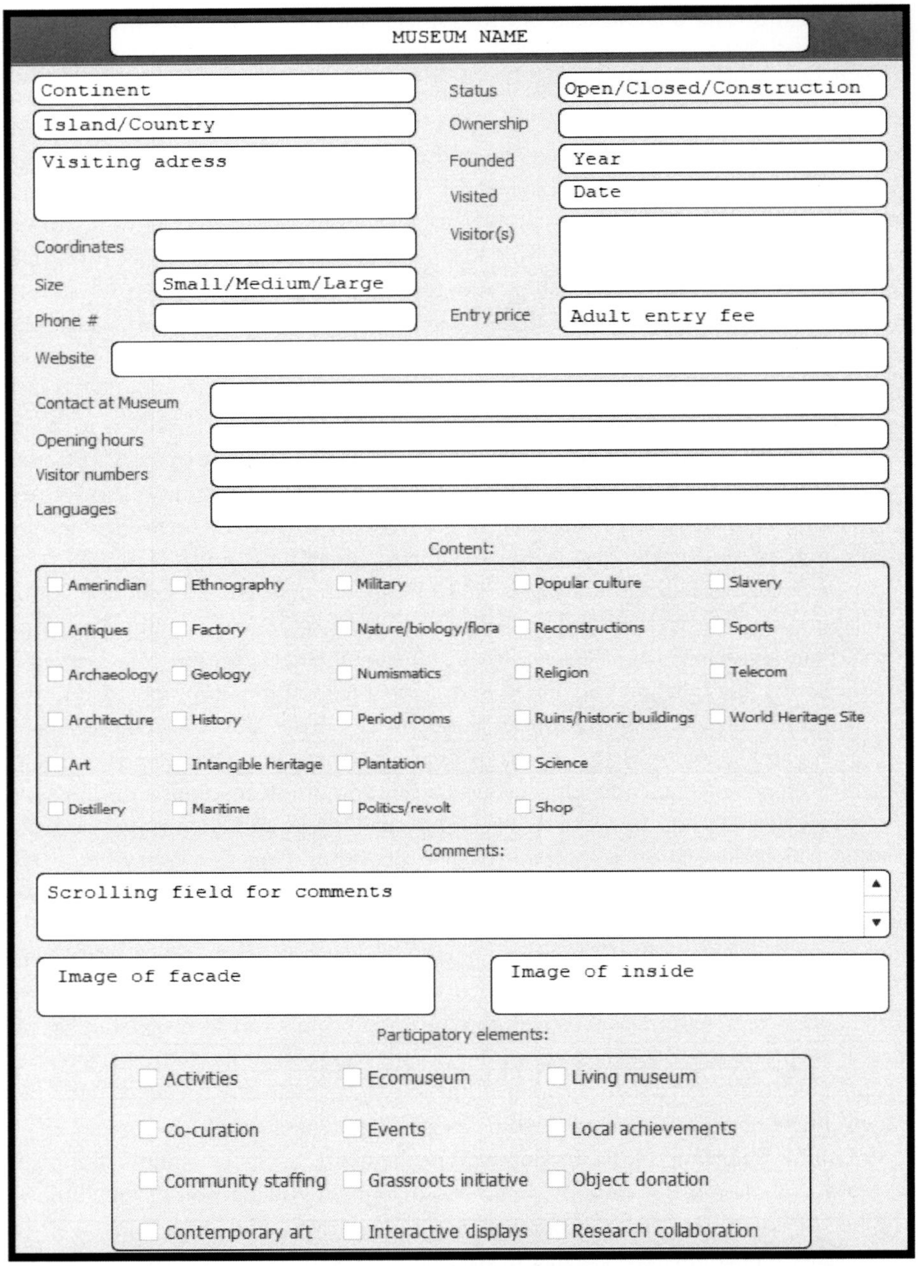

MUSEUM NAME		

Continent	Status	Open/Closed/Construction
Island/Country	Ownership	
Visiting adress	Founded	Year
	Visited	Date
Coordinates	Visitor(s)	
Size	Small/Medium/Large	
Phone #	Entry price	Adult entry fee

Website

Contact at Museum

Opening hours

Visitor numbers

Languages

Content:

- ☐ Amerindian
- ☐ Ethnography
- ☐ Military
- ☐ Popular culture
- ☐ Slavery
- ☐ Antiques
- ☐ Factory
- ☐ Nature/biology/flora
- ☐ Reconstructions
- ☐ Sports
- ☐ Archaeology
- ☐ Geology
- ☐ Numismatics
- ☐ Religion
- ☐ Telecom
- ☐ Architecture
- ☐ History
- ☐ Period rooms
- ☐ Ruins/historic buildings
- ☐ World Heritage Site
- ☐ Art
- ☐ Intangible heritage
- ☐ Plantation
- ☐ Science
- ☐ Distillery
- ☐ Maritime
- ☐ Politics/revolt
- ☐ Shop

Comments:

Scrolling field for comments

Image of facade

Image of inside

Participatory elements:

- ☐ Activities
- ☐ Ecomuseum
- ☐ Living museum
- ☐ Co-curation
- ☐ Events
- ☐ Local achievements
- ☐ Community staffing
- ☐ Grassroots initiative
- ☐ Object donation
- ☐ Contemporary art
- ☐ Interactive displays
- ☐ Research collaboration

Figure 4: Fields from the database constructed for the regional museum survey, with clarifications.

Category	Meaning
Amerindian	Relating to the Amerindian population of the Caribbean region.
Antiques	Objects from 'grandmother's era' c. 40-100 years old.
Archaeology	Relating to archaeology from any era/culture.
Architecture	Relating to noteworthy architecture or structural design.
Art	Artworks, whether historical or contemporary, in any medium.
Distillery	A distillery is part of the museum.
Ethnography	Objects or intangible heritage from non-historically-distant cultures.
Factory	A factory is part of the museum.
Geology	Relating to geology.
History	Relating broadly to history, whether local or global.
Intangible heritage	Intangible heritage is included in the museum.
Maritime	Relating to maritime heritage.
Military	Relating to military heritage.
Nature/biology/flora	Natural heritage, biology, or flora is included in the museum.
Numismatics	Relating to numismatics, currency.
Period rooms	Rooms are decorated with objects to represent a past era.
Plantation	A plantation is part of the museum.
Politics/revolt	Relating to politics and revolt or resistance.
Popular culture	Relating to popular culture, *e.g.* food, music, dance, drink.
Reconstructions	Replicas or reconstructions of objects/structures are included.
Religion	Relating to any religion.
Ruins/historic buildings	The museum is located in, or encompasses ruins or historic buildings.
Science	Relating to any of the natural sciences.
Shop	A shop is a prominent aspect of the museum.
Slavery	Relating to slavery and the abolition of slavery.
Sports	Relating to sports.
Telecom	Relating to telecommunication technologies.
World Heritage Site	The museum is designated World Heritage.

Table 1: Meaning of the categories in the 'content' field of the Caribbean Museums Database.

by museum type, ownership, or linguistic area did not reveal much detail, as some categories are overrepresented while others are underrepresented. For this reason, it was decided to develop visualizations based on the relative frequencies of participatory practices (see figures 50-52). These visualizations are able to show which percentage of museums of a certain type employ a particular participatory practices.

Finally, to aid analysis, matrices were developed which showcase the participatory practices per individual museum. Essentially, this data is directly available in the Caribbean Museum Database and its 'participatory elements' field. However, in order to see if there were any patterns, it was useful to view the participatory practices of all the museums in one glance (see figure 5).

The outcomes of the analysis and interpretations of the data and the visualizations can be found in the remainder of this dissertation. The Caribbean Museums Database forms the core of Chapter 4 which showcases the twelve participatory practices identified in Caribbean museums along with ample examples of each. The computer science collaboration and resulting analysis and interpretation are discussed in detail in Chapter 7 and the visualizations are included as figures 44-56.

Case Studies

The two case studies provided the framework in which the micro level research data was collected. Again, fieldwork was a major component of this data collection, re-quiring collaborative preparation beforehand as well as data management, coding of qualitative data, and descriptive statistical analysis afterwards. Case study fieldwork was conducted 2015-2016, and, as mentioned earlier in this chapter, it involved three phases: exploratory visit, main study, presentation of results. The main study phase was where the majority of the data was collected through a combination of interviews, participant observation, and community surveys.

The main goal of the case studies was to gain an in depth understanding of how community engagement processes happen and develop in Caribbean museums. As the regional museum survey had revealed a prevalence of grassroots initiatives in the Caribbean, and as they are relatively understudied in favor of governmental initia-tives, it was decided that the case studies should focus on such grassroots initiatives. Following this decision, a number of parameters were developed for the case studies. Firstly, the aim would be to research two different types of community engagement processes, with different kinds of museums involved. Secondly, it was the intention to work with communities who are minority populations within their respective island or country and as such are characteristic for the diversity of Caribbean societies. This was noted as an important parameter also because some Caribbean museums had been critiqued for marginalizing communities of non-African descent (Farmer 2013). Thirdly, to be able to investigate different stages of community engagement processes, it was suggested to include both a newly started and an already ongoing community engagement project. Finally, noting the available time frame in which the case studies could be conducted, and the need to develop an in depth understanding of community perceptions, feasibility was a crucial parameter. This meant that any case study would need to allow a concise research question which it would be possible to answer by means of rapid assessment methods. Participatory rapid assessment requires preparing

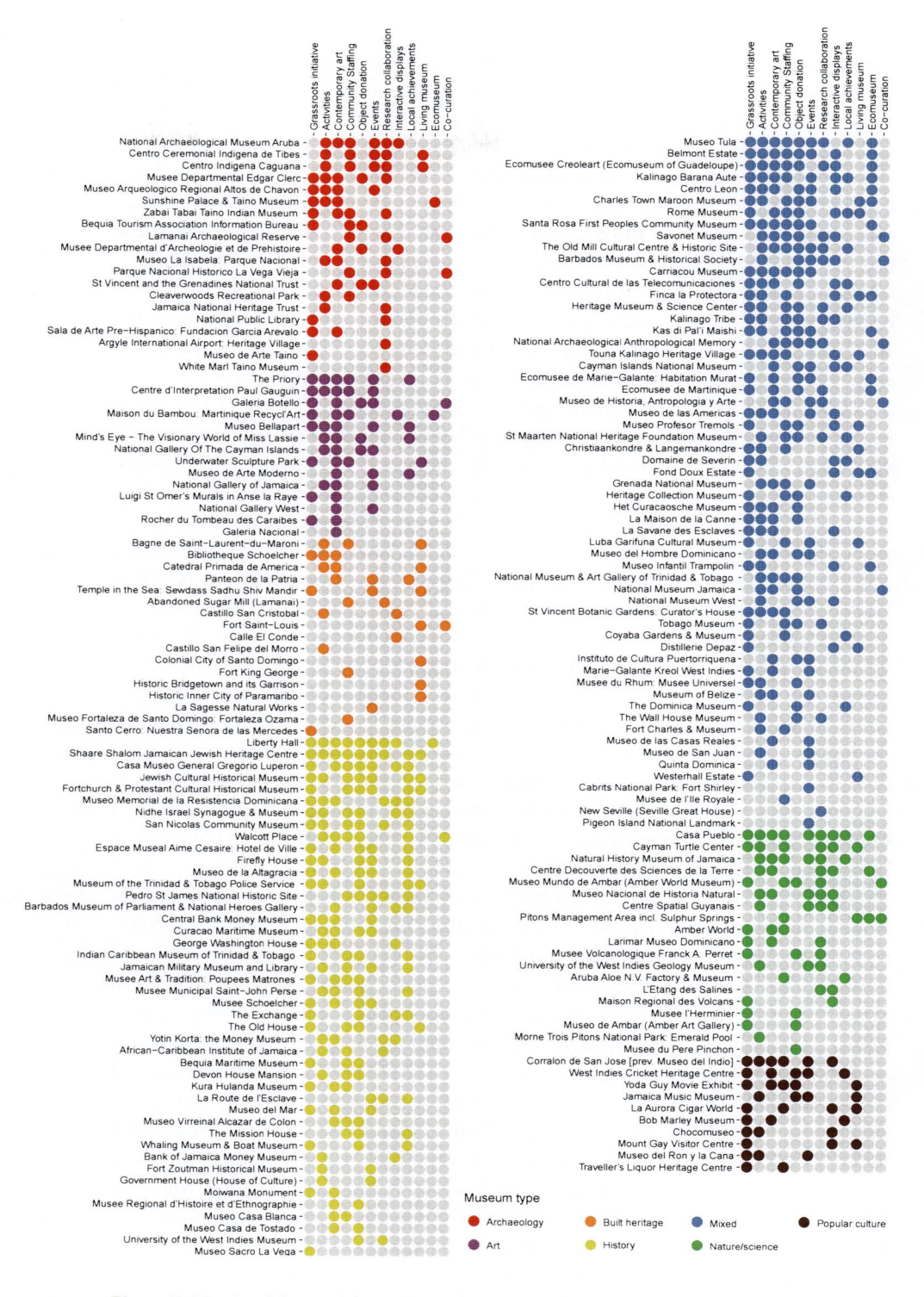

Figure 5: Matrix of the participatory practices per museum, colored by museum type. The museums are sorted by type and then from most to least participatory practices.

clearly defined research questions and a limited amount of variables before entering the field, structuring participatory observation to answer a specific set of questions, rather than observing the community more freely (Bernard 2006: 353). Feasibility also demanded a high level of extant proficiency in the language spoken by the community in question. Along with these four parameters for the selection of case studies, an invitation by the museum and community in question was indispensable. I was determined not to conduct case study research without the explicit consent of the communities involved and made sure that any case study plan was deemed beneficial not only for this research but also for the participating community and museum.

Throughout the course of the regional museum survey, several invitations were received to return to a museum and community for such a case study. However, not all of these invitations aligned with the parameters which had been set, and yet others were not possible within the timeline of the research project. Ultimately, the two case studies which were selected were based in Dominica and in Barbados. In Dominica, in the Kalinago Territory, the case study revolved around the *Kalinago Barana Autê*, a museum which was conceived as a grassroots initiative by the Indigenous Kalinago community, but was ultimately constructed and is currently still owned by the national government, while the daily management of the museum is run by the Kalinago. It showcases an ongoing community engagement project between a national government and a local community. In Barbados, the case study was centered on the *Bengal to Barbados* exhibition project, a co-curated exhibition which was devised by members of the East Indian community in Barbados who reached out to the *Barbados Museum & Historical Society* for their participation. It showcases the beginning of a community engagement project between a national museum and a local community. It bears repeating that the goal of the case studies was to gain an in depth insight into community engagement processes. Considering the wide diversity of Caribbean museums revealed through the regional museum survey, there is no way in which these case studies could be considered representative of Caribbean community engagement processes as a whole. They function as merely two examples on a wide spectrum and do not aspire to be representative or all-encompassing.

The first phase of fieldwork for each case study effectively began during the regional museum survey when the museums in question, the *Kalinago Barana Autê* (KBA) and the *Barbados Museum & Historical Society* (BMHS) were first visited and initial conversations occurred with potential case study participants. Preparation began in earnest afterwards through discussions and meetings with community members and/or museum staff. These discussions were very important for planning the second phase of fieldwork and for collectively developing a research question that this fieldwork would aim to answer. In Dominica, the main aim of the case study research was to assess the value and importance of the KBA for the Kalinago community and to identify how they felt the museum could improve for the future. This topic was deemed important by the management of the KBA as well as political leaders in the community who were looking to alter the operation of the museum and possibly its ownership structure. In Barbados, the main aim of the case study research was to understand the heterogeneity of the East Indian community and the participants' diverse goals for and attitudes towards the exhibition project. This topic was deemed of fundamental importance for the early phase of the co-curation project by both BMHS staff and East Indian community members who were all not yet certain about the collective aims of the project and how they could best be met.

Practical preparation for the second phase of the case study fieldwork consisted of the development of a survey in the form of a paper-based questionnaire. For both case studies, the surveys had some similarities. The surveys contained ten questions, of which the last three concerned the respondent's age, gender, and an option to leave their contact information for a longer interview. Both surveys also contained questions which asked respondents for positive and negative keywords related to the museum/exhibition project. Similarly, respondents were asked about the importance and perceived or potential benefits of the museum/exhibition. Specifically for the KBA, respondents were asked about visitation of the KBA, as well as for suggestions for improvements. In the case of the Bengal to Barbados exhibition project, respondents were asked questions about their sense of community belonging, as well as their involvement in the project and their desired outcomes of the exhibition. These differences were designed with the collectively developed research questions in mind. The surveys were reviewed and tested by case study participants, and suggestions for alterations were incorporated. These paper-based questionnaires were designed on two pages so that they could fit on a single piece of paper and would not take more than five to ten minutes to complete. This was to ensure a low threshold for participation and to hopefully allow a larger number of responses.

This second phase of fieldwork was conducted in both cases over the course of roughly a month, in July-August 2015 in Dominica and February-March 2016 in Barbados. Administering the survey was a major component of these studies, along with rapid assessment participant observation (Bernard 2006: 352-353). For the former, the aim was to use the street-intercept method: approaching potential survey respondents freely in the street or around their homes, thereby ensuring that all parts of the community could be surveyed in a random pattern (Bernard 2006: 257). For the latter, the key is to already have specific research questions when entering the field, so that answers may be found in a relatively short amount of time. I lived locally during this time, engaging frequently with members of the respective communities and spending time in or working at the museums. Community gatherings, lectures, events, and meetings were attended whenever possible. In addition, interviews were conducted. In the end, 150 surveys were administered in Dominica and 51 in Barbados. Although a similar fieldwork methodology was developed for both case studies, the communities, museums, and settings of each were unique and necessitated a specific approach in the field. These particularities are described in detail in the respective case study chapters.

Collaboration with case study participants was vital for the collection of this micro level data. In Dominica, the efforts of the Development Officer of the Ministry of Kalinago Affairs in planning the case study and a presentation of results, the willingness of the KBA's manager to provide detailed information about the museum, and many members in the community for their openness and hospitality were particularly appreciated. In Barbados, the BMHS director and deputy director were instrumental in assisting in the preparation of the case study and reflecting on its results, as well as for providing a place within the institution for me to work. Three East Indian community members were essential research participants and community gatekeepers, as they distributed surveys to relatives, friends, students, colleagues, and other community

Figure 6: Presenting and discussing survey results, 2016. Left: Kalinago Barana Autê. Right: Barbados Museum & Historical Society.

members. In both Dominica and Barbados, many others provided assistance, in terms of conversation, accommodation, or transportation. Of course, neither of the case studies would have been possible without the 201 respondents who dedicated their time and freely shared their insights.

While in the field, survey data was digitized and the responses were aggregated per question (see *Questionnaire Results: Kalinago Barana Autê*, page 258; *Questionnaire Results: Bengal To Barbados*, page 264). For open ended questions, responses were recorded as originally stated, but also coded and grouped according to categories. This made it possible to compare answers to all of the questions, whether the data was qualitative (*e.g.* why respondents considered the museum important or not) or quantitative (*e.g.* how many times they had visited the museum). Afterwards, descriptive statistical analysis was undertaken of all of the questions, using the answers as variables. In the case of the Bengal to Barbados questionnaire, analysis was consequently also performed by separating the responses of the East Indian respondents from the Barbados Museum & Historical Society staff in order to see whether their surveys were significantly different. These analyses were complemented by the participant observation that had taken place during the entire main phase of the case study fieldwork. By compiling this data, preliminary results were formulated.

The final phase of case study fieldwork consisted of the presentation of results (see figure 6). The preliminary results of the Dominican case study were presented during a special community meeting held at the *Kalinago Barana Autê* in March 2016. All Kalinago present were invited to ask questions about the results as well as confirm whether the results were in line with their own perceptions. While no results were contested, they were accepted as useful information and taken onboard for the future development of the KBA. As part of this presentation, the future of the KBA was discussed in detail and its value for the community and not just for visitors was emphasized in the suggestion for a new mission statement. In addition, the ownership of the KBA was candidly discussed, providing deeper insights into the community's contested views on this matter. Also in March 2016, preliminary results of the Barbadian case study were presented during a meeting of the Exhibition Planning Committee at the *Barbados Museum & Historical Society*. Again, committee members present were asked for their input and any questions. There was general consensus as to the validity of the results, and a point was made to take on suggestions for the continued development of the exhibition project. Committee members were particularly worried about their representativity and discussed a number of possible solutions to this issue – both in terms of the committee and wider community involvement. In addition, they reflected on their own influence on potential project participants, which led to new awareness of their personal biases. For both case studies, these presentations of preliminary results were very useful, on the one hand to confirm the analysis and interpretations of the data, and on the other hand to provide practical suggestions for how the data could be used by community members and museum staff in the continuation of their community engagement processes.

Research Ethos

> *Participating in the unmapped territory of engagement zones is risky and has real consequences for the participants, museums, and communities involved.*
> Bryony Onciul (2013: 93)

As a researcher, participating in engagement zones or in community engagement projects falls into a similar position. A researcher can never be entirely neutral, and their presence can never be without effect or impact on the subject of study. For this research project into community engagement in the Caribbean, I was aware of this risk and took on a research ethos couched in the New Museology and post-colonial theories. This ethos informed the general attitudes, philosophies, and codes of conduct that guided my fieldwork as well as the research project as a whole. From this ethos, I approached this research as an arena for debate, used community engagement approaches, worked self-reflexively, positioned myself as an open-minded outsider, championed accessibility, and employed survey ethics. In all of these matters, I complied with the NEXUS1492 Ethics Code (NEXUS1492 2013) and the Netherlands Code of Conduct for Scientific Practice (VSNU 2004).

Similar to the New Museology which characterizes museums as arenas for debate, I took on a comparable perspective for this research and made sure to welcome input, feedback, and debate throughout the entire course of the project. I made an effort to present the research in all stages to museologists, archaeologists, heritage professionals, and historians, working either in the Caribbean or elsewhere in the world. Partially, this was achieved by presenting at several international conferences per year, and partially by being open about my research while working in the field. To be able to receive feedback on my project was crucial for the development of my research, my thought processes, and to evaluate my interpretations. By asking critical questions at conferences and elsewhere, I was able to draw global museological debates to consider the Caribbean.

Community engagement is not only the topic of this research project, but indeed its approaches also informed my research ethos. Community participation and power sharing were important aspects which I sought to bring into the execution of the project. Thus, the explicit participation of people in the project was encouraged – not only to develop transdisciplinary research with colleagues, but also to involve Caribbean museum staff and community members into directing the research. Caribbean individuals were asked to recommend museums to include in this study, and in the two case studies intense local participation was welcomed. For this, being able to share power is a key issue, for instance by asking community members to edit survey questions. Community engagement was very important in providing feedback, but also in the developmental stages of the research.

Working self-reflexively is a characteristic of both the New Museology and of post-colonial theories, which urge the researcher to reveal themselves, their biases, and actively work towards countering them. I was strongly aware of my origins as being colonial. I am half Dutch and half Hungarian, having lived most of my life in Europe, with shorter periods of time spent in Australia and the USA. My perspective has been characterized by these cultures and by being a woman. Academically, my studies in archaeology and museology have both been couched in post-modernist lines of thought. Although I was trilingual as a child, and became quadrilingual in the course of my university studies, I could communicate better in some areas of the Caribbean than in others. Awareness of my cultural and colonial background spurred me to a constant evaluation of my role in my research and my own impact. I was purposefully open about my background to research participants and others, and made sure to note that the research project as a whole had received European funding. This awareness helped me to work towards making sure that the outcomes of the research project would be sure to benefit the Caribbean directly. I was acutely aware of the risk of perpetrating colonial power imbalances and exploiting the knowledge and resources of the region for European gain.

With this awareness, I decided to position myself deliberately as an open-minded outsider. Listening was key. This research project was the first to take me to the Caribbean, an area of the world which I had no personal knowledge of beforehand – so I made sure to closely pay attention to those who did know the region and let their knowledge guide mine. Realizing the gaps in my own linguistic proficiencies, I took extra language courses. Even though it was not feasible to gain fluency in all main Caribbean languages – not to mention the creole or patois languages which are widely spoken – I hoped that even a basic proficiency of a language could reduce conversational barriers and at least eliminate the need for interpreters. The reception of my Dutch identity varied throughout the Caribbean. Despite my own concerns, mostly it was met positively – especially my fieldwork during the 2014 World Cup when the Netherlands had impressed football fans throughout the Caribbean. The sensation of being an outsider persisted throughout the whole course of the research project, reminding me of my own identity and ensuring that I kept checking my biases and privileges. Over time, I was able to develop a role as a partial insider in terms of my knowledge of museums in the region, which was institutionalized by my election to the Board of the Museums Association of the Caribbean in 2015. Although I did not consider myself to be the appropriate person for this position, I ultimately accepted as a chance to repatriate, as it were, my knowledge and research to the region.

In this vein, accessibility was an important part of my research ethos. On the one hand, I wanted to be accessible as a researcher. I made sure to share my contact information with people I worked with in the field and worked hard on being personally approachable. On the other hand, it was important that my research results would be accessible. To this end, the dissertation, the online accessible Caribbean Museums Database, and the data are designed and visualized in a way to be readable, usable, and digital. Digital open access is key to ensure that the research can be read in the Caribbean in particular and be of use to people working in Caribbean museums.

Finally, I employed survey ethics to ensure that information was shared on the basis of informed consent. During case study fieldwork, participants were asked for their willingness to participate in the surveys and were free to decline or retract their knowledge. Although survey respondents were generally not anonymous to myself, the digitized survey data is anonymized as are all references to survey responses in this dissertation. Interviews explicitly asked for oral consent, and consent was also solicited separately to approve any audio recording. All information obtained from meetings and (in-)formal interviews is referenced anonymously. More detailed information on how the case studies were conducted in the field is described in Chapters 5 & 6. Photographs within museums were only taken when permission had been granted either orally or in writing. In some cases museums allowed me to take photographs only for personal use and consequently these images have been excluded from publication in the Caribbean Museums Database.

4

Caribbean Participatory Practices

Community is not a commodity. [Participation] *is not cheap. It's not easy. It's the work we feel driven to do to build a museum that is of and for our community.*
Nina Simon (2014)

Nina Simon is seen by many in the museological field as the person who spearheaded the practical exploration of community participation in museums. Her experiences as a museum consultant, and her particular interest in making museums more participatory, were bundled in her book *The Participatory Museum* (Simon 2010). While the book considers community engagement and participation theoretically, its uniqueness lies in the vast collection of practical examples from museums which wanted to be more participatory in a specific way and the steps they took to achieve that goal.

As Simon stresses, participation is neither cheap nor easy. Although small projects can be undertaken in short amounts of time and with minimal budgets, her point is that true participation and community engagement takes deep dedication. Thus, while her book contains a collection of practical examples for smaller and bigger participatory projects, building a museum that is truly "of and for our community" will take many projects and a deep investment of time, passion, and commitment. This is the case for museums wishing to engage in participatory practices everywhere in the world, including the Caribbean. Yet, individual projects which are relatively cheap and easy to achieve, can of course lead to deeper community engagement in the long term. It is with this in mind, that this chapter hopes to provide concrete examples for those Caribbean museum staff who wish to find regional practices that can be adapted to their own institutions. While the chapter shows that participatory practices already occur widely throughout the Caribbean, participation is an ongoing process that benefits from continued investment and reassessment.

Thus, this chapter presents a wide range of participatory practices from the Caribbean and discusses how each of these practices may best be applied. It functions as an extensive answer to the sub question "what are the characteristics of contemporary Caribbean museums and how are they adopting and adapting participatory practices?" (see *Research Questions and Objectives,* page 18). This collection of practices does not claim to be complete. However, it does reflect the most commonly occurring methods of community engagement in the Caribbean. The categories according to which the participatory practices have been grouped were designed for this research. Many of these practices are established in the field of museum studies, which has supported my definition of each practice. However, it is important to point out that these categories were specifically designated for this research based on experiences in the field. In addition, it was part of the fieldwork of the regional museum survey to identify the presence of any participatory practice in each visited museum. In other words, museum staff or another visitor might not identify the same participatory practices in each museum, depending on their definition. The categories of participatory practices range from fundamental, such as ecomuseums, to complementary, for instance in the case of activities or events. Each section begins with a definition and description of the participatory practice as categorized for this research, along with any noted difficulties concerning their application or identification. Then a few specific approaches or key aspects are highlighted and illustrated with examples. All of the examples are from the Caribbean museums that were visited during the regional museum survey 2013-2016 (see *Regional Museum Survey*, page 49). Nearly every museum contained at least one type of participatory practice. There were only eight cases where it was not possible to identify participatory practices with certainty, because the museum was still under construction, closed incidentally for refurbishment, or permanently closed. Besides these cases, only three other museums did not have any participatory practices: *Fort St. Louis* on St. Martin, *Morne Fortune: Apostles Battery & The Powder Magazine* on St. Lucia, and *L'Église du Fort* on Martinique. All of these are open air sites of built heritage with informative text panels, but without on-site staff or non-structural objects. All data used in this chapter was taken from the Caribbean Museums Database of all of the 195 museums visited (see *Index: Caribbean Museums Database*, page 251; see also the online accessible Caribbean Museums Database).

Museum Foundation & Organization

Grassroots Initiatives

Museums in the Caribbean are commonly the result of grassroots initiatives. This means that the initiative for the establishment of the museum (the concept, the creation, and the collection) lies solely or mainly with a community or individual and not with the (local) government, ministries, or existing public institutions (*e.g.* national trusts). Some of these museums may still be managed by communities or individuals today and are still grassroots museums. Others may have changed ownership or management over time and are no longer grassroots museums. However, their history and origin remains the same. Museums that are the result of grassroots initiatives are generally highly participatory as they have been founded by a community or a community member to answer a perceived lack or a specific need. In many cases, these museums will also incorporate other participatory practices, for instance with regards to their collections or with staffing. Of the museums visited during the regional museum survey, 98 museums (50%) were grassroots initiatives. These initiatives are not restricted to any specific part of the Caribbean or to any linguistic area. Instead, we find grassroots initiatives throughout the entire Caribbean.

Figure 7: A display case made from a jukebox showcases geological collections at Museo Profesor Tremols, Dominican Republic.

Grassroots initiatives in the Caribbean may be the result of a single individual's passion for heritage and history. For instance, *Museo Profesor Tremols* in the small municipality of Laguna Salada (Valverde province, Dominican Republic) was set up by prof. José de Jesus Tremols Acosta in 1965. Passionate about archaeology, history, geology, and local heritage, he had been collecting objects and artefacts for many years before deciding to open his collection to the public.[9] He realized that many people living in the area had little knowledge of their own heritage and that many traditions, especially related to agriculture, were disappearing due to modernization. He transformed part of his home into a museum space, with self-made shelves, displays cases, and object labels (see figure 7). The museum and its collection have continued to grow over the decades and in this rural area they are important resources for school children and adults alike by providing access to their past, stretching back to pre-colonial times.

Other grassroots initiatives are the result of the efforts of multiple people, for instance a religious community, cultural community, local community, or a community with a shared interest, such as a historical society or artists' collective. In some cases these communities have set themselves up as foundations or non-profit organizations, while others are more informally organized. For instance, the *Santa Rosa First Peoples Community* in Trinidad set up their museum or community center in 1974. The main aim of this first peoples community is to protect their Indigenous cultural heritage, transmit it to younger generations, and teach it to other visitors.[10] The museum space is located on communal lands in a building that is also a community gathering place and office.

A grassroots initiative may be funded or supported by private corporations, thus placing it in the category of 'private museum.' Directors, CEOs, or a board of directors may choose to reinvest the profit from their businesses into the creation of a museum or to extend the reach of their company by expanding into the heritage sector. For instance, the *Museo Bellapart* in the Dominican Republic was founded in 1999 by the president of the local Honda dealership, Juan José Bellapart.[11] The museum exhibits Mr. Bellapart's privately acquired art collection but is located within the building of the Honda dealership. Another example of a common practice in the Caribbean are businesses that have expanded their shop or factory with a museum. Rum distilleries are the most common of these private grassroots initiatives, such as the *Distillerie Depaz* on Martinique. The visit often contains a tour of the estate or factory along with displays related to the sugar cane process and its local history. Amber museums, such as the *Museo Mundo de Ambar* in the Dominican Republic, provide information about amber and its inclusions from a natural science perspective. In most of these cases, the museum supports the shop by drawing visitors who then become customers. The majority of these private museums do not charge entrance fees.

Finally, there are a number of cases in which grassroots initiatives have been handed over to the government since their creation. For a number of reasons, most often to

---

9   Conversation with founder of *Museo Profesor Tremols* (Laguna Salada, Dominican Republic, 21 January 2015).

10   Conversation with guide at *Santa Rosa First Peoples Community* (Arima, Trinidad, 9 January 2015).

11   Conversation with director of *Museo Bellapart* (Santo Domingo, Dominican Republic, 15 January 2015).

do with practical staffing motivations related to keeping the museum open and operational, a grassroots initiative may be passed on to governmental ownership. This has been the case with the *Musée Schoelcher* in Guadeloupe, the oldest grassroots initiative visited that is still open to the public. The museum was opened in 1887 fulfilling the ambitions of politician and abolitionist Victor Schoelcher to house his sculpture and travel collections (panel texts, Musée Schoelcher). For the longevity of the museum, it became governmental and is now managed by the Conseil Régional de la Guadeloupe.

As mentioned previously, not all museums that have started out as grassroots initiatives continue to be owned in the same manner. In some cases, museums founded by single individuals have expanded and become community projects. Other museums, as stated above, have transferred to governmental ownership. Some community groups may have, since founding the museum, organized themselves in non-governmental organizations (NGOs) that may or may not be for profit. However, the majority of the grassroots initiatives, are still grassroots (53%) or private (24%) museums, if perhaps in a different set-up. Only a small percentage of these grassroots museums are now entirely governmental (15%) or have mixed private and public (*i.e.* governmental) ownership (4%).

Identifying a grassroots initiative is, in most cases, fairly straightforward. Many museums have information about their own history which can be found either within the museum itself, in the museum's brochure, or on the museum's website or social media page. Certainly, museum staff can usually also answer questions related to the origin of the museum. Of course, applying the participatory practice of a grassroots initiative is more difficult. Setting up a museum from the conception of the idea to its execution requires persistent effort and hard work. Fortunately, there are many handbooks or step-by-step guides to setting up and managing a museum, for example *Museum Basics* (Ambrose & Paine 2012) or *Running a Museum: A Practical Handbook* (Boylan 2004), both published through ICOM. Therefore, the focus here will lie on best practices to sustain a grassroots initiative, rather than to create one.

One of the major challenges with grassroots museums is sustainability (although for a counterpoint on the value of the ephemeral museum, see the discussion on *Sustainability*, page 198). This is particularly evident with museums managed by individuals, where the museum, its collections, and its narratives are brought to life by the founder. Naturally, this is jeopardized if the founder passes away or is no longer able to manage the museum. To investigate the best practices related to the sustainability of grassroots initiatives, the focus will lie on two aspects: the narrative and the overall operation of the museum.

The narrative is one of the most characteristic aspects of a grassroots initiative. Oftentimes, the museum is the result of a particular interest in collecting or has been set up to tell a specific story. This story might not align with the national narrative visible in governmental museums. In the case of an individual's museum, the narrative is usually strongly linked to that individual and to a personal history. The origins of the collection, the structure of the museum, the object categories, and object biographies may all be entwined with personal stories and choices. Over time, "the collector has literally put a part of self into the collection" (Belk 1994: 321). These stories and the collections are, of course, best narrated by the founder. With community grassroots museums, the narrative is linked to a community history and perspective. Although community members are very important in portraying their narrative, the museum's narrative might not depend as strongly on personal histories as it depends on a collective history.

Narrative sustainability in an individual's grassroots museum could be achieved by creating a video or audio guide of the founder narrating a visit to his or her museum. For example, Nick Maley, the founder of the *Yoda Guy Movie Exhibit* in St. Maarten, has created a video guide for his museum. Small TVs are placed throughout his museum which loop footage of him pointing out various displays and recalling personal anecdotes related to objects in his collection. This provides a personal connection and tells the narrative of the museum without the need for Maley to always be present. Naturally, this could also be achieved with an audio guide. Thus, it could be useful to conduct oral history projects to collect and preserve the narratives and stories of grassroots museum founders for the future.

In community museums, narrative sustainability can be realized in a number of manners. For instance, at the *Museo Tula* on Curaçao, members of the Afro-Caribbean community work as tour guides to tell the history of Tula and their community from their own perspective. These guides provide an additional layer to the narrative already present in the museum panels and labels by entwining the community history with personal histories. Also on Curaçao, at *Savonet Museum*, an oral history project led to the production of a documentary film which is shown in the museum exhibition. In this film, various local community members who have lived or worked on the estate recall old ways of life or talk about traditions. As long as the museum succeeds in making its value clear to its community, it should be quite feasible to achieve community investment.

The second aspect of sustainability is the overall operation of the museum. This point is mainly related to staffing and funding. Grassroots initiatives in the form of private museums are generally the most robust in this regard. Especially when the museum is incorporated into a business, such as with the distilleries and amber museums mentioned above, museum staff is employed and paid through the company. However, grassroots museums without such long-term financial support may face operational sustainability challenges.

Community grassroots museums can approach funding and staffing in a number of ways. For instance, *Casa Pueblo* in Puerto Rico is a local community collective that engages in environmental and heritage projects. Their operation is funded entirely by individual donations or out of the revenues from their self-produced coffee beans and their crafts shop.[12] They do not accept donations from governments or organizations, wishing to remain self-sufficient and independent. With regards to staffing, they rely entirely on a rotating schedule of community members who donate their time voluntarily. Grassroots museums can function under a foundation or other formal organization structures, making it easier to apply for funding from governmental agencies or private sources. In some cases it might be useful to collaborate with tour operators or cruise ship travel agents to guarantee a stable influx of visitors. The *Charles Town Maroon Museum* in Jamaica has linked up with tour operators to include their museum as part of the tours into the Blue Mountains National Park.

---

12   Conversation with founder of *Casa Pueblo* (Adjuntas, Puerto Rico, 29 January 2015).

Staffing and funding issues are arguably most challenging for grassroots initiatives by individuals. Operating these museums, owned by a single founder, may only be feasible if the founder is retired or otherwise with limited opening hours. If the founder passes away, the museum may have to close altogether. Even if the museum is valued by the surrounding community, it is still not always possible to find another person to take over the museum's operation. As such, the best way to ensure the continuation of such a grassroots museum is to plan ahead and involve other people. On Bequia, harpooner Mr. Athneal Ollivierre founded the *Whaling Museum* (or *Athneal's Private Petite Museum*). As he became older, he passed on his collection, his stories, and his knowledge of whaling to his nephew, Mr. Harold Corea, who then continued running the museum after the loss of Mr. Ollivierre. Unfortunately, no sufficient plans were made to keep the museum open after Mr. Corea's death and subsequently the collection is currently unavailable to the public while the local historical society looks for new staff to reopen the museum. Of course, as mentioned earlier, plans can also be made to donate the museum and its collections to a governmental body. Ultimately, the best approach for the sustainability of grassroots initiatives depends on the specific circumstances of each case.

Ecomuseums

The ecomuseum is a specific museum model that can be found around the world (see *Defining the Museum*, page 33). These museums are frequently the result of grassroots initiatives and they tend to focus heavily on a particular community, usually a local community. The main aim of an ecomuseum is "to link the past with the present as a strategy to deal with the future needs of that particular society" (Fuller 1992: 328). In general, it can be said that an ecomuseum is more a community *process* rather than a *product* (Davis 2008: 403; Fuller 1992: 331). Ecomuseums can be identified by four main aspects. First of all, the ecomuseum tends to extend beyond the museum building, encompassing a wider landscape. Secondly, there is a strong emphasis on environmental sustainability. This runs parallel to the third aspect, namely a collective effort towards cultural sustainability or the preservation of culture and its transmission to younger generations. Finally, ecomuseums are heavily invested in the future of their target community and work towards skill development or training.

During the regional museum survey, 19 ecomuseums were visited throughout the Caribbean, two of which were under development at the time of visiting. Seventeen of these (89%) are grassroots initiatives and almost all of these are still managed by a community; four are currently governmentally run and owned. Although the ecomuseum concept originated in France, Caribbean ecomuseums can also be found in the Dutch-, English-, and Spanish-speaking Caribbean. However, only the museums on the French-speaking islands actually carry the name 'ecomuseum' (*ecomusée*). As such, the other ecomuseums were identified according to the abovementioned four aspects. This section will provide examples from these ecomuseums to illustrate the four key aspects and to highlight best practices for each.

The ecomuseum can often be recognized from a distance by its first aspect, which is the extended museum landscape. Depending on the community and the orientation of the museum, this landscape can vary in size, content, history, and use. The *Ecomusée de Marie-Galante: Habitation Murat* on Marie-Galante is set on a former plantation

Figure 8: Ecomusée de Marie-Galante: Habitation Murat, Marie-Galante, consists of an extended museum landscape.

estate. The museum extends beyond the exhibits in the reconstructed former great house and encompasses the ruins of a sugar refinery and a windmill, as well as a garden, kitchen, and other auxiliary buildings (see figure 8). The *Museo Tula* on Curaçao is similarly located on the grounds of what used to be a plantation estate. In this case the grounds are incorporated as a natural resource and an extensive walking tour through the gardens and wider landscape links to the museum. In both of these examples, the ecomuseum is created in an existing heritage landscape with ruins and historic buildings. However, it is also possible to set up an ecomuseum in a location and then develop the landscape around it. The *Ecomusée CreoleArt* on Guadeloupe is an example of this second approach. In this case, the museum was not located on a geographically remarkable site or housed in historical ruins. Instead, the ecomuseum landscape developed over time, beginning with a small didactic garden of plants and their uses. As the ecomuseum project expanded, the garden was extended and other cultural elements were included, such as historical dioramas and craft workshops. The *Charles Town Maroon Museum* in Jamaica forms the final example. This ecomuseum was built within the residential area of the Charles Town maroon community. The museum building is located next to an *asafu* yard, which is an enclosed open air space for music and dancing.[13] Besides the asafu yard, a craft workshop, and the museum building with a library, it could be argued that the ecomuseum extends into the surrounding town and encompasses the whole community. The museum, as a result of its activities, programs, and other participatory practices involves, as well as affects, the entire community.

---

13   Conversation with relative of founder of *Charles Town Maroon Museum* (Charles Town, Jamaica, 26 July 2014).

The second key aspect of ecomuseums is that they strive for greater environmental sustainability. This might be achieved by reducing the human impact on nature, teaching more sustainable methods of agriculture, or learning to live with dangerous natural phenomenon. In Grenada, the *Belmont Estate* has been transformed from a traditional plantation to an eco-farm. Local community members are employed at the estate and work with sustainable agricultural methods. There is a strong emphasis on creating awareness for the value of local produce in an attempt to both boost local production and reduce import. The estate produces fair trade chocolate as well as involves visitors in the process. *Casa Pueblo* on Puerto Rico began as a small collective environmental movement to protect the local community and landscape from the harmful impact of a proposed mining operation (panel texts, Casa Pueblo). After successfully shutting down the mining plans, the community moved on to tackle other issues related to environmental sustainability. Among others, they advocate the use of solar panels and they have developed highly energy efficient LED-lights in a university collaboration. They have also set up a program to teach children about the forest and nature by organizing classes in the forest. *Museo Infantil Trampolín*, in the Dominican Republic, is a museum for children of all ages. Several didactic rooms of the museum are dedicated to environmental sustainability. Through games, videos, and interaction with the guides, children learn how humans impact nature and how we can work to reduce this impact. Two miniature cities show how the future would be different if we continue as we are doing now or if we become more environmentally active. As a final example, the *Centre de Découverte des Sciences de la Terre* on Martinique can be mentioned. This ecomuseum was set up in 2004 at the foot of the Mt. Pelée volcano. Not only is it a geological survey station monitoring the behavior of the volcano, it is also an educational center focused on teaching local populations how to live in such a dangerous area. It shows the benefits of living in this area, while providing tips on how to plan for a possible eruption.

Although it is often assumed that the *eco* prefix in ecomuseums refers to the natural environment, it actually refers to the entire ecology surrounding a given community, including its cultural environment. This brings us to the third key aspect which is the preservation and transmission of culture. This is especially important to communities who feel that their traditions, knowledge, language, and their way of life is being lost. The *Santa Rosa First Peoples Community* in Trinidad has a community center or museum building in which they show craftwork and traditional subsistence strategies, such as the cassava baking process. Their craftwork is mainly basketry or other woven objects, beaded jewelry, and woodwork, and the objects are used as museum displays but are also for sale. This creates a consistent need for new items to be made and enables the community to invest in practicing these craft skills and pass on the knowledge of these skills to the younger generation. Additionally, the community is working on plans to develop their community center into a larger heritage village.[14] In traditional buildings they could have their current museum display as well as a craft workshop. Ideally, they would also like to house a few families in the heritage village so that they can practice traditional subsistence and agricultural methods and teach these to both visitors and younger community members. The *Luba Garifuna Cultural Museum*

14   Conversation with guide at *Santa Rosa First Peoples Community* (Arima, Trinidad, 9 January 2015).

in Belize is similarly devoted to preserving and transmitting cultural knowledge. The founder of this museum is one of the branch presidents of the National Garifuna Council of Belize (NGC) and connects the aims of the museum with the mission of the council. Collaboratively, they have engaged in a number of projects to preserve craft techniques, for instance by recording video footage of older community members practicing crafts that are currently only known to a few people.[15] The NGC and the museum are also strongly focused on preserving other intangible cultural elements such as the Garifuna language, music, and dance. The NGC has, for instance, initiated the creation of Garifuna primary schools where children are taught both in English and in Garifuna. The museum has been involved in assisting with these language programs and in connecting older community members with cultural knowledge and skills to younger community members who want to learn this heritage.

Cultural sustainability and teaching cultural practices ties in closely to the final key aspect of ecomuseums, namely the focus on community skill development. In some cases, as demonstrated in the examples above, community skill development is tied to cultural sustainability. However, there are other cases where community skill development is not necessarily related to cultural transmission; *Liberty Hall* in Jamaica provides an example of the latter. Liberty Hall is dedicated to the legacy of National Hero Marcus Garvey, the founder of the Universal Negro Improvement Association (UNIA) in 1914 (panel text, Liberty Hall). The museum continues in the spirit of Marcus Garvey and works on community development through education and inspiration. Several educational programs are run through the museum, many of them serving as outreach activities in communities where people may not be able to visit the museum. One of the museum's programs is for literacy and targets school-going children, another has an adult audience and teaches computer skills. The museum dedicates a large portion of its work to such community skill development as a way to improve the quality of life of its community members. Certainly, the examples of ecomuseums mentioned above which are working for environmental or cultural sustainability also involve community skill development. One may think of sustainable agricultural methods, recycling, energy preservation methods, cooking recipes, traditional food production practices, and, of course, the development of craft and language skills. Going back to the definition of the ecomuseum mentioned above, it is not surprising that community skill development is such an integral aspect of the museum's work. After all, the ecomuseum is a long-term community process which requires constant dedication and development.

Living Museums

Living museums are museums in which a significant part of the museum's narrative and content is relayed through living agents. These people could be employees who work in the organization attached to the museum or inhabitants of a heritage site or house museum. They may also be community members involved in the museum's practice, for instance community members demonstrating crafts within the museum space. Considering the fact that there is such a great diversity of living museums, there

---

15 Conversation with founder of *Luba Garifuna Cultural Museum* (Belize City, Belize, 29 October 2013).

THE SOCIAL MUSEUM IN THE CARIBBEAN

is no straightforward single participatory practice. Thus, this section will focus on four groupings of these types of museums: places of residence, religious sites, ecological sites, and places of work. Living museums which contain craft workshops or showcase other forms of intangible heritage through community participation are also discussed in three other sections of this chapter: *Ecomuseums* (page 73), *Community Staffing* (page 79), and *Interactive Displays* (page 95).

The first category of living museums is places of residence, such as city centers inscribed as World Heritage Site, heritage tours in villages, or museums located within an individual's home. Although the sizes of these places may differ significantly, they have in common that each of these sites contains more or less permanent habitation. This means that there are unique possibilities for interaction between visitors and residents. On the one hand this can enhance the museum experience for visitors because they can engage with people living on the site who are personally involved in that particular heritage. On the other hand, community members can choose to pass on their personal stories and community heritage to visitors without having to leave their homes and yards. The dual village of *Christiaankondre & Langemankondre* in Suriname is an example in which an organized heritage tour is embedded into the local community and its place of residence. A visit to these villages is guided by one of the community members who will lead a walking tour through the village, its gardens, and the communal buildings. This several hour tour provides many opportunities for visitors and community members to interact, for instance in the school, the store, the clinic, or any of the residencies along the way. This allows for the transmission of a multi-vocal community heritage narrative. The tours organized in Dominica in the *Touna Kalinago Heritage Village* operate in a similar manner. Here the tour ties more strongly to the residences of particular households that are visited one at a time. In each house, the visitors are invited into the yard and a specific cultural tradition is demonstrated and discussed. Such living museums are often great for showing and telling heritage that is embedded in the present and by providing a platform to answer visitors' questions. Community interaction is less structured and more spontaneous in World Heritage listed city centers, but these places also have the potential to provide multi-vocal heritage perspectives. Finally, personal interaction vitally characterizes the entire museum visit for museums located in homes.

Religious sites are the second grouping of living museums and refer to a museum or interpretation center combined with a religious building such as a synagogue, church, or temple. This category also includes archaeological sites where religious practices are performed. Unlike with places of residence, there is not necessarily a permanent presence of community members. When community members are present, this is generally for a brief time but for a (highly) significant event. Depending on the museum, visitors may be a part of or witness such events which might otherwise be restricted for non-community members. It is possible that visitors are asked to dress or behave in a certain way, requiring visitors to some extent to assimilate with the community. This is a highly participatory practice in which visitors temporarily participate in the community. For instance, the *Synagogue Mikvé Israel-Emanuel and Jewish Cultural Historical Museum* in Curaçao allows visitors to enter the synagogue as well as the museum. However, men entering the synagogue are required to cover their heads and *kippot* are provided at the entrance. Visitors are also restricted with regards to which events they may attend. While the Shabbat on Friday evenings and Saturday mornings is open to attendance by (appropriately dressed) visitors, Jewish Festivals are off limits except on the first day. This allows participation in religious and cultural events of the local Jewish community within limits set by the same community. In Puerto Rico a slightly different participatory dynamic can be found in two Amerindian archaeological sites: the *Centro Ceremonial Indígena de Tibes* and the *Centro Indígena Caguana*. Both of these sites contain ball courts and are associated with the former Indigenous population of the island, the so-called Taíno. There are currently growing communities in Puerto Rico which self-identify as Taíno (for a debate on this issue of identity, *cf.* Forte 2006; Haslip-Viera 2013). These so-called neo-Taíno communities wish to retain Taíno traditions, use their iconography, and perform religious and cultural ceremonies, ideally on actual pre-colonial Amerindian sites (Oliver 1998: 214-216). Since both sites are managed governmentally, neo-Taíno groups must ask for permission to perform ceremonies or rituals on the archaeological sites.[16] It seems that in most cases this permission is granted, generally during the regular opening hours of the archaeological park. As such, other visitors are able to participate in these ceremonies and interact with this cultural community if they desire.

Ecological sites such as heritage farms, national parks, marine parks, and eco-tourism sites are the third grouping of living museums. These sites are characterized by a high level of engagement with the natural environment, often mediated through guides or employees in the park, farm, or site. On eco-tourism sites or heritage farms there tends to be a high amount of participation in the agricultural and production process. This active participation is coupled with engagement with the employees working on the site who guide visitors on the estate and answer questions. This provides unique natural knowledge and awareness of local traditions related to agriculture and cooking. National and marine parks have a strong focus on creating awareness for the protection of natural environments and species. This awareness is mediated through guides and rangers who show visitors both the beauty and fragility of nature. The *Underwater Sculpture Park*, just off the coast of Grenada, forms a unique example (see figure 9). This park was the initiative of artist Jason de Caires Taylor, who created concrete sculptures and submerged them in a bay that had been damaged by hurricane Ivan in 2004. His idea was to stimulate the reef to recover from the hurricane by providing the reef with new surfaces to grow on. Now, the bay is a marine protected area and visitors dive, snorkel, swim, or boat to the sculptures under mandatory guidance and are taught to protect the reef and marine life. Visitors thus actively participate in the protection of this particular living environment during their visit.

Places of work are the final category of living museums discussed here: museum factories, shops, distilleries, police stations, or military bases. Although again there is a great amount of variety in these living museums, a visit to them is greatly characterized by the employees working there and the limitations of each particular working environment. Although many of these museums have ample opportunities for engagement between visitors and employees, this interaction can be restricted or guided by rules. For instance, in some working environments it may not be possible or safe to

---

16   Conversation with guard at *Centro Ceremonial Indígena de Tibes* (Ponce, Puerto Rico, 28 January 2015).

Figure 9: When diving in the Underwater Sculpture Park, Grenada, visitors participate actively in protecting the reef.

interrupt employees with questions. In other cases, such as with the active military base of *Fort Saint-Louis* on Martinique, parts of the site may be entirely off-limit to visitors. Here, visitors are restricted to the historical parts of the fort and there is no interaction with the modern military base and its employees. However, in many other cases it is possible to observe ongoing production processes. The *Distillerie Depaz*, also on Martinique, allows visitors to follow a clearly marked path through the factory and other production areas and watch the rum production process in action. Such demonstrations are very common in this category of living museums and provides a specific type of participation. Naturally, this participation is increased in those places of work where it is possible to engage directly with employees, which is most common for museums with shops, such as the *Chocomuseo* in the Dominican Republic. Here, engaging with visitors is the core job and there is a high level of interaction. Focus lies less on production and more on the final product, so rather than see a demonstration of the process, visitors are allowed to taste or test the product. Ultimately, it is activity and human interaction that typifies these living museums.

Community Staffing

Any museum needs staff, of course, even if this is just one person. However, museums about a particular history, heritage, or culture benefit if they are staffed partially or entirely by members of that same community. In some museums, particularly grassroots museums, community staffing is often self-evident. However, in other museums, community staffing is not as common or may only happen in certain positions. It is certainly not always easy to identify whether a museum has community staffing, especially as a visitor and outsider. In practice, this meant that for the regional museum survey it was often only possible to identify community staffing with certainty in the front-of-house positions. In some cases, community staffing was confirmed by the staff directly, or apparent through the museum's website or on exhibition labels. An additional challenge is that identity and community belonging can be determined differently by community members or outsiders. In total, 76 (highly likely) cases could be identified in which museums had community staffing, although a higher number is certainly possible. Still, not all museums have content that is specifically tied to a specific community and in these cases the communities targeted by the museum may be so diverse that they can be reflected in the museum staff without being overly apparent. This section will discuss a number of best practices related to community staffing. Staff here encompasses all persons working at a museum, regardless of whether this is paid labor.

One of the most obviously engaging ways of incorporating community members into the museum is by appointing them as guides. This has the clear benefit that community members are often best equipped to tell the community's history and traditions from a personal perspective. This approach resonates with visitors who connect on a personal level with their guide and can feel more involved in the museum and its content. *Kura Hulanda Museum* on Curaçao – which focuses on the African diaspora, its great civilizations, and the history and legacy of slavery – has a number of community guides who offer to take visitors through the museum. They speak about their own place in the African-diaspora and their personal experiences. This incorporates multi-vocality in the exhibition spaces and allows community members to be an integral part of the museum and participate towards creating the museum narrative. For visitors, it increases participation by providing a place for discussion, learning, and interaction with community members.

For museums that include intangible heritages, a good approach can be to include community members as performing staff. This is the case at the *Charles Town Maroon Museum* in Jamaica where community members demonstrate music, song, and dance in the museum space. Visitors are strongly encouraged to join in with the dances and are taught some of the basic steps. This provides a unique window for participation between visitors and community members. The *Museo Tula* on Curaçao also involves community members to relay intangible heritages. The museum is an initiative of the local Afro-Caribbean community and preserves and teaches their syncretic[17] traditions while focusing on the history of Tula's slave revolt. Although they also have community members working as museum guides, they have expanded their inclusion of community expertise by employing community members in the museum's kitchen to cook Afro-Caribbean meals and snacks. When visitors pay their entrance fee to the museum, they can choose to add a warm lunch to their museum visit.

Community members can also be incorporated into the staff as caretakers of the museum or heritage site. At *Lamanai Archaeological Reserve* in Belize, members

---

17 There has been extensive academic debate about the meaning and use of the term *syncretism*. Here it is used to echo one of the staff members who referred to her culture as syncretic, as a mix of African and Caribbean elements.

from the local community who self-identify as Mayan have been offered training through the National Institute of Culture and History (NICH) and its Institute of Archaeology. Interested community members have learned about archaeology, history, biology, geology, and other subjects relevant to the Archaeological Reserve. They are now responsible for guiding visitors through the site and protecting both the visitors and the archaeological remains. Only these caretakers have the authorization to guide visitors on the site which are their ancestral lands. Because they are personally invested in the archaeological remains and their preservation, they are very careful to protect them. A similar situation can be found at *Parque Nacional Histórico La Vega Vieja* in the Dominican Republic, where colonial archaeological remains are maintained and cared for by members of the local community. Family members living around the site are responsible for admitting visitors as well as protecting the ruins, either from careless visitors or looters. A third example can be found at the *Underwater Sculpture Park* just off the shore of Grenada, mentioned previously. Although the park does not have any staff as such, a non-profit group of volunteers was formed to maintain and rejuvenate the sculptures. They actively work to seek sponsorship for the replacement and reno-vation of existing sculptures or the creation and submersion of new installations. Of course, in addition to this, a large group of people are part-time caretakers of the site, such as all the dive instructors, fishermen, tour operators, and others who take visitors to the site. During the visit, they are responsible for the visitors under their supervision and must make sure that no one damages the reef, the marine life, or the sculptures.

It is also possible to include community members into the museum as part of an art installation or artist in residency program. This kind of artistic staffing tends to be tem-porary and project based. *Centro León* in the Dominican Republic organizes an annual art competition in which they are very attentive to meet the artists' wishes. They have a large gallery in which winning submissions are exhibited as envisioned by their makers. In 2014/2015, one of the artists wished to continue making similar artworks within the gallery.[18] Centro León agreed and the artist set up a workbench with materials and tools next to his submissions. He regularly worked within the gallery and interacted with visitors. *The Priory* in Grenada, which is still under development, will convert this beautiful home into a center for art and culture. One of the most popular plans is to invite artists to take up residence and work freely on their art for a number of months. Their resulting works will then be exhibited within The Priory itself.

Certainly, community members can be a part of the regular museum staff: as curators, educators, collections managers, directors, or in any other position. Any ap-pointment of community staff will of course incorporate their community perspectives into that particular aspect of the museum work. A curator from the community may influence an exhibit by using the community's language, tone, or highlight community interests. On Curaçao, Dutch, English, and Papiamentu are all official languages and a large part of the population is bi- or multi-lingual. However, most museums choose to present their exhibitions in Dutch (the language of government) and English (the language of visitors). At *Museo Tula* (also discussed above) many labels are presented only in Papiamentu (the first language of the majority of the local population) or with

---

18   Conversation with coordinator of exhibitions at *Centro León* (Santiago de los Caballeros, Dominican Republic, 23 January 2015).

Dutch or English translations in second place. This choice of language reflects the curators' ties to the local community and the museum's place within it. Of course, beyond the language, the contents of the exhibition are also intimately tied to the Afro-Caribbean community. Educators may develop programs and activities that specifically attract members of their community or work towards tackling their specific issues. As mentioned earlier, *Liberty Hall* in Jamaica has specific programs that target children's literacy. They also work with adults to increase their computer skills, enabling them to not only maintain social ties, but also to gain practical skills such as submitting online job applications. Besides the abovementioned, there are of course many other examples of community members working as museum staff.

Museum Collections & Exhibitions

Research Collaboration

Research collaboration between community members and a museum is another way for the community to contribute directly to the creation of exhibitions and knowledge. This kind of collaboration could be identified as a method of crowdsourcing, in which the goal is to collect knowledge or data. As summarized by Mia Ridge, "crowdsourcing is emerging as a form of engagement with cultural heritage that contributes toward a shared, significant goal or research area, by asking the public to undertake tasks that cannot be done automatically, in an environment where the tasks, goals (or both) provide inherent rewards for participation" (Ridge 2013: 437). Of the museums visited, 48 examples were found in which such research collaboration had taken place. Naturally, there may have been many more cases, but the results of this research collaboration may not have been on display at the time of visitation.

When museums seek out research collaboration with community members, they may be interested in the specific personal knowledge or experiences of individual people. In many cases, personal stories or experiences may be used to enrich and personalize exhibitions, or oral histories may be collected and kept in the museum's archives. The *San Nicolas Community Museum* in Aruba has a collection of artefacts, most of them dating to c. 50-100 years ago.[19] Many of these objects have been bought or donated following the death of local residents. The museum focuses heavily on collecting personal stories related to these objects, for instance by asking relatives for information about the previous owner of the artefact. In this way, they aim to construct object biographies based on personal knowledge or experiences from local community members. This is long-term research, just like the crowdsourcing project run by the *Museo Memorial de la Resistencia Dominicana* in the Dominican Republic. This museum uncovers the hidden, conflicted, and bloody history of the dictatorship of Rafael Trujillo (1891-1961) and a turbulent time in the recent history of the country (De Peña Díaz 2013). Throughout the exhibition, forms can be found that encourage people to write to the museum with their personal experiences of the regime. As the dictatorship was characterized by secrecy and misinformation,

---

19 Conversation with manager of *San Nicolas Community Museum* (San Nicolas, Aruba, 21 January 2014).

the museum aims to voice the events as they really happened (panel texts, Museo Memorial de la Resistencia Dominicana). Certainly, they gain much credibility by telling the story through first-hand accounts. In addition, they can also provide comfort to people whose stories are now being heard and whose grief is now accepted (guestbook entries, Museo Memorial de la Resistencia Dominicana).

Museums may also collaborate in seeking personal knowledge or experiences on a more short-term basis. The *University of the West Indies Museum* in Jamaica engaged the visiting public for a temporary project called *Freeze Frame*.[20] Within the museum, a video from 1953 about campus life was shown. Visitors were asked to write the names and some information about any persons they recognized in the footage on paper copies of stills from the film. The museum relied on the personal knowledge of visitors, and of alumni and their relatives in particular, to add more knowledge to the video. As such, many people who had been anonymous figures in the film were identified. Visitors were also encouraged to recount experiences they may have had of particular places on the campus and to write these down too. Temporary research collaboration also took place at *Savonet Museum* on Curaçao. For the creation of the museum, which was opened in 2010, an oral history project took place to preserve the specific knowledge of people who had lived on or around the estate. In video interviews, these former inhabitants talked about the work they used to do as well as their knowledge of the land and its plants and animals. The video is shown in the exhibition in several fragments.

Community members may also collaborate with museums in providing data beyond what the museum could collect on its own. In some cases the research may have taken place externally at the initiative of a university or organization, but the results are displayed within a museum. At the *National Archaeological Museum Aruba*, the local population is on display in an exhibition about identity and genetics. DNA studies of the population have been able to determine the different genetic percentages of Aruban ancestry, for instance, that "Arubans are 40% Amerindian" (panel text, National Archaeological Museum Aruba). Besides demographics, another common collaborative research area concerns archaeological excavations. Excavations are usually led by a group from the scientific community but often take place in collaboration with a museum where the finds will ultimately be stored and exhibited. In some cases, the wider public may be invited to assist with the excavation. In Puerto Rico, both the *Centro Ceremonial Indígena de Tibes* (opened in 1982) and the *Centro Indígena Caguana* (opened in 1965; see figure 10) are archaeological sites that have become museums which may be visited by the public. In each case, the museum consists of an open air part with the visible archaeological structural remains, as well as a museum building with artefacts. These museums have collaborated over a number of decades and excavation seasons with many different members of the archaeological and scientific communities. The museum stores, houses, and displays the finds and is concerned with conservation and education. Scientists contribute to the museum by engaging in further excavations or research, uncovering artefacts, or adding new knowledge to the museum's repository. Data collection also takes place at *Yotin Kortá: The Money Museum* on Curaçao, which encourages students of any age

---

20   Conversation with curator at *University of the West Indies Museum* (Kingston, Jamaica, 31 July 2014).

Figure 10: The site at Centro Indígena Caguana, Puerto Rico, was first excavated in 1915 and opened to the public in 1965. Archaeological investigations continue to contribute objects and information to the exhibitions.

to come and research their collections and archives. If these school students present an oral report or write a short paper, they are asked to share this with the museum and these reports are collected on the museum's website. In this way, the museum encourages young students to do research in their archives and to add their findings and knowledge to the museum's repository.

Finally, it must be stressed that research collaboration will require that ethical considerations be taken into account. In every case, but especially regarding sensitive matters, genetic materials, or information that might be in any way harmful, participants' consent is vitally important. Additionally, transparency of the use and display of data and information is imperative. It may be desirable to collect data anonymously and to protect the donor's identity when disclosing any information.

Object Donation

Community members may also participate in the museum process by contributing objects towards the museum's collections. Whether the museum actively encourages community collecting or only accepts incidental donations, it is necessary for the museum to have a collections management plan and for staff to be committed to the long-term safekeeping of these objects. It is essential to have a policy on how these items will be handled, catalogued, stored, and possibly exhibited. It must also be decided if the objects require any conservation or special care. If there is a possibility that the object(s) may be put on display, this should be discussed with the donor, if feasible. Unless the donor wishes to remain anonymous, it is good practice to place the donor's name on the object label. Besides showing gratitude and personally crediting the donor for their contribution to the museum's collection, this has added benefits. At the basic level, it indicates to visitors which objects have been donated and which are part of the museum's own collecting endeavors. Perhaps more importantly, it may also encourage additional donations: by showing visitors what kind of objects are valued by the museum, people may be inspired to consider the potential public value of their own property. Secondly, if donations are well cared for in a museum environment, this may encourage possible donors to bestow objects for better safekeeping than they can provide at home. Of course, in some countries there are laws which state that certain types of objects must be handed over to a museum: this is often the case with archaeological finds. However, this section will only consider voluntary donations. A minimum of 76 cases of object donation were identified although it is more than likely that the actual number is higher, as donated objects on display are not always indicated and donations may also be kept in storage.

It is possible to separate object donations into a number of categories. First of all, we can distinguish incidental donations from active community collecting. Incidental donations cover those cases in which one or more objects are donated to the museum on the initiative of the donor without the museum placing a specific request. This type of donation is sporadic and generally the museum decides whether or not to accept the donation. The donor may be an individual or a group of people and the donation may comprise of one object or an entire collection. At *The Wall House Museum* on St. Barthélemy such an incidental donation is on display. The island is currently an overseas collectivity of France, but belonged to Sweden from the concession in 1785 until it was returned to France in 1878 (panel texts, The Wall House Museum). There is still Swedish heritage on the island and the ties to Sweden are visible in the museum in the form of a Swedish flag. It was made by artist Marianne Lundahl as an exact copy of the flag which was flown on St. Barthélemy 1819-1878 (object label, The Wall House Museum). The replica was donated in 1996 and is displayed with labels in both Swedish and French.

The objects donated to the *Ecomusée de Marie-Galante: Habitation Murat* on Marie-Galante have a different collection history. When the museum existed only conceptually, the local community was asked to donate objects to create the museum's collection (panel text, Ecomusée de Marie-Galante: Habitation Murat). Between 1976-1980, object collection took place throughout the island based on a collection plan: community members were requested to donate items related to the home, work, celebrations, music, and medicine. Particular urgency was expressed to donate objects which reflected ways of life that were rapidly disappearing from the island. The museum could not have been created as was envisioned without the active and large-scale community collecting of artefacts. As basically the entire collection was donated, labels do not identify individual donors. Instead, a panel explaining the history of the museum expresses gratitude to the entire population of Marie-Galante for their past and continued donations.

Secondly, we can differentiate donations of single objects from the donation of entire collections. At the *St. Maarten National Heritage Foundation Museum* many examples can be found of single object donations. For instance, the "very old ship lantern donated by Mr. Al Deher," the clock "donated by Judith Codrington," or the "VOC coins dating 1736-1792 donated by Simone Halley and family" (object labels, St. Maarten National Heritage Foundation Museum). A donated object may also have been made specifically for display at the museum: "This small piroque [dugout canoe] was carved from a gommier tree in the interior of Dominica for our museum by a Carib Indian with the name of Chalo in 2005" (object label, St. Maarten National Heritage Foundation Museum). Depending on the object, it is not necessarily challenging to manage and maintain individual donations, as they can be catalogued rapidly. However, it may not always be easy to place them in the right context, or they might require significant conservation and care. In addition, if the museum receives many single donations, it can become more difficult to find space for all of them and to manage and display each of them in accordance with the wishes of the donor.

Donations of entire collections can prove to be more challenging to a museum, although they may also be considered more valuable thanks to their cohesive narrative. Yet, when an entire collection is donated, it might require a whole room to be dedicated to, or even built for it, if the collection needs specific maintenance or conditions for preservation. On the other hand, it is possible that the collection is already catalogued and labeled for display. Naturally, a collection as a complete unit can provide significant extra depth to the museum. The *Musée du Rhum: Musée Universel* on Guadeloupe began as a museum of rum distillation and has expanded with a number of different exhibitions on various topics since its opening in 1990, now calling itself a universal museum (panel text, Musée du Rhum: Musée Universel). Perhaps most expansive was the addition of the collection of natural scientist Fortuné Chalumeau in 1994. This collection consists of hundreds of preserved insects and butterflies, neatly pinned on cushions and displayed in hanging frames. The collection is vast and is housed in a separate room. Because of the fragile nature of the artefacts, the room is kept under strict climate control, requiring long term financial support.

As in this latter case, donations may not naturally fit within the original scope or content of the museum. However, by accepting and displaying these collections, the museum can expand upon its reach and its appeal. A comparable example can be found at the *National Museum & Art Gallery of Trinidad & Tobago*, which has an extensive art collection as well as exhibitions of archaeology, history, social history, petroleum, and geology. The museum also has a room that is the Sports Hall of Fame, established by the WITCO Sports Foundation in 1984 (panel text, National Museum & Art Gallery of Trinidad & Tobago), extending the scope of the museum to include sports history. A similar situation is the case at the *Musée Départemental d'Archéologie et de Préhistoire* on Martinique. The museum's collections are archaeological and ethnographic, focusing on the Amerindian past of the island and the rest of the Caribbean. However, a section of the museum is dedicated to a collection of 62 pieces of pre-Columbian gold jewelry from Colombia donated by Mr Alain Ho Hio Hen (panel text, Musée Départemental d'Archéologie et de Préhistoire). The gold jewelry, although from a similar time period, comes from South America and differs from the Caribbean exhibitions. The panel text explains that this collection invites a deeper understanding of the Americas as a whole and closer ties to Colombia in particular.

While donations can result in some eclecticism within the museum, it is also possible that they fit perfectly within the museum's content and scope. This is more likely to happen with donations that have been requested by or occur on the initiative of the museum. The recently opened *Museo de la Altagracia* in the Dominica Republic is dedicated to the history and veneration of the Virgen Altagracia. It is closely connected to the Basilica Higüey, where the Virgen Altagracia is worshipped, which is located on the same grounds. Part of the museum tells this specific religious history and displays objects related to this past. However, another part of the museum focuses on today's veneration and the objects that are used in ceremonies or offered by the public, so called ex-votos. These ex-votos are often valuable items, such as jewelry or objects made of precious metals. Individuals donate these objects to the Virgen in the Basilica, and make a sacred vow if their wish is granted, or in gratitude after their wish has been fulfilled. Periodically, some of the objects amassed at the Basilica are, in turn, donated to the museum. For the donors, the value of the object lies in the act of the donation; what happens afterwards to the material object is less relevant.[21] So, in this case, the museum takes initiative to, albeit indirectly, collect objects from the community. The objects selected in this way by the museum form an integral part of the museum's exhibitions.

Finally, it is also possible that the donation of a collection, for instance to a (local) government, leads to the creation of a museum. This was the case with the *Musée Schoelcher* in Guadeloupe. Viktor Schœlcher donated his collection of statues and reliefs, as well as objects he had collected on his many voyages, to the Conseil Général of Guadeloupe in 1883 (panel text, Musée Schoelcher). The donation was accepted unanimously and the municipality of Pointe-à-Pitre proposed a location. The museum was inaugurated on 21st July 1887 and exhibited part of Schoelcher's donated collection which contained 980 pieces. The donation was considered so valuable and so extensive that it not only warranted exhibition, but indeed required its own institution. Today, the museum is still open to the public and displays part of this original collection, although it has grown with additional donations, purchases, and loans.

To summarize, object donations can be valuable assets to the museum: by growing the existing collections, extending the scope of the museum, anchoring the museum more strongly within the community, or even by being the raison d'être of the museum's existence. For community members, object donation may increase their perception of the value of their heritage, it may safeguard fragile objects, it may tie them more strongly to their museum, leave behind a personal legacy after an individual's death, or create a sense of pride at having property on display in the museum. Fiona Candlin has noted that "simply accepting and housing objects *is* a public service" (Candlin 2016: 115). However, it must be reiterated that accepting object donations should not be taken lightly. If a museum accepts a donation, it takes on the responsibility for that donation for the long-term. This means that the museum is responsible for the safety, security, preservation, and use of the object. A collections management policy is necessary to make sure the donations are taken care of. Such a policy is also useful to set criteria to determine which objects the museum will or will not consider accepting. The *National Museum & Art Gallery of Trinidad & Tobago*, for instance, has such a policy on their website along with a donation form. ICOM's *Code of Ethics for Museums* (ICOM 2017) is also a good starting point to setting up guidelines and rules for object donations and collections management.

---

21 Conversation with director of *Museo de la Altagracia* (Higüey, Dominican Republic, 20 January 2015).

Contemporary Art

Museums may wish to collaborate with members of the artistic community by including and exhibiting contemporary art. Beyond representing a local or regional community, artists may also incorporate other identities into their work, reflecting particular social, political, or other interests. Artists, who speak through their work, can visualize the interests, issues, and emotions of the communities that they are a part of. As such, the inclusion of contemporary art may be a way for museums to visually, or in other media forms, include community voices in their exhibition spaces. Of course, contemporary art can be included on a small or large scale, there is a difference between commissioned pieces or freely inspired works, and there are other criteria which influence the level of community engagement achieved by this practice. Of the museums visited, 89 contained contemporary art within the public spaces of the museum. For this study, contemporary art was identified if: it was termed 'modern' or 'contemporary' by the museum itself, if it was made by a living artist, or if it was made in the last 100 years.

There are a number of common ways in which contemporary art is included in Caribbean museums. First of all, an artist might be commissioned to provide work that illustrates objects that are on display in the museum. This can commonly be seen in archaeological museums, where the purpose or use of some of the objects may not be self-explanatory to the visitors. Illustrations or paintings of the objects can be used as a didactic tool. This method for the inclusion of contemporary art has been applied in the *Museo Arqueológico Regional Altos de Chavón* in the Dominican Republic. Dominican artist Boris De Los Santos was hired for a series of illustrations to accompany the refurbished exhibitions. The idea was that these illustrations would help visitors follow the narrative without relying on text, especially for visitors whose native language is not Spanish or English, or for younger children. The illustrations turned out to be so successful, that the director decided to build the exhibitions around them.[22] The founder of *Rome Museum* on Grenada, Mr. Joseph Rome, is a sculptor who has created a number of wooden pieces to illustrate objects in his museum. Among others, he has made several wooden feet which show certain illnesses or wounds that were commonly contracted in the bush and he uses the sculptures to illustrate various traditional bush remedies. The *Bob Marley Museum* in Jamaica is a similar example of visual art used to illustrate the main exhibits – of course, in addition to the major role his music plays. The museum is housed in the artist's former home, as well as in some newer buildings on the grounds. In the outside areas, the focus resonates in a series of large painted or photographic murals featuring images of Bob Marley and Rastafari symbolism. The use of these artworks on the walls effectively projects the message of the museum beyond its exhibition spaces and illustrates the theme and style of the museum to the outside world. Beyond illustration, art works may also be commissioned for various production purposes: exhibition design, website design, or a logo. Approaching artists from a local or other community may be a good way to make sure these designs reflect the community which the museum is a part of.

Naturally, a part of the museum can be dedicated to contemporary art, with permanent space for (rotating) contemporary art or by temporarily installing an art

---

22 Conversation with director of *Museo Arqueológico Regional Altos de Chavón* (La Romana, Dominican Republic, 18 January 2015).

exhibition in a gallery that is not reserved for art. The *St. Vincent and the Grenadines National Trust* has an area available as public exhibition space, which is usually occupied by display cases with archaeological materials recovered on the islands served by the trust. At the time of visitation in 2015, a photo exhibition by Robert Charlotte was just opened, featuring portraits of Garinagu. These large photos were hung throughout the room, spread between the archaeological artefacts. Although the space was not originally set up for such an exhibition, it could be adapted on a temporary basis. A temporary location for art was also created at the *Museo Virreinal Alcázar de Colón* in the Dominican Republic. Here, paintings by a local artist were propped up on easels in an open gallery on the second floor. In other museums, a gallery that is used for all manner of temporary exhibitions could also house contemporary art every now and then. If space for the inclusion of contemporary art is allocated on a temporary basis, it is important to assess whether this space is actually suitable for this purpose. Contemporary art may require different security measures, lighting levels, or larger viewing distances.

Issues related to the suitability of a space may be avoided by dedicating an area permanently to the display of contemporary art. In *Het Curacaosche Museum* on Curaçao, a number of hallways have been reserved as art galleries. Local artists can display their artworks here on a temporary basis and paintings are frequently rotated. This gives local artists the opportunity to showcase their work. By changing the artworks frequently, the artistic community is able to keep participating in the museum. In the Dominican Republic, *Centro León* encourages deep participation of local artists by hosting an annual art contest, mentioned previously. The museum has two massive galleries dedicated to art: one with key pieces from past years of the competition, another for the winners of the current edition. The artworks on display in the gallery of former entries are curated by the museum staff around their selection of themes and works. On the other hand, the gallery with the current winners is curated in close contact with the respective artists, some of whom spend months in the exhibition space creating their pieces, perhaps directly onto the gallery wall.[23] For those artists who have been selected by the committee, there is a high level of participation with the museum while they work on creating, curating, and installing their work in the gallery.

Certainly, there are also museums that are dedicated entirely to contemporary art. Some of these museums might also be 'galleries' in the sense that they have art for sale as well as for display. The *Galería Botello* is an example in Puerto Rico: set up in 1953 as a for-profit gallery by artist Angel Botello, it is now also partially a museum. It has a number of pieces for sale by local artists, but also displays some of Angel Botello's works as well as other well-known local pieces. At the other end of the spectrum one can identify large art museums such as the *Museo de Arte Moderno* in the Dominican Republic. Sprawling on four enormous floors, the museum is able to display contemporary art in both permanent and temporary galleries, and in various media. The inclusion of contemporary art in this museum reflects engagements with a wide range of artistic communities over several decades.

---

23   Conversation with coordinator of exhibitions at *Centro León* (Santiago de los Caballeros, Dominican Republic, 23 January 2015).

Local Achievements

This section considers those museums that exhibit the noteworthy achievements from members of their local community. Although many museums recall important community events or achievements, they do not always celebrate individual community members personally. In the museums visited, 44 cases were identified of community achievements being including in the museum's public displays. This participatory practice can anchor the museum more strongly within the community in a number of ways. First of all, it openly pays tribute to community members for valued deeds. Secondly, these exhibits may be a source of pride to the community. Thirdly, it can be an inspiration to community members who may also want to be exhibited. Finally, it localizes the museum by making it of particular personal interest to members of the community. In addition, visitors from outside the community may learn more about, and increase their appreciation of, the community.

A museum may choose to celebrate contemporary local achievements or commemorate historical accomplishments. The *Heritage Collection Museum* on Anguilla, which narrates the history of the island and its people, also includes achievements of the local community from recent times. The museum contains many photographs showing the more recent history of the island. Among these photos, there is a section dedicated to local centenarians: Anguillans who have reached their 100th birthday. This small wall of fame celebrates the oldest members of the local community. Contemporary achievements are also displayed at the *Museum of the Trinidad & Tobago Police Service*. Roughly half of the museum space is dedicated to a chronological exhibition of the history of the police service and the islands, centering on the succession of the commissioners of police. Each commissioner is featured in a portrait with his name and years of service as commissioner inscribed below. These portraits are surrounded by images of political or military events that took place in the same time period: royal visits, group photos, big sporting events, or riots. The history of the country is placed in direct connection to the personal achievements of the commissioners, sometimes accompanied by personal items such as insignia or pieces of their uniforms.

Historical accomplishments are a common feature in museums anywhere in the world, but here we will consider those by individual community members that are exhibited in the museum. In Jamaica, the *Shaare Shalom Jamaican Jewish Heritage Centre* tells the history of Jamaican Jews and part of the exhibition consists of a series of panels titled 'Jewish Achievements/Contributions to Jamaican Society' (panel text, Shaare Shalom Jamaican Jewish Heritage Centre). These panels relate the individual achievements of Jamaican Jews since the 17th century in the areas of industry, commerce, the arts, education, professions, and public service. Also on Jamaica, the *Charles Town Maroon Museum* pays tribute to historic achievements by maroons (see figure 11). The maroons were principally enslaved Africans who escaped from plantations or from slave ships into the interior of the island (panel text, Charles Town Maroon Museum). With the help of, and together with, Indigenous survivors, they established new societies. Fighting for their freedom, survival, and to repel the colonizers, they often found themselves in conflict and hardship. In the museum, panels discuss personal accomplishments of the "Maroon Heroes," often related to military strategy and battle.

By including community achievements, museums may wish to draw attention to otherwise unsung or unknown individuals. At the *St. Maarten National Heritage*

Figure 11: The maroons' resistance to slavery is also shown on the outside of the asafu yard of the Charles Town Maroon Museum, Jamaica.

Foundation Museum a stairwell has been turned into a community hall of fame. Portraits of local community members are posted on the wall along with extensive biographies including their accomplishments. Most of these achievements are related to the improvement of conditions on the island. For instance, the biography of a midwife commends her for her many years of safe deliveries. Other people on the wall have worked in education or religion. Such a wall of fame can have a strong impact on the community, awarding specifically those people who have spent their lives working in the interest of the community. Other museums might take the opposite approach by claiming popular or well-known individuals as belonging to the community connected to the museum. For instance, the *Coyaba Gardens & Museum* on Jamaica has a panel titled 'Famous sons of St. Ann' (panel text, Coyaba Gardens & Museum), dedicated to two famed individuals who were born in the parish of the museum. The museum tells the lives and achievements of these two parish members: 'National Hero Marcus Mosiah Garvey and Robert (Bob) Nesta Marley.' By pointing out that they came from *this* parish, the museum effectively adds their fame to the narrative. A similar narrative can be found at the *West Indies Cricket Heritage Centre* on Grenada. The museum has an extensive collection of bats, kit, uniforms, photographs, and memorabilia from famous members of the West Indies cricket team. The museum has chosen to include achievements from team members from the entire West Indies, not only Grenada, and it connects itself to a regional community.

Finally, there are also museums that are dedicated entirely to the accomplishments and life of a single individual, which generally reflect a narrow yet deep engagement. Jamaica's *Bob Marley Museum*, mentioned before, is a well-known example. The museum is dedicated to his life, career, and music, showcasing his platinum records,

Figure 12: Mind's Eye: The Visionary World of Miss Lassie, Grand Cayman, is dedicated to the preservation of the home and other artworks of Gladwyn K. Bush.

awards, and newspaper clippings from around the world. The museum was founded by his wife with the aim to preserve and carry on his legacy (panel text, Bob Marley Museum). Several other museums can be found in the Caribbean that are dedicated to the accomplishments of a single individual. The *Casa Museo General Gregorio Luperón* in the Dominican Republic, is centered on the political and family life of Luperón. As military and political leader, he was instrumental in the restoration of the Dominican Republic in the 19th century. The museum focuses mainly on this political history, although it also includes some personal and familial artefacts and narratives. It is strongly tied to the local municipality where he was born and where they feel most proud of his legacy. A third example is the *Musée Municipal Saint-John Perse* in Guadeloupe. Set in a historical house, the museum exhibits the life of diplomat and Nobel laureate poet Alex Leger, whose pseudonym was Saint-John Perse. Leger grew up in Point-à-Pitre and the municipality decided to honor his literary and diplomatic achievements by creating this museum (panel texts, Musée Municipal Saint-John Perse). *Mind's Eye: The Visionary World of Miss Lassie* on Grand Cayman, preserves the extraordinary painted home of visionary intuitive artist Gladwyn K. Bush (see figure 12). The foundation who owns the museum also works to retain her artworks in Cayman by restricting their sale abroad – by doing so, they hope to locally preserve her work.

Co-curation

Co-curated exhibitions are those which have been created through collaboration between a museum and the members of one or more communities. Most commonly, the resulting exhibitions are temporary rather than permanent. Although it is possible for such a collaboration to take place between the museum staff and a single community member, for instance an artist whose work will be exhibited, it is more often a collaboration between a group of people. Co-curation tends to require deep commitment and engagement, both from museum staff and community members. Projects may take months or years of work, even if the resulting exhibition is only open to the public for a relatively short time. In many cases, the initiative lies with the museum who has decided to involve a community in their exhibition process. As co-curation tends to require more of a commitment than most other participatory practices, it occurs more rarely. In the museums visited, only 12 examples of co-curation were identified, although certainly more museums have created co-curated exhibitions in the past or may have been working on one behind the scenes. If done well, co-curation can give community members a voice in all aspects of the exhibition process and can result in a high level of participation. However, there is also a danger that participation may be perceived as an empty promise or a box-ticking exercise. This section will focus on four important aspects of the co-curation process: the power balance, representativity, multi-vocality, and the time frame. Each aspect is illuminated using the same example, chosen because of the conversations with the museum director and a community member, which provided a greater understanding of the processes leading to the exhibition's creation. Most of these aspects are not openly visible in the exhibition space, so insider knowledge of the process is needed in order to provide these examples. Critical discussions related to power balance, representativity, multi-vocality, and the investment of time can be found in Chapter 7.

> *When we invite in outsiders, of any kind, we have to do it on their terms. Not ours. It's their key. It's their door. They have given us the gift of their participation, and they deserve our interest and respect. Even if that requires learning new ways of working, speaking, or connecting.*
> Nina Simon (2016: 75)

The power balance between museum staff and community members can lead to problems, conflict, or friction if not approached carefully (see *Community Engagement*, page 39). Usually, the power balance favors the museum staff, especially when they have already taken the initiative to invite community members to participate in co-curation, and it takes purposeful effort on the side of the museum staff to share power with community members. If not, community members fall into an advisory role, while museum staff has all the decision-making power. In such collaborations, if one side feels that they are not allowed to actually contribute in a meaningful way, they will rapidly perceive the process as a waste of time and effort. As co-curation usually occurs on a voluntary basis or with minor compensation, participants must get satisfaction out of the project itself. Secondly, it is also important to decide on which aspects of the exhibition process community members will be participating in. For instance, are community members engaged from the start in deciding the topic of the exhibition or only at a later point? Will the co-curation project encompass object selection, content creation, narration, design, layout, marketing, mounting, or guiding visitors? The *National Museum Jamaica* co-curated an exhibition called *Rastafari* together with members from several Rastafari communities. Community members were not involved at the very beginning of the process, as the museum had already decided on the exhibition topic.[24] However, community members were involved in the consecutive stages of the exhibition process and some of them were also active as guides within the exhibition space once it opened to the public.

Representativity may be a complex issue when co-curating an exhibition: who is representative for a community? It is entirely possible that the museum might approach individuals who are not supported by their community, or that the community actually consists of several sub-communities who may have different or conflicting opinions and desires. Internal disagreements or conflicts are a common characteristic of all kinds of communities (Lavine 1992: 145). Ultimately, it is important to be aware of the fact that participation always occurs between individuals: individual members of staff and individual community members (Watson 2007: 18). In the case of the Rastafari exhibition, finding representative community members was a challenge.[25] Several different Rastafari communities exist in Jamaica that do not necessarily see eye to eye. The museum attempted to contact community members from several of these communities, in order to represent most of them. However, community members did not always want to work together, choosing instead to liaise with the museum staff rather than to collaborate with each other. This made the co-curation process rather lengthy as it took a long time to reach consensus on many issues. In this respect, it may be easier for a museum to engage with a community that is organized into a foundation or an society, which may already have a structure implemented for decision making as well as a hierarchy of power.

This brings us to the third aspect, namely multi-vocality. For many museums engaging in co-curation, one of the main goals is to include other voices into the exhibition space besides the curatorial voice. A simple way might be to include quotes of community members within the design of the exhibition, but one may also think of community members recording the audio guides. When community engagement occurs throughout the museum process, the voices of community members ideally become embedded in every aspect of the exhibition, including the objects, design, and narratives. Within *Rastafari* it was decided to physically represent this multi-vocality by presenting the main narrative in a series of parallel panels. One series of panels was worded by museum curators, while the other was written by Rastafari community members. Due to the particular Rastafari use of language and tone, the museum staff found it necessary to include their curatorial version. As mentioned above, not all community members were in agreement with each other about various aspects of the exhibition, including the panel texts. Some of them chose to voluntarily work in the exhibition space as guides to tell another narrative to balance it out. One of these guides expressed that it was great that this exhibition existed, because people could learn the full version of the story, and not the way it was told in other places.[26] He also said that it was very important that the museum decided to make this exhibition to

24   Conversation with director of *National Museum Jamaica* (Kingston, Jamaica, 24 July 2014).
25   Conversation with director of *National Museum Jamaica* (Kingston, Jamaica, 24 July 2014).
26   Conversation with guide at *National Museum Jamaica* (Kingston, Jamaica, 24 July 2014).

speak for and amplify the voices of the Rastafari who have been a marginalized group in Jamaican society.

The final aspect of co-curated exhibitions has to do with the time frame. At a bare minimum, co-curation already requires a significant investment of time by museum staff and community members alike. If a large group of community members are involved as representatives, decision-making can be slow. In addition, community members and museum staff must take the time to learn about, understand, and trust each other. This is essential for co-curation, although it is often approached by the museum as optional. Community members need time to learn the museum process and understand what is or is not possible. Staff members need to listen to the community to understand what issues are important to them and to learn what their goals are with the exhibition. To make the co-curation project work best, it is moreover important for staff and community members to trust each other. Building trust may take a very long time, particularly with communities who may have had bad experiences with (governmental) organizations or who have been marginalized. It is necessary to make sure that the museum dedicates sufficient time and resources to the co-curation project: first to build trust with the community, then to collaborate together on the exhibition, and finally to continue the engagement after the exhibition is completed. This last step is particularly important to make sure that community members have achieved both their short-term and long-term goals with the exhibition and to maintain a good relationship for possible future collaborations.

Museum Visitation

Interactive Displays

The previous sections of this chapter were concerned with participatory practices that largely take place outside the museum visit: the museum's foundation, staffing, co-curation, or contributions to exhibitions with objects, research, art, or achievements. Interactive displays, however, accommodate participation during the museum visit. For this reason, interactive displays are often the first thing that comes to mind when thinking of museum participation. We tend to think of interactive displays as computer screens or tablets that allow visitors to interact with the exhibition through a game or information database. However, there are plenty of other, non-digital ways for visitors to actively participate in the museum experience. This section will discuss interactive displays in the broadest sense covering opportunities for visitors to interact with the museum and its staff during the visit. Of the museums visited, 46 cases were found in which such visitor activity was supported by the museum. Once again, this is a conservative number: more museums support interaction, but not always on a permanent basis in the galleries. Some museums might have more infrequent participation, in the form of activities or events. The following examples have been grouped into a number of types of interaction: demonstrations, experimenting, listening, tasting, playing, researching, and farming.

Under the grouping of demonstrations, one can think of staff demonstrating the use of objects or craft-making to visitors. Depending on the interaction between visitors and demonstrators, this may be more or less participatory. In some cases, visitors may be encouraged to follow the example of the staff and try their hand at crafting or other activities. The *Kalinago Barana Autê* in Dominica demonstrates traditional subsistence methods of the indigenous Kalinago people, such as a sugar cane press, a cassava grater, and the baking of cassava bread. Visitors learn about making and using objects that are part of the Kalinago traditional way of life. By interacting on site with members of the Kalinago community, they can learn even more about their culture and heritage. Mr. Rome of *Rome Museum* in Grenada has many items to demonstrate, mentioned also before. Some of these objects were used traditionally by people living in the bush, such as a pit latrine, a mud earth oven, or a coconut comb. Others are electronic appliances that are no longer commonly in use, such as old radios or gas pumps. He has also made a number of sculptures that represent wounds or illnesses occurring in the bush. With these sculptures he demonstrates traditional medicines and remedies. The *Ecomusée CreoleArt* on Guadeloupe provides space for half a dozen workshops for various demonstrations. There are not always live demonstrations in these workshops, but if the crafts(wo)men are not present there is a video that shows the same processes. These workshops show a variety of activities related to traditional subsistence strategies on the island as well as several professions and household chores: cocoa processing, making wooden toys, shoemaking, cashew nut roasting, and doing the laundry or the dishes outdoors.

Interaction in terms of experimenting most often occurs in museums that have natural or scientific content. At the *Bank of Jamaica Money Museum* and at *Yotin Kortá: The Money Museum* on Curaçao visitors can test the validity of their own bank notes under UV light. At *Yotin Kortá* there are also a number of cases in which visitors can compare real bank notes to forgeries and find the differences. The *Centre de Découverte des Sciences de la Terre* on Martinique has set up a small station where visitors can learn to identify various geological materials. A number of samples are placed around a microscope and an information sheet helps visitors to classify these samples. Knowledge-oriented visitors are often interested in not only learning what something is, but also how to identify it or recognize it by themselves. Museums may provide the means and the setting to teach this kind of skill. It might also be possible for visitors to engage in small experiments as research collaboration.

Visitors commonly engage in listening activities in museums, some of which may be more participatory than others. Naturally, when visitors follow a guided tour, a large part of their visit will concern listening and communicating with their guide. Listening activities may also take a digital form, such as with audio guides or headset installations. These activities give visitors more freedom of choice regarding which content they will engage with. For instance, the *Museo Casa de Tostado: Museo de la Familia Dominicana Siglo XIX* is a historic home with period room style exhibits. By using an audio guide and no written labels, the museum can provide information in several languages and keep the atmosphere of the home as authentic as possible without marring the walls with texts. Visitors can choose in what way they interact with each room and its objects: by immersion through observation or with guidance from the audio tour to look at particular things. Other audio guides may provide visitors with the option to learn more about certain topics or objects. Listening activities may also occur incidentally throughout the museum, rather than consistently in the form of a tour. At *Centro León*, also in the Dominican Republic, the atmosphere of certain exhibition spaces is enhanced with soundscapes. One exhibit, related to the market place, comes to life: when you move one of the vendors, they start calling their wares. In this example, it is the action of the visitor that starts or stops the audio. Visitor participation is thus essential to get the audio experience.

Tasting might not seem like a common sensory activity in a museum. However, in the Caribbean, due in part to the large number of hybrid museums, tasting and product testing is a regular occurrence for visitors. One may think, first of all, of the many rum distilleries. Some of these estates have separate shops with a tasting counter, such as the *Westerhall Estate* on Grenada or the *Domaine de Séverin* on Guadeloupe. Other distilleries might have rum tasting available within the museum space. Besides rum distilleries there are plenty of other products to taste, such as chocolate or cocoa tea at the *Chocomuseo* in the Dominican Republic. At *La Aurora Cigar World* in the Dominican Republic, visitors are encouraged to smoke or 'enjoy' a cigar during their visit of the factory and museum. The *Kalinago Barana Autê* in Dominica, also mentioned above, offers visitors a taste of cassava bread as well as herbal tea. All of these examples provide visitors with a sensory experience to better understand the products showcased in the museum and the processes that go into making them.

Museums are incorporating more games into their exhibitions, not only for children but also for adult visitors. Playing within the museum space may help visitors engage with the museum's content in a different way. In addition, playing may make the museum visit a more social activity by setting up visitors to play together or against each other. At the *Centro Cultural de las Telecomunicaciones* in the Dominican Republic, part of the exhibits are about computers, robotics, and future technologies. As an interactive display they set up an Xbox game console with a Kinect motion sensor. Visitors can play a racing game while attempting to steer the car with the movement of their bodies, rather than using a hand-held controller. Visitors, including adults, were drawn to this activity, because they were intrigued to test this technology. Within the context of this museum, it showcased the direction in which technology is headed and the versatility of applying such technologies. However, playing does not have to be digital. The *Museo Infantil Trampolín* in the Dominican Republic is a museum geared towards children that incorporates many games (see figure 13). The prehistoric section has visitors play an archaeological and paleontological game by placing fossils and artefacts in the right places on a stratigraphic wall. In the section concerning the human body, children can climb up a wall representing human skin on a gigantic scale, while holding on to the massive hairs. The *Centre Spatial Guyanais* in French Guiana also has a number of games, especially for children visiting in school groups. A whole floor is dedicated to children's activities: tables for coloring and drawing space shuttles, LEGOs for building space shuttles, and big space-themed board games on the floor to play collectively. Playful interaction can be helpful to understanding, and engaging with, the museum's content.

Researching or finding additional information beyond that presented in the exhibitions might also be interaction provided for visitors. Some museums contain reference libraries or archives that are publicly accessible. In other museums, there may be multimedia screens or documents that visitors can access for additional information. The activity of researching additional information lets visitors engage more deeply with the content of the exhibition. A digital solution is present at the *Museo de las Américas*

Figure 13: Interactive displays in the human body gallery at the Museo Infantil Trampolín, Dominican Republic.

in Puerto Rico. In the first exhibition space, dedicated to contemporary and past Indigenous populations of the Americas, sculpture casts of individuals from different Indigenous cultures are on display. Within the same gallery, video touch screens are installed where you can click on each sculpture to learn more about that cultural group. The screens also show a bibliography or provide further information on a number of subjects, such as the prehistoric settlement of the Americas. Similar screens are installed in the *Museo Nacional de Historia Natural* in the Dominican Republic. In 2006, interactive and digital elements were incorporated into the museum's galleries to enhance the visitor experience and to be able to provide more information to those who are interested.[27] Among others, the physical exhibition of taxidermy birds is now extended with digital information about each species. Analogue research interaction is facilitated within the *Tobago Museum*. In several of the exhibition rooms, tables and chairs are set up with research binders with copies of historic documents. Many of these are related to the plantation-era on the island, listing the estates and their inhabitants. Visitors interested in historical or genealogical research can take their time to go through these documents for their own research.

Finally, a number of museums related to nature and agriculture support farming activities. As with the examples related to tasting, this kind of activity mainly occurs in hybrid or ecomuseums where gardens or farms form part of the museum landscape. At *Finca la Protectora* in the Dominican Republic visitors can learn ecological farming methods. Coffee, banana, and other crops are grown on the site and farmed together

---

27   Conversation with curator at *Museo Nacional de Historia Natural* (Santo Domingo, Dominican Republic, 14 January 2015).

with visitors so they can gain a stronger connection to the land and its produce. It is the aim to connect these farming activities to heritage hikes in the area to also understand the archaeological past of the land. Cocoa is produced at the *Fond Doux Estate* in St. Lucia. Although visitors are not involved in the farming of the cocoa, they may contribute to part of the processing of the cocoa beans. Schoolchildren may visit the *Ecomusée CreoleArt* on Guadeloupe to work in the traditional gardens known as *'jardin créole'* and learn farming skills. This type of activity provides another dimension to the museum visitor, often a very active one, in which visitors actively contribute to the museum and shape its landscape.

Activities

Activities and events are the final two participatory practices discussed in this chapter. As with the interactive displays discussed above, they provide community engagement integrated into the museum visit or as part of an exceptional museum visit. Activities are characterized by action, often occurring on a regular basis. One may think, for instance, of monthly programs that the museum offers. There is usually a high level of interaction between participants and museum staff. 90 museums were identified where activities were organized. Of course, more museums probably organize activities, but these may not have been visible during this regional museum survey.

Perhaps the most commonly known museum activities are those related to visiting school groups. These educational activities may be adjusted to the age of the students or their curriculum, while remaining in line with the content of the museum. The *Musée Départemental Edgar Clerc* on Guadeloupe focuses on the archaeological past of the island. A special activity room lies between the two main galleries. At the time of visitation, a school group was crafting with clay in this room. The goal of the activity was to make a modern object, but to decorate this in an Amerindian style that the children had seen in the museum galleries. This combined elements from the museum and its Amerindian collection while encouraging children to make something that they might be able to use in the present. The *University of the West Indies Geology Museum* in Jamaica also has a special activity room for school groups. Based closely on the curriculum of the schools, the museum provides different programs for children of different ages, relating geology to the environment, recycling, or mining.[28] The museum also provides excursions or activities for university students to learn about geology outside the museum.

Museums also provide activities for many other communities and target audiences. The *Museo Bellapart* in the Dominican Republic has an activity planned every Saturday. The program is rotated weekly, so that it always targets a different community: children, teenagers, adults, or those with reduced mobility.[29] The activity itself is also different each time: one month the teenagers might work with graffiti, next month with photography, and after that with digital art. As such, the museum aims to continuously draw in members of these four targeted communities to develop their interest in art

---

28   Conversation with director of *University of the West Indies Geology Museum* (Kingston, Jamaica, 21 July 2014).

29   Conversation with director of *Museo Bellapart* (Santo Domingo, Dominican Republic, 15 January 2015).

as well as their skills. Museums may also provide special tours as activities. The *San Juan National Historic Site: Castillo San Cristóbal* in Puerto Rico provides special tours on a weekly basis. One of these tours focuses on exploring the tunnel system of the fortress while another tour is held after opening hours by lantern light. Not geared to any specific community, various workshops can be completed at the *Chocomuseo* in the Dominican Republic. Those interested can enroll in a workshop to learn about the cocoa process and how to make their own chocolates.

Although many museum activities take place in and around the museum building, museum staff may also engage in outreach activities. While their exhibition space was closed for refurbishment, the *Central Bank Money Museum* on Trinidad decided to experiment with community outreach. With a box containing some of the museum's objects, staff approached communities outside the capital to talk about money, trade, and banking.[30] They also approached the local community of Port of Spain by setting up a stand during a major event on the Savannah. The community's feedback was so positive to both of these pilot tests that plans are underway to expand the museum's outreach activities into a regular program. Such a program is already implemented by the *Jamaica National Heritage Trust*. As guardians of the island's heritage, the trust has vast storages of archaeological artefacts, but many of them are not exhibited by the trust or by the connected Institute of Jamaica. Instead, the staff uses some of these artefacts, taking them around to schools and showing them to school children.[31] Oftentimes, the schools are the ones who call the trust to request an outreach activity on a specific subject, such as the Amerindian past or the legacy of slavery. The trust also engages children in exploratory excavations to pique their interest in the archaeological field. Outreach activities are a good way to involve community members in the museum who might otherwise not be able to visit the museum or do not think they have an interest in doing so.

Events

Unlike activities, events are occurrences or happenings that are generally incidental in nature, such as an event for the opening of a new exhibition. Visitors to events may participate uniquely in the museum visit, for instance by being at the museum after hours or in parts of the museum otherwise restricted from visitors' view. Community members may also be asked by the museum to perform as part of the event. The regional museum survey found 70 museums which hosted events, although again a higher amount is likely.

Museums may choose to organize events for the public within the museum space. *Centro León* in the Dominican Republic organizes a weekly 'videocafé' on Friday evenings. Anyone can come to the museum's café and the lawn just outside to watch music videos that are projected on the wall of the building. Every week the focus of this event is on a different artist or musical style. This kind of event draws community members to the museum who might otherwise not visit the museum. Public events usually take place more infrequently. The *Santa Rosa First Peoples Community Museum*

---

30   Conversation with curator at *Central Bank Money Museum* (Port of Spain, Trinidad, 7 January 2015).
31   Conversation with archaeologist at *Jamaica National Heritage Trust* (Kingston, Jamaica, 23 July 2014).

on Trinidad organizes events to celebrate Indigenous Heritage Day on 14th October.[32] On this day, they organize a communal breakfast, a craft fair, and a musical evening. They invite Indigenous and first nations communities from other countries as well as hosting over a thousand school children for the day. As such, the museum also supports interaction between various communities. The *Grenada National Museum* organizes and hosts a cultural event every first Friday of the month in the evening.[33] For these events, various members of the local community may be invited to perform, to lecture, or to enhance the event in another way. These monthly events usually draw the local community to attend and interact with each other within the museum space. Museums may also choose to host private events within their facilities. Many museums are housed in historical buildings or in beautiful settings and form perfect locations for weddings, parties, or other ceremonies. Hosting such private events may not only be a source of income, but can also turn the museum into an important community place. Museums may also host events specifically for (potential) funders and donors, providing a unique opportunity for interaction with the museum and its staff. Finally, living museums may already be engaged in events in which museum visitors might be allowed to participate. As an example one could think of religious services held in churches, synagogues or temples that are connected to museums and heritage centers. While some of these services might not be accessible to outsiders, others may welcome visitors if they follow certain rules. Participation in such events engages visitors with the specific religious community in a way that is often felt as highly meaningful.

Besides cultural events, museums may also organize scientific events for visitors. The *Museo del Hombre Dominicano* in the Dominican Republic is a very active participant in the local and regional archaeological community.[34] Every year, the museum organizes a symposium to attract scholars from around the world to present their current archaeological research. In addition, the museum also hosts smaller weekly conferences to discuss new research or new exhibitions. In this way the museum brings its research staff in frequent contact with other members of the scientific community to improve participation in scientific projects and archaeological research. A different type of scientific event is organized at the *Centre Spatial Guyanais* in French Guiana. Here, visitors have the possibility to observe the launch of a satellite from a special observation area close to the launch platform. Of course, this is a special event for which people have to apply beforehand for security reasons. During this event they interact with the staff monitoring and observing the launch event.

Summary

Caribbean museums are so diverse it is impossible to characterize them or define them according to only one aspect. Couched in the specific history of museums in the region, this diversity has partially been influenced by colonial legacies and cultural, museological differences. Even more so, this specificity is due to the differences in

---

32 Conversation with guide at *Santa Rosa First Peoples Community* (Arima, Trinidad, 9 January 2015).
33 Conversation with director of *Grenada National Museum* (St George's, Grenada, 13 July 2014).
34 Conversation with director of *Museo del Hombre Dominicano* (Santo Domingo, Dominican Republic, 16 January 2015).

the communities which are at the heart of these museums and/or their missions. As we have seen, nearly every Caribbean museum is participatory to a greater or lesser extent and it is this community engagement which defines part of its character. Yet, as the introduction to this chapter emphasized, museums that wish to remain dedicated to their communities need to continuously commit to engaging, and therefore can benefit from regularly reconsidering and adjusting their participatory practices.

Thus, the aim of this chapter was twofold. Primarily, it sought to answer the sub question: "what are the characteristics of contemporary Caribbean museums and how are they adopting and adapting participatory practices?" (see *Research Questions and Objectives*, page 18). Secondly, it aimed to provide a collection of Caribbean participatory practices as a resource to museums in the region. The regional museum survey formed the core data for this chapter; of this survey an index of museums included can be found in the appendix and the full Caribbean Museums Database is accessible online. As mentioned in the introduction to this chapter, at least one type of participatory practice was identified in almost every museum visited during the regional museum survey. Community engagement is thus applied by museums in the Caribbean very frequently and with great variety. This chapter presented twelve categories of participatory practices that range from the foundation and organization of the museum, to collection and exhibition processes, as well as participation during the museum visit. Within each of these twelve categories, a wide range of examples was presented to showcase how each community engagement method can be applied in numerous ways depending on the institution and its connected communities. Previously, participatory practices were described mainly with examples from European and North American museums, most notably in Nina Simon's influential book *The Participatory Museum* (Simon 2010). However, this chapter has expanded on this museological discussion by showing through which participatory practices Caribbean museums are engaging with their respective communities. A critical discussion of these results, from both a macro and a micro level perspective, is found in Chapter 7 and is based on the visualizations which show the social museum in the Caribbean in a series of regional overviews (see figures 44-56).

5

Case Study: Kalinago Barana Autê, Dominica

Arguably, grassroots action is the most significant form of "community action."
Elizabeth Crooke (2015: 487)

Quite possibly indeed there is no greater community engagement than when independent interest in heritage inspires an individual or community to create their own museum as a grassroots initiative. Such grassroots action will require decision-making on most, if not all, aspects of the museum and its work. Yet, collaboration and negotiation will still be necessary as the museum project develops. This is even more pronounced when other participants who are seen as outsiders become involved. Thus, for grassroots initiatives as well as other community engagement projects, the *process* also requires close attention as it can be complex and subject to change over time.

Whereas the previous chapter assessed the participatory practices employed throughout the Caribbean on a wider scale, the aim of the two following chapters is to provide a more detailed analysis of two specific community engagement processes, as they are applied in the Caribbean, by zooming in on two distinct case studies. These case studies are not intended to function as contradictory examples or polar opposites; they also cannot reflect the entire scope of community engagement projects that are taking place in the region. Instead, these case studies each highlight a single point on the spectrum of Caribbean community engagement processes. Each case study provides a unique answer to the sub question: "how are community engagement processes, including their value and outcomes, perceived by Caribbean communities?" (see *Research Questions and Objectives*, page 18). The answers should not be seen as all-inclusive, but rather understood in their respective context. The two case studies are centered around different types of museums and focus on two distinct communities that each have their own characteristic cultures and histories. The community engagement project conducted in each case had different goals, as well as different outcomes. These differences are also visible in the length and the scope of the community engagement projects, and additionally in the development of the participatory process.

The focus of this chapter is on the case study conducted in the Kalinago Territory on the island of Dominica in the Lesser Antilles. The Kalinago Territory is home to Dominica's Kalinago community and contains the *Kalinago Barana Autê* (KBA), an open air museum that is an ongoing community engagement project which began as an Indigenous grassroots initiative (see figure 14). The KBA is currently operated by Dominica's Ministry of Tourism but managed by the Kalinago, requiring long-term collaboration between government and local community. The main aim of the case study is to assess the value and importance of the KBA for the Kalinago community and to identify how they feel the museum could improve for the future.

The chapter will begin by providing a brief (pre-)history of the Kalinago and their current community. Afterwards, the creation and foundation of the KBA will be discussed along with a description of the museum today. The fieldwork conducted for this case study will be detailed, with specific focus placed on the aims of this fieldwork period and my experiences in the Territory. Implications of fieldwork strategies, adjustments, and fieldwork experiences will also be incorporated throughout the remainder of the chapter. The fieldwork results are the core of the chapter, namely the perceptions of the Kalinago community in relation to the value that the KBA holds for them. These perceptions provide insights into the present outcomes of the community engagement project. The chapter will conclude by discussing the Kalinago community's hopes for the future of the KBA and any further outcomes they still wish to attain.

Brief History of the Kalinago in Dominica

Wai'tukubuli, known as Dominica after its English naming, is an island in the Eastern Caribbean and part of the Lesser Antilles (Boomert 2014; Honychurch 2000: 9). The island is of volcanic origin and is characterized by its extremely mountainous terrain and dense forest cover (see figure 15). The earliest human interactions in the Windward Islands have been dated to c. 3000 BC and show the settlement by Amerindian peoples possibly originating from the Northern coast of the South American continent (Bérard 2013; Honychurch 1995: 15; Honychurch 2000: 9; Keegan & Hofman 2017: 37-38). Over the next few millennia, various Amerindian peoples speaking Arawakan languages settled throughout the region. Archaeologists have debated the nature of this settlement and the cultural, technological, and linguistic characteristics of these Amerindian peoples for decades (Keegan & Hofman 2017). In many cases, the naming of pre-historic peoples and cultures has followed an archaeological classification based on pottery styles (*e.g.* Saladoid or Suazoid; Rouse 1992). The naming of the Amerindian peoples from the period of contact with Europeans was frequently based on historic accounts, either using the (often misguided or blatantly negative) terminology of the Europeans for various peoples or using Amerindian vocabulary and language families to identify groups (*e.g.* Carib, Arawak, or Taíno; Keegan & Hofman 2017: 11-15). Archaeologists now believe that the settlement of the region did not occur in rigid waves of ever more technologically advanced peoples, as had been hypothesized in the early 20th century (Hofman & Carlin 2010: 110; Siegel 2013: 24). Instead, it is argued that the Lesser Antilles in particular consisted of a mosaic of Amerindian peoples, speaking related Arawakan languages with at times markedly different cultural traditions (Hofman 2013: 214; Honychurch 2000: 25; Keegan & Hofman 2017: 236-237; Siegel 2013: 39).

The Amerindians who lived in the Lesser Antilles during the period of contact with the Europeans were for many centuries referred to as 'Caribs' or 'Island Caribs' (to distinguish them from 'Caribs' on the mainland; Boomert 2000: 4; Honychurch

Figure 14: Entry to the Kalinago Barana Autê, Dominica.

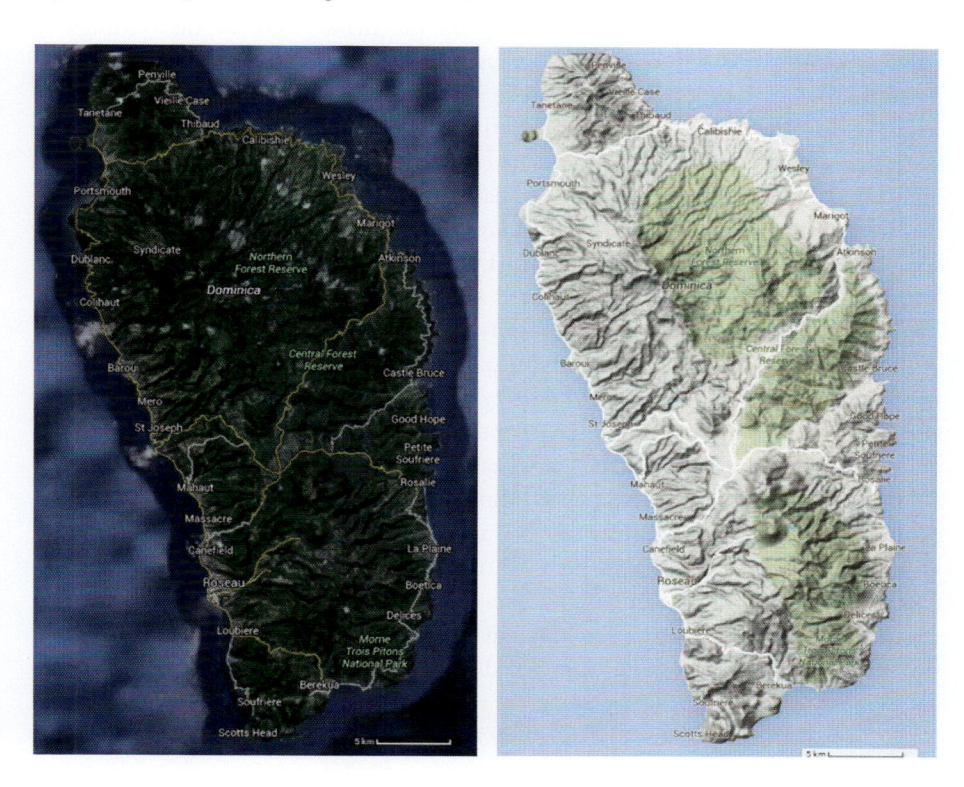

Figure 15: Dominica. Left: satellite image. Right: map with a terrain view showing elevations.

2000: 24). The term was derived from the Indigenous word *Cariban*, which is used today to identify a group of languages spoken in lowland South America (Keegan & Hofman 2017: 14-15). The term was appropriated by the Spanish and used to signify the Amerindians they did not get along with, as opposed to what they deemed to be the more friendly and welcoming 'Arawak,' now more properly referred to as 'Taíno' (Allaire 2013: 97; Honychurch 2000: 14). This terminology is confusing, as both the 'Caribs' and 'Arawak' spoke Arawakan – not Cariban – languages (Taylor & Hoff 1980: 302). Of course, "the Spaniards did not come here as anthropologists."[35] Indeed, scholars have argued that this was a conscious process of othering that had implications in Europe related to the perceived validity of the colonization of the region (Boucher 1992: 6; Lenik 2012: 84). The term 'Carib' carried strong negative connotations, linked with the practice of cannibalism and 'Caribs' were frequently described as warlike and ferocious (Honychurch 2000: 15; Keegan & Hofman 2017: 14 & 240). The myth of the friendly and peaceful 'Arawak' and the violent and cannibalistic 'Caribs' can still be found to persist in schoolbooks and in the mindset of people throughout the region today (Con Aguilar *et al.* 2017: 337).

Caribbean Indigenous communities, archaeologists, (ethno) historians, linguists, and other scholars have done extensive research, and undertaken political and educational lobbying since the 1940s to put a halt to spreading this stereotypical dichotomy and to reflect newer perceptions of identity (Honychurch 2000: 3). As part of this process, the renaming of some Amerindian peoples has been proposed and in some places this has been politically and officially implemented. In the case of Dominica, the contemporary Indigenous community on the island revisited the writings of French missionary Raymond Breton who visited the island in 1642 and extensively recorded the language of the Amerindian population (Breton [1665] 1892; [1666] 1900; [1667] 1877). He had written that the people there called themselves *Callinago* or *Calliponam* (in the men's and women's languages respectively; *cf.* Allaire 2013: 97; Honychurch 2000: 14). Although the female term, *Karifuna*, was initially adopted by the Indigenous activists in the 1980s, today they primarily refer to themselves by the male term, *Kalinago* (Honychurch 2000: 14). The renaming of the community from 'Carib' to 'Kalinago' was officially passed in Dominica on 20th February 2015 and also led to the renaming of the community's collective lands from 'Carib Reserve' to 'Kalinago Territory' (Carib Reserve (Amendment) Act 2015). Dominican historian Lennox Honychurch had previously already interpreted this renaming of communities and locations as being an important part of the Indigenous revival movement occurring on the island and elsewhere in the Caribbean region (Honychurch 2000: 4).

Having sketched the intricacies surrounding the naming of various Amerindian peoples, we will now consider the history of the Kalinago in particular. The Kalinago are believed to have settled Wai'tukubuli and the neighboring islands between AD 1250-1400 (Allaire 2013; Bérard 2008; Boomert 1986; Boomert 2009; Honychurch 1995: 21; Keegan & Hofman 2017: 232-233). The Kalinago lived a life strongly connected to the ocean and they did not restrict their movements to individual islands, instead utilizing the resources of different areas, often seasonally (Bérard *et al.* 2016: 133; Callaghan 2013: 290-293; Hofman 2013: 209; Hofman & Carlin

---

35   Conversation with guide at *Centro Indígena Caguana* (Utuado, Puerto Rico, 29 January 2015).

106

THE SOCIAL MUSEUM IN THE CARIBBEAN

2010: 107-108; Hofman & Hoogland 2012: 69; Hofman & Hoogland 2015: 102; Shearn 2014: 368). With the European settlement in and invasion of the Caribbean region, this pattern of trade and movement in the Lesser Antilles was disrupted – initially only irregularly, later more and more destructively (Hofman & Hoogland 2012; Hofman *et al.* 2014: 602; Shafie *et al.* 2017: 65). In the early 16th century, mainly the Spanish interacted with the Kalinago: landing on their islands, engaging in skirmishes, and capturing Kalinago to transport them as slaves to other islands (Bright 2011: 47; Honychurch 1995: 33-34; Lenik 2012: 84). The active resistance of the Kalinago coupled with the mountainous terrain of the island is often cited as the reason that European influence in Dominica was kept minimal for several centuries. It is estimated that by 1569 around 70 Europeans and Africans were living among the Kalinago – presumably many of these had been taken in after being shipwrecked – with no European settlement on the island (Honychurch 1995: 37).

The British were the first to officially 'claim' the island in 1627, with the French following soon after (Honychurch 1995: 38-39). Despite these claims, both the French and the British were mainly stationed on other islands, only infrequently interacting with the Kalinago on Dominica for trading or raiding. In the 1640s, French missionaries visited the island for longer periods and left records of the Kalinago and their culture (*e.g.* Raymond Breton, mentioned above). In 1660, the French signed a treaty with the Kalinago, promising not to colonize Dominica and St. Vincent (Honychurch 1995: 43). This was a period in which the French and the British fought extensively over control of the Lesser Antilles (Shafie *et al.* 2017: 65-66). The Kalinago on Dominica and the neighboring islands were directly entangled in this struggle by joining into battles and varyingly supporting one or the other side, as well as indirectly by having their usual movements in the region restricted by Europeans (Honychurch 1995: 46; Shafie *et al.* 2017). When France and Britain signed a peace treaty in 1686, Dominica was designated as a neutral island to be left to the Kalinago (Honychurch 1995: 47). However, although settlement was prohibited by this treaty, nothing was said about temporary use of the island, for instance to collect wood or other resources. It was the French who first began to slowly encroach on Dominica's Kalinago population over the course of the 18th century. Initially, families and individuals were stationed there temporarily, but as these became permanent settlements, a commander was appointed in 1727 (Honychurch 1995: 49-50). The non-Kalinago population of the island was rapidly increasing, with the French settlers and planters outnumbered by enslaved Africans in 1745 (Honychurch 1995: 54-55). Despite the signing of a new treaty of neutrality between the French and the British in 1748, the French kept their influence on the island. By 1750, the living space of the Kalinago had been restricted to the leeward side of the island (Honychurch 1995: 50).

The Seven Years War between France and Britain (1756-1763) was mainly fought at sea or on other islands, with the exception of the capture of Dominica by the British in 1761 (Honychurch 1995: 58). It was officially ceded to the British in 1763 after the French had gradually expanded their influence on the island for over 100 years (Honychurch 1995: 60). During this period of unrest, many enslaved Africans escaped inland and formed maroon communities (Honychurch 1995: 93). It was British surveyor John Byres in 1776 who first officially set aside a piece of the island for the Kalinago, 134 acres on the Eastern coast (see figure 16; Honychurch

2000: 173). In a later map made by surveyor Hesketh Bell, this lot was erroneously calculated to be 232 acres. The first map legally bound the Kalinago not only to one island – while they had previously been mobile in a wide seascape – but to a small acreage on the rugged East coast of the island. The end of the 18th century and the beginning of the 19th century were characterized by even more uncertainty and colonial violence: the French briefly recaptured the island (1778-1783), they invaded again in 1795, and the British and local maroon communities were engaged in a number of wars between 1785-1815 (Honychurch 1995: 84-116). The Kalinago were involved in several of these struggles, either choosing to fight on one side or being unintentionally affected by the conflict (Bright 2011: 47).

At the start of the 20th century, Hesketh Bell brought up the issue of the Kalinago's land and delineated a much larger area, 3700 acres or roughly 2% of the island, as a 'Carib Reserve' in his 1901 map (Honychurch 2000: 173). This plan not only officially gave the Kalinago a much larger tract of land, but also supported the appointment and official recognition of a Kalinago chief who would receive a governmental allowance (Honychurch 1995: 161). Although the boundaries of the land remained an issue, this did give the Kalinago a small amount of political autonomy and also served to make the community slightly more visible to the government. Despite the initial positive effects of this governmental interference, the situation exploded violently in 1930 with an event that became known as the Carib War (Honychurch 2000: 183-185). Police came into the reserve searching, as they said, for smuggled goods such as liquor and tobacco. The Kalinago had been used to trading by canoe with Guadeloupe, for instance, and selling items without license. Now, the police decided to seize some goods and arrest suspects. The Kalinago grouped up around the policemen, throwing sticks and stones. The police fired back at the crowd, killing two Kalinago and injuring two more, before escaping from the 'Reserve.' Violence escalated when the Administrator of Dominica asked the Royal Navy for assistance, who stationed a frigate off the coast of the 'Reserve.' The Navy threatened and frightened the Kalinago by prohibiting their movement on sea, firing star-shells, displaying searchlights at night, and searching for suspects on land by day. After an inquiry, a commission demoted the chief and the Kalinago were stripped of the administrative rights they had had (Honychurch 2000: 186). Today, a Kalinago Memorial for the two men who were killed can still be visited in the Salybia area.

Since this violent clash between the Kalinago and the government, the position and autonomy of the Kalinago community has slowly improved. In 1937 a 'Carib Council' with a chairman was established by the government and, after many years of petitioning by the Kalinago, the Administrator approved the installment of a new chief in 1952 (Honychurch 2000: 207). Following the independence of Dominica in 1978, the responsibilities of the council and the regulation of the election of chiefs was consolidated even further by an Act of Parliament (Carib Reserve Act, Chapter 25:90, 1978). As mentioned previously, the communal lands were officially renamed to 'Kalinago Territory' as recently as 2015. It consists of seven settlements, from North to South: Bataka, Crayfish River, Salybia, St. Cyr, Gaulette River, Mahaut River, and Sineku (Honychurch 2000: 179).

Today, Dominica is one of the most sparsely populated island countries in the Caribbean region with a population of just over 71,000 (Commonwealth of Dominica

THE SOCIAL MUSEUM IN THE CARIBBEAN

Figure 16: Surveyor John Byres' map of Dominica, 1776.

2011: 6). In the official census of 2011, 2145 persons were registered as living in the Kalinago Territory, although the Kalinago themselves estimate their number to be approximately 3000, which is also echoed elsewhere[36] (Commonwealth of Dominica 2011: 18; Smith 2006: 74). Marked by this low population density, and turning its underdevelopment into an asset, the island with its many high peaks, jagged valleys, and lush natural parks has been branded 'the nature island' (Smith 2006: 73). While most of the Caribbean tourist destinations are known for their sandy beaches and comfortable resorts, Dominica is described in opposite terms, as a pure, simple, natural, and adventurous place. In the Kalinago Territory, some say that "if Columbus returned, Dominica would be the only island he'd recognize."[37] The same sentiment was also expressed at a meeting in the Kalinago Territory by Prime Minister Roosevelt Skerrit: "Where in the world, where in the world today, has such utopia been realized [as in Dominica]?" (Skerrit 2015: min. 23:13) This representation of Dominica as 'the nature island' is in no small part strengthened by the presence of the Kalinago. Initially, in advertisements in the 1960s, the image of Dominica as the "home of the last of the Caribs" (Honychurch 2000: 73) was propagated by the Dominica Tourist Association beyond the control of the Kalinago. Today, similar vocabulary can still be found on Dominica's official tourism website: "Dominica is the only Caribbean island with a remaining population of pre-Columbian Carib Indians."[38] However, the same language is also echoed by the Kalinago themselves: "Dominica is the home of [...] Kalinagos, the remaining survivors of the first inhabitants of the island."[39] It is in this complex history of settlement, colonization, marginalization, cultural revival, identity formation, and representation that one must place the creation of a museum in the Kalinago Territory.

The Kalinago Barana Autê

The Kalinago Barana Autê (meaning 'Kalinago Village by the Sea'; KBA) is an open air museum located in the Kalinago Territory, overlooking the Atlantic Ocean. It is a grassroots initiative, as the plans for the project were developed within the Kalinago community. These first plans and proposals called the KBA a "Carib Cultural Village." Today, the KBA can be characterized as an ecomuseum. This section will first provide a history of the development of the KBA, then describe the ecomuseum as it appears to visitors today, and finally characterize the KBA as an ongoing community engagement project.

The idea for the (model) cultural village first appeared on paper in a proposal written by visiting anthropologist Arthur Einhorn in 1972 (Smith 2006: 78). Einhorn stated that the concept was already envisioned by several individuals in the Territory. Indeed, interest in the development of Kalinago cultural heritage can also be identified

---

36 *About Us,* Kalinago Territory website: http://kalinagoterritory.com/about-us/ (Accessed: 22 January 2016)

37 Conversation with interviewee KBA#16 (Kalinago Territory, Dominica, 10 August 2015).

38 *History & Culture,* Discover Dominica Authority: http://www.dominica.dm/index.php/history-a-culture (Accessed: 22 January 2016)

39 *About Dominica,* Kalinago Territory website: http://kalinagoterritory.com/getting-here/about-dominica/ (Accessed: 22 January 2016)

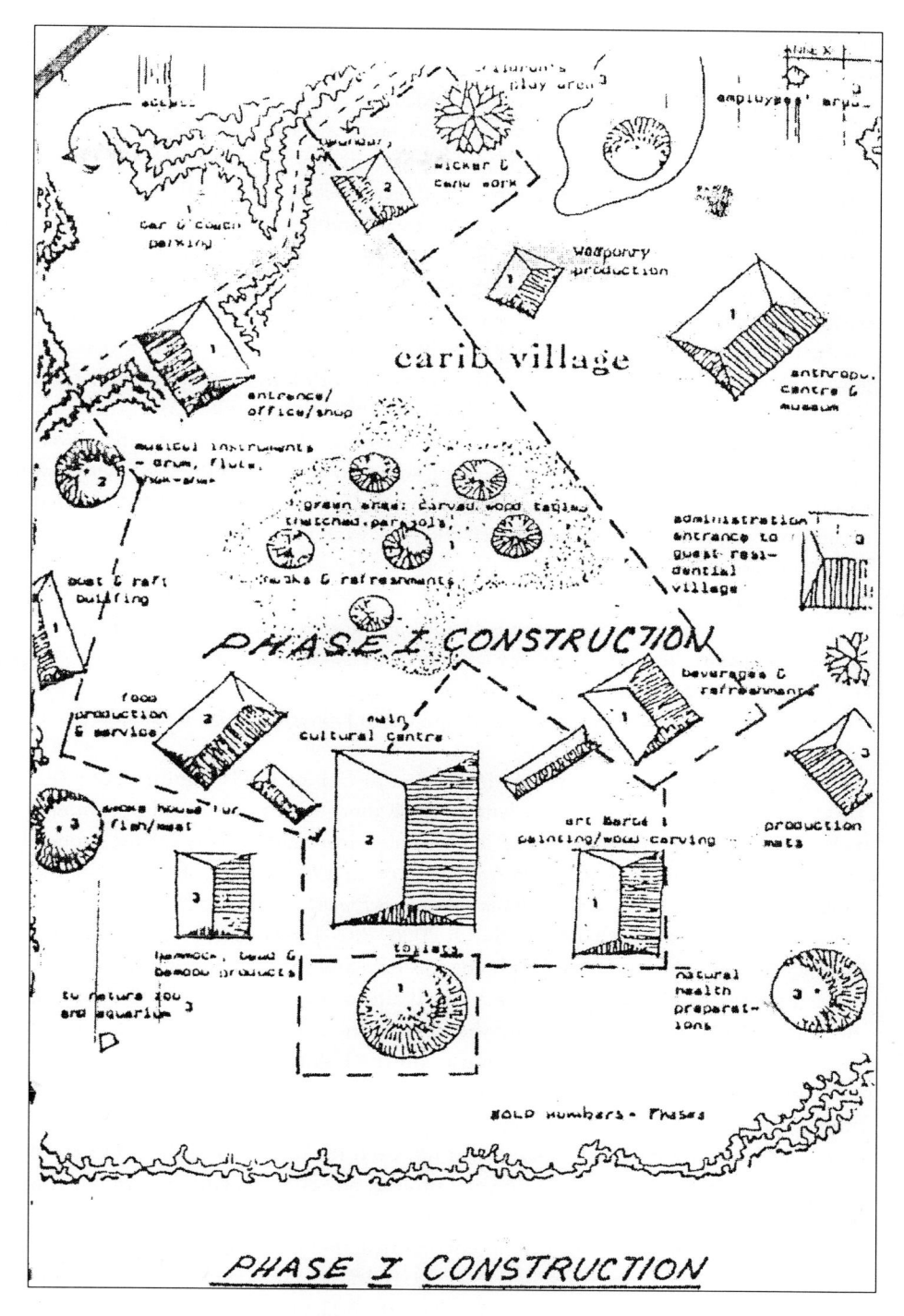

Figure 17: Plans for the design of the 'Carib Cultural Village,' 1987.

in the story of the children's book *In Our Carib Indian Village* written by then Chief Faustulus Frederick and Elizabeth Shepherd (1971). Frederick developed these ideas into his own proposal for a cultural village, which was submitted to the government of Dominica in 1976 (Honychurch 2000: 214). According to his idea, the village would consist of thatched houses, containing craft workshops, canoe building sheds, a small restaurant, and a kitchen for preparing cassava meals (see figure 17). The main aim of the project, as envisioned by the Chief, was to create employment within the Territory, a part of which would be achieved by including huts for overnight visitors. Although most literature credits Frederick as being the first Kalinago to present the idea of the cultural village, this is contested by some other families in the Territory who claim they came up with the idea first.[40] Ultimately, it was Frederick's proposal which first got the attention of the government and was reworked by a team of consultants from the International Labour Organisation (ILO) in 1982 (Smith 2006: 214). This team prepared a report, which outlined a number of recommendations for the further development of the project. A proposal for funding was then attached to the 1987 *Report on Carib Cultural Village* by the National Development Corporation. This proposal stated an aim of the project that echoed Chief Frederick's intention, albeit in more openly economic terms:

> *The main objective of the project is to develop a tourism product around indigenous resources that will ensure job creation as well as a viable tourist attraction that is in keeping with Dominica's tourism strategy.*
> National Development Corporation (quoted in Honychurch 2000: 213)

The project stagnated in the late 1980s due to lack of funds (Smith 2006: 78). This was caused by the fact that the land in the Kalinago Territory is held in common ownership which, at the time, made it impossible to receive a loan against property. The plans for the cultural village were revived in 1994 as part of the Caribbean Development Bank's *Upgrading of Ecotourism Sites Project* (UESP) that provided loans to tourist sites around the country (Smith 2006: 78). The government, through the Minister of Tourism, was able to apply for this loan and thus, at this point, took over and ran the development project. It was noted already by the ILO in 1982 that both the chief and his council were aware of the fact that the development of such a heritage site would inevitably have a cultural impact on the Kalinago community and would result in local changes. It was reported that "they were more than willing to accept [these changes] in order to obtain increased income" (ILO Carib Village Report 1982, quoted in Honychurch 2000: 214). It had not been the intention of the Kalinago to have the cultural village as a governmental project, but due to financial restraints this proved to be the only way (at the time) that the project could be completed.

As a project headed by the government, construction of the actual heritage village itself was put out for competitive tender. Effectively, this excluded the Kalinago from building their own project, as they did not have the financial resources to put in a bid. Besides not giving the Kalinago the chance to invest their own time and energy into the construction of the site (thus creating a sense of involvement), this also meant that the

---

40   Conversation with interviewee KBA#16 (Kalinago Territory, Dominica, 10 August 2015).

Figure 18: Map of the Kalinago Barana Autê, posted near the entrance.

village was built without the use of Kalinago tools, skills, and cultural traditions – such as cutting timber during a dark moon to avoid rotting. It has been argued that the resulting model village is a construction "that could never have been built by Caribs" (Smith 2006: 80). Furthermore, some Kalinago argue that the site was constructed poorly and therefore requires extensive – and expensive – maintenance.[41] Although a project manager from the Kalinago community was appointed in 2002, the KBA ultimately falls under the responsibility of the Ministry for Tourism. It was stated at the time that the intention of the Ministry was to eventually hand over responsibility for the heritage site to the Kalinago Chief and Council, once they had met certain requirements. The KBA was opened to the public in 2006. Since then, the ownership of the ecomuseum has remained the same, falling under the government and the Ministry of Tourism, while being managed locally by a member of the Kalinago community. Naturally, this has complicated the degree to which the Kalinago community can feel connected to the site and has also influenced the value that the KBA has for them (see *Perceiving the Kalinago Barana Autê*, page 119).

The KBA today contains fewer buildings than were initially planned for the site (see figure 18). Visitors most often come to the site in groups as part of island tours, cruise packages, or in school groups. Visitors who come to the site on their own, without a guide, are less common. For all visitors, the experience of the KBA follows a similar plan. Visitors are greeted by a tour guide and gathered in the interpretation center. This small building contains a number of panels with images and information,

---

41   Conversations with interviewee KBA#1 (Kalinago Territory, Dominica, 31 July 2015) & interviewee KBA#48 (Kalinago Territory, Dominica, 12 August 2015).

which tell visitors about the prehistory of the Kalinago on the island and in the whole region, as well as the more recent history of the Territory and its Chiefs. Whenever a tour guide is available, she or he will meet the group of visitors here and discuss these topics. The guide will also show a number of Kalinago objects to the visitors, such as a cured snake skin, a woven fish trap, or basketry. Upon leaving the interpretation center, the rest of the visit takes place in the form of a tour through the model village. Due to the sloping terrain of the KBA and the generally hot weather, the tour has a slow pace, with frequent stops to discuss cultural elements and examine different structures and natural features. Thus, the tour passes over the small Crayfish River, while the guide describes traditional fishing methods, and past a canoe where shipbuilding and the Kalinago connection to the sea are explained. Then, the group visits the *karbay*, also called *taboui*, the large house or hall where the men would gather. In the karbay, visitors learn about the traditional organization of the Kalinago. Often, craft vendors can be found here, selling jewelry made of seeds and plants, as well as basketry and decorated calabash. On the stage inside the karbay traditional dances and music are sometimes performed by one of the Kalinago cultural groups, but this generally has to be arranged beforehand. Further along the path are a number of smaller *ajoupa*s (shelters against sun and rain) and *mouina*s (family houses). In these smaller houses or huts, visitors learn about traditional food and drink, as well as family life. It is also here where visitors can learn how cassava and sugar cane are produced and prepared, and taste cassava bread and herbal tea. The tour continues along the coast past panoramic coastal views to explore the trees and plants that are endemic to the island. When visitors pass along the river a second time, they will learn about the ways in which the Kalinago dye *larouma* reeds which are used for weaving. The tour concludes at the viewpoint over the ocean, near the entrance to the site. This is where visitors will find the facilities, a picnic area, and small restaurant, all of which are in traditionally styled buildings. This is also where the guide talks about the previous Chiefs while visitors can view the wooden sculpted heads that are on display, representing each Chief. The slow-paced stop-and-go nature of the tour following a number of different topics allows visitors plenty of time to interact with the guide and ask questions. Observations by myself, as well as the staff of the KBA, note that visitors are generally satisfied with the tour. However, on occasion, there is a disparity between visitors' expectations of the KBA and reality. Namely, visitors sometimes expect the KBA to be a *living* Indigenous village where they will encounter the Kalinago community living in traditional fashion in the houses on the site (as opposed to a non-inhabited model village). This misunderstanding might stem from the fact that the visiting public does not always distinguish between the advertisements of the Kalinago Territory (as the place where the Kalinago live) and the Kalinago Barana Autê (as a model of a traditional Kalinago village).

The experience of these non-Kalinago visitors to the KBA is markedly different from the use of the site by the Kalinago community themselves. The Kalinago rarely visit the KBA as part of a tour, only as part of a school outing, for instance, or to bring visiting friends. Instead, the Kalinago use the site in other ways and the accessibility of the site for the community is maintained by providing unrestricted and free entry for community members. Even before the KBA was built, the Kalinago living in the surrounding area were used to visiting the mouth of the Crayfish River, the falls, and the pools. This tradition is still kept today, with people visiting the pools to meet friends and family, to bathe in the river or sea, and to relax. However, with the construction of the KBA, the community has added new ways in which they use the site. Most obvious, perhaps, is the use of the site as a place of employment, for instance for tour guides, guards, cooks, or craft vendors. Indirect employment has also been created for people to deliver goods or services to the KBA, for instance the dancers of the cultural groups, the cassava bread bakery, the people who maintain the site, or those who sell the vetiver grass that is used as thatching on the roofs. In addition to employment opportunities, the KBA has also become a venue for community events. Workshops, gatherings, or meetings are organized regularly and some people stop by the KBA just to visit their friends or family who are working there. Festive events, such as birthday parties, graduations, or weddings are also celebrated within the KBA. Thus, while for visitors the KBA is mainly a cultural and educational experience, for the Kalinago community it is principally a place that supports community socializing and creates employment opportunities.

The Kalinago Barana Autê fits the definition of an ecomuseum as described in an earlier chapter (see *Ecomuseums*, page 73). It is a museum that was developed as the result of a grassroots initiative with a strong focus on a particular community, in this case the Kalinago community. The KBA extends beyond the walls of the museum building (the interpretation center) into a wider landscape, encompassing both structural and natural elements. Environmental sustainability is emphasized in the traditional materials used on the site, while cultural preservation and transmission (to younger generations of Kalinago and to visitors) form the core of the tour of the KBA. Cultural preservation is also encouraged by some of the employment opportunities that support traditional crafts and skills, such as basketry or woodworking. This leads to the fourth aspect of ecomuseums, skill development, which is again encouraged by employment opportunities related to the KBA, but also by hosting training sessions and workshops for community members on site. The KBA is not a finished community engagement project, but rather an ongoing and long-term process of collaboration and negotiation between Dominica's government (Ministry of Tourism) and the Kalinago community.

Fieldwork: Aims and Experiences

The Kalinago Territory and the Kalinago Barana Autê (KBA) were first visited in March 2015 during a week-long stay in Dominica. During the regional survey of Caribbean museums, the KBA was identified as a complex case of an ecomuseum that began as a grassroots initiative, but was taken over and developed as a governmental project. As part of the aim to investigate a wide range of types of communities, it was preferred to also include modern Caribbean Indigenous communities.[42] The Kalinago Barana Autê was selected as a case study based on a number of parameters (see *Case Studies*, page 58). The complex position of the KBA, as being guided by both governmental and community influence and desires, led to the hypothesis that this might be an area of

---

42   It should be noted here that the Kalinago are not the only living Caribbean Indigenous community, nor is the KBA the only Caribbean Indigenous heritage site included in the regional museum survey. Other examples include Belize's *Luba Garifuna Cultural Museum*, the *Santa Rosa First Nations Community Museum* in Trinidad & Tobago, or the Indigenous inhabitants of the dual villages of *Christiaankondre & Langemankondre* in Suriname.

contention or conflict. This could possibly provide thought-provoking insights into the dynamics of the process of community engagement between the Kalinago and government over the KBA.

This particular study of the KBA was framed by other fieldwork studies conducted in roughly the same time period by colleagues in the NEXUS1492 and associated research projects. Around this time, multiple colleagues worked within the Kalinago Territory: Eldris Con Aguilar (teacher workshops on indigenous heritage), Jimmy Mans (oral histories and indigenous legacies), Samantha de Ruiter (archaeological fieldwork of settlement patterns), Eloise Stancioff (heritage and landscape changes), and Amy Strecker (indigenous rights). Although they were couched in different disciplines and collected different types of data, all of these studies were based on community collaboration. While this study of the KBA did not directly overlap with any of these previous studies, the presence of these researchers will have impacted the community and may have engaged the same community members in surveys, interviews, or other interactions with researchers. When asked, community members were generally positive about contributing to foreign-based research projects, but clearly stated their wish for research results to return to the Territory for their benefit.

The main fieldwork was set up to take place in the Kalinago Territory from July 28th – August 21st 2015. I spent this time living in the territory as part of the community and taking part in a number of community events to provide context to the fieldwork by means of participant observation. This method enables the fieldworker to experience a community and the behavior of its members and also to intellectualize everything that has been seen or heard; to be able to place things into perspective (Bernard 2006: 344). Being able to do this requires a certain amount of 'insider knowledge' and firsthand experience. Secondly, it has been noted in many fieldwork campaigns that presence builds trust (Bernard 2006: 354). This also proved to be true in this case. I was frequently asked where I was staying as I moved through the Territory and spoke to people. When I replied that I was renting a room with a well-known community member (rather than staying outside the Territory), this frequently led respondents to feel more at ease and more willing to engage in a conversation. In addition, this allowed community members to come by at a later time to answer questions when it was more suitable, or to simply stop by to ask how the research was progressing. It cannot be overemphasized how important 'hanging out' is to build rapport (Bernard 2006: 368). In the case of this fieldwork, it was also valuable for establishing a common ground to initiate conversations. For instance, it was an excellent ice breaker to start a conversation based on both having been to the cricket game last weekend.

Although traditional anthropological field research often takes a year or longer, many studies can be completed in a number of weeks or months (Bernard 2006: 349). If the fieldworker, for instance, already speaks the native language and is familiar with (some of the etiquette of) the community, this reduces a number of boundaries between fieldworker and community members and fieldwork can thus be sped up. This was the case for me in the Kalinago Territory. In addition, having visited the Territory once before, I was already in contact with a number of Kalinago community members, which again facilitated access to the community. Due to the short time frame available for the fieldwork for this case study, participatory rapid assessment was used, which requires having clear questions and a limited amount of variables ready before entering the field (Bernard 2006: 353).

Besides participant observation, I had arranged a survey to be completed as a self-administered questionnaire and also prepared questions for interviews with members of the community who were particularly involved in the KBA. The full survey can be found in the appendix (see *Questionnaire: Kalinago Barana Auté*, page 257). The questions that were incorporated in the survey and the oral interviews were derived from information gathered from informal open interviews conducted during the first visit to the Kalinago Territory and the KBA. Such informal interviews are particularly helpful at the start of a fieldwork campaign to identify which topics are valuable to explore in more detail (Bernard 2006: 211).

At the outset, I planned to complete the survey/self-administered questionnaire by using a street-intercept method (Bernard 2006: 257). The plan was to walk around the Kalinago Territory, asking people to "please answer a few questions about the KBA," and then giving them the survey on paper with a pen. For this reason, the survey was kept brief and the questions were short and relatively easy to answer as they were opinion-based. However, it became apparent from the first day of trying to administer the survey as a questionnaire, that this method was not preferential to the community. The first respondent requested that I read the questions out loud and write down his answers.[43] I gave the next several respondents the choice of either filling it out themselves or having me read out the questions and write down the answers; each respondent preferred the latter. After having established this to be a general preference, I decided to read the questions and write down the answers myself by default, unless the respondent indicated that they wished to self-administer the questionnaire. Thus, the survey ultimately became a series of face-to-face interviews, with a few self-administered questionnaires as exceptions. Low literacy levels can be identified as one of the reasons for this preference by community members: although not stated overtly by respondents, discomfort with writing was observed in those cases where persons did self-administer the questionnaire, regardless of age.

The survey contained closed questions (with multiple choice options), open-ended questions, and 5-point scales (Bernard 2006: 269 & 273). Depending on how the survey was conducted (self-administered questionnaire or face-to-face interview), differences may have occurred in how some questions were answered. For instance, question #7 "Is there anything you would like to see changed about the Kalinago Barana Auté?" offered a number of categories as answers on paper. However, when verbally asked this question, the respondent would generally begin to answer without hearing the options and in these cases I would select an appropriate category (or 'other'). On the other hand, answers written by respondents to open-ended questions were often more brief than those written down ad verbatim by me. Indeed, in the case of a few self-administered questionnaires, some questions were skipped by respondents altogether.

The street-intercept method was applied on roughly half of the fieldwork days. On these days, I mainly approached people who were on their land, around their homes, in the shops, or walking on the main roads. Although community members were often

---

43   Conversation with interviewee KBA#1 (Kalinago Territory, Dominica, 31 July 2015).

Figure 19: The Kalinago Territory cricket tournament was a wonderful event for hanging out with the community and also offered opportunities for conducting surveys.

occupied when approached in these places, hanging laundry, working, farming the land, doing crafts, or engaged in social activities such as hair braiding or dominoes, many were very willing to participate in the survey – often continuing their ongoing activity in the meantime. Many people in the community spend a significant part of the day outside their homes, on their terraces, in their yards, on their land, or in public spaces. Thus, I chose to approach people in these spaces, rather than to knock on doors and intrude on people inside their homes. On the remainder of the days, different methods were applied to approach community members in other situations. For instance, I visited the local clinic in Salybia on a few days, surveying patients in the waiting room. I also approached community members during a number of events, such as during the games of the Kalinago Territory cricket tournament (played on the weekends in the Territory; see figure 19) or prior to the start of the "Keeping it Real" public meeting of Dominica's Cabinet of Ministers with district members held at the Salybia Primary School. By combining these methods, it was possible to survey both men and women of all ages, throughout large parts of the community.

Most community members approached throughout the fieldwork campaign were willing to participate in the survey. In a couple of cases, people were hesitant and stated that they "don't know anything about that." When I explained that the survey was more a matter of opinions than facts, most people agreed to answer the questions. Sometimes people would prefer to first see someone else, such as a family member, do the survey ("Granny, you go first"), before offering to also answer the same questions.

Over the course of the fieldwork campaign, only 6 people declined to participate in the survey. In total, 150 surveys were completed.

Additionally, one in depth interview was completed with the then manager of the KBA. Although more interviews had been planned initially, due to the change of the survey to a mainly interview format, this one interview was deemed salient to understand the workings of the KBA, some of the ongoing issues, as well as planned changes. In actuality, many of the surveys conducted as face-to-face interviews contained more questions than the ones on the paper, as respondents naturally turned these interviews into longer conversations. In many cases, they were very interested in me and the overall purpose of the survey and its initial results. Some community members insisted to first ask me a few questions, before answering the questions in the survey.

The aim of this case study was to understand the Kalinago community's perceptions of the KBA. Firstly, I wanted to know more about the issue of governmental ownership: did this affect community members' visitation of the site? Was this something that community members resented? Secondly, the aim was to uncover the importance of the site and its benefits for the community as they perceived it. Was the museum an important locus of community identity? Did it create employment opportunities? Or did all the income leave the Territory to the Ministry? Finally, I wanted to find out how community members would like to see the KBA changed or improved. At the outset, I had anticipated that community members might be dissatisfied with the ownership of the KBA, its entry fees (as being too high), or that they might overall not feel very involved or invested in the museum. However, this did not prove to be the case for the majority of the Kalinago community surveyed.

Perceiving the Kalinago Barana Autê

This following section will present the results of the survey and interviews held in the Kalinago Territory as part of the case study fieldwork. The collated, categorized, and calculated survey responses can be found in the appendix (see *Questionnaire Results: Kalinago Barana Autê*, page 257). This section begins by presenting the basic statistics and demographics of the survey respondents, before delving more deeply into the community's perceptions of the Kalinago Barana Autê (KBA) based on values and benefits that were identified in the fieldwork data. Following the methodology described in the previous section, 150 surveys were conducted along with one in depth interview. This interview was with the then manager of the KBA, a member of the Kalinago community who lives in the Territory. The majority of the surveys were conducted as face-to-face interviews, with only c. 20 of them completed as self-administered questionnaires. Although only a small segment of the Kalinago community was surveyed, namely 5-7%,[44] both genders are well represented and the age groups are fairly well represented.

---

44 This percentage depends on how one measures the size of the Kalinago population. If one uses the 2011 census of a population of 2145 persons, the survey included 7% of the community (Commonwealth of Dominica 2011: 18). Instead using the approximation of 3000 persons from the Kalinago Territory website, gives a 5% representation of the community.

The results of the survey were presented, for feedback and discussion, to members of the Kalinago community during a special meeting held at the KBA, 18 March 2016 (see *Case Studies*, page 58). Community members present at this meeting, many of whom work at the KBA, noted that they considered the 150 surveys to be a representative sample size. Furthermore, they noted that they found the results themselves also to be representative, based on their own conversations about the KBA with other community members. They were interested in recommendations on how to move forward with the future plans of the KBA by incorporating these results. They stated that many of the issues revealed in the survey results were known to them through conversations, but that they had until now lacked the data to support these notions. This enabled the usage of the preliminary survey results, for instance, to rework their mission statement or to apply for funding to make certain changes or improvements to the site.

Survey Demographics

Kalinago community members from all parts of the Territory were surveyed, by conducting surveys along the main roads, as well as at community gathering places such as important meetings, sporting events, and the central health clinic. In order to assess the value of the KBA for the Kalinago community as a whole, it was deemed necessary to ensure that community members of all ages and genders were represented. Furthermore, fieldwork aimed to achieve a demographic balance as much as possible, in order to eliminate the results being biased to specific groups within the community.

The gender balance in the survey respondents was almost exactly even with 74 female respondents and 76 male respondents (see figure 20). The age distribution of the respondents shows a lower representation by children (under 15) and those aged over 65, while there is a higher amount of teenagers (aged 15-24). Young children were surveyed less frequently, as they had some difficulty answering some of the open-ended questions, specifically related to the importance and benefit of the KBA for the community. Community members aged over 65 were approached as frequently as community members of other age groups, however several of them declined participating in the survey. Those who declined either believed that they did not have the knowledge required to answer the questions or only spoke Creole. The overrepresentation of teenaged respondents (aged 15-24) can be explained by, on the one hand, the extent to which they were curious about me and approached me (instead of vice versa), and, on the other hand, the extent to which this group socializes collectively in public – playing sports and attending events or just hanging out on the street. Especially the latter reason often led to several individuals of this age group wishing to be surveyed one after the other.

Visitation of the KBA

In identifying the value of the Kalinago Barana Autê for the Kalinago community, the first criteria was set as the visitation of the KBA by community members. It was hypothesized that community visitation of the site would not be high and that, therefore, the value of the KBA as a place to visit would not be particularly significant. This hypothesis was based on the (in retrospect) erroneous assumption that the entry fee of the KBA would be too steep for community members to visit on a regular basis. The error of this assumption was pointed out early in the course of the fieldwork: although not openly advertised, members of the Kalinago community can enter the site free of charge and freely. Using the walking trails and the old coastal road, they are able to access the site without having to use to main entrance. The site is not fenced off in any way, but is overseen by security guards after hours. Community members can and do

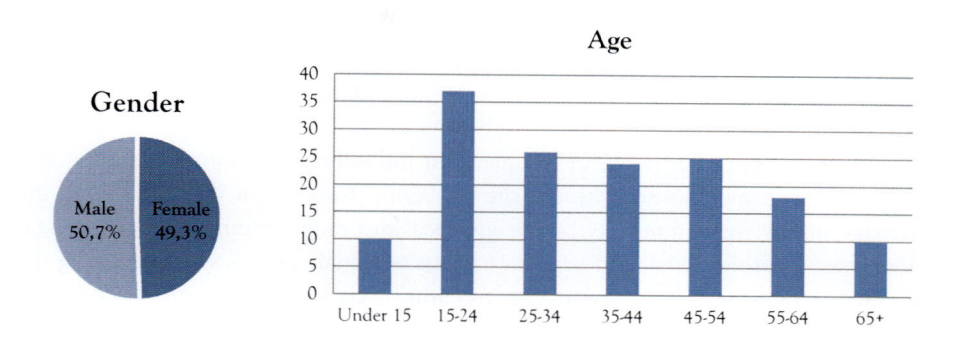

Figure 20: Gender and age distributions of survey respondents in Dominica.

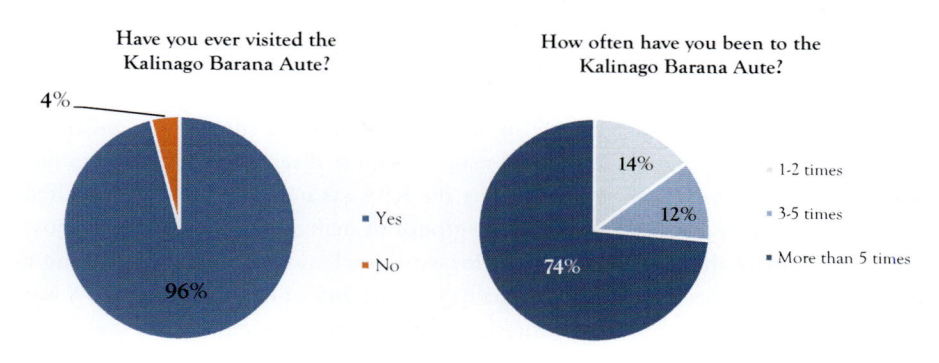

Figure 21: Respondents' visitation percentage and number of visits to the Kalinago Barana Autê.

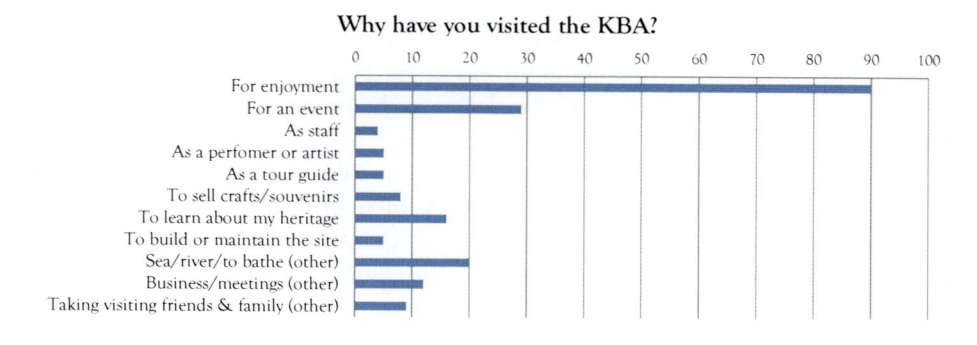

Figure 22: Respondents' reasons for visiting the Kalinago Barana Autê.

use the site at any time of the day. The manager explained that "the intention was to leave the facility a hundred percent accessible to the local residents."[45]

The importance of the KBA for the Kalinago community was reflected in the survey results related to visitation of the site. Except for six respondents, everyone else stated that they had visited the KBA since its opening in 2006 (see figure 21). Those who had not visited the KBA, alternately said it was too difficult to go there (physically, because of the access road), that they pass through there but do not specifically 'visit' the place, or that there was no particular reason that they had not been to the KBA. Of those respondents who had visited the KBA, an overwhelming majority stated that they had visited more than 5 times, exclaiming "oh! Many times!" "hundred times!" or "ten, twenty, fifty times."

It is clear, then, that the KBA is a place for the Kalinago community to visit and that most of them choose to visit the site frequently. Reasons for the visitation of the heritage site by the community can be grouped into roughly four categories: recreational, social, professional, and educational. Recreational reasons, such as visiting the site "for enjoyment," "for an event," or "to bathe" were mentioned most often by the respondents and were clearly the first major association with visitation of the KBA when asked (see figure 22). These recreational reasons sometimes overlapped with, or were closely tied to, social reasons, such as visiting the KBA "for an event," "for meetings," or for "taking visiting friends or relatives." However, overtly social reasons were stated much less frequently than reasons of recreation. Professional reasons were also less frequently stated, noting visitation "as staff," "as a performer or artist," "as a tour guide," "to sell crafts/souvenirs," "to build or maintain the site," or for "business/ meetings." This grouping of professional reasons is quite diverse and reflects community members who are employed directly by the KBA (as staff or guides), those hired incidentally by the KBA (such as the dance groups or maintenance workers), or those who use the site of the KBA as their place for work (such as the craft vendors or those attending business meetings on site). Finally, the category of educational reasons was the least important for community visitation of the heritage site, reflected in the survey by the response "to learn about my heritage." Ultimately, the Kalinago community most of all associates visiting the KBA with recreation.

Importance of the KBA
The importance of the KBA for the Kalinago is already implicitly clear in the survey results from the frequency of community visitation. However, this result is echoed strongly in the responses to the direct question of the importance of the KBA (see figure 23). Almost all of the respondents, 97%, stated that they considered the KBA to be "a lot" or "extremely" important to the community. None of the respondents felt negatively about the importance of the KBA. In an open question, respondents were asked to elaborate and explain why they felt that the KBA was important for their community (in total 132 responses, some with multiple reason). It is interesting to note that in answering this question, respondents only rarely thought of their own personal visitation of the site for recreational or social reasons as a reason for the

---

45   Interview with manager of *Kalinago Barana Autê* (Kalinago Territory, Dominica, 15 August 2015).

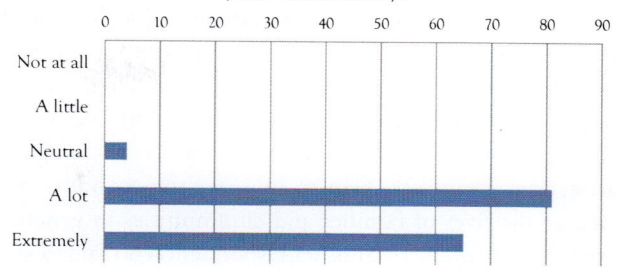

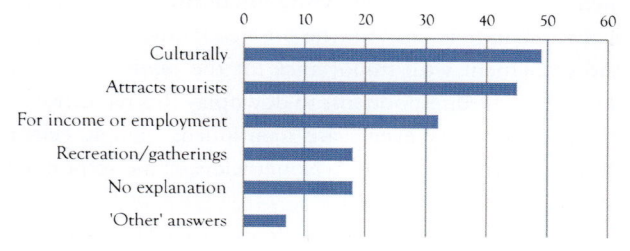

Figure 23: Respondents' assessment of the importance of the Kalinago Barana Autê.

KBA's importance. Instead, communal importance was more frequently associated with other reasons.

Chief of these reasons are those that can be termed internal cultural reasons, for instance related to the preservation of the Kalinago heritage, knowledge of the ancestors, or the teaching of Kalinago history within the own community. One respondent stated that the KBA "is important because this is the only place you could know about the Kalinago history."[46] Another respondent noted its importance by saying that "it has helped to reidentify the Carib people."[47] The importance of the KBA as a place to learn about the community's ancestors was also noted: "because it is an Indigenous place and there we get a lot of information about our ancestors."[48]

An almost equally important category of reasons was the one related to the attraction of tourists or visitors from outside the community. The KBA is thus considered an important hub that draws people to the community "because so many people come all the time to visit."[49] The importance of the KBA as such an attraction was usually not stated specifically in economic terms, but rather as bringing people together and creating awareness for the Kalinago: "it brings a lot of visitors to our island to visit our people and heritage"[50] or "we have visitors worldwide every day."[51] The KBA is seen as

46   Survey KBA#3 (Kalinago Territory, Dominica, 7 August 2015).
47   Survey KBA#39 (Kalinago Territory, Dominica, 11 August 2015).
48   Survey KBA#89 (Kalinago Territory, Dominica, 13 August 2015).
49   Survey KBA#24 (Kalinago Territory, Dominica, 10 August 2015).
50   Survey KBA#49 (Kalinago Territory, Dominica, 12 August 2015).
51   Survey KBA#76 (Kalinago Territory, Dominica, 12 August 2015).

the focal point of the whole Territory, specifically for drawing in visitors from beyond the community, it is the "most important site in the Territory."[52]

Separately grouped are the responses that are specifically related to economic importance, either the direct employment opportunities at the KBA or the increased income to the Kalinago Territory as a whole thanks to its attraction of visitors. One respondent said that the KBA was important "because of the employment for the Kalinago people and for tourism."[53] Another respondent explained that "as a tourist attraction site, it can help to improve the economy of the Territory, which could change the lives of families and communities in general."[54] This sentiment was put even more strongly by another respondent who said "I view the KBA as the economic artery of the Territory."[55]

Importance related to the enjoyment of the KBA or the use of the museum for events or meetings was less frequently overtly stated by the respondents, despite (as mentioned above) the high visitation of the site by community members. It is possible that while individuals visit the site frequently, they do not associate *personal* recreation and enjoyment with importance for the *community*. It is likely that the phrasing of the question led respondents to downplay this recreational/personal importance. More often, community events are mentioned: "people celebrate anniversaries there and things are well attended."[56] Nonetheless, some respondents noted the importance of "the pool to bathe and fish."[57]

Finally, a number of respondents gave other reasons that do not fall in the above-mentioned categories. For instance, one respondent stated that the KBA was "an important tourism tool to help create sustainable development."[58] This respondent pictured the KBA as a model or good example for the development of other sustainable businesses in the Kalinago Territory. On the other hand, another respondent indicated that the community did not sufficiently appreciate the importance of the KBA: "we don't participate as locals, we take it for granted, but it is important."[59] The KBA can also function as a place to encourage talent, for dancers or crafts(wo)men, "because it helps them display talents and skills."[60] One respondent stated the importance of the KBA in terms of its uniqueness, because "apart from the Barana Autê I don't think there is any other place that has these kinds of activities and things."[61] Ultimately, it can be said that the communal importance of the KBA is most often seen in cultural terms and as a point of attraction for visitors, while employment or economic reasons are of less importance.

52   Survey KBA#132 (Kalinago Territory, Dominica, 16 August 2015).
53   Survey KBA#7 (Kalinago Territory, Dominica, 7 August 2015).
54   Survey KBA#84 (Kalinago Territory, Dominica, 13 August 2015).
55   Survey KBA#45 (Kalinago Territory, Dominica, 12 August 2015).
56   Survey KBA#83 (Kalinago Territory, Dominica, 13 August 2015).
57   Survey KBA#35 (Kalinago Territory, Dominica, 10 August 2015).
58   Survey KBA#144 (Kalinago Territory, Dominica, 18 August 2015).
59   Survey KBA#130 (Kalinago Territory, Dominica, 15 August 2015).
60   Survey KBA#97 (Kalinago Territory, Dominica, 13 August 2015).
61   Survey KBA#115 (Kalinago Territory, Dominica, 15 August 2015).

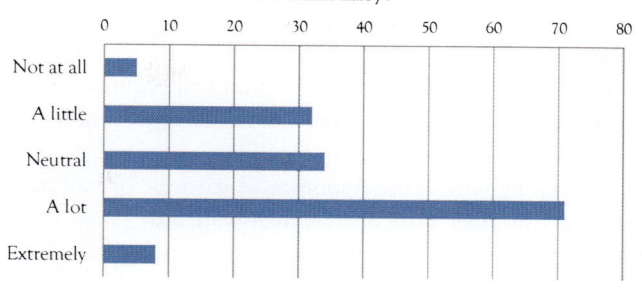

Do you feel that the KBA benefits your community?

Figure 24: Respondents' assessment of the benefits of the Kalinago Barana Autê.

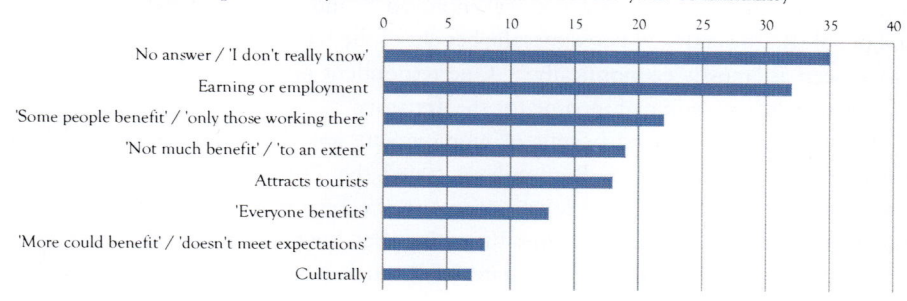

Please explain how you feel that the KBA benefits your community

Benefits of the KBA

When respondents were asked to discuss the *benefits* of the KBA for the community, rather than its importance, responses were more diverse and included negative reactions (see figure 24). The responses indicate that the *intrinsic values* of the KBA are not contested, while the Kalinago community is more conflicted about the *instrumental values* of the KBA. Following the definition by John Holden, intrinsic values are those which pertain to "a subjective experience of culture" (Holden quoted in Scott 2009: 196). Instrumental values, on the other hand, are more clearly utilitarian and are associated with specific outcomes. This type of value is often also more tangible, quantifiable, and easier to measure, for instance economically. In her research, Carol Scott has identified intrinsic values in categories such as: well-being, empathetic, historical, spiritual, or social (Scott 2009: 201). Instrumental values are categorized as economic, capacity building, or learning, among others. In this survey, 'importance' was more often seen as a "subjective experience" and associated with intrinsic values. As mentioned above, the Kalinago community was overwhelmingly positive about these value. However, the communal 'benefit' of the KBA is seen as referring to tangible benefits and clear outcomes. When considering these values, the Kalinago community was much more divided. It appears that the Kalinago intrinsically (subjectively, emotionally) highly value the KBA, but that they are not all pleased with the actual, quantifiable outcomes that the KBA has generated.

A slight majority of the respondents, 53%, considered the KBA to be "a lot" or "extremely" beneficial. However, there is also a significant number of respondents, 25%, who stated that the KBA was "not at all" or "a little" beneficial. The remainder of the respondents were neutral. This picture becomes more complex when one looks at the responses to the open question, asking respondents to elaborate on their perception of the KBA's communal benefit. These responses have been categorized in different groups, largely relating to the tone of positivity or negativity of the response or by the specific reason indicated, such as a cultural or economic reason. Some respondents (35) did not answer this open question or said something like "I don't know much about that"[62] or "not too sure of that."[63]

Beginning with those responses which were overall more positive in tone, we can identify a number of benefits which were also stated in the question regarding importance: cultural, employment, and attracts tourists. Employment is stated exactly as often as a positive benefit to the community as it was given as the reason the KBA is important to the community, namely by 32 respondents. Respondents noted: "the community benefits because people get employed"[64] and "people go there and work, and people do the crafts."[65] For some, the benefit of the KBA for the Kalinago community is seen as "mostly economically."[66] One respondent noted that the benefit of the KBA is that it is a "source of income for the Territory."[67]

Linked to the perceived benefit of employment was the benefit of the KBA in attracting tourists or visitors. Respondents stated that "people come to visit"[68] and that because of the KBA "more tourists come to the Territory."[69] This was sometimes directly related to economic outcomes by stating that "tourists come to the shop."[70] In most cases, respondents did not elaborate much further on this point beyond stating that the KBA brings in visitors.

Cultural benefits were stated least of all, possibly because cultural values were perceived to be largely intrinsic and intangible and thus not associated with a more quantifiable term such as 'benefit.' When cultural values are mentioned, they are described in strongly positive terms. Respondents noted that the KBA is "a part of the culture of the Territory"[71] and that it "reminds us of who we are as a people."[72] Besides relating these benefits to identity, they are also connected with cultural preservation: "it helps educate the children and people, causing the Kalinago culture to remain active."[73] However, ambiguity of the community regarding the benefit of the KBA can be seen in one response which stated that "the community benefits from the preservation [of culture] but not financially."[74]

Besides the positive responses indicating benefits of the KBA for cultural reasons, employment, or attracting tourists, some respondents more generally stated that "everyone

62   Survey KBA#134 (Kalinago Territory, Dominica, 16 August 2015).
63   Survey KBA#82 (Kalinago Territory, Dominica, 13 August 2015).
64   Survey KBA#3 (Kalinago Territory, Dominica, 7 August 2015).
65   Survey KBA#147 (Kalinago Territory, Dominica, 18 August 2015).
66   Survey KBA#77 (Kalinago Territory, Dominica, 12 August 2015).
67   Survey KBA#132 (Kalinago Territory, Dominica, 16 August 2015).
68   Survey KBA#65 (Kalinago Territory, Dominica, 12 August 2015).
69   Survey KBA#21 (Kalinago Territory, Dominica, 10 August 2015).
70   Survey KBA#17 (Kalinago Territory, Dominica, 10 August 2015).
71   Survey KBA#129 (Kalinago Territory, Dominica, 15 August 2015).
72   Survey KBA#141 (Kalinago Territory, Dominica, 16 August 2015).
73   Survey KBA#92 (Kalinago Territory, Dominica, 13 August 2015).
74   Survey KBA#39 (Kalinago Territory, Dominica, 11 August 2015).

benefits."[75] It was noted of the KBA, that beyond being a museum, "it's more community tourism, so most of the people are benefitting."[76] One respondent explained that "directly or indirectly, they do [benefit]; it gives the Territory a good image."[77]

Despite these positive responses, and the abovementioned comment that in some way everyone in the community benefits, this is not perceived to be true by everyone. Some responses occupy a more negative middle ground, stating that the community is "not [benefitting] in the way that it should."[78] One respondent felt that "more people could be employed"[79] and in the words of another respondent: "I feel that the Kalinago Barana Autê is under-exploited."[80] These responses indicate that some community members, although seeing that there is a benefit of the KBA for the community, feel that this benefit could and should be greater.

More strongly negative responses come from community members who feel that *others* are benefitting from the KBA but they themselves, personally, are not. These responses frequently carry tones of envy: "much of the community does not benefit, only those who work here"[81] or "we don't really benefit, but the manager does."[82] Some even feel that the community does not benefit from the KBA at all, only the government: "it benefits the people who run it, not the community."[83] Other responses note injustice in the division of the benefits of the KBA throughout the community: "so far, I have not seen it [the benefit], there are not enough jobs there, it is unfair."[84] This same feeling was stated by another respondent who said that the KBA "creates some employment for some people in the Territory, a handful, the chosen ones from the management body. You feel left out."[85]

Finally, a group of respondents simply did not perceive there to be much or any benefit for the community from the KBA. These responses do not contain emotions related to envy or unfairness, but simply note a lack of benefit. Most of these responses were very brief. Respondents said the benefit of the KBA for the community was "not too much."[86] Others said that the community benefitted "to an extent,"[87] "not really,"[88] or "not at this point."[89]

Ultimately, it is clear that while the community has no problems identifying the *importance* of the KBA, there is a greater division when it comes to assessing the *benefits* of the KBA. Some community members feel that everyone benefits, for instance by the good image which the KBA creates of the Territory or as a site that preserves Kalinago culture. Employment is clearly a contested benefit, with some respondents

---

75   Survey KBA#28 (Kalinago Territory, Dominica, 10 August 2015).
76   Survey KBA#58 (Kalinago Territory, Dominica, 12 August 2015).
77   Survey KBA#100 (Kalinago Territory, Dominica, 13 August 2015).
78   Survey KBA#57 (Kalinago Territory, Dominica, 12 August 2015).
79   Survey KBA#9 (Kalinago Territory, Dominica, 7 August 2015).
80   Survey KBA#91 (Kalinago Territory, Dominica, 13 August 2015).
81   Survey KBA#4 (Kalinago Territory, Dominica, 7 August 2015).
82   Survey KBA#25 (Kalinago Territory, Dominica, 10 August 2015).
83   Survey KBA#119 (Kalinago Territory, Dominica, 15 August 2015).
84   Survey KBA#136 (Kalinago Territory, Dominica, 16 August 2015).
85   Survey KBA#144 (Kalinago Territory, Dominica, 18 August 2015).
86   Survey KBA#6 (Kalinago Territory, Dominica, 7 August 2015).
87   Survey KBA#11 (Kalinago Territory, Dominica, 10 August 2015).
88   Survey KBA#24 (Kalinago Territory, Dominica, 10 August 2015).
89   Survey KBA#45 (Kalinago Territory, Dominica, 12 August 2015).

stating employment in fully positive terms, others more negatively noting that the site could be exploited more, and yet again others enviously describing the employment of a handful of 'chosen ones.' One of the issues with the community's perception of benefits related to employment is that the original aim of the KBA, when it was first designed and developed, was to provide employment to the community. That has always been stated as one of the main aims for the Kalinago community of this community engagement process. However, over time, it has become clear that not every community member can economically benefit directly and in quantifiable ways from the existence of the KBA. This has created conflict and contention. During the meeting at the KBA when these survey results were presented, members of the new management team of the KBA stated that creating employment was not (anymore) a main goal for the museum. It was suggested to develop a new mission statement which could express its aims on the one hand for the Kalinago community and on the other hand for outside visitors. A mission with a clear goal for the Kalinago community, unrelated to economic gain or employment, may make it easier in the future to demonstrate communal benefits and outcomes.

Associations with the KBA

As part of the survey, respondents were asked to "please characterize the Kalinago Barana Autê in three *positive* keywords" and to then do the same exercise with three *negative* keywords. Many respondents initially needed help in answering the question, as they did not fully understand the way it was phrased. In these cases, I would prompt them by asking "how would you describe the KBA to someone in three positive words? The KBA is…." and then encourage the respondent to "say the first three words that pop into your mind." I purposefully did not prompt the respondents by providing examples of keywords, to make sure respondents made their own associations.

The survey respondents overwhelmingly associated the KBA with positive keywords. Of all the respondents, only 6 did not answer the question. Most of the respondents mentioned two or three keywords, giving a total of 392 responses to this question (or 2.7 keywords per respondent). These keywords were manually counted for duplicates and then categories were identified (see figure 25). Any respondent could give up to three different words, but these could all be in same category, for instance they could all be 'aesthetic' keywords. The positive keyword most often associated with the KBA was 'beautiful' (36 respondents). Most of the keywords mentioned related to intrinsic values, meaning values that follow from a subjective experience of the site. The responses to this question reflect the responses to the question of the importance of the KBA for the community (see above). In both cases, responses are overwhelmingly positive and based on personal experiences. The positive keywords are more closely connected to their own visitation of the museum, reflecting their emotions and experiences of the site itself, personally and subjectively.

Many of the responses were linked to the aesthetic (90), experiential (65), recreational (39), and natural (38) qualities of the landscape and the site of the KBA. Aesthetically, community members commented on how the KBA is *beautiful, attractive,* and has a *wonderful view*. In the experiential category are keywords that are more general positive words of appreciation of the site, such as *nice, exciting,* and *interesting*. Related to the community's recreational use of the site of the KBA are keywords such

Please characterize the KBA in three *positive* keywords

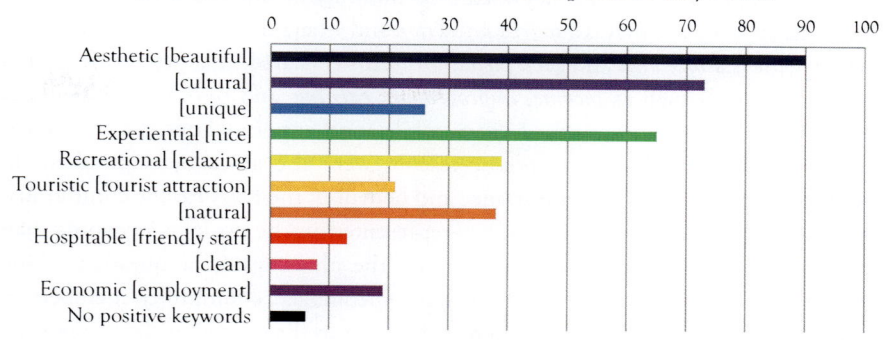

Figure 25: Respondents' positive keywords for the Kalinago Barana Autê. In brackets the top keyword for each category.

Please characterize the KBA in three *negative* keywords

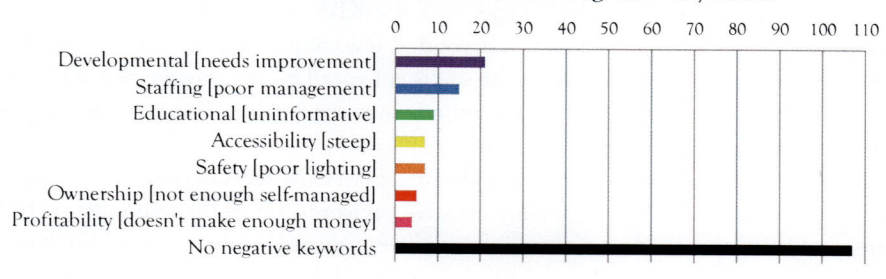

Figure 26: Respondents' negative keywords for the Kalinago Barana Autê. In brackets the top keyword for each category.

as *relaxing, peaceful,* and *quiet.* Keywords specifically related to the natural aspects of the landscape were *natural, cool,* and *good location.* All of these keywords show the intrinsic values that community members place on the KBA, mostly related to their own experience of the site. These are therefore also clearly related to how the community uses the site: for recreational purposes in an aesthetically pleasing and experientially enjoyable place.

Respondents also noted cultural keywords (73), referring to the KBA as a *cultural, historical,* and *traditional* place. Many of these keywords related also to education, identity, and the preservation of heritage and ancestors. These values can be considered to be both intrinsic *and* instrumental, as on the one hand they reflect subjective experiences of the KBA (*e.g. traditional* or *authentic*) while one the other hand they refer to outcomes of the community engagement process of the KBA (*e.g. preserving* or *educational*). Many of the cultural keywords also refer to specific activities that take place at the KBA, such as the *local bread* and *delicious meals* which are made there, the opportunities to *learn different crafts* and the dancers who *help visitors dance to the music.*

A mix of intrinsic and instrumental values can also be found in the categories of touristic (21) and economic (19) keywords. Community members associated the KBA instrumentally as a place that is a *tourist attraction* and where they conduct *private tours*. Intrinsically, it is a *nice visit* and *good for visitors*. This is related to largely instrumental economic keywords such as *income, improvement, earning,* and *cash*. One respondent described the KBA by saying that it *helps us*, while another pointed out that it *enhances the reserve*. Both touristic and economic reasons were also given by respondents in relation to the questions of the importance and benefit of the KBA for the community. However, both of these categories are less represented in the positive keywords than they are as responses to those other questions. The phrasing of the question asking for positive keywords was more likely to have encouraged community members to consider their own visitation and experience of the site as the source for their responses. Thus, it is likely that mostly respondents who actually personally receive income or employment at the KBA would mention economic keywords, while other community members would use different keywords.

Finally, community members described the KBA in a few other intrinsic categories, noting its uniqueness (26), cleanliness (8) and the hospitable atmosphere (13). Community members subjectively experience the KBA to be *unique, special,* and an *icon* within the Territory and the world beyond. A few community members particularly pointed out that the experience of the site is enhanced by the *friendly staff*, and that the KBA is *welcoming* and *inviting*. Cleanliness was the smallest category, containing keywords such as *clean, tidy,* and *neat*.

Whereas almost all respondents were able to describe the KBA in positive keywords, the majority was unable to provide any negative keywords. Of all the respondents, 107 were unable or unwilling to say a single negative keyword, saying "I wouldn't know anything negative to say about that." Of those who did describe the KBA with negative keywords, this was often only one or two keyword(s). In total, 68 negative responses were given by 43 respondents, an average of 1.6 keywords per respondent. Just as with the positive keywords, words were manually counted for duplicates and separated into a number of categories (see figure 26). Several of these keywords were phrased as a "lack of.." or "poor…" implicitly stating how these perceived negative values could be countered or alleviated. Negative keywords were mainly related to instrumental values, where a lack of a specific outcome or state is perceived. It can be inferred that a majority of the Kalinago community does not have significant negative subjective experiences of the KBA and therefore chose not to answer this question.

Negative keywords were frequently directed towards the physical state of the site, referring to its development (21), accessibility (7), and issues of safety (7). Regarding the development of the site, respondents noted that the KBA *needs (some) improvements*, is *incomplete,* and *outdated*. Most of these comments were accompanied by suggestions for maintenance of the site and expansion of the KBA and its scope (see *Improvements for the KBA*, page 131). Negative keywords related to the accessibility of the KBA were all about the physical location of the site on the old coastal road and the difficulty of using the connecting access road from the new coastal road. Respondents noted that the KBA was *too far down, too far,* and that the road was *steep* making it a *tiring walk*. The issue of the access road is one that has also been discussed by the management of the KBA, with various solutions having been suggested over time (more on this below). Regarding safety, a few respondents said that the KBA has *poor lighting*, that the *river crossing is difficult*, and that the site is *dangerous*. Most of these comments related to safety have to do with the fact that community members are used to using the site regardless of the weather or time of day. Therefore, they may have difficulty maneuvering the site after heavy rainfall or in the dark. Most of these negative keywords, as mentioned before, already imply solutions and are not expressed in overtly negative tones.

A few respondents offered negative keywords related to the content of the heritage of the KBA, categorized as educational values (9). These respondents said that the KBA *lacks information, lacks authenticity*, or *needs more pictures*. Although many of the community members do not often visit the KBA in the same manner as visitors from outside the community, some individuals still wish they could learn more from the site about their own culture. These comments were expressed by teens and young adults, for instance, who suggested that the KBA should have more information, more pictures, and more cultural elements.

Finally, community members stated negative keywords related to the business side of the KBA, about staffing (15), ownership (5), and profitability (4). Some members of the Kalinago community feel that the KBA has *poor management*, is *disorganized*, or that there is a *lack of communication* (for example between the management and the rest of the staff). Of course, issues of staffing and management are closely related to (or sometimes seen as responsible for) some of the other negative values mentioned above, such as the (lack of) development of the site or the perceived lack of information. These problems are also tied to the issue of ownership. I had assumed prior to this fieldwork that the governmental ownership of the KBA would be a major source of contention. However, only 5 respondents specifically stated that the KBA is *not enough self-managed* and that it is negative that the *government runs it*. A few respondents commented negatively on the profitability of the KBA, saying that it *doesn't make enough money* and that it is *slow as* [the] *season closes*. One of them felt that the KBA is *expensive* for visitors.

Improvements for the KBA

Although the members of the Kalinago community responded overwhelmingly with positive keywords associated with the KBA, of course this does not mean that they do not see room for improvement regarding the continued operation and existence of the site. Those respondents who provided negative keywords frequently phrased these in ways that already implied suggestions for improvement or problem-solving. Many respondents who did not want to give negative keywords, nonetheless provided suggestions for changes to the KBA. The survey asked respondents "is there anything you would like to see changed about the KBA?" and respondents could pick multiple options from a number of categories, add their own category, and elaborate on their suggestion(s). Respondents could also choose 'nothing' as their answer to this question. Of all the respondents, 45 said that they would not like to see anything changed about the KBA. In these cases, respondents either said they didn't know of anything to change or that the KBA is nice or good the way it is. One respondent explained: "maybe as

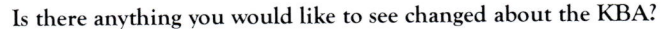

Is there anything you would like to see changed about the KBA?

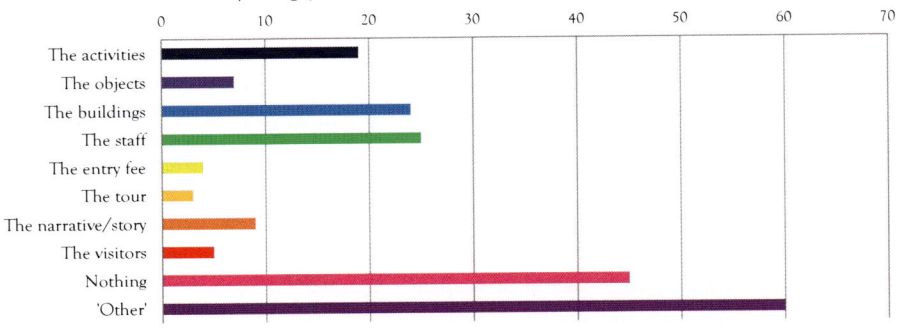

Figure 27: Respondents' suggested improvements for the Kalinago Barana Auté.

time goes by, do some changes to better it up, but it is going on good."[90] A majority of the respondents, 70%, suggested changes and many of them also suggested changes in other categories than those provided on the survey form (see figure 27). As respondents were able to elaborate, they often provided extensive details of the changes they proposed and how they felt these should be implemented. Some respondents provided a list of suggestions, others only suggested one change. In the remainder of this section, each category will be discussed one by one, with the category of 'other' responses being discussed last as this contains a multitude of different suggestions in itself.

In the category of activities (19), community members mostly suggested the addition of more activities or creating different activities. One respondent explained that "they should always have some new things, [now] every time people go it's the same."[91] Another respondent agreed, saying the KBA should have "more live shows, educational meetings, more of an attraction, see [that] there's always something to do."[92] A more specific suggestion was given by another respondent who said that "more cultural activities could be done at the site, especially shows for Carib week."[93]

Many of these suggestions were already known to the staff and management of the KBA and had been taken under consideration. The intention to add more activities to the cultural output of the KBA was expressed in the interview with the manager. However, he noted that all these plans must also be reviewed in terms of their financial viability.

> *One of the focus is to have more activities on the spot, on the facility. [...] we have been able to have the cassava bread circling on a fairly steady basis. We have engaged the dancers. Once the weavers are there, they do their thing, so that is not a problem. But there are other traditional activities we would love to have more, on a more steady basis, including the construction of a canoe. [...] because that is something that visitors always have an interest in, the construction of the canoe.*

---

90   Survey KBA#83 (Kalinago Territory, Dominica, 13 August 2015).
91   Survey KBA#60 (Kalinago Territory, Dominica, 12 August 2015).
92   Survey KBA#98 (Kalinago Territory, Dominica, 13 August 2015).
93   Survey KBA#94 (Kalinago Territory, Dominica, 13 August 2015).

There are other activities that we are looking at, for example traditional fishing, the processing of all things such as cocoa and coffee, that sort of thing, so these are things we are looking at doing. And of course, other activities such as face painting, especially for the children, right, and storytelling.

Again they are brilliant ideas, very good ideas but the next challenge is the financing. Because while we would love to have all these things one time or today, but there appears to be financial implication. So we need to know that, I mean, we have the required financing to meet these costs, once we start engaging the people.[94]

Some respondents suggested that the KBA could benefit from the addition of more objects (7) or archaeological artefacts. Currently, the museum mainly consists of the buildings of the model village, as well as the landscape, and the interpretive center. The latter contains panels with texts and images as well as some objects, all of which are ethnographic. One respondent said that the KBA should have "more historical stuff"[95] and another respondent echoed the sentiment, saying that they should "bring back the ancient things the Caribs used to use."[96] Another respondent said that "they need a better museum with all the past chiefs and their personal items."[97] The KBA could benefit from adding more objects to their collection and displays, whether these are archaeological artefacts (some of which are currently held in the capital, Roseau, while others are in museums overseas), more ethnographic materials, or historic objects belonging to ancestors and chiefs.

The buildings (24) were also suggested as a part of the KBA that could be changed. Some community members suggested the addition of new buildings, "maybe some guesthouses for people to overnight."[98] However, responses were more often related to the maintenance of the current buildings. It is understood within the community that the current use of vetiver thatching on the roofs of the buildings is expensive to maintain. One respondent suggested that "shingles would last longer & improve the buildings."[99] Another respondent, who has worked on maintaining the buildings, made a similar comment to switch to "more modern materials that still look traditional, [it] would need less maintenance."[100] According to the manager, the maintenance of the buildings is currently one of the biggest consistent expenses of the KBA.

One of the questions I am usually asked is where in maintenance […] do we spend all that money? Or so much money? Because we are using thatch, right, the local thatch, there is a challenge, right, because it takes […] quite a bit of grass to cover the structures. And the lifespan, it's at the most about two-and-a-half to three years. So then you have to start changing that, and it is not one structure, it is several structures. So you see, when you add it up, it means that a significant

94 Interview with manager of *Kalinago Barana Autê* (Kalinago Territory, Dominica, 15 August 2015).
95 Survey KBA#123 (Kalinago Territory, Dominica, 15 August 2015).
96 Survey KBA#114 (Kalinago Territory, Dominica, 15 August 2015).
97 Survey KBA#60 (Kalinago Territory, Dominica, 12 August 2015).
98 Survey KBA#82 (Kalinago Territory, Dominica, 13 August 2015).
99 Survey KBA#17 (Kalinago Territory, Dominica, 10 August 2015).
100 Survey KBA#1 (Kalinago Territory, Dominica, 31 July 2015).

amount of money goes into that. [...] we are exploring different avenues in which the material that we use can be supported or where the lifespan can be extended with various techniques [...] keeping as close as possible to the traditions.[101]

However, he pointed out that the current use of thatch actually provided indirect employment to members of the community. Certainly, changing the materials used on the roofs of the buildings would therefore affect the economic situation of the community as a result.

All the thatch which is bought, it is purchased from the local residents, of the community. Because again given the demise of the agricultural sector in the community, once upon a time more than 90% of the revenue or the income of families in the community was generated [...] from the agriculture sector, primarily banana. But since [...] the collapse of the banana industry, it meant that a lot of people have become almost paralyzed as it were with regards to income generation. So [...] a number of residents in the community have seen the cultivation of the thatch as a very good avenue for them, where they could generate revenue for themselves. So it means that the more we can buy, the better for the residents.[102]

The staff (25) was another category in which respondents suggested change. Some respondents felt that the KBA should change "the amount of staff, [have] more people who know more about the culture."[103] Several respondents specifically indicated that more young people should be working at the KBA, either to provide employment to this generation, "give young people more jobs to do,"[104] or to make them more invested in the community. To that extent, one respondent said that they should have "more young people helping the community & the KBA go further. [The] chief should encourage young people."[105] Another respondent said that the staff should improve their internal cohesion and communication, "to come together as a whole with the staff and have meetings."[106] Financial management of the KBA was also suggested for improvement. One respondent said that the KBA should change "the salary, especially [for] the guides."[107] Another respondent was dissatisfied about the management saying that "they take too long to pay people who sell the vetiver, sometimes months."[108] Thus, for some respondents negative personal experiences in dealing with (the management of) the KBA influenced their suggestions for improvements specifically, while other respondents made more general suggestions for the staff to expand or improve.

The entry fee (4) was not an issue to most of the respondents. This is understandable since the Kalinago community has free access to the site, so they are not confronted with a fee. Only a couple respondents considered the price that visitors pay: "I just find

101 Interview with manager of *Kalinago Barana Autê* (Kalinago Territory, Dominica, 15 August 2015).
102 Interview with manager of *Kalinago Barana Autê* (Kalinago Territory, Dominica, 15 August 2015).
103 Survey KBA#119 (Kalinago Territory, Dominica, 15 August 2015).
104 Survey KBA#138 (Kalinago Territory, Dominica, 16 August 2015).
105 Survey KBA#2 (Kalinago Territory, Dominica, 3 August 2015).
106 Survey KBA#6 (Kalinago Territory, Dominica, 7 August 2015).
107 Survey KBA#62 (Kalinago Territory, Dominica, 12 August 2015).
108 Survey KBA#16 (Kalinago Territory, Dominica, 10 August 2015).

that it's too high, it could attract a lot more if the price was lower."[109] One respondent suggested that the entry price should also be free for Kalinago from other islands, such as Guadeloupe or St. Vincent, not only for those living on Dominica: "make it easy for Kalinago people to access, free for all Kalinago."[110]

The guided tour (3) was brought up by only a few respondents as something that could be changed. Again, this is understandable as most community members do not take the tour when they visit the site. One respondent did elaborate on their suggestion to change the tour, saying that there should be "more tour guides who speak different languages."[111]

Closely related to the previous category, is that of the narrative (9) or story told at the KBA, mostly consisting of comments about the need for more cultural content. One respondent said that "more history [is] needed down there,"[112] another felt the same way that "they should have more aspects of the Kalinago."[113] Specifically, it was suggested that the KBA should have "more information and pictures, [to be] more in depth and about the culture."[114] A different suggestion was provided by another respondent who said that there should be "more information and plaques at various places, like at the cassava mill"[115] This would allow visitors to visit the KBA by self-guided tour, following signs to information plaques, rather than with a tour guide. This suggestion was brought up during the presentation of the preliminary survey results. One of the community members asked whether visitors would be willing to pay the entry fee for the KBA if they did not receive a guided tour, a concern which was discussed collectively. While visitors may expect to have a guide when they are visiting museums as part of an organized tour or large group, many would not be surprised to visit without a guide if they come alone or in a small group. Thus, community members considered the potential benefits of a self-guided tour and of adding informative plaques throughout the route followed on the site and the management of the KBA will consider these possibilities in developing future plans.

Regarding visitors (5), respondents only commented on the fact that the KBA should have more visitors. One community member said that "we need more tourists,"[116] another saying that "more visitors should visit the site."[117] Respondents did not make any suggestions regarding where visitors are coming from or if visitors are coming as part of tours or individually.

As mentioned, many respondents suggested changes that did not fit into one of the provided answer categories. These 'other' answers (60) are quite diverse, although some points were iterated by multiple respondents (see table 2). Some respondents stated a general need for improvements (7). One respondent said "the whole facility need improving."[118] Another felt that "they have it carelessly, [they must] keep it up to date

109 Survey KBA#8 (Kalinago Territory, Dominica, 7 August 2015).
110 Survey KBA#80 (Kalinago Territory, Dominica, 13 August 2015).
111 Survey KBA#81 (Kalinago Territory, Dominica, 13 August 2015).
112 Survey KBA#43 (Kalinago Territory, Dominica, 11 August 2015).
113 Survey KBA#61 (Kalinago Territory, Dominica, 12 August 2015).
114 Survey KBA#115 (Kalinago Territory, Dominica, 15 August 2015).
115 Survey KBA#148 (Kalinago Territory, Dominica, 18 August 2015).
116 Survey KBA#12 (Kalinago Territory, Dominica, 10 August 2015).
117 Survey KBA#92 (Kalinago Territory, Dominica, 13 August 2015).
118 Survey KBA#57 (Kalinago Territory, Dominica, 12 August 2015).

'Other' suggested improvements	Amount of times suggested
Access road/trails, wayfinding, bus system, wheelchair access	15
Marketing & visitors' expectations	14
More local foods/drinks/music/souvenirs, authenticity, less modernized	10
General improvement	7
Herbal garden	4
Stronger community bond	4
Employment	3
Expansion	3
Living experience	3
Local management	2
Ocean access	2
Implement a business plan	1
Improve the bridge over the river	1
Improve washrooms	1
More tours linked to the cruise ships	1
Open in the evenings	1
Organized craft association	1
Pipeline for fresh water	1
Zoo with parrots and peacocks	1

Table 2: 'Other' suggested improvements for the Kalinago Barana Autê.

and keep it interesting."[119] However, it was pointed out that "there is always place for improvement, but you need the financial collateral first."[120] Other respondents more generally spoke about expanding (3) or enlarging the KBA. This was often also coupled to suggestions for more employment (3). A few suggestions were made only by single individuals, for instance to include a small zoo with peacocks and parrots or to organize a craft association for all the weavers. Other such suggestions were to install a fresh water pipeline, for use by the bathers, and to create more tours that link directly to visitors disembarking from the cruise ships. One respondent suggested improving the washroom, another commented on the bridge over the river that was slippery at times. One community member felt it would be nice if the site was also open (to visitors) in the evenings. Another felt that the current management of the KBA did not have an actual business plan in place and suggested that one be implemented.

Other suggestions were voiced by multiple respondents, such as the physical accessibility of the site (15). This is a serious and well-known concern, on the one hand for community members to walk down there and on the other hand for the visitors' coaches and buses. Many solutions have been offered over the years, such as creating a scenic route over the old coastal road, starting at the Salybia church. In the words of one respondent, the KBA should change "the road down there, people don't always

---

119 Survey KBA#79 (Kalinago Territory, Dominica, 12 August 2015).
120 Survey KBA#129 (Kalinago Territory, Dominica, 15 August 2015).

find the turn. [They should] improve the old coastal road from the north end."[121] Another suggested to use "maybe this road [from Jolly John] and open up the [old] coast road."[122] Wayfinding is also an issue, so it was suggested that the KBA should have "more signs to show the way."[123] One respondent had noticed that "wheelchairs cannot go through it."[124] Besides the fact that the current access "road is too steep,"[125] they should "upgrade the trails, they can be dangerous."[126] The issue has been problematic since before the KBA was constructed.

> *The accessibility to the facility is a major concern and again it shows one of our flaws in our planning. Because when that was being conceptualized it was never ever thought that coaster size vehicles would be transporting any passengers down here. [...] The thought was that only small cars would be coming down here so there was no need to have in place a two-lane type of road. And given the sharp corners that you have... So it is a major concern. Because I know there are drivers who have expressed to me that they are not driving down here. [...] There was consideration to connect the facility with another access road going straight across to the Salybia church. [...] But for whatever reason, the road was constructed where it is right now and it is just not the best point of access to the facility. Because, as I said, you have sharp corners, steep hills and deep drains, so that's a major challenge. [...] As to any immediate plan to enhance access, this would not be a distant dream.*[127]

Second most mentioned in the category of 'other' improvements, were the marketing (14) and advertising of the KBA. A respondent noted that the KBA needs "more publicity, advertising. Let the wider world know what it's all about."[128] One of the members of staff said "perhaps, if I must say, the expectations of visitors: they think they will find Kalinago living in the village in the old ways."[129] This point resonated with other staff members at the KBA when the preliminary survey results were presented. They discussed the reasons why visitors are sometimes disappointed when their expectations do not align with the reality of their visit. Staff and management agreed to reconsider how they brand the KBA and with what visual imagery they represent themselves, for instance on their website and Facebook page. Featuring photographs of the dancers in traditional clothes in the *karbay* creates certain expectations, while photos of a tour guide in regular clothes demonstrating the sugar cane press creates others.

The need to be more authentic and less modern was expressed by a number of respondents who suggested that the KBA should have more local foods, drinks, music,

---

121 Survey KBA#146 (Kalinago Territory, Dominica, 18 August 2015).
122 Survey KBA#108 (Kalinago Territory, Dominica, 15 August 2015).
123 Survey KBA#77 (Kalinago Territory, Dominica, 12 August 2015).
124 Survey KBA#64 (Kalinago Territory, Dominica, 12 August 2015).
125 Survey KBA#56 (Kalinago Territory, Dominica, 12 August 2015).
126 Survey KBA#99 (Kalinago Territory, Dominica, 13 August 2015).
127 Interview with manager of *Kalinago Barana Autê* (Kalinago Territory, Dominica, 15 August 2015).
128 Survey KBA#11 (Kalinago Territory, Dominica, 10 August 2015).
129 Survey KBA#3 (Kalinago Territory, Dominica, 7 August 2015).

and souvenirs (10). As one respondent said, the KBA should have "more Indigenous flavor: music, food, and the guides in uniforms."[130] Another respondent agreed that "the snackette must be more traditional and not American, using our local provisions. Only natural souvenirs."[131] Someone else suggested adding "hammocks made from natural materials."[132] In general, it was felt by these respondents that the KBA "should be really how they had it in the past (not modernized)."[133] Although management is not convinced about the need to implement some of these traditional elements, such as guides in traditional clothes, they do support the idea of providing visitors with more traditional cuisine.

> *Even for some of the folks who we have operating here, they sometimes forget the image [...] that we are supposed to be portraying [...] One of the concerns that they [visitors] have, for example, is when they come, they don't get enough of the Kalinago cuisine. [...] while they like the food, the food is good, but they would have preferred if it was more traditional, something more Kalinago. And that is the reason why [...] we give them a complementary sampling of the cassava bread and a local herbal tea or local coffee or cocoa-tea. And that has been assessed very, very, very well.*[134]

Related to the feeling that the KBA should become more authentically Kalinago, a few respondents suggested adding a garden (4). One respondent explained that the KBA "needs [a] vegetable garden, [and] grow the plants for the crafts."[135] If the site would grow traditional plants, vegetables, and herbs, the KBA could provide the materials for the basketry and weaving on site as well as produce all the food and ingredients needed to cook local dishes and make local drinks in the snackette. Additionally, a few respondents felt that the KBA could offer more of a 'living experience' (3): "maybe have people living there in the traditional outfit."[136] However, not everyone agrees that this would be a good idea, as it might confuse visitors even more if the model village becomes a living village.

A few individual respondents remarked on the fact that the KBA should build a stronger bond within the Kalinago community and not just provide services to visitors. One respondent said that the KBA should be "more community oriented."[137] This suggestion was also discussed then the preliminary survey results were presented and received agreement from those present: the KBA should consider in what ways it can be of more relevance to the Kalinago community. One person present at the meeting suggested perhaps language lessons could be provided. Staff and management of the KBA are considering how they can include the Kalinago community into the mission of the KBA and create activities or programs that will support the community. In

---

130 Survey KBA#103 (Kalinago Territory, Dominica, 13 August 2015).
131 Survey KBA#80 (Kalinago Territory, Dominica, 13 August 2015).
132 Survey KBA#72 (Kalinago Territory, Dominica, 12 August 2015).
133 Survey KBA#61 (Kalinago Territory, Dominica, 12 August 2015).
134 Interview with manager of *Kalinago Barana Autê* (Kalinago Territory, Dominica, 15 August 2015).
135 Survey KBA#104 (Kalinago Territory, Dominica, 15 August 2015).
136 Survey KBA#75 (Kalinago Territory, Dominica, 12 August 2015).
137 Survey KBA#45 (Kalinago Territory, Dominica, 12 August 2015).

line with one of the most common uses of the KBA by the Kalinago community for bathing, two respondents suggested improvements relating to the access to ocean. The KBA could "make the river more suitable for bathing and [provide] easier access to the ocean, maybe with steps and railings."[138]

The need for more local management was also raised during the survey, with a handful of respondents indicating that they felt the KBA should be governed locally. One respondent felt very passionately that "the Kalinago people have got to rise and take ownership of it."[139] Another statement was clear that the KBA should have "people here more involved in running it and the government not being involved."[140] Part of this desire for self-governance of the site is the fear that the government is benefitting financially from the KBA and the efforts of the Kalinago community, thus: "[it] should be managed by the Kalinago themselves, maybe the fund [income] is going to the government."[141] This concern has been voiced by community member before and was known to the manager.

The intention was always to pass over the facility to the people. [...] The sole reason why it has not yet been done it's [...] based upon the sustainability of the facility. [...] Because it is presently under the supervision of the Ministry of Tourism slash government, periodically when we have major works to be done or when there is a significant drop in revenue during the lull, it means that the Ministry of Tourism, government, will come in to meet the financial shortfall. [...] Because actually, all the revenue that the facility generates, it stays largely in the community. The revenue is spent on maintenance. Maintenance, staff salaries, the little promotion that can be done, so these are the primary areas that we spend the money.

Interviewer: "And those people who are employed in maintenance and so on, are from the community?"

Everything. The only finance that goes out of the Territory, it's utilities. [...]

Interviewer: "So there is no overhead profit or anything that goes back to the Ministry of Tourism?"

No. Certainly not, certainly not. Actually we are very happy when we are able to meet our expenditures on the monthly basis and [...] we do not have to be calling in the government.[142]

Summary
Taking the Kalinago Barana Autê (KBA) as a case study of an ongoing Caribbean community engagement project, this chapter has attempted to provide and illustrate

138 Survey KBA#19 (Kalinago Territory, Dominica, 10 August 2015).
139 Survey KBA#144 (Kalinago Territory, Dominica, 18 August 2015).
140 Survey KBA#18 (Kalinago Territory, Dominica, 10 August 2015).
141 Survey KBA#58 (Kalinago Territory, Dominica, 12 August 2015).
142 Interview with manager of *Kalinago Barana Autê* (Kalinago Territory, Dominica, 15 August 2015).

one possible answer to the sub question: "how are community engagement process-es, including their value and outcomes, perceived by Caribbean communities?" (see *Research Questions and Objectives*, page 18). The KBA was a grassroots initiative by the Kalinago community in Dominica, planned by the community since the 1970s. It was ultimately funded, developed, and constructed by Dominica's Ministry of Tourism and opened to the public in 2006. It is currently managed and staffed by members of the Kalinago community. As a participatory practice, the KBA can be characterized as an Indigenous grassroots initiative which was governmentally developed and is currently collaboratively operated.

Firstly, how is the *process* of the KBA perceived by the Kalinago community? The answer to this must be sought in the various statements and comments made by community members regarding the management or lack of local management of the KBA. Certainly, a number of respondents consider that the KBA in its current state is not independently financially viable and thus needs to remain under the Ministry of Tourism. Some community members felt that if the KBA were to be administered by the current chief and council, this would actually be detrimental to the museum. These individuals feel that the chief and council are not taking care of other community matters and thus adding the KBA to their responsibilities would be unwise. However, other members of the Kalinago community are convinced that the KBA should be en-tirely communally owned. For them, the community engagement project of the KBA remains incomplete until it is self-governed. It is important to note that this is also the intention of the government. When the plans for the KBA were created, a set of criteria were developed to measure financial and managerial viability. Once these criteria are met by the KBA management and the Kalinago chief and council, ownership of and responsibility for the KBA will be handed over to the community. However, as was indicated also by the manager, the KBA is now still dependent on occasional financial support. Ultimately, the process of the KBA is perceived to be working well according to the majority of the respondents. However, parts of the community would welcome local ownership of the heritage site – either now or in the future when financial viabil-ity has been achieved.

Secondly, how is the *value* of the KBA perceived by the Kalinago community? Focusing on intrinsic values, the Kalinago community is overwhelmingly positive about the KBA. These intrinsic values can be separated further into direct values, the results of the use of the site by the community members themselves, and indirect val-ues, namely value for the community resulting from the use of the site by other visitors. The latter, indirect intrinsic values, can be characterized as the perceived importance of the KBA on a global scale, the prestige associated with such an attraction, and the value of creating global awareness of the existence of the Kalinago Indigenous community. Respondents frequently noted the importance of the KBA, its uniqueness, and the cultural qualities. These comments along with the perceived importance of the KBA as an attraction for visitors reveal such values.

The community attaches even greater importance to the direct intrinsic values of the KBA which are described more frequently and highly positively. Almost all members of the community habitually visit the site, revealing the importance of the KBA as a place for recreation and relaxation in an environment that is aesthetically and naturally appealing. The KBA is an important focal point of Kalinago cultural identity and helps community members to strengthen their cultural awareness and maintain an ancestral connection. For the community, the site of the KBA was already a social gathering place in the past, but this has been aided by the construction of the model buildings and the creation of new social spaces. As such, it is an important tool in the facilitation of social cohesion, as a place where community members can meet, celebrate events, and conduct business. Thus, the intrinsic values of the KBA are perceived to be highly important and are greatly appreciated by the Kalinago community, even if not always on a conscious level.

Thirdly, how are the *outcomes* of the KBA perceived by the Kalinago community? Focusing on outcomes, and thus on instrumental values, the Kalinago community is much more conflicted about the KBA. On the one hand, the community recognizes that the KBA has succeeded in becoming a community hub where social events can be celebrated and business meetings can be held. It is also widely understood that the KBA has been instrumental in preserving certain aspects of Kalinago culture and has supported cultural preservation and education. However, the community is much more conflicted and divided when it comes to outcomes such as employment and income. It is understood that the visitors attracted to the KBA create direct employment opportunities (*i.e.* the staff at the KBA) as well as encourage other sources of income to the Kalinago Territory (*e.g.* craft vendors along the main road, guest houses). Nonetheless, members of the community feel that these sources of income are not benefitting the whole community or are unfairly distributed. While some people feel that in some way everyone benefits, others speak with envy. The shortfall of this outcome is particularly painful as the original aim of the KBA (when first stated in 1976) was to generate income and employment for the Kalinago.

Looking overall at the process, intrinsic values, and instrumental outcomes, it is clear that the KBA is not a finished community engagement project. There is room for improvement and a need to continue developing the project. As of 1ˢᵗ January 2016, the overall manager of the KBA was succeeded and, in addition, a new day-to-day manager was appointed together with a new administrative assistant. Thus, some changes have already taken place regarding the management structure of the KBA. The new management will have to consider and create a mission statement for the KBA that includes aims to fulfil the needs of the community *and* its visitors. Regarding visitors, the KBA will consider how to represent and brand itself, somewhere on the spectrum from traditional to modern. Additionally, the KBA will develop a stronger community focus, for instance on cultural transmission, linguistic preservation, or cultural sustainability. Currently, with income as the main goal, it is understandable that people are disappointed if their income has not (noticeably) increased. Ultimately, the KBA will need to work to become a financially viable organization, for instance by finding ways to reduce their maintenance expenses. If they reach such organizational sustainability, the community as a whole can collectively consider whether they wish to make the change towards self-regulation of the Kalinago Barana Autê and its independence from the Ministry of Tourism, as was always the plan.

6

Case Study: Bengal To Barbados Exhibition, Barbados

The process of engagement can be as important, and sometimes more important, than the practical outcome of a heritage project.
Laurajane Smith & Emma Waterton (2009: 116)

At the beginning of a community engagement project, participants often have clear ideas about practical outcomes: such as the development of an exhibition or the organization of an event. However, as Smith & Waterton point out (above), the process itself can be of even greater importance. This is because generally throughout a community engagement process, new or unexpected outcomes can be achieved. Many of these outcomes may not be practical in the same way, but might have long term impact on participants, such as with increased social cohesion. These intrinsic values and effects of the process of engagement may be valued much more than practical outcomes by participants.

Following on the previous chapter, the aim of this chapter is also to provide a detailed analysis of a community engagement process, as it is applied in the Caribbean, through a second case study. As mentioned at the start of the preceding chapter, these two case studies are not presented as contradictory examples or dichotomies. Similarly, they do not pretend to cover the entire spectrum of community engagement projects that are taking place in the region. This case study has as its purpose to give a unique answer to the sub question: "how are community engagement processes, including their value and outcomes, perceived by Caribbean communities?" (see *Research Questions and Objectives*, page 13). Once again, this case study must be understood in its specific context: the particular communities that are involved and the specific museum and its history that are the focal point for this engagement. The community engagement project of this second case study differs from the first with regards to its aims and outcomes, as well as the length and scope of the project, and the development of the participatory process.

The focus of this chapter is the case study conducted on Barbados in the Lesser Antilles. Whereas the previous chapter was concerned with the value of a museum within a particular community, this chapter zooms in even further to focus on the collaborative process of co-curation and the roles of the participants involved. This exhibition project was the initiative of a few members of the Barbadian East Indian community who approached the *Barbados Museum & Historical Society* (BMHS) for collaboration. The main aim of the case study was to understand the heterogeneity of the East Indian community along with the participants' diverse goals for and attitudes towards the exhibition project.

The chapter will begin by briefly describing the history of the East Indian community in Barbados and their current position in Barbadian society. Afterwards, the history of the BMHS will be discussed along with its key changes and developments throughout the 20th century. The context of the case study will be expanded by discussing the origins of the co-curation project and how this relates to the New Museology. These theoretical underpinnings are used to explain the interest of the BMHS in participating in the exhibition project and to identify which aims the museum staff and East Indian community had with the project. The undertaken fieldwork will be detailed, with specific focus placed on the goals of this fieldwork period and the actual experiences in Barbados. Implications of specific fieldwork strategies, any adjustments that were made, and the fieldwork experiences will also be visible throughout the remainder of the chapter. The essence of the chapter lies in the fieldwork results, namely the perceptions of participants in relation to the value this exhibition might hold for them. These perceptions provide insight into the heterogeneous identities of the East Indian community, which underlie their differing aims with the project. Ultimately, the chapter will conclude with a discussion of some of the more recent developments of the community engagement project and consider implications for future plans for continued community involvement.

Brief History of the East Indian Community in Barbados

Ichirouganaim, known as Barbados following its Spanish/Portuguese naming, is the Easternmost island in the Lesser Antilles chain. This Arawakan name is often translated as meaning 'red island with white teeth' (the teeth symbolizing reefs), although according to recent research by a Martinican anthropologist, it could also be translated as 'the extremity to the windward,' characterizing the island's extreme position to the East (Honychurch 2016). Whereas most of the islands in the Southern Lesser Antilles are volcanic, Barbados consists entirely of non-volcanic sedimentary rocks, primarily limestone (Fitzpatrick 2011: 598). Barbados was thought to be settled by Amerindians in the Archaic Age around 2000 BC, although a single radiocarbon date may place settlement as early as 3000 BC (Fitzpatrick 2011: 601; Keegan & Hofman 2017: 200-201). While there are only a few scarce remains recovered from this first period of settlement, more complete evidence has been found from a later settlement wave of the so-called Saladoid peoples. These settlers appear to have rapidly spread throughout the Caribbean region, starting around 350 BC from Trinidad and moving towards the North (Boomert 2014: 1222). During the time of the first European voyages throughout the region, Barbados was home to Kalinago people, similar to those who were living in Dominica (see *Brief History of the Kalinago in Dominica*, page 136). They adapted their lifestyles to the particular conditions of the island(s) they lived on. In the case of Barbados, this meant that they used stacked bottomless pots to protect their wells in the dry coral limestone (Boomert 2014: 1223; Hofman & Hoogland 2015: 109). Unlike the jagged, volcanic islands in the chain,

Barbados is mostly flat creating a markedly different landscape which also encouraged different use of the land and surrounding seascapes.

Brief histories of Barbados regularly begin with the arrival and subsequent settlement of the island by the English. In these cases, any preceding Amerindian existence and European interference is simply skipped over: "[Barbados] was originally inhabited by Amerindian Arawak people. When the first English ship arrived in 1625, its crew found the island to be uninhabited" (Russell 2013: 181). Of course, more detailed histories attempt to bridge this gap. Lennox Honychurch has explained the lack of inhabitants on the island in the early 17th century as a result of the Spanish, and to a lesser extent Portuguese, incursions into the Lesser Antilles to raid and capture Amerindians to work elsewhere in the region in mining and pearl diving (Honychurch 2016; *cf.* Martin 2013). Following this line of thought, it is presumed that initially Amerindians in Barbados may have been caught off guard by European raids, leading to their enslavement and forced emigration (Fisher 2014: 103). The largely flat landscape of the island would have made it difficult for them to hide from the Europeans inland in rugged terrain, as was the strategy elsewhere in the Lesser Antilles. Thus, Amerindians may have also emigrated on their own initiative to these other islands, where they could more easily escape from European enslavement. The centrality of Dominica and St. Vincent in the Kalinago islandscape – as bases for survival *and* resistance – may have contributed to their position as strongholds for Indigenous populations (Shafie *et al.* 2017: 67). Ultimately, the fact that Barbados was uninhabited (or at least *appeared* uninhabited) was the result of European interference in the island and the region and certainly no natural situation. Of course, this did make claiming the island for the English relatively 'easy,' as they could argue that it belonged to no one. Settlement was also easier than elsewhere in the region, because they did not have to contend with or defend themselves against an Indigenous population. Instead, they could focus their attention on other European powers or on Amerindian peoples on other islands. In this historical period, Barbados was consistently under British rule until its independence in 1966. During the first few centuries of British rule, Barbados was characterized by a minority population of white Europeans (although not all of these were wealthy whites) who had placed themselves above a majority population of enslaved Africans. Complex race, class, color, and caste issues following from the plantation system have marked Barbadian society until this day (Degia 2007: 23). The perceived lack of continuity with the Amerindian population, which is also reflected in classroom education, has led to Amerindian heritage "not [being] part of the collective inheritance of the average Barbadian" (Honychurch 2016).

East Indians first entered the Caribbean region after the abolition of slavery in the British Empire and the successive abolition of the apprenticeship system in 1838. In this setting, plantation economies were struggling to attract new sources of cheap labor and sought replacement work forces from India. The first indentured laborers from India arrived in Guyana in 1838, and significant populations would be shipped to Trinidad, Guadeloupe, Jamaica, Suriname, and other Caribbean islands and countries. After the last indentured transport to the Caribbean in 1918, just over half a million[143] Indian laborers had been brought to the region under

---

143 553,316 Indians arrived in the Caribbean under British rule in 1838-1918.

British rule (Ramtahal 2013: 121). Those of Indian descent who initially entered the region through the system of indentured labor are known as Indo-Caribbeans. In Trinidad & Tobago, this Indo-Trinidadian community has been able to construct a strong collective identity based around 'mother India' as a point of cultural reference (Jayaram 2003: 127). This is remarkable, considering the linguistic, religious, caste, economic, ecological, and cultural differences of the migrants who originally hailed from different areas in India. It has been suggested that the physical isolation and ethnic stereotyping of Indians who were lowest in the island's hierarchy during the period of indenture, effectively kept them from cultural borrowing or creolization, leading to this development of a collective ethnic identity (Jayaram 2003: 124). Particularly in Trinidad & Tobago, the immigration of Indian indentured laborers has had a significant impact on the current composition of the population. In the 2011 census, of a total population of 1.3 million, East Indians constituted the biggest ethnic group at 35.4%, with Africans accounting for 34.2% (Government of the Republic of Trinidad and Tobago 2012: 2 & 15). The desire to strengthen the position of the Indo-Trinidadian community is also reflected in the creation of the *Indian Caribbean Museum of Trinidad and Tobago* in 2006 (Ramtahal 2013: 123).

Unlike Trinidad & Tobago, Barbados did not directly receive any Indian indentured laborers. Thus, the history of the East Indian community in Barbados is characterized by more recent migration, roughly over the last 100 years, of a different nature. Upon closer investigation, it is possible to determine five specific strands of migration, each characterized by the geographic location from which migrants originated, as well as their purpose for migration (see figure 28). In fact, several of the earliest migrations of Indians to Barbados could be called accidental migrations: migrants who intended to travel elsewhere, but ended up in Barbados instead.

Migrations to Barbados have consisted of a combination of both push and pull factors. Push factors for migrants to leave India included general conditions of poverty and famine, specifically for farmers, resulting from colonial land use and policies which had disrupted traditional ways of life in the 19th and early 20th century (Degia 2007). The Great Famine of 1899 was particularly disastrous and pushed many Indians to new ways of life. In the province of Gujarat, the reduction of the role of Surat as a port city played a role as well. In the case of the Hindu Sindhis, the partition of India (see more below) led many to flee from the now majority Muslim population in Pakistan. Pull factors were largely the possibilities to create a better life for migrants and their families (whether by sending money home or by bringing their families with them). Most often, pull was specifically known to migrants through local newspapers advertising the abundance of work elsewhere in the world, for instance in cutting timber in Brazil (Nakhuda 2013: 34). As mentioned, many migrants initially set out for other places (Brazil, Guyana, Trinidad, Panama) and ended up more or less accidentally in Barbados. During later periods of migration, pull factors were strengthened by the possibility to join relatives and kin already located in the Caribbean: to have these relatives arrange necessary permits and help new migrants to find work.

The first Indian migrant, from West Bengal, arrived in Barbados c. 1910 (Nakhuda 2013: 20). Bashart Ali Dewan was a Muslim who had left his wife behind in the village of Jinpoor, India, to travel to Trinidad. There, it is likely that he met other Bengalis who were working in Trinidad as itinerant traders, selling goods door-to-door.

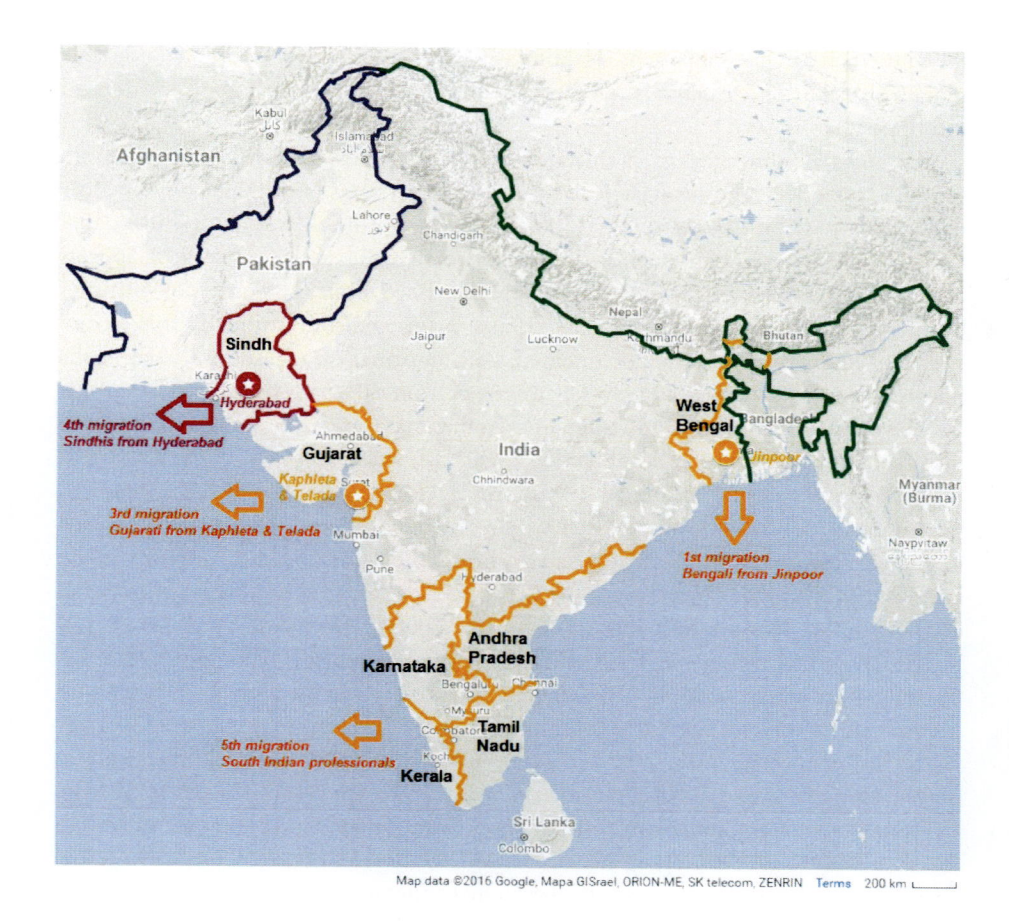

Map data ©2016 Google, Mapa GISrael, ORION-ME, SK telecom, ZENRIN   Terms   200 km

Figure 28: Map showing the areas from which Indians migrated to Barbados, corresponding to four strands of Indian migration to Barbados. First: Jinpoor, West Bengal. Third: Kaphleta & Telada, Gujarat. Fourth: Hyderabad, Sindh (today Pakistan). Fifth: Andhra Pradesh, Tamil Nadu, Kerala & Karnataka. The second strand (not pictured) was Indian migration within the Caribbean.

Travelling on to Barbados, he began working in the same fashion as an itinerant trader, later opening up a small shop. Despite having a family in India whom he supported financially, he married again in Barbados in 1920 (Nakhuda 2013: 21). His new wife and daughter moved to Calcutta, India, a few years later, where his wife passed away in 1925. He travelled to his Indian family in Jinpoor in 1926 where he stayed for a year before returning to Barbados, marrying again and having three more children (Nakhuda 2013: 23). Finally, in 1937, possibly as a result of debt, he left Barbados for good, moving back to Jinpoor and leaving behind his Barbadian family and his business. The history of Bashart Ali Dewan is fairly characteristic of the first strand of Indian migration to Barbados. This Bengali migration, which ended in 1938, was rather small and short-lived. Sabir Nakhuda has estimated that the total Bengali migration consisted of fewer than two dozen individuals (Nakhuda 2013: 28). All the Bengali migrants were Muslim men, none of their female relatives or wives travelled with them to Barbados. Many of these Bengalis married Christian women in Barbados and also raised their children as Christians (Nakhuda 2013: 30). Although the original migrants remained Muslims themselves, these Bengalis and their descendants rapidly assimilated into Barbadian society.

Around the same time, c. 1910, some Indo-Caribbeans arrived in Barbados from Guyana to work in the sugar factories (Nakhuda 2013: 67). Although there is little documentation of the movement of Indo-Caribbeans within the region, it is likely that for purposes of trade they may have travelled to Barbados earlier as well. It appears that Indo-Caribbean migration to Barbados remained limited, mostly consisting of businessmen arriving in the 1960s and 1970s, primarily from Trinidad. This second strand of migration is poorly documented, with information mainly restricted to the business ventures and lives of a few key migrants from these two decades.

The third strand of migration originated from Gujarat and, more specifically, for the most part from two villages: Kaphleta & Telada. The first handful of Gujaratis arrived in Barbados in 1929 by accidental migration (as had been the case with the Bengalis) (Hanoomansingh 1996; Nakhuda 2013: 34-35). These Gujaratis had initially travelled to Brazil, where they were told that a significant Indo-Caribbean community could be found in Guyana. Travelling on to Guyana, they learned that bringing coal and coconuts by schooner to Barbados was a lucrative trade. They made a number of trips to Barbados, where they met the small community of Bengalis who appeared to be, for Indian standards, well off. The Gujaratis decided to stay in Barbados, picking up the itinerant trade and moving in with the Bengalis. Like the Bengalis, the Gujaratis were Muslim and one of these new migrants was a Hafiz who could lead the group in prayer, strengthening their religious identity and knowledge (Nakhuda 2013: 37). The Gujaratis encouraged more migrants to travel from Gujarat to Barbados, providing entrance permits and setting up new arrivals in the itinerant trade. Gujarati migrants arrived in a number of waves, with the first female migrants arriving in 1948 (Nakhuda 2013: 38). Afterwards, Gujarati migration changed in character from being a purely male migration intent on earning money to be able to support extended families at home, to a migration intent on starting a new life in Barbados. In this later stage, Gujaratis were able to create a stronger cultural community due to the presence of women who were better at upholding various cultural traditions, for instance related to cooking (Degia 2016). Women molded cultural traditions, innovating them and combining them with Barbadian cultural elements. Although the stories of women are particularly difficult to uncover, in part because they often kept to the private sphere of the household, their passivity should not be assumed. Compared to their original roles in India, they expanded their social roles, worked alongside their husbands in trade, and were often responsible for the family's agriculture (Degia 2016).

Roughly simultaneously, a fourth strand of migration began from Sindh (current day Pakistan) in 1932. The Sindhis, in particular those from the city Hyderabad, had been setting up a global trade network since the mid-19th century (Markovits 2000: 110). This merchant network or 'trade diaspora' had its center in Hyderabad, with other branches throughout the world, mainly along maritime routes (Markovits 2000: 125). The network worked under a steady circulation of goods, money, and men. Men were sent out with temporary contracts to work at one of the branches around the world, usually for 5 years, followed by a year at home in Hyderabad with their families (Markovits 2000: 168). These Sindworkies, as the merchants were known, dealt initially in exotic items or 'curios' and silks (Markovits 2000: 120). Later, they expanded their products to more general goods, textiles, and consumer electronics (Markovits 2000: 194 & 282). The network was based strongly on kinship ties and the Sindhi were predominantly Hindu. By the early 20th century, the network had a truly global reach, with branches and shops in Asia, Africa, the Mediterranean, South America, the Caribbean, and Australia (Markovits 2000: 122-124). Within the Caribbean region, Sindworkies were located in Trinidad and Panama at least as early as 1915 (Markovits 2000: 127).

The first Sindhi to arrive in Barbados in 1932 was a businessman who had retired from a South Asian branch of the network and wanted to set up his own business (Nakhuda 2013: 50). After visiting kin with a shop in Bermuda, he decided to settle in the Caribbean, ending up in Barbados. Unlike the Gujaratis, who had been farmers in India and had picked up itinerant trade in South America and the Caribbean, Jivatram Atmaram arrived with knowledge of trade and ties to an existing network of goods, cash, and employees. He soon set up a shop and regular long-term visits from kin kept the store going until he returned to India in 1937 and fell ill (Nakhuda 2013: 52). This first enterprise opened the way to Barbados for other Sindhi. Still operating on a kinship basis for business, Sindhi migrants encouraged relatives to follow them to Barbados. Today, many of the Barbadian Sindhi can be traced to two families who were at the core of the Sindhi migration in the late 1930s: Kessaram and Thani (Nakhuda 2013: 52). After the partition of India, many Hindus from what had now become Pakistan fled from the country's Muslim majority. For the Sindhi, who had such a well-established trade network, this meant that many families fled abroad in their entirety, often beyond India, to places where Sindworkies were already established (Markovits 2000: 277). Whereas previous Sindhi migrants had all been male, with frequent visits home to their families, in 1947 the first female Sindhi migrated to Barbados (Nakhuda 2013: 56). This also led to a change in the nature of the Sindhi merchant network, from a constant circulation of men to a more sedentary state: Sindhis went from sojourners to settlers (Markovits 2000: 279 & 284). Naturally, this also led to a change in the character of the Sindhi community which now consisted of family groups and not merely male kin. As such, although the network itself may have weakened, the sense of community grew.

Finally, the fifth strand of migration originated from the states of Andhra Pradesh, Tamil Nadu, Kerala, and Karnataka in South India. Today, each of these four states has a majority Hindu population (56% in Kerala, over 80% in the other three provinces) (Office of the Registrar General India 2001). Migration from Southern India to Barbados began recently, in 1968 (Nakhuda 2013: 64). These migrants are often known as the South Indian professionals, consisting primarily of doctors, with some migrants specialized in other professions such as I.T., accounting, or banking. This final group of migrants is relatively small: according to Sabir Nakhuda's research, it consists of only about 160 individuals (Nakhuda 2013: 64). The community is predominantly Hindu and has strong ties to India, frequently returning to visit relatives and friends. They tend to teach their children the mother tongue spoken in their state of origin, along with English, rather than Hindi.

These five strands of migration have led to the existence of the East Indian community in Barbados today. Although the Indian diaspora in general has been widely researched, as has the East Indian community of nearby Trinidad, very little research has been completed on the history and current identity of this Barbadian community. So far, only three researchers have published on this subject. Peter Hanoomansingh conducted an ethnographic study of the Gujaratis and Sindhis in Barbados focusing on their commercial activities (Hanoomansingh 1996). Sociologist Haajima Degia focused her Master's thesis on the contemporary position of the Gujaratis and Sindhis as ethnic minorities in Barbados (Degia 2007). Her PhD dissertation continued on this topic, focusing on identity construction among the Gujaratis specifically (Degia 2014). She is especially interested in uncovering female oral histories to counter the dominance of male migration narratives. Most recently, Sabir Nakhuda published his book *Bengal to Barbados*[144] which includes personal histories from each migratory strand, mainly drawn from oral histories conducted in Barbados and in India/Pakistan. Both Degia and Nakhuda are members of the Gujarati community: Degia is the daughter of Gujarati emigrants, Nakhuda emigrated from Gujarat in 1957.

Today's East Indian community in Barbados is far from homogeneous. Migrants and their descendants have travelled from vastly different areas in India, from different religious, linguistic, economic, and cultural backgrounds. Thus, the five migratory strands are more or less still recognizable within the fabric of the community (of which the Bengalis are least visible as they were the smallest group and largely merged with Barbadian society or the Gujaratis). Each of these migrations was characterized by a different geographical origin, as well as different professions upon arrival in Barbados. The Bengalis & Gujaratis are predominantly Muslims who were farmers by origin, but who retrained themselves in Barbados to work as itinerant traders. The Indo-Caribbeans, arriving from elsewhere in the region, worked in Barbados following the period of indentureship mainly in factory settings, such as sugar factories, and the inter-island trade. The Sindhis are predominantly Hindu and work in and own stores, a profession they were already familiar with before arrival in Barbados. This group views themselves as businessmen. Finally, the South Indian professionals are also predominantly Hindu but work in highly educated or skilled professions such as medicine and IT. Of all of these groups, the Sindhi and the Gujarati are the biggest in number and also the most visible pillars of the East Indian community in Barbados.

It is interesting to note that these two bigger groups of migrants also held different positions within the stratified society of Barbados which was strongly based on race, color, and class. Bengalis and Gujaratis, as itinerant traders, fit into the hierarchy above the previously enslaved Africans but below the impoverished whites (Degia 2007: 49). With a higher status than the majority black population, these itinerant traders were able to receive goods on credit from white store owners who treated Indians preferentially because of their lighter color. They then sold these goods, again on credit, to rural populations and the working classes living throughout the island, often traveling many kilometers a day by foot (Nakhuda 2013: 40). This population relied on itinerant traders for goods as they often did not have the leisure time to travel to town to the stores, nor could they receive goods on credit from shopkeepers. However, buying goods on credit created debt for these individuals, who were then indebted to the

---

144 The book itself contains few in text references which makes it difficult to correlate some of its information.

traders, often owing weekly repayments. Certainly, this position in society, as well as their work relying on providing credit and collecting dues, led Gujaratis to struggle with their identity. Much of Barbadian society (their black customers), may have stereotyped the Gujaratis as cunning or shady, suspecting them of adding extra charges to their bill, charging a high markup, or collecting debt after it had been paid off. These stereotypes of East Indians are still voiced by Afro-Barbadians today (Degia 2007: 76). The Gujaratis, however, preferred to see themselves not as exploitative, but rather as heroes or saviors of the black population willing to walk long distances, willing to risk not being paid, and often lenient towards their debtors, sometimes even cancelling a debt when the situation warranted (Degia 2016). From their perspective, it was thanks to the itinerant traders that the Afro-Barbadian population was able to afford clothing and other goods which helped improve their lives.

The Sindhis, upon arrival, immediately set themselves apart from the Gujaratis: the latter were farmers peddling wares on credit as itinerant traders, the former were businessmen who owned shops and participated in an international trade network. Indeed, the Sindhi were often educated and had some knowledge of English (Markovits 2000: 138) whereas the Gujaratis often knew no English at all upon arrival (Nakhuda 2013: 39). It is on these grounds that a distinction in status was made between Gujaratis and Sindhis that is still visible in the East Indian community today. Nonetheless, similarities can, of course, also be found between these two major groups in this heterogeneous community. Primarily, both groups tie themselves to common cultural imaginations of 'mother' India, often essentializing aspects of the homeland (Degia 2007: 50). More specifically, both Sindhis and Gujaratis still frequently return to India to find marriage partners, often finding the local community too small (and consisting of too many kin) to find a suitable spouse (Degia 2007: 50-51). In many cases, these marriages are traditional marriages arranged through the parents. However, within both groups, gender imbalances have been noted, with women being less visible in public society and generally less empowered (Degia 2016; Markovits 2000: 265-276). When asked about value systems contributing to success, both East Indians and other Barbadians noted the East Indians' sense of community as a positive force (Degia 2007: 138). Thus, despite significant differences, it may still be possible to speak of an East Indian community in Barbados.

To conclude, the East Indian community of Barbados is quite heterogeneous, originating from five strands of migration of varying size, from different geographical locations, and with unique histories. Within this community, the Gujarati-Muslims and the Sindhi-Hindus form the two major pillars. In the 2010 census of Barbados, out of a total population of 226,193, 3018 individuals (or 1.3%) self-identified as being of East Indian ethnic origin (Barbados Statistical Service 2013: 51). In the same census, 1055 Hindus and 1605 Muslims were noted (Barbados Statistical Service 2013: 59). Certainly, the size of the East Indian community may be larger if it includes individuals who marked their ethnic origin as 'mixed' or another category. Issues of identity are often sensitive and, in census enumeration, they frequently lead to problems related to the phrasing of the questions as well as the response (Christopher 2013: 327). The intricacies of the identities of the members of the East Indian community will be discussed below in the presentation of the results of this case study (see *Perceiving the Bengal to Barbados Project*, page 161). Despite being a small minority in Barbados, the East Indian community has (or is perceived to have) considerable influence as well as (disproportionate) wealth (Degia 2007: 28). Although this leads to friction at times, it also provides the community with significant standing in Barbadian society. Ultimately, with their unique yet recognizable history of migration, the East Indian community shares a Caribbean identity founded on a "culture of migration" (Hope, quoted in Premdas 2002: 57).

The Barbados Museum & Historical Society

A history of the *Barbados Museum & Historical Society* (BMHS) cannot be separated from its colonial context and its roots in the early collections, Great Exhibitions, and museums which were created in the Caribbean as extensions of empire during the 19th and 20th centuries (Cummins 2013; see *Museum History*, page 13). Alissandra Cummins has extensively researched and written about the history of museums in the English-speaking Caribbean, charting their development in line with historical, political, scientific, and theoretical shifts (Cummins 1992; 1994; 2004; 2012; 2013). Within this framework, she has also specifically investigated the history of the BMHS (Cummins 1998), of which she is currently the director. Thus, this section draws significantly on her research, as well as the publications of others who have been professionally related to the BMHS: current deputy director Kevin Farmer (2013) and previous director David Devenish (1985).

As mentioned above, the development of the BMHS in the 20th century had its roots in earlier centuries and the Enlightenment-model of museums which was applied by the British Empire throughout its colonies (Cummins 2013: 11). These early museums had a number of purposes. Primarily, the predominantly natural history collections were intended to serve commercializing and advertising purposes. Highlighting the natural assets of each colony, these collections were meant to attract investors or to encourage emigration to these areas (Cummins 2013: 15). Thus, many early Caribbean institutions were built around the geological or natural history collections accumulated through systematic surveys of the islands. Similar natural history collections were amassed by agricultural societies and other upper class groups with the aim to contribute to the multitude of Great Exhibitions occurring during the 19th century (Cummins 2013: 18). Again, these collections had the aim to show off the industry of the colony, as well as its products, to the wider Empire and world. In addition to commerce, these early museum institutions also had a 'civilizing' purpose, aimed to educate the 'lower classes' (Bennett 1995; Cummins 2013: 14). As such, they were supposed to be instruments of social salvation, providing (black) working classes with a moral and intellectual culture, all within the system of colonization (Cummins 2013: 33).

It is in this setting that plans were first voiced for the creation of a museum (and library) in Barbados. Lt. Col. Reid, appointed Governor of Bermuda in 1839, created the legislation for the establishment of a public library and a museum (Cummins 2013: 12). The commercializing purpose was dominant in his endeavors: these institutions were deemed necessary to identify, categorize, and promote colonial products and thus to improve the condition of Bermuda's agriculture. Within a few years, he had successfully established libraries with museum collections in Bermuda, the Bahamas, and St. Lucia (Cummins 1998: 2). Reid, who was consecutively appointed

Governor of Barbados and the Windward Islands in 1846, continued to expand this idea and initiated similar bills for the creation of such institutions in Barbados, as well as Grenada and St. Vincent (Cummins 2013: 14). Despite these plans, such a museum was not opened in Barbados. A public library was established only much later, in 1904, and without a museum collection (Cummins 1998: 2).

New plans for a museum were developed in 1910, when a colonial report suggested the acquisition of the former residence of the Governors of Barbados to be used as a museum (Cummins 1998: 2). Although this initiative, again, did not lead to the creation of a public museum, it was noted at the time that several Amerindian collections[145] existed on the island. It is one of these private collections, Rev. N.B. Watson's collection of natural history, that became the seed for the creation of the BMHS (Cummins 1998: 5). In 1926, the Civic Circle of Barbados, a society ladies' organization, became the custodians of this collection and began to raise funds for its acquisition and for a grant to house the collection. Fundraising ran into problems and negotiations stopped, until in 1933 two Carnegie Trust museum commissioners visited Barbados while conducting a survey of Caribbean museums (Bather & Sheppard 1934; Cummins 1998: 6). These commissioners strongly supported the creation of a museum in Barbados based on the Watson collection and in the same year the BMHS was incorporated by an act of legislation and a first exhibition was opened in Queen's Park House. By the next year, government agreed to give the BMHS a long term leasehold of the old military prison at St. Ann's Garrison (Cummins 1998: 7). In this building, the museum was able to finally open to the public in May 1934 (see figure 29).

For the first decades of its existence, the BMHS was frequently debated in terms of its accessibility and representativeness, primarily with the government. As an institution mainly envisaged and run by upper class individuals, it tended to reflect a vision of Empire, rather than represent the emergent West Indian societies which had gained power and a sense of identity since WWI (Cummins 2004: 234; Cummins 2013: 38). The BMHS was deemed Eurocentric, and members of government, such as Sir Grantley Adams, voiced their concerns about the "exclusivity of the Society" and proposed that the museum should be run by government (Cummins 1998: 8-9). It was stated that governmental ownership was necessary in order to have the public in its entirety benefit from the museum, rather than it remain the recreation of a select few (Cummins 1998: 10). Naturally, an underlying sentiment was the understanding that those who owned the museum would have "the power to define cultural and community identities within it" (Cummins 1998: 10).

The conflict about the accessibility/exclusivity of the BMHS continued. The museum attempted to demonstrate its accessibility by providing free entry to school children and tours for school groups, ultimately adding a Children's Museum in 1945 (Cummins 1998: 17). However, its collections (as well as its buildings) remained Eurocentric in focus (Cummins 1998: 11). This focus could be seen on a wider scale throughout the region, when in the 1950s, as a response to the tourist industry, a heritage industry developed focused on the preservation of (European) historical sites (Cummins 1992: 41). National Trusts were formed in the region, with one set up in

---

145 In 1914, archaeologist Jesse Fewkes reported a cabinet of curiosities at Codrington College, Dr. John Hutson's collection, and Mr. Evan K. Taylor's collection (Cummins 1998: 2).

Figure 29: Entrance of the Barbados Museum & Historical Society, Barbados.

Barbados in 1960 (Cummins 1992: 41). Failing to fight the allegations of social exclusivity, the BMHS collections around this time contained only a few brief references to the majority black population (Cummins 2013: 39). The collections did not reflect the significant "black renaissance of political awareness and socioeconomic consolidation" (Cummins 1998: 14) which had been developing in the region and culminated in the independence of Barbados in 1966.

Independence forced the BMHS to, once again, confront the issue of relevance for this new society and to consider their role in the creation of a national identity in the 1970s and 1980s (Cummins 1992: 47; Cummins 1998: 24). On a governmental level, it had become clear that national identity creation went beyond designing a flag and writing a nation anthem: it "became a core mandate of cultural institutions" (Farmer 2013: 170). Initially, identity creation was by no means intended to be inclusive, but rather relied on the rejection of anything European. Slowly, museums sought to be more accessible to all. Museums were aided by a new generation of Caribbean historians who had stepped away from a perspective of Empire and adopted post-colonial and gendered theories (Farmer 2013: 172). These historians gave voices to the majority population; museums, including the BMHS, were able to expand upon their narratives and be more inclusive. As Kevin Farmer has noted, "Caribbean nationalism, as constructed in the post-independence era, sought to combat the issue of colonial self as inferior, replacing it with a notion of self as superior" (Farmer 2013: 174).

In the case of the BMHS, these new histories and the drive to national identity creation, along with concerns that the museum was not representative of Barbadian life as a whole, led to the establishment of a Museum Development Plan Committee in

THE SOCIAL MUSEUM IN THE CARIBBEAN

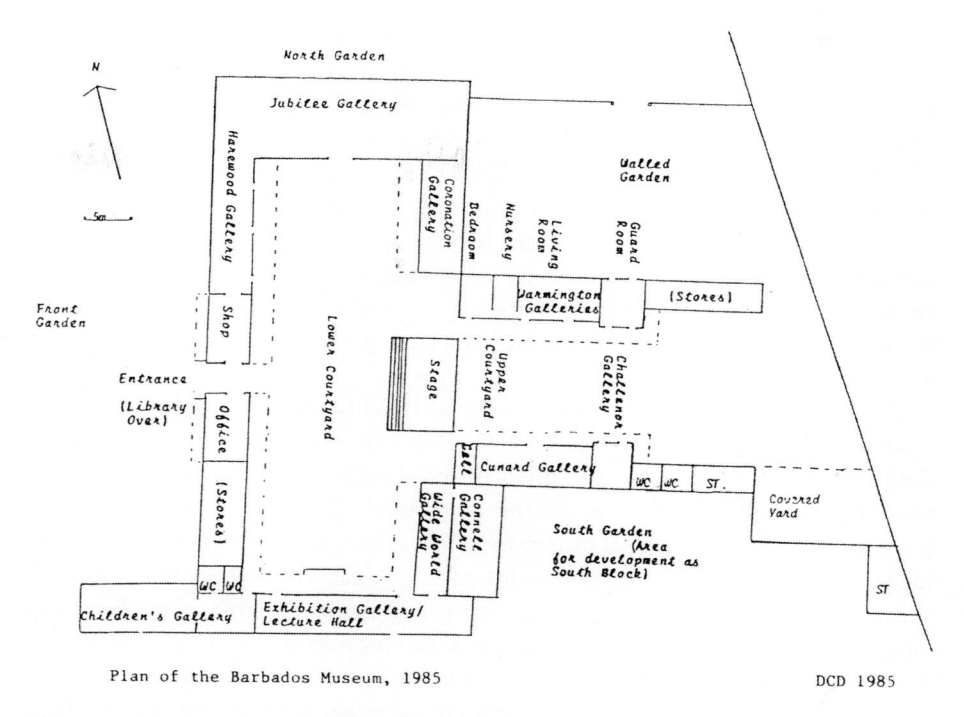

Plan of the Barbados Museum, 1985

DCD 1985

Figure 30: Plan of the Barbados Museum, 1985.

1980 (Cummins 1998: 27). At this time, the BMHS mission was "to collect, preserve, and publish matter relating to the history and antiquities of Barbados, to gather and preserve appropriate articles for collections, and to promote a knowledge of Barbadian history, culture and related matters" (Whiting 1983: 33). Thus, the proposal for development, submitted by the Committee in 1982, was focused on inclusivity and to make the museum more reflective of Barbadian culture. This plan was implemented from 1983-1984, with the appointment of several new staff members, the extensive renovation of the buildings, the construction of new service blocks, and the redesign of some exhibitions (Devenish 1985: 66; see figure 30). The current mission statement was adopted in 1990: "The Barbados Museum is a non-profit institution. Its mandate is to collect, document and conserve evidence of Barbados' cultural, historical and environmental heritage and to interpret and present this evidence *for all sectors of society*" (my emphasis, Cummins 1998: 27). The Children's Gallery was renewed in 1992 (Cummins 1998: 28) and the latest permanent exhibition, called *Africa: Connections and Continuities,* opened in 2005 to emphasize the history of the Afro-Barbadian population (Russell 2013: 182). With each of these developments, the museum has attempted to open itself up towards the wider Barbadian society and to demonstrate its relevance. Yet, Kevin Farmer has warned that the creation of Caribbean national identities, as centered upon an image of the region as consisting primarily of descendants of Africa, has marginalized other ethnic groups (Farmer 2013: 173). To alleviate this marginalization, in the case of the BMHS, social inclusivity has been most visible in the temporary exhibitions "co-created with special interest groups within the community" (Cummins 1998: 29-30) that have been successfully developed since the mid-1980s.

The Bengal to Barbados Exhibition Project

The *Bengal to Barbados*[146] exhibition project was initiated by members of the East Indian community. Their motivations to approach the BMHS with this idea for an exhibition, along with an identification of their desired outcomes for the project, will be explained in more detail below. The willingness of the BMHS to collaborate should be seen within the context of the museum's dedication to temporary co-curated exhibitions since the 1980s. In turn, the BMHS' approach to the exhibition project fits within their own particular history and development, as well as reflects more global museological trends. From the point of view of the staff of the BMHS, it is possible to identify three main goals for participation in co-curation: social inclusivity, multi-vocal national identity, and reflexivity.

As was shown in the previous section, the BMHS historically struggled to demonstrate its relevance for the wider Barbadian society. Writing in 1998, Alissandra Cummins reflected that "the perception of social exclusivity is a stigma which the Museum has fought hard to erase for over fifty years" (Cummins 1998: 11). Thus, it is not difficult to identify social inclusivity as a key motivation for the BMHS staff to engage in co-curation projects such as this one. After decades of accusations of exclusivity, the museum strongly emphasizes that it is accessible (physically, intellectually, culturally) to 'all sectors of society' and that it also presents the heritages of Barbados as a whole. Collaborating with multiple communities throughout Barbados, whether for temporary exhibitions, programs, events, or activities, has been the way in which the BMHS works towards social inclusivity. This approach helps on the one hand to include diverse communities' heritages in the museum and, on the other hand, to reach out to these communities and make the museum accessible to them. The benefits and necessity of social inclusion have been noted within the wider museological field (see *New Museology*, page 24). Carol Scott has argued that relevance and social inclusivity are essential for museums that wish to be sustainable in the long term (Scott 2015: 105). Graham Black noted that relevance and social inclusion are particularly important to reach out to marginalized communities, in particular people who do not visit museums (Black 2015: 136). Certainly, sustainability and widening the audience base of the museum are also reasons for the BMHS to focus on social inclusivity through this exhibition project. In the words of Nina Simon, the aim is "to matter more to more people" (Simon 2016: 21).

Issues of identity, sense of belonging, and community cohesion are particularly relevant in today's world of global human mobility and migration (Black 2015: 126). In the Caribbean, which is characterized by plural societies and diverse, heterogeneous communities, these issues may be even more pressing. National identity has to be constructed multi-vocally. As Rex Nettleford argued, "diversity is one of humanity's greatest strengths" (Nettleford 2008: 4) and museums should especially help to promote "mutual respect and understanding between peoples of differing race, class and creeds within nations" (Nettleford 2008: 17). How, then, can a national identity be

---

146 At the time of this case study, the exhibition project did not formally have a title. The Exhibition Planning Committee suggested that I could use the title of Nakhuda's book 'Bengal to Barbados' as a working title for the exhibition project.

constructed out of such diversity? According to Alissandra Cummins, the answer lies in shared experience rather than any shared tangible culture:

> *The heritage of the Caribbean is not so much valued therefore for the tangible remains and artefacts which litter the galleries, corridors and basements of so many European museums, but rather is a shared, lived, defining (intangible) experience of Indigenous extirpation, slavery, migration, indenture, plantations and colonial control stretching over a period of some 500 years. It is this shared human heritage of our historical experience which [...] defines who we are as a people.*
> Alissandra Cummins (2012: 26)

National museums and heritage institutions are key players in creating national histories and, thus, in validating nationally-constructed identities (Cummins 2004: 227). In the case of the BMHS, as can also be seen in its current mission statement, the exhibitions are intended to (re-)present Barbados as a plural society (Cummins 1992: 51). Kevin Farmer has urged Caribbean museums to echo the diverse voices of the people they represent without any bias or favor (Farmer 2013: 176-177). In order for museums to be truly multi-vocal, curators need to adopt participant action: not merely speaking in the voices of others but inviting those others in to speak for themselves (Arnold 2015: 330). Thus, the BMHS' participation in this co-curated exhibition is also clearly motivated by their desire for the East Indian community to represent themselves as an element of Barbados' plural society, to promote mutual understanding, and to highlight the shared experience of migration.

Finally, the BMHS' motivations for participation in the project can also be understood as a desire for greater reflexivity. As part of the school of thought of the New Museology, reflexivity is an important element. Museum staff are encouraged on the one hand to critical self-reflection of their actions and their museum, and, on the other hand, to make museums more democratic by inviting external participation (Butler 2015: 177). As part of the latter, co-curation is seen as one of the most effective, if intensive, processes. Ideally, throughout this process, the community becomes part of the museum, as the museum becomes part of the community (Phillips 2003: 161).

The motivations for the members of the East Indian community can also be identified in their history, as well as in their current position in Barbadian society. The starting point for the exhibition project was the publication of Sabir Nakhuda's book *Bengal to Barbados* (Nakhuda 2013) and its positive reception in the East Indian community in Barbados and in the wider Indian diaspora. Nakhuda, together with his friend Suleiman Bulbulia of the Barbados Muslim Association, approached the BMHS in 2015 to make an exhibition on the same topic. The BMHS staff, Nakhuda, and Bulbulia agreed to work on this exhibition based on the research done for the book.[147] Farmer, as deputy director of the BMHS, was the museum's main contact person and organized two initial meetings with a number of community leaders. Early on, he expressed his concern with the representativity of Nakhuda and Bulbulia (both Gujarati-Muslim men) for the East Indian

---

147 Meeting with deputy director of *Barbados Museum & History Society* (via Skype, 7 February 2016).

community as a whole. Thus, he approached Haajima Degia (who has researched the female Gujarati community) as well as Sindhi community leaders to be part of the Exhibition Planning Committee. The initial timeline was to open the exhibition in 2016, marking Barbados' 50th anniversary of independence which the BMHS was honoring with a series of exhibitions and events. Ideas were developed to accompany the exhibition with events tied to different religious feasts such as Eid, Diwali, and Holi. Although possibly unknown to the East Indian community members prior to approaching the BMHS, the museum does have some Indian objects in its collections (Devenish 1985: 65).

The BMHS intended co-curation to be highly participatory, inclusive, multi-vocal, and reflexive. Their view was that "we facilitate, it is driven by them" and that the project would be a test for the museum to see "how open we can be."[148] Regarding the inclusivity of the project, the deputy director was concerned that not all committee members were consistent in attending the planning meetings and he also noted that women did not always speak. The meeting time, which fell on Mondays just after lunch, was frequently reconsidered to see whether more community members would attend otherwise and thus improve the multi-vocality of the process. To assist with the reflexivity of the project, the BMHS had invited me to be part of the project and to "lend your experience in ensuring that it is a community driven exhibition."[149] This idea of the community engagement process aligns with Nina Simon's 'hosted' participatory model in which power lies largely with the community and the museum is minimally involved as support (Simon 2010: 190-191).

The East Indian community, most frequently represented at the planning committee meetings by Nakhuda and Bulbulia, had somewhat different intentions for the project. They preferred a more moderately participatory role, placing more decision-making power with the museum staff. Their ideas were more in line with Simon's 'contributory' participation model in which community members create and submit content, while the project as a whole is managed by the museum (Simon 2010: 190-191). As an example, regarding the panel texts, Farmer suggested that BMHS staff could write an essay text based on Nakhuda's book, which Farmer would then turn into panel texts for the community members to edit and revise. Bulbulia responded that "this is good, since we are unfamiliar with this sort of text, so we can edit and revise."[150] Just as Farmer had, they also expressed concerns with the absence of representatives from other parts of the East Indian community and suggested including additional individuals who might be able to attend the set meeting time. Not particularly concerned with reflexivity, they instead focused on concrete practical tasks: *e.g.* the collection of objects from the community, the identification of exhibition themes, and communication with potential sponsors. A more detailed analysis of the perceptions of the East Indian community in relation to the exhibition project and its outcomes is presented further on in this chapter.

---

148 Meeting with deputy director of *Barbados Museum & History Society* (via Skype, 7 February 2016).
149 Meeting with deputy director of *Barbados Museum & History Society* (via Skype, 7 February 2016).
150 Meeting with Exhibition Planning Committee (Bridgetown, Barbados, 29 February 2016).

Fieldwork: Aims and Experiences

The Barbados Museum & Historical Society was first visited in October 2015, as part of a conference in Barbados. It was during this visit that contact was established with a number of staff members of the BMHS, including the director, deputy director, and curator. As part of the conference, I had held a presentation on the regional museum survey and the case study conducted in Dominica, and showed conference delegates the Caribbean Museums Database. Following this presentation, the deputy director approached me to suggest a number of upcoming BMHS projects that might be suitable as a second case study. In particular, he mentioned that the museum had recently been approached by members of the East Indian community for a co-curation project. Based on the parameters identified for the case studies, this project was ultimately selected (see *Case Studies*, page 58). It would be able to showcase a community engagement process between a national museum and a minority community based on their grassroots initiative and the dynamics of this collaboration would be very different than those of the previous case study in Dominica. The fact that the project was just beginning provided a unique perspective as well. By including such a relatively recent migrant community, additional insights into the diversity of Caribbean communities could be made.

After a number of initial exchanges and online meetings, fieldwork took place on Barbados from February 25th – March 23rd 2016. In the course of this fieldwork, I lived relatively close to the museum, but not in a neighborhood that was particularly associated with the East Indian community. As participant observer, I worked in the offices of the BMHS during this time and took part in a number of museum and community events, as well as joining the Exhibition Planning Committee meetings. For reasons related to access, observations were more often related to the BMHS and museum staff, than to the East Indian community. As such, my contextual perception of the museum staff as participants in the project was more developed than my insights into the East Indian community.

As with the other case study, participatory observation was employed through participatory rapid assessment by preparing clearly defined research questions and a limited amount of variables before entering the field (Bernard 2006: 353). The nature of the case study, focused as it was on a short-term project of a temporary exhibition, was suitable in this respect. Similar to the other case study as well, I prepared a survey to conduct as self-administered questionnaires containing a total of ten questions which can be found in the appendix (see *Questionnaire: Bengal to Barbados*, page 264). These questions were adjusted at the start of the fieldwork period together with the East Indian members of the Exhibition Planning Committee. To exemplify, I had listed many possible categories of response to the question regarding the respondent's identity which they then narrowed down to include only the categories they considered relevant. In the end, the survey contained a mix of open-ended questions, closed-ended questions (with multiple choice options), and 5-point scales (Bernard 2006: 269 & 273). In total, the survey was completed by 51 respondents: 7 of whom were BMHS museum staff and the remainder members of the East Indian community.

Initially, I planned for a similar fieldwork approach as in Dominica, namely a mix of visiting community gathering places and the street-intercept method. However, it became clear in meeting with the Exhibition Planning Committee that such an approach would not be sufficiently valuable. Primarily, it would not be very useful, as it turned out that the community in general was largely unaware of the exhibition project, whereas the questions were geared towards individuals with a basic awareness of the existence of the project. Secondly, street-intercept surveying was not as straightforward in Barbados as the East Indian community lives spread out over multiple parishes. On the recommendations of the East Indian members of the Exhibition Planning Committee, it was decided to adjust the survey strategy.[151] Copies of the survey were given to three members of the Exhibition Planning Committee who offered to operate as community gatekeepers and survey administrators: Suleiman Bulbulia, Haajima Degia & Sabir Nakhuda. These gatekeepers offered to hand the survey to relatives, friends, students, and attendants at community events whom they were in contact with. They were also asked to make an effort to reach out to other parts of the East Indian community, rather than only their Gujarati group. Gatekeepers were instructed to tell respondents briefly about the exhibition project, if the respondent did not yet know about it, and to assure respondents to fill out the survey as best they could and to skip any questions they could not answer. They were not given instructions to focus on obtaining an age or gender balance, but rather to prioritize persons who knew of the project and/or were from other parts of the community. I approached members of the museum staff directly to fill out the survey. Thus all surveys were completed as self-administered surveys and the majority of these were handed out, supervised, and collected by the three community gatekeepers. In analyzing the survey results, it is possible to identify the perspectives of the respective community gatekeepers as a bias in the responses of their respondents. This is discussed in more detail later (see *Representativity*, page 173).

In addition to the survey, information was gathered from participant observation. Working from within the museum, it was possible to observe the museum staff and to attend meetings of the Exhibition Planning Committee, as well as engage with staff in project discussions. I also attended several public events organized by the museum, such as the *Barbados Museum and Historical Society Lecture Series 'Becoming Bajan'* and the *Heritage Treasures 5K Walk & Run*. In addition, I visited a public lecture held at the University of the West Indies by Haajima Degia (2016) about her research into the ethnic identity of the Barbadian Gujaratis. These events provided greater contextual understanding of both participating communities.

The overall aim of this case study was to understand the perceptions of the East Indian community and the BMHS museum staff in relation to this co-curation project. Firstly, I was interested in charting the communities' awareness of the exhibition project and their involvement in it. Did people know about the exhibition project? Were they able to voice their project ideas or was the project perceived as exclusionary? Secondly, did participants have clearly defined participatory roles? Did museum staff and members of the East Indian community agree in their expectations of what the other party would contribute to the project? Thirdly, to investigate what project aims these participants had. Did different community members have different expectations of the project's aims and its outcomes? Could such differences lead to conflict or friction? Finally, I focused on the identities of the participants, also to assess their

---

151 Meeting with Exhibition Planning Committee (Bridgetown, Barbados, 29 February 2016).

representativity. At the outset, I had hypothesized that a possibly unequal balance of power between the East Indian community and the BMHS could be a main point of conflict. However, as discussed below, problems seemed to be more often related to the heterogeneity of the East Indian community.

Perceiving the Bengal to Barbados Project

This following section will present and discuss the results of the surveys conducted among staff of the BMHS and members of the East Indian community in relation to the *Bengal to Barbados* exhibition project. The categorized and collated survey results can be found in the appendix (see *Questionnaire Results: Bengal to Barbados*, page 264). In total, the survey was completed by 51 respondents, 7 of whom were BMHS museum staff plus 44 members of the East Indian community. As such, results are clearly marked whether they apply to all respondents ('*total*'), to BMHS museum staff only ('*BMHS*') or only to members of the East Indian community ('*EIC*'). Along with the survey responses, this analysis and interpretation of the case study data also draws on contextual information obtained through participant observation. The section begins by presenting the demographics of the survey respondents, afterwards focusing on the heterogeneous identities of the members of the East Indian community. The identities of the East Indian community members are essential to keep in mind for all the following interpretations of results: such as, the awareness of and involvement in the project, the importance and benefits of the project, positive and negative associations with the project, representativity, and the planned outcomes.

Preliminary results were presented for feedback and discussion at a meeting of the Exhibition Planning Committee, held at the BMHS, on 21 March 2016. These initial results were paired with suggestions for the continuation of the exhibition project. Many of these suggestions had already been considered by the committee, but could now be connected to practical approaches and solutions. The committee was happy to hear that community members were positive about the project and agreed to focus their initial energies on expanding their reach and being more inclusive.

Survey Demographics

Respondents were not evenly balanced by gender or by age, due in part to the survey methodology and partially to the nature of the communities surveyed. To exemplify the latter, the BMHS has a majority of female staff, which was reflected – if in a more uneven ratio – in the gender balance of the BMHS survey respondents (6:1). As an example of the former, the community gatekeepers had not been instructed to focus on a gender or age balance in administering the survey, but rather to try to reach out to community members from the five different migration strands and thus from different sub-communities. Although the gatekeepers were all Gujarati, two of them attended Sindhi community gatherings specifically for the survey. Besides this, the gatekeepers handed out the survey to their own students, relatives, and friends who were (nominally) aware of the exhibition project. Thus, they prioritized surveying respondents with some prior knowledge of the project and/or who identified with diverse migration strands. Consequently, the results are not statistically reflective of the

Barbadian East Indian community as a whole.[152] It is also not possible to know whether the gatekeepers consciously or subconsciously focused on gender or age balances in distributing the survey, or whether they were biased towards respondents of certain age groups or genders in collecting survey responses.

The total results show a modest gender imbalance, with more female respondents (59%) than males (see figure 31). As mentioned above, the gender imbalance was particularly pronounced with the BMHS respondents, due to the composition of the staff and ability to participate in the survey. However, the results are more balanced in relation to gender division among the East Indian community respondents, and are therefore able to more evenly reflect any gendered perceptions.

An imbalance can also be seen in the age distribution of survey respondents (see figure 32). Overall, roughly half of the respondents were aged 15-24 or 25-34 (each age group corresponding to 25.5% of the total), with the other age groups being less represented. In order to see differences between 'younger' and 'older' respondents, it was possible to divide them almost equally into two groups with half aged under 35 (n=27) and the other half aged 35 and up (n=24). With the exception of one young family member, children under the age of 15 were not included by the community gatekeepers in the survey. Naturally this age group was not at all represented among BMHS staff; they are all of working age. The relatively small sample size of BMHS staff does not significantly impact the EIC age distribution in relation to the total age distribution.

Community Identities

It became apparent that the heterogeneous composition of the East Indian community, especially along religious lines, had significant impact on the survey responses and on perceptions of the exhibition project. Despite five strands of migration, the current East Indian community in Barbados has two major pillars: the Gujaratis and the Sindhis. The Bengalis historically assimilated with the Gujaratis or mainstream Barbadian society, the Indo-Caribbeans are poorly documented but may have similarly merged, and the South Indian professionals remain primarily aligned with Hindu communities in India and secondarily with the Sindhis because they are often only temporarily in Barbados. Thus, it is possible to tentatively and roughly identify members of these two pillars by their religious identity: Hindus are mainly Sindhi-Hindus and Muslims are mainly Gujarati-Muslims. The respondents from these two religious groups had markedly different perceptions of the exhibition project. This section only focuses on the EIC responses (n=44).

The question related to identity asked: "which communities do you consider yourself a part of?" Respondents could provide multiple answers in three geographic-cultural categories (Barbadian, Caribbean, East Indian), three religious categories (Christian, Hindu, Muslim), indicate that they considered themselves part of 'none' of these, or add 'other' options. As mentioned earlier, these categories had been determined together with the East Indian members of the Exhibition Planning Committee. A few immediate observations can be made regarding the responses (see figure 33). First

---

152 In the 2010 census, 3018 individuals self-identified as East Indian, 1055 as Hindu and 1605 as Muslim (Barbados Statistical Service 2013: 51 & 59). The 44 EIC respondents represent 1.5% of the total community, or 1.7% (n=18) of Hindus and 1.5% (n=24) of Muslims.

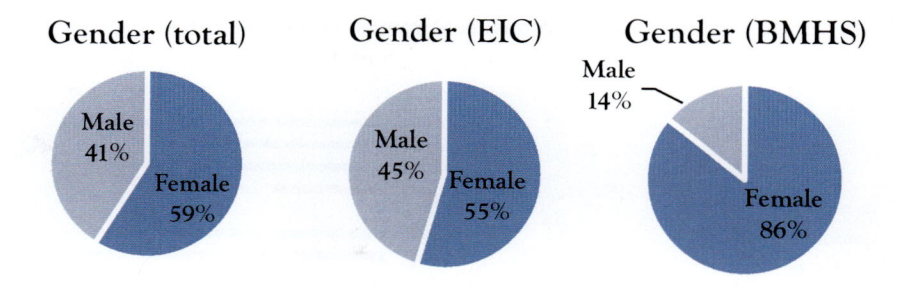

Figure 31: Gender distributions of survey respondents in Barbados: total numbers, only East Indian community members, and only BMHS staff.

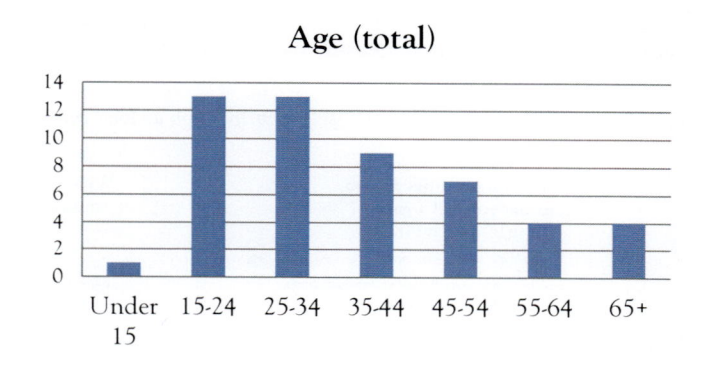

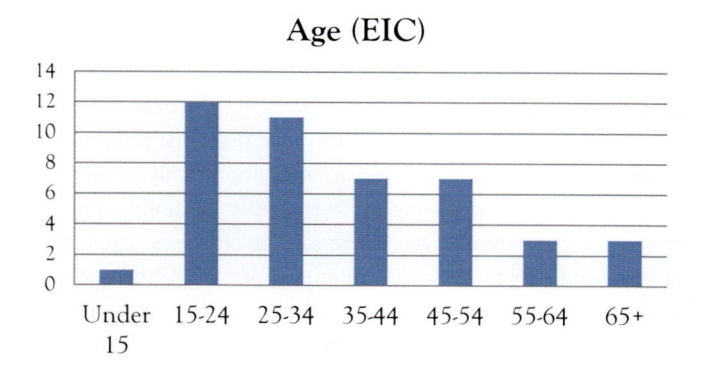

Figure 32: Age distributions of survey respondents in Barbados: total numbers, only East Indian community members, and only BMHS staff.

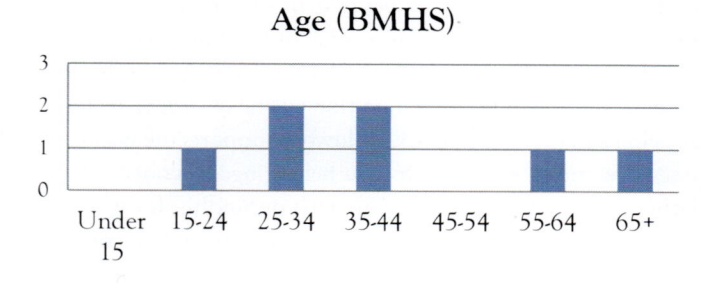

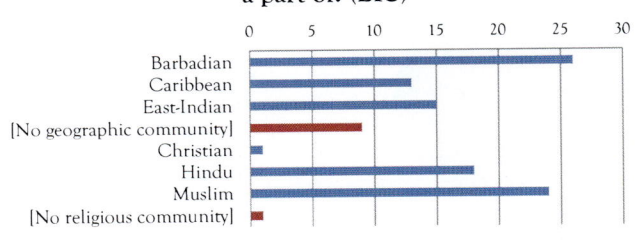

Which communities do you consider yourself a part of? (EIC)

Figure 33: East Indian respondents' self-identification with given communities.

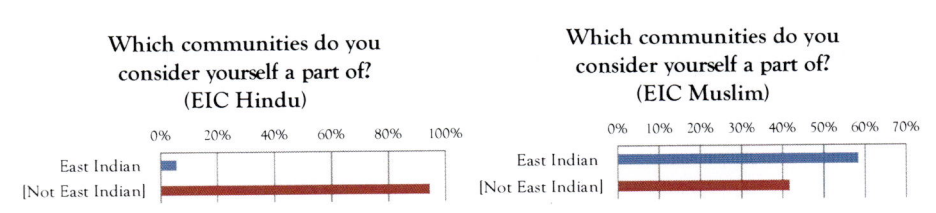

Which communities do you consider yourself a part of? (EIC Hindu)

Which communities do you consider yourself a part of? (EIC Muslim)

Figure 34: East Indian respondents' self-identification as East Indian, divided by religion.

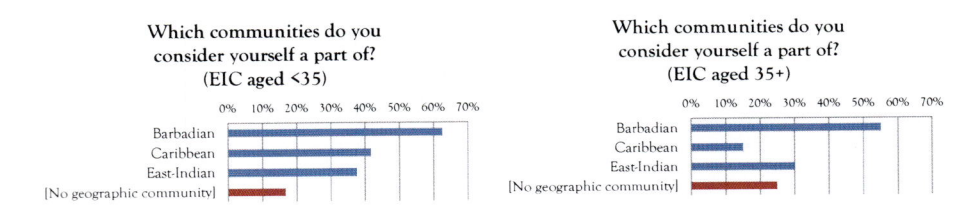

Which communities do you consider yourself a part of? (EIC aged <35)

Which communities do you consider yourself a part of? (EIC aged 35+)

Figure 35: East Indian respondents' self-identification with geographic communities, divided by age.

of all, not unexpectedly, religious identity is an exclusive category, meaning that no respondent indicated to belong to more than one religious community. On the other hand, geographic-cultural identity was not perceived to be exclusive and respondents frequently indicated belonging to multiple categories resulting in a higher amount of responses (54 responses by 35 respondents for these categories). Secondly, respondents were more likely to indicate a religious identity. Only one respondent did not indicate a religious community, whereas 9 did not select a geographic community.

Following these two immediate observations, of obvious interest is the fact that although these respondents had been identified as fellow community members by the gatekeepers, for instance by being their own family members or by attending a community gathering or religious service, only a minority of respondents self-identified as East Indian (34%). One possible interpretation is that this low level of response has to do with the phrasing of the question as one of '*belonging* to a community' rather than as being a matter of ethnicity. Fieldwork supports the notion that this community does not have strong ties of collective belonging. In conversations, community members rather speak of themselves as Gujaratis or Sindhis, for instance, than as East Indians.

This lack of perceived belonging to the East Indian community is furthermore pronounced along two divisions: religion and age. Regarding religion, specifically Hindu respondents indicated a near total lack of belonging to the East Indian community (see figure 34). Muslim respondents were more divided, with a majority selecting a belonging to the East Indian community. This difference was also supported by further observations, in which Gujarati-Muslims more often spoke as representing the East Indian community, while this was not the case for Sindhi-Hindus. Although both of these pillars may ethnically identify as being East Indian (which seems to be supported by the Barbados census data), the former group has more deliberately constructed a sense of belonging in the form of an East Indian community. In fact, the exhibition project as a whole, aiming to present the history of the East Indian community collectively, was initiated by Gujarati-Muslims and they were, during this case study fieldwork, also more frequently present at Exhibition Planning Committee meetings. Bias due to the community belonging of the gatekeepers who administered the survey might have impacted results as well.

Regarding the division of identity along age lines, it was hypothesized by Degia,[153] based on observations from her own research, that younger East Indians more strongly self-identify as Barbadian and less often as East Indian. She suggested that this might be due to the fact that they will more often have been born and raised in Barbados and thus have weaker ties to India. With these survey respondents, this hypothesis did not hold true (see figure 35). In fact, while the respondents aged under 35 did more frequently self-identify as Barbadian, they also more often self-identified as East Indian. Especially pronounced is this group's sense of Caribbean identity. The older respondents, aged 35 and over, less frequently indicated a sense of belonging to Barbadian, Caribbean, or East Indian communities. On the whole, this older group was more likely not to select any geographic community at all. In conclusion, it can be tentatively interpreted that the younger members of the East Indian community have stronger, and more often plural, geographic-cultural identities.

To summarize, the discrepancy between the low amount of responses regarding self-identification to the East Indian community, by individuals who were nonetheless all perceived to be part of this community, can be explained in three ways. Namely: first of all, ethnic origin may not lead to a sense of community belonging, secondly this sense of belonging seems to lie almost exclusively with the Muslim part of the community and, finally, older community members identify more moderately on a geographic-cultural basis. These three reasons may also have implications for estimating the overall size of the East Indian community, as certainly the earlier mentioned numbers from the 2010 Barbados census could similarly be affected by these dynamics.

Despite being able to identify some of the reasons for this discrepancy, it still raises the question whether it is relevant at all to speak of 'an East Indian community' as a collective group. Although in some respects it might seem more accurate to polarize the community into a Gujarati-Muslim and a Sindhi-Hindu pillar, in other respects it is still useful and valid to speak of an East Indian community. The latter is true particularly with regards to similarities in histories of recent migration, their particular relationship to the topic of the exhibition, as well as when one considers how this group is seen

---

153 Meeting with Degia (Bridgetown, Barbados, 10 March 2016).

by outsiders or its separation from other Barbadian communities. Nonetheless, in the remainder of this chapter, the reader should be aware of the fact that the East Indian community should be seen as heterogeneous with segments that are more strongly or more weakly tied to the group as a whole. Where relevant, community perceptions that differ strongly between the two pillars will be highlighted.

Project Awareness & Involvement

The *Bengal to Barbados* exhibition project, at the time of this fieldwork, had not been publicly announced. Despite the desires of the whole Exhibition Planning Committee to work inclusively and participate with many members of the East Indian community, involvement in the project was still limited. The gatekeepers administering the survey focused on including those who were already aware of or involved in the project and explained the project to those who were not. Even within the walls of the Barbados Museum & Historical Society, some staff members were not aware of the project until asked to complete the survey. In total, only 12 respondents indicated that they were involved in the exhibition project (see figure 36). Of the 39 not involved in the project, when asked why they were not involved, many provided no explanation (15) or indicated that they were not aware of the project (13). Some stated that they had not been asked to be involved (6) or were not aware how they could be involved (2). A lack of project awareness was apparent, with respondents stating that they were "not aware of the project,"[154] that it was "not known to me,"[155] or that they "had no idea about it."[156]

Certainly, the lack of project awareness had direct implications for the amount of participants the project could hope to engage. Despite this low level of awareness, verbal and written responses indicated that there was a *potential* for participation and that respondents were positively inclined to being involved (if only they knew how or were asked to). As one respondent noted: "I'm not directly involved but should the opportunity arises [sic], I would like to be involved."[157] When this was discussed with the Exhibition Planning Committee, some plans were made as to how public awareness of the project could be improved and how community involvement could be increased.

Respondents who indicated that they were already involved in the project were asked in what way they were involved. Both involved BMHS staff members stated that they were researchers for the exhibition, whereas the East Indian community members noted a diversity of involvements, from being on the Exhibition Planning Committee, to transporting donated artefacts, or assisting with culinary aspects of the exhibition.

Imbalanced community engagement projects can lead to participants feeling that their voices are not being heard or that their actual involvement is tokenistic. As such, the Exhibition Planning Committee and I wanted to know whether participants were pleased or dissatisfied with their degree of involvement. Thus the survey asked those who indicated involvement in the project: "do you feel that your voice is being heard?" Of the involved BMHS staff members, one refrained from answering and the other

154 Survey BtB#39 (Barbados, 12 March 2016).
155 Survey BtB#26 (Barbados, 8 March 2016).
156 Survey BtB#45 (Barbados, 15 March 2016).
157 Survey BtB#38 (Barbados, 12 March 2016).

Are you involved in the *Bengal to Barbados* exhibition project?

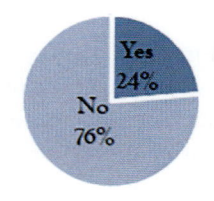

Figure 36: Respondents' involvement in the Bengal to Barbados exhibition project.

responded positively, elaborating that "I've only recently become involved in the project, so thus far I haven't been able to contribute as much as I possibly can."[158]

Among the involved members of the East Indian community, responses were more divided. The majority responded *yes* (6), with the remainder stating *sometimes* (2) or *no* (2). Although not all of these respondents elaborated, a tentative explanation is possible due to additional observations. As had been indicated within the Exhibition Planning Committee, East Indian participants expected to be consultants within the project with a limited decision-making role. As such, they anticipated to have relatively less decision-making power within the project as compared to the BMHS staff. The point of contention, instead, seemed to be in the balance of power *within* the East Indian community, rather than between the community and staff. Positive responses all echoed expectations of consultation that were met: "I offer suggestions that are taken into consideration"[159] or as another respondent said "I am told of the plans & ask [sic] for opinion."[160] The one negative response is specifically about power imbalances between community members: "generally, at the meetings, certain individuals monopolise the discussion."[161] Although one could assume this power imbalance within the community is due to the two pillars, this is not the case. In fact, all 10 involved members of the East Indian community were Muslim and may tentatively be identified as Gujarati-Muslims. Instead, the imbalance in power might be based on gender. Those who felt their voices were being heard were mostly male (5:1), while both of those who indicated that their voice was *not* being heard were female. This concern had already been voiced by the BMHS prior to this fieldwork.[162] Renewed efforts were planned to improve inclusivity of female East Indian community members.

Exhibition Aims, Importance & Benefits

Making sure that co-curation participants are aware of their respective project aims is an important step in avoiding possible conflict and misunderstandings while working towards desired outcomes. Thus, as part of the survey, respondents were asked "what do you hope the exhibition will achieve?" and asked to pick up to three of the twelve listed aims or to add 'others.' In general, East Indian community members and BMHS staff prioritized similar project aims, although there are also some notable difference in responses between the two (see figure 37).

First of all, despite the instructions given on the survey, many respondents (16) picked more than three exhibition aims. This over-selection of exhibition aims was

---

158 Survey BtB#1 (Barbados, 3 March 2016).
159 Survey BtB#35 (Barbados, 12 March 2016).
160 Survey BtB#29 (Barbados, 9 March 2016).
161 Survey BtB#49 (Barbados, 15 March 2016).
162 Meeting with deputy director of *Barbados Museum & History Society* (via Skype, 7 February 2016).

particularly pronounced among BMHS staff, with 6 out of 7 respondents indicating more than three aims. The East Indian community members selected 3.8 aims on average (167 responses for 44 respondents), while BMHS staff selected 7.1 aims on average (50 responses for 7 respondents). In comparing the results, the relative importance should be kept in mind rather than the percentage of responses per se.

BMHS staff members indicated that *awareness* (100%), *education* (86%), and *understanding* (86%) were the most important outcomes they hoped the exhibition would achieve. Of secondary importance were a *stronger community* (71%) and *unity* (71%). BMHS staff considered *enjoyment* (29%), *empowerment* (14%), and *pride* (14%) to be the least important aims of the exhibition. The East Indian community also indicated that *awareness* (70%), *education* (52%), and *understanding* (41%) were the most important outcomes they hoped the exhibition would achieve. However, of secondary importance they indicated different aims namely *cultural celebration* (39%) and *pride* (32%). Finally, the East Indian community similarly considered *enjoyment* (16%) and *empowerment* (2%) to be the least important aims of the exhibition.

For both the East Indian community and BMHS staff, the three primary aims of the exhibition were the same: awareness, education, and understanding. At the opposite end of the scale, both groups of respondents also agreed that the least important aims were empowerment and enjoyment. Differences occur primarily in the medium ranges of the results. For instance, whereas pride was of secondary importance to the East Indian community, it was deemed of little importance to BMHS staff. On the other hand, while BMHS staff considered recognition and dispelling myths to be secondarily important outcomes of the exhibition, these were valued lower by the East Indian community.

Thus, in the eyes of all the respondents, the primary aim of the exhibition was educational and outward focused towards Barbadian society as a whole: to raise awareness and to educate. As one respondent argued, "this is an opportunity for us to educate, enlighten fellow Barbadians about us."[163] A BMHS staff member noted that "this would enable the general public to be more educated about the customs and the culture of the East Indians."[164] Of secondary importance, and more inward-looking, was the aim to celebrate East Indian culture and to build a stronger community. Some respondents specifically commented on inter-generational education: "it will be nice for the young ones to know the history of our arrival here."[165] Finally, it was clear that the exhibition should not be geared towards political aims such as empowerment, nor that it should focus especially on enjoyment. These interpretations had clear implications for the exhibition development process by indicating that the primary tone of the exhibition should be educational and that the primary goal audience would be 'the Barbadian public' at large, with the East Indian community as a secondary audience for the purpose of community bonding.

Beyond exhibition aims, respondents were also asked to evaluate the exhibition based on how they perceived its importance and its potential benefits. On a five-point scale, the survey asked participants "do you feel that this exhibition is important for

---

163 Survey BtB#36 (Barbados, 12 March 2016).
164 Survey BtB#6 (Barbados, 10 March 2016).
165 Survey BtB#19 (Barbados, 8 March 2016).

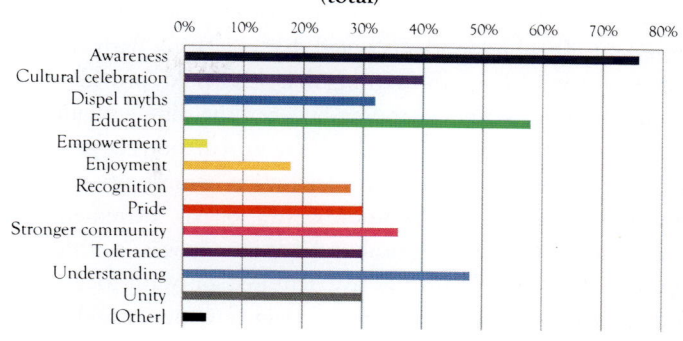

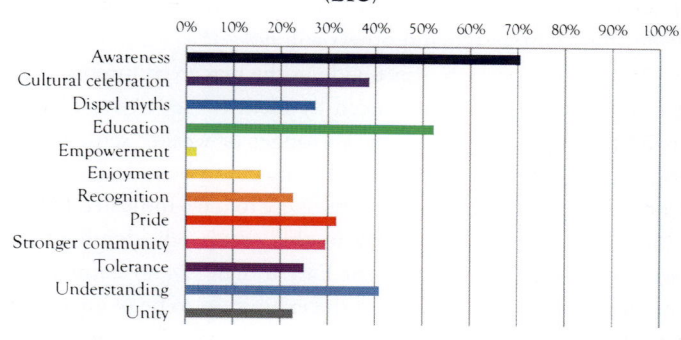

Figure 37: Respondents' expectations for the Bengal to Barbados exhibition project: total numbers, only East Indian community members, and only BMHS staff.

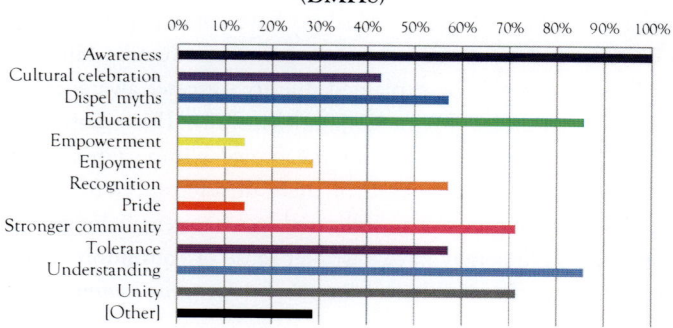

your community?" (see figure 38). Responses greatly differed depending on which community or pillar they belonged to. BMHS staff in general were quite positive about the importance of the exhibition, mostly stating that it was "a lot" or "extremely" important. These respondents noted that educating Barbadians about the East Indian community was important, arguing that this would "provide an opportunity for greater communication & understanding between the different cultural groups"[166] and thus, hopefully, lead to more tolerance. These explanations largely echoed the main exhibition aims presented above. The East Indian community was highly divided between those who felt that the exhibition was "a lot" or "extremely" important (n=23), and those who were more skeptical and felt that it was "a little" or neutrally important (n=21). Those who were positive repeated outward-focused educational outcomes in elaborating this question, noting again how this would educate and enlighten the wider Barbadian public. Those who were more negative about the importance of the exhibition were often uncertain ("not sure") or questioned the reach and therefore the impact of the exhibition. One respondent said "it might bring awareness, but only a few people come to these exhibitions."[167] Another respondent noted neutrally that "some will be interested and others will not."[168]

On closer inspection, this divide in the perceived importance of the exhibition can be interpreted as being influenced by identity (see figure 39). The division is characterized by religion as well as by a stronger or weaker sense of geographic-cultural belonging. Those who perceived the exhibition to be of less importance were more often Hindu than Muslim (14:6) and less likely to have indicated belonging to a geographic-cultural community. Only 43% of this group self-identified as Barbadian and even fewer noted Caribbean (24%) or East Indian (24%) community belonging. On the other hand, those who perceived the exhibition to be of greater importance were more often Muslim than Hindu (18:4) and also more often indicated a geographic-cultural belonging. Of this group, 74% self-identified as Barbadian, with also more frequent selections of Caribbean (35%) and East Indian (43%) community belonging. As discussed above, this division aligns with the two pillars within the community, as well as by the fact that the Gujarati-Muslims have constructed a stronger sense of belonging to the East Indian community than is the case for the Sindhi-Hindus. Beyond this, the division can also be explained due to a greater awareness of and involvement in the exhibition project by the Gujarati-Muslims. This group is both more aware of the project, increasing their sense of the project's importance, as well as more involved in it, quite possibly as a result of their already perceived importance of the project. Additionally, the group who indicated less frequent belonging to geographic-cultural communities, thus may have a weaker sense of community and therefore is less likely to indicate that the exhibition is important *for your community*" as the survey question was phrased.

As a follow up question, respondents were also asked "do you think the exhibition will benefit your community?" (see figure 40). In general, responses to this question were more evenly divided among the four points on the scale, ranging from "a little"

166 Survey BtB#1 (Barbados, 3 March 2016).
167 Survey BtB#49 (Barbados, 15 March 2016).
168 Survey BtB#26 (Barbados, 8 March 2016).

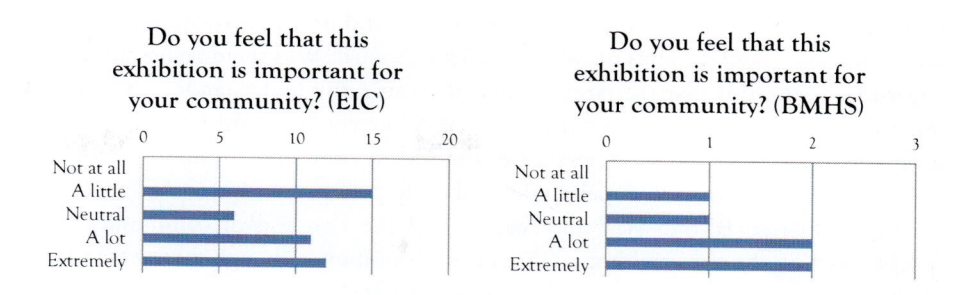

Figure 38: Respondents' assessment of the importance of the Bengal to Barbados exhibition project: only East Indian community members and only BMHS staff.

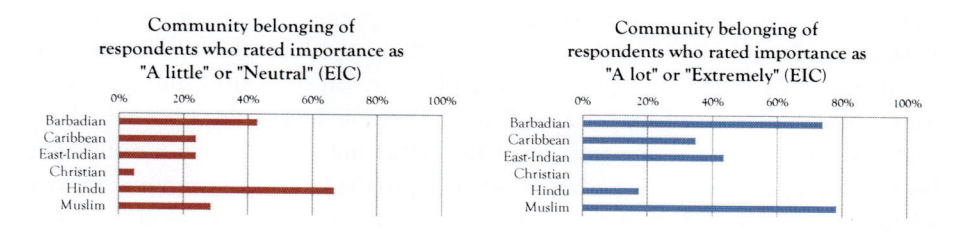

Figure 39: East Indian respondents' self-identification with given communities, divided by the extent to which they rated the Bengal to Barbados exhibition project as important.

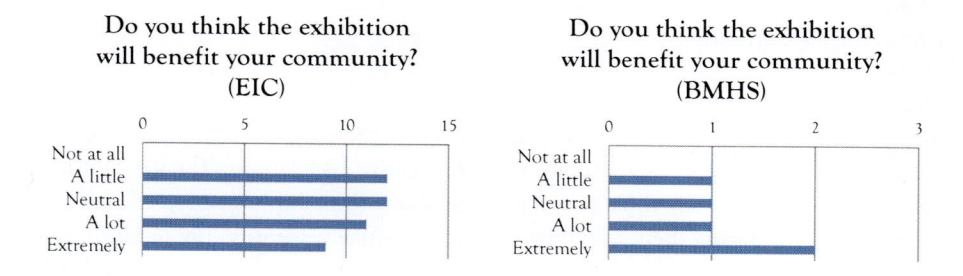

Figure 40: Respondents' assessment of the benefits of the Bengal to Barbados exhibition project: only East Indian community members and only BMHS staff.

to "extremely" beneficial. The respondents overall were slightly less positive regarding the benefits, but at the same time fewer respondents were as negative and more were neutral. BMHS staff noted that the exhibition could benefit the Barbadian public and that the content would benefit the East Indian community. However, one staff member questioned the scale and impact of the exhibition, saying "I think a lot will depend on marketing and communication in order to achieve a significant audience size for maximum impact."[169] The East Indian community was divided almost evenly as well and several respondents commented that they were "not sure about benefits."[170]

169 Survey BtB#4 (Barbados, 9 March 2016).
170 Survey BtB#47 (Barbados, 15 March 2016).

One respondent also noted that benefits would depend on the content and style of the exhibition: "it all depends on what is being exhibited. Will there be literature or/ and audio visual aids that the targeted audience can easily understand?"[171] Of those respondents who elaborated their response, many presented inward-focused benefits noting that it would improve tolerance of the Indian community, build bridges between communities, help to dispel myths, and "help preserve our history."[172]

To summarize, BMHS staff and members of the East Indian community had similar views on the aims and importance of the exhibition, although there were some differences between these groups and more notably among the East Indian respondents. Primarily, both groups were concerned with educational exhibition aims and had outward-focused perspectives to educate the Barbadian public at large. The East Indian community also found cultural celebration and pride important, showing a secondary need for the exhibition to result in community strengthening. These aims were largely reflected in the perceived importance of the exhibition, although respondents were greatly divided in this matter between those who were largely positive and those who were more skeptical of this importance. This divide could be explained partially along the religious divide of the two pillars of the community and also by a distinction between stronger and weaker perceived belonging to the East Indian community as a whole. In addition, BMHS staff was more positive regarding the exhibition's importance. Finally, responses were overall more evenly distributed regarding the potential benefit of the exhibition, with fewer negative & positive responses and more neutral responses. In answering this question, respondents were alternatively more uncertain about possible benefits or were more inward-focused on benefits for the East Indian community specifically.

Project Associations

The perceptions of the survey respondents towards the exhibition project were also evaluated by asking them for their positive and negative associations. The survey asked respondents to "please say three positive things about the exhibition project" and followed this up by asking them to do the same for negative keywords. The question was intended to specifically get insight into the perceptions of the respondents towards the project and therefore to understand some of the dynamics of the collaborative process. However, during the course of the fieldwork it became apparent that a significant amount of respondents were not, or only minimally, aware of the project. Therefore, they found these questions particularly difficult to answer and many did not submit any responses to these two questions. Of all the respondents, 23 did not indicate any positive associations and an even higher number of respondents, 41, did not submit any negative associations. Those who noted positive associations frequently wrote down terms which had been listed as multiple choice options to the previous question "what do you hope the exhibition will achieve," thus repeating their aims for the exhibition as project associations.

To begin with analyzing the positive responses, 28 respondents (55%) answered this question and the majority indicated three positive terms, with an average of

171 Survey BtB#7 (Barbados, 4 March 2016).
172 Survey BtB#38 (Barbados, 12 March 2016).

2.5 positive terms per respondent (see figure 41). BMHS staff and members of the East Indian community responded relatively equally often to this question. Respondents primarily associated the exhibition project as being educational and creating awareness, echoing the main exhibition aims. Another major grouping of association were general positive comments about the project as an idea. Respondents noted it was *interesting*, a *good idea*, *fun*, *inspirational*, and *exciting*. Beyond these general positive comments, a few respondents noted that the project was *innovative* and that such a project had not been attempted before. Some also stressed that the project was *timely*, *needed*, and *important*, stressing the necessity of the project being undertaken.

In analyzing the negative responses, it is apparent that negative associations were mentioned exclusively by members of the East Indian community. Negative responses were given by 10 respondents, corresponding to 23% of the respondents from the East Indian community. Most of these respondents only indicated one negative term, resulting in an average of 1.3 negative terms per respondent (see figure 42). There are two primary points of contention which were given as negative associations. First of all, respondents felt that the project was *biased*, *one-sided*, or *monopolized* and therefore did not reflect the community as a whole. Secondly, and closely related to the first point, respondents noted that the project was *unknown by many*, stating that it was *private* and *exclusive*. Two respondents also noted that the project was *overdue*.

To summarize, many respondents were unable to provide their associations with the project, primarily due to their lack of familiarity with the project. Those who did respond noted mainly positive associations, with negative associations only being mentioned by members of the East Indian community. Whereas the positive associations were concerned with the project as an *idea* or its aims, the negative associations point towards conflict related to the *process* of the exhibition project. Again, responses indicate friction within the East Indian community and point towards the fact that certain community members felt either excluded from the project due to the low awareness of the project or that the project was monopolized by some community members at the expense of others. Thus, whereas respondents felt that the idea of the project was good and timely, the process was deemed biased and exclusive by some members of the East Indian community.

Representativity

The representativity of the East Indian community members involved in the project was a point of concern from the outset, for three reasons. First of all, the heterogeneous East Indian community was not sufficiently represented by the members of the Exhibition Planning Committee. Secondly, not all community members who are in fact involved in the process felt equally heard. Thirdly, the personal perceptions and associations of the three community gatekeepers biased the respondents they administered the survey to.

The first two points have already been brought up. Despite efforts by the members of the Exhibition Planning Committee, not all parts of the heterogeneous East Indian community are sufficiently represented or can equally participate in the project. There are multiple reasons for this. The heterogeneity of the East Indian community makes it particularly challenging to find persons who can be representative along multiple dividing lines (female/male, Hindu/Muslim, Gujarati/Sindhi, young/old). Even though individuals representing some of these segments of the community sit on the committee, due to the meeting time and location (at the BMHS) not all members are able to be present for all meetings, therefore in effect giving those who can be present more decision-making power. Certain members, even when they are present, do not feel that their voices are being heard, indicating that community members are not equally valued or equally listened to. Representativity was highlighted as a major concern for the success of the co-curation project in moving forward. Committee members were also concerned with this issue and agreed to work on making the project more inclusive by expanding the amount of East Indian community members involved through wider public events and consultation. It was noted that these events should happen in locations that were more central to the residential neighborhoods of the East Indian community. They also agreed to look into the meeting times and locations, to try to attract new members to the committee, and to encourage attendance of existing members.

The final point is related to bias due to the perceptions of the community gatekeepers. Bulbulia & Nakhuda visited community events and gatherings and administered the survey together at these events and also individually to family members and friends. Degia administered the survey independently among students, family members, and friends. When introducing the survey, the gatekeepers explained the exhibition project and the aims of the survey in their own words. It was apparent, already in my first observations, that Degia's stance towards the project was different than that of Bulbulia and Nakhuda. Whereas Degia experienced friction in the co-curation project between East Indian community members and described the project in both negative and positive terms,[173] Bulbulia and Nakhuda were overall more positive and did not recognize any conflict, only the low meeting attendance.[174] Some of the survey results, related to the perceived importance and benefit of the exhibition project and specifically the question about negative project associations, could be read as having been influenced by the differing perceptions of these gatekeepers. It is likely that survey respondents, when introduced to the exhibition project by the gatekeeper administering the survey, understood the project to some extent in the tone in which the gatekeeper chose to describe the project. There is a marked difference in how Degia's survey respondents (n=8) indicated the exhibition project's importance and its benefits, as opposed to Bulbulia/Nakhuda's respondents (n=36) (see figure 43). Namely, Degia's respondents were more negative.

The differences in perception were also visible in the question related to negative project associations. Of the 10 respondents who gave any negative associations, 7 of these were Degia's respondents (or 88% of her respondents). Degia's respondents were those who noted that the exhibition process was biased, monopolized, exclusive, and private. The remaining 3 respondents, who had been surveyed by Bulbulia/Nakhuda, noted negative associations of a different kind, namely that the project was overdue and that it was unknown by many. In presenting the preliminary survey results to the Exhibition Planning Committee, this issue was discussed and a suggestion for mediation was made. Different participants presenting the project differently to outsiders – influencing public perception of the project – could lead to conflict as the project progressed.

---

173 Meeting with Degia (Bridgetown, Barbados, 10 March 2016).
174 Meeting with Exhibition Planning Committee (Bridgetown, Barbados, 21 March 2016).

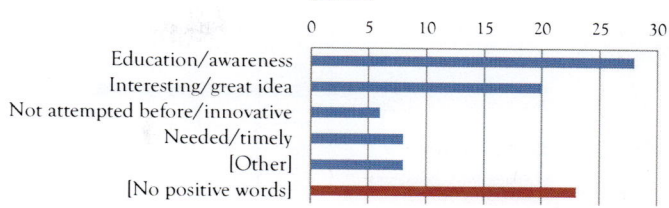

Please say three *positive* things about the exhibition project (total)

Figure 41: Respondents' positive keywords for the Bengal to Barbados exhibition project.

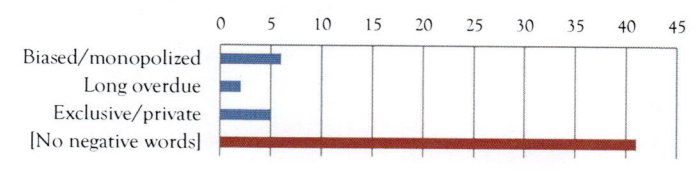

Please say three *negative* things about the exhibition project (total)

Figure 42: Respondents' negative keywords for the Bengal to Barbados exhibition project.

Project Development

Since finalizing this fieldwork, development of the project has continued. In discussing the preliminary survey results, the Exhibition Planning Committee noted the need for wider engagement with the East Indian community and mediation between participants; thus more time would be needed to build connections with potential participants and bridges between current participants. A decision was made to push back the date of the exhibition opening (originally 6 July 2016 – now proposed August 2018). Initially the exhibition was planned within Barbados' yearlong celebration of 50 years of independence, with the opening of the exhibition falling on the last day of Ramadan. It would be open for three months, with events and programming continuing for longer and the exhibition potentially traveling throughout the island afterwards.

At the time of writing (fall 2017) the plan for the exhibition opening is for it to take place in August 2018 to coincide with the start of the school year.[175] Programming will specifically focus on allowing Barbadians to engage with the East Indian community and their heritage. As part of the efforts to make the exhibition project more inclusive and to reach out to a wider audience and potential participants, a meeting was held at the BMHS to invite more East Indian community members to provide their input into the project. 12 persons attended this meeting and left inspired to encourage friends and family to become involved. One of these persons will be doing research to provide a gendered understanding of the community. A follow up meeting will be planned in a more neutral location. Although they had not had meetings in a while, the Exhibition Planning Committee members are in regular contact, deepening their relationship into one of trust. They are working primarily on content research and object collection. In

175 Meeting with deputy director of *Barbados Museum & History Society* (St. Croix, 28 July 2017).

Do you feel that this exhibition is important for your community? (EIC)

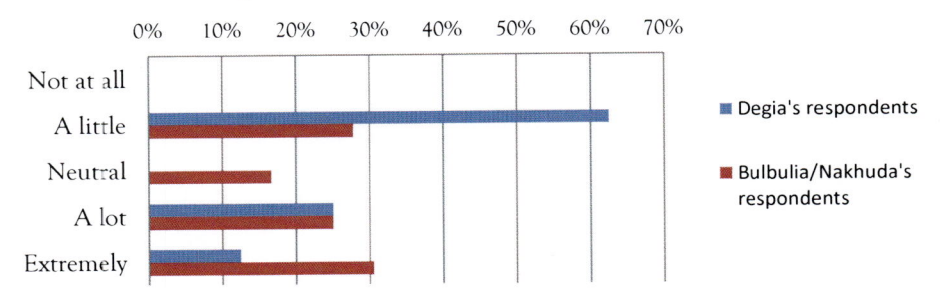

Do you think the exhibition will benefit your community? (EIC)

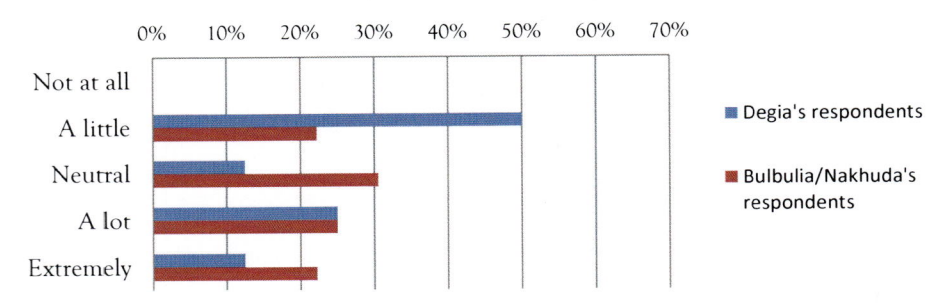

Figure 43: East Indian respondents' assessment of the importance and the benefits of the Bengal to Barbados exhibition project: divided by who administered the survey.

addition, some of the participants have begun working on their own genealogy projects alongside the exhibition project. BMHS staff stressed that buy in from the whole community is essential, so that neither the museum nor the East Indian community is pushing the project down an isolated path. For all of these reasons, additional time was invested in the project to ensure that nothing happens until all participants feel ready: "the key thing for us is not to try to impose that curatorial rigor, but to be a bit more organic and flexible in order to engage."[176]

Summary

We're learning as we're going on, we're not doing it the traditional way.[177]

This chapter took the *Bengal to Barbados* exhibition project as a case study of an ongoing Caribbean community engagement process and attempted to provide and

---

176 Meeting with deputy director of *Barbados Museum & History Society* (St. Croix, 28 July 2017).
177 Meeting with deputy director of *Barbados Museum & History Society* (St. Croix, 28 July 2017).

illustrate an answer to the research question: "how are community engagement processes, including their value and outcomes, perceived by Caribbean communities?" (see *Research Questions and Objectives*, page 18). The idea for the Bengal to Barbados exhibition project resulted from the publication of Sabir Nakhuda's book (2013) of the same name and was initiated by his subsequent request to the *Barbados Museum & Historical Society* (BMHS) to co-curate a temporary exhibition. Centered on the topic of this book, the focus of the proposed exhibition would be the five migratory strands through which East Indians travelled to Barbados, their 100 year history on the island, and their current role within Barbadian society. The exhibition project was conceived in 2015 and is currently still in development, scheduled to open in August 2018. It is co-curated by staff of the BMHS and members of the heterogeneous East Indian community, who are learning to adjust and adapt the process flexibly along the way. Originating as a grassroots initiative, the exhibition project is co-curated by a national museum and a minority community.

How is the *process* of the Bengal to Barbados exhibition project perceived by the East Indian community and by BMHS staff? Due to the limited awareness of the project and small number of project participants at the time of this study, many community and staff members could not comment deeply on the process of the exhibition project. Of those who could, BMHS staff was generally positive about the process, although they noted that wider community participation was necessary and they hoped to place more power and responsibility with the East Indian community. East Indian community members were generally positive about the collaboration with the museum and preferred the museum to have relatively more decision-making power, as they felt that museum staff had more appropriate expertise. However, some community members were negative about the collaboration process within the East Indian community, noting that conversations and decision-making could be biased or monopolized by certain individuals.

How is the *value* of the exhibition project perceived by the East Indian community and by BMHS staff? The East Indian community saw the aim of the exhibition to primarily be an outwards-focused one, namely to educate the Barbadian public about the community's history and heritage. As a secondary aim, cultural celebration and pride were noted, indicating that inward-focused aims were also seen as an integral part of the exhibition. As an idea, the exhibition was generally valued positively. However, in valuing the importance of the exhibition, the community was deeply divided between those who felt that the exhibition was of little importance and those who felt it was very important. This separation aligns with existing divisions within the community: partially between the two pillars of Gujarati-Muslims and Sindhi-Hindus, partially between respondents with stronger or weaker ties to the East Indian community as a whole, as well as along age and gender differences. BMHS staff was overall positively inclined towards the exhibition project, primarily also stating the aim to be educational for all Barbadians. Secondarily, they hoped the exhibition would lead to unity and a stronger (Barbadian) community. Generally, staff rated the importance of the exhibition to be high and were also positive about the idea of the project. As outsiders, BMHS staff was not personally conflicted about how the history of the East Indian community should or should not be told, as long as this was balanced and correct.

How are the *outcomes* of the Bengal to Barbados exhibition project perceived by the East Indian community and by BMHS staff? As the project was still in a very early stage during the course of this fieldwork, project participants and survey respondents were largely uncertain about the outcomes of the project. At the time, they rather noted the potential benefits of the project and how it could support bridging between communities and increased tolerance among Barbadians. However, respondents did say that benefits would be highly dependent on the process of the project, as well as the actual outcomes in terms of the resulting exhibition and related programming. Those involved in the process emphasized that any outcomes would depend on how inclusively or exclusively the project would progress. In general, both East Indian community members and BMHS staff had a rather undecided outlook on the outcomes of the project.

Ultimately, the positive continuation of the co-curation process depends on the extent to which the project is successfully made more inclusive (and thus more representative of the heterogeneous East Indian community) and the successful mediation by BMHS staff between East Indian individuals separated along dividing lines of identity, religion, age, and gender. Contention and sources of conflict in this exhibition project do not lie *between* the museum staff and community but rather *within* the community. In order for BMHS staff to take on the role of mediator, it is instrumental that more time is invested to understand the dynamics of the East Indian community and to be able to work towards bridging. Participating East Indian community members will need to be equally invested in bridging and willing to shift the power balance within the community. With continued and increased inclusivity and mediation, the Bengal to Barbados exhibition has significant potential to not only educate the wider Barbadian public about a specific history, but also to strengthen the bonds of the East Indian community and encourage a more tolerant Barbadian society. Along the way, flexibility and adaptation are necessary, constantly learning as the process continues. If successful, the exhibition could form the beginning of an East Indian community museum in Barbados.

Figure 44: Map of the studied museums in the Caribbean.

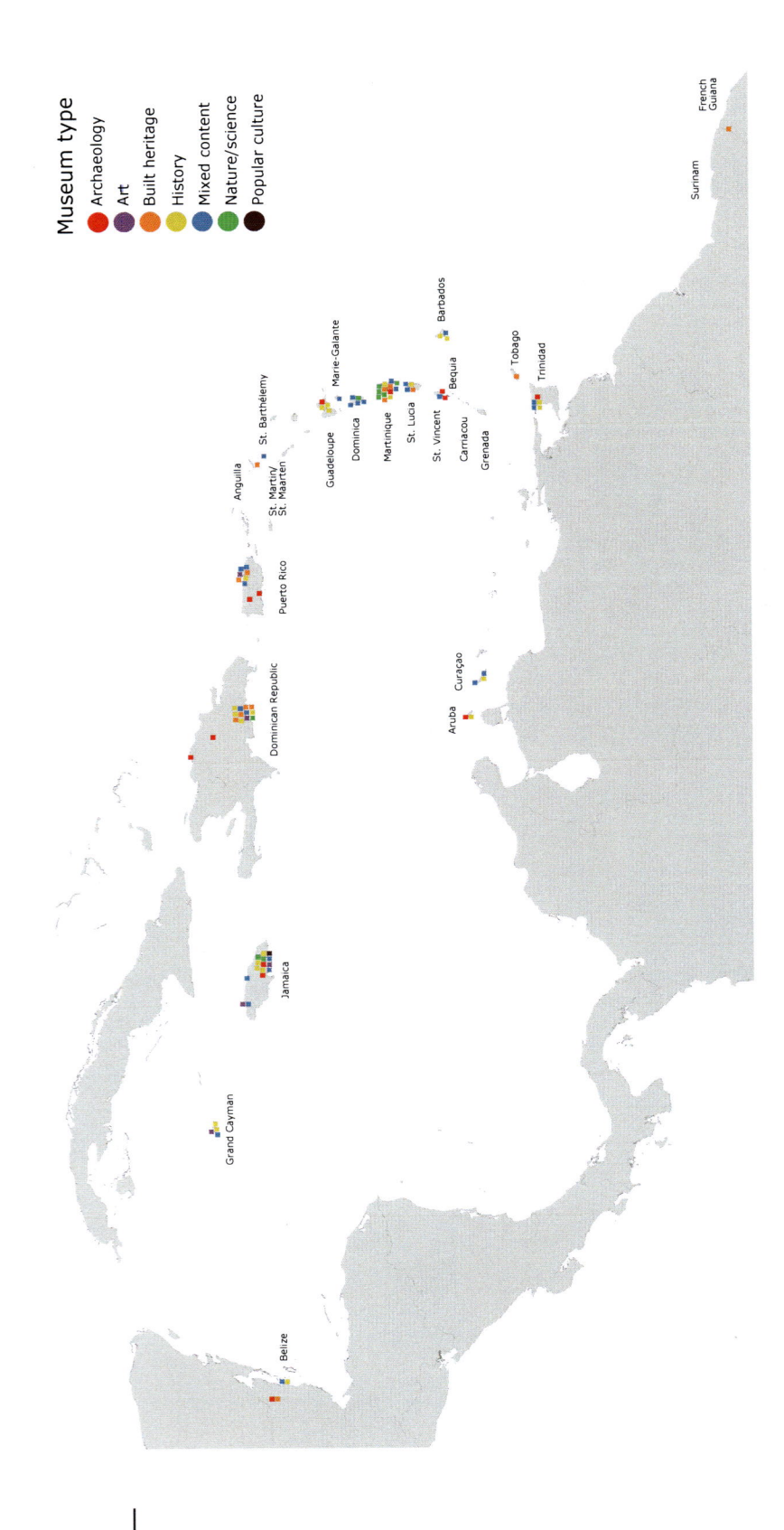

Figure 45: Map of the studied governmental museums in the Caribbean

Figure 46: Map of the studied grassroots museums in the Caribbean.

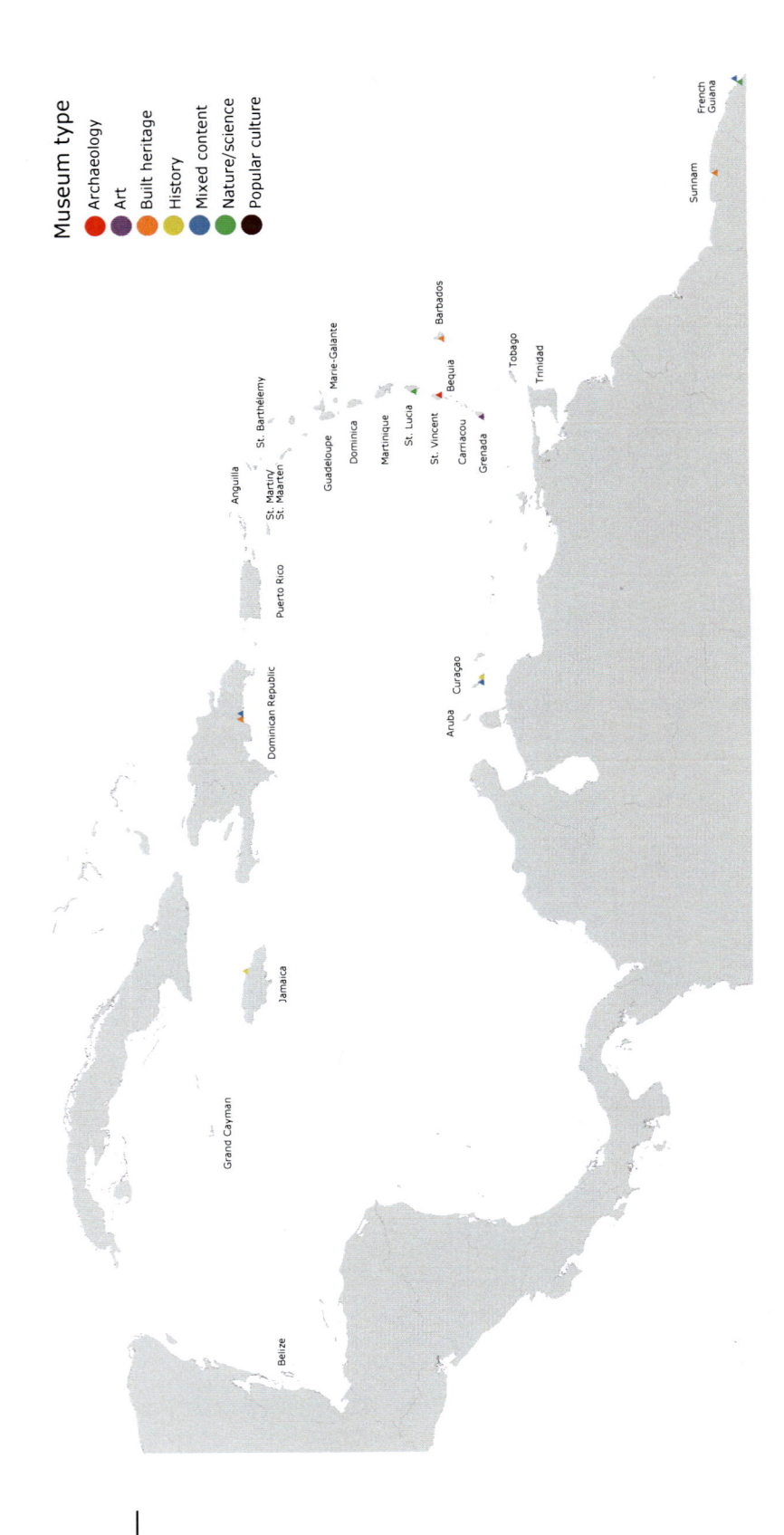

Figure 47: Map of the studied museums of mixed ownership in the Caribbean.

Figure 48: Map of the studied private museums in the Caribbean.

Figure 49: *Map of the studied museums of unknown ownership in the Caribbean.*

THE SOCIAL MUSEUM IN THE CARIBBEAN

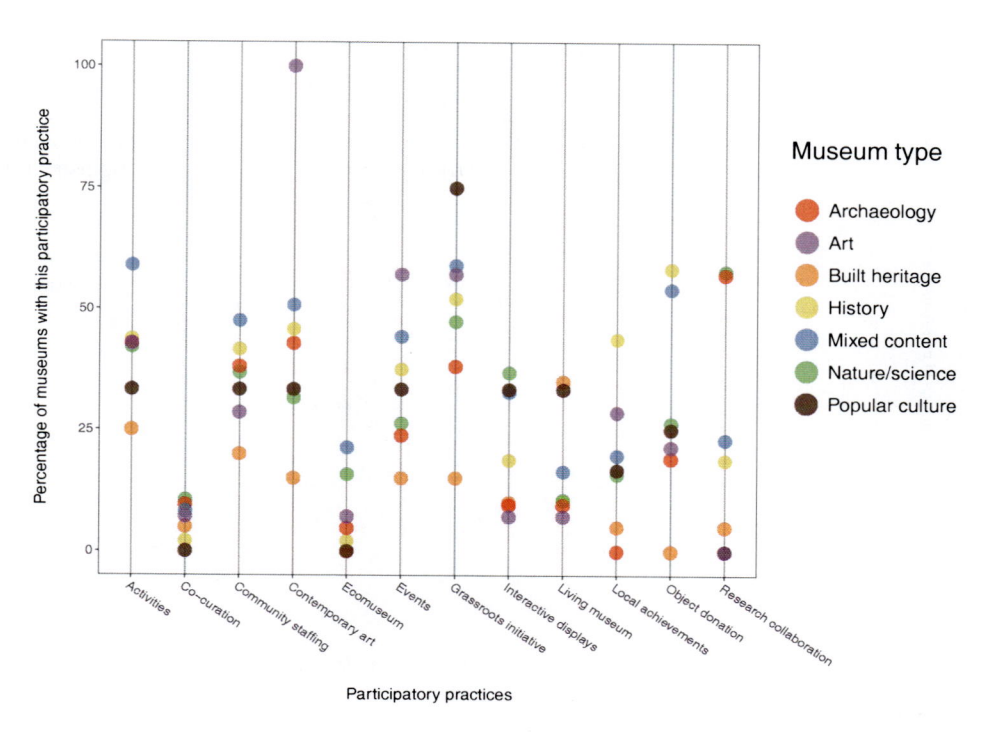

Figure 50: Percentage of museums which have any of the participatory practices. Museums are separated by type (of content).

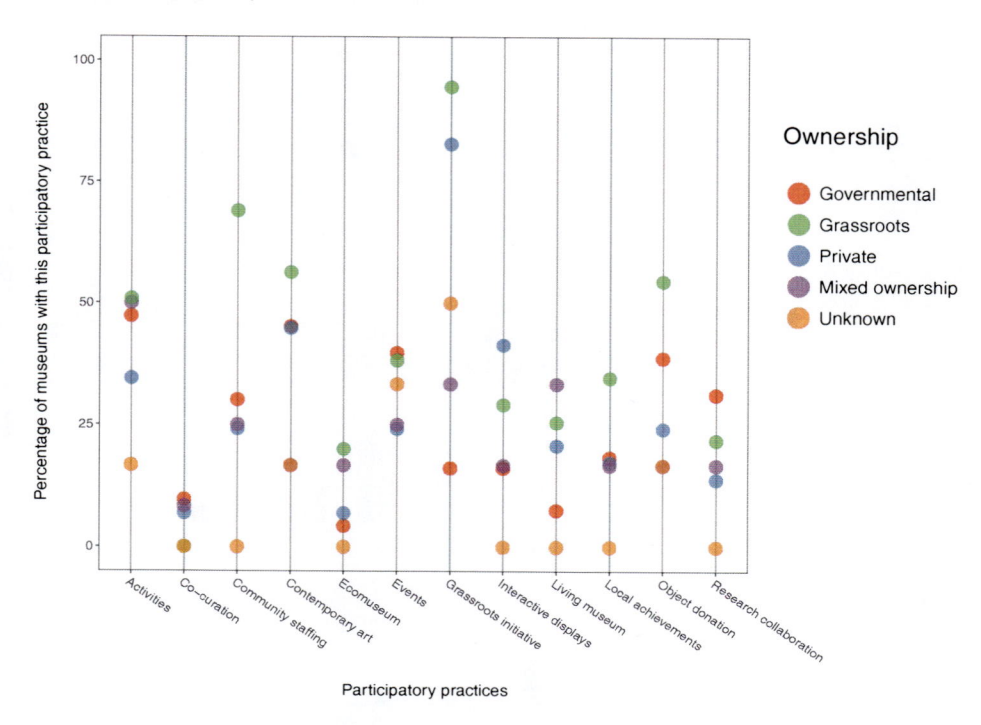

Figure 51: Percentage of museums which have any of the participatory practices. Museums are separated by ownership.

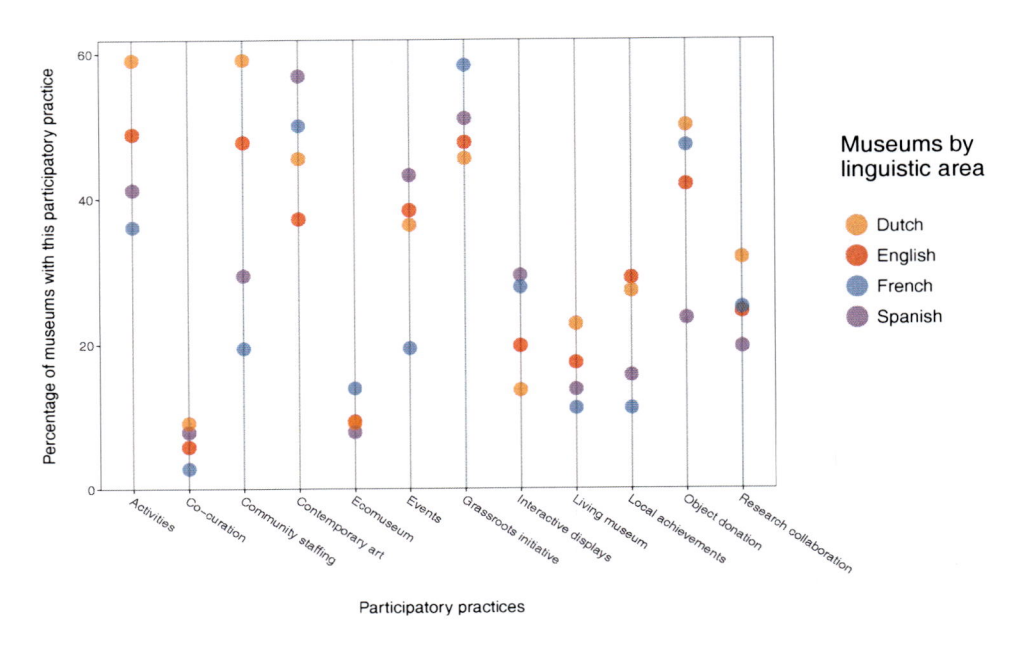

Figure 52: Percentage of museums which have any of the participatory practices. Museums are separated by the linguistic area they are located in.

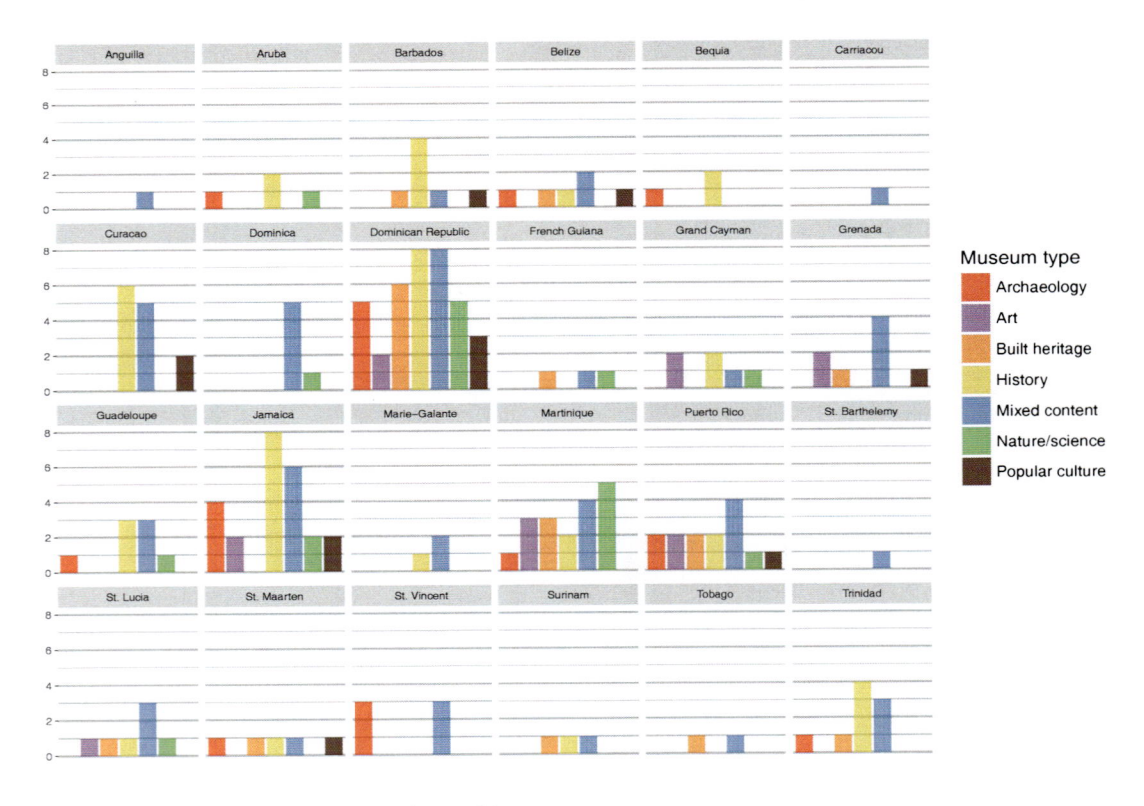

Figure 53: The studied museums per place and by type.

THE SOCIAL MUSEUM IN THE CARIBBEAN

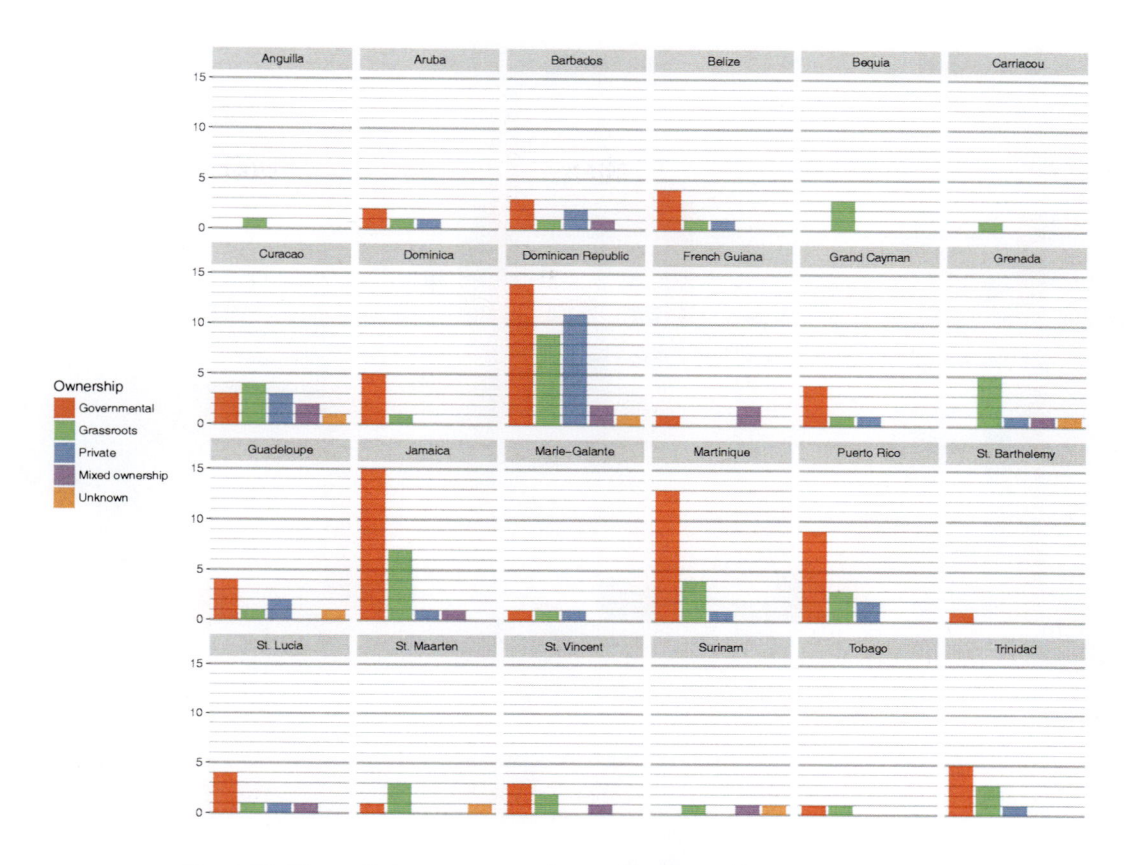

Figure 54: The studied museums per place and by ownership.

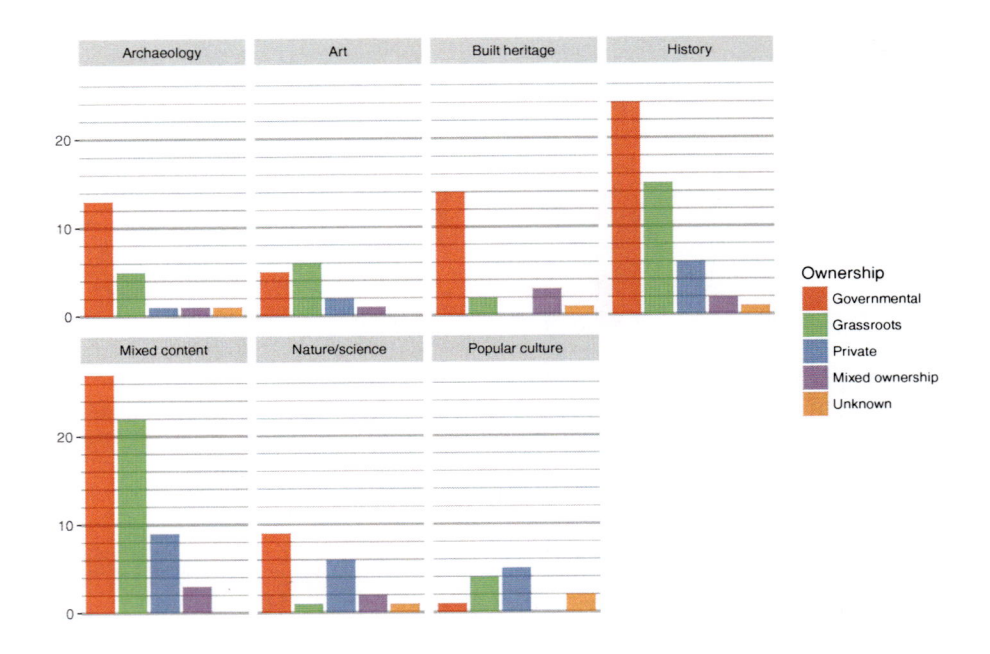

Figure 55: The studied museums per type and by ownership.

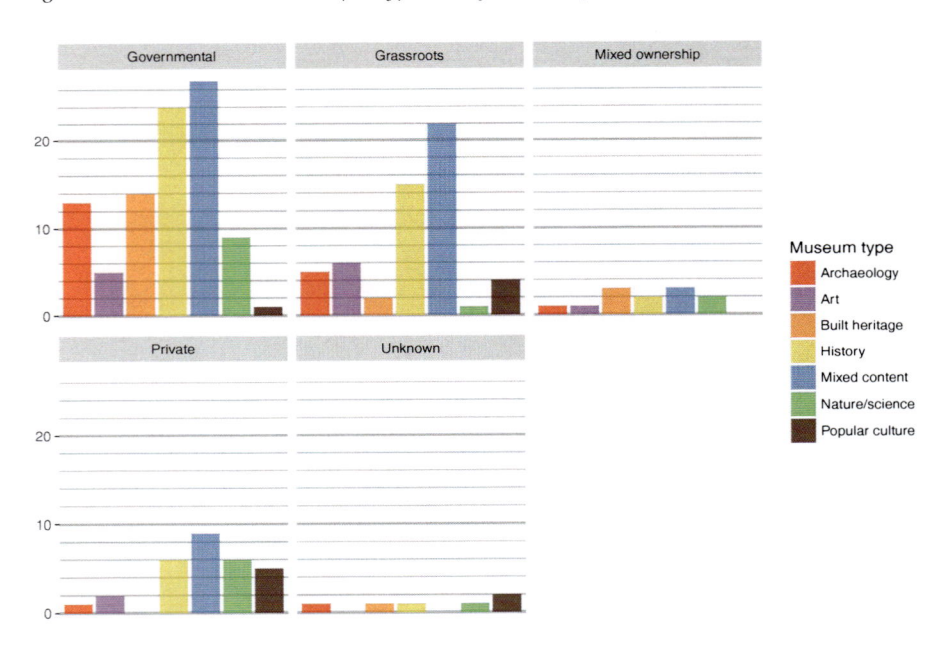

Figure 56: The studied museums per ownership and by type.

THE SOCIAL MUSEUM IN THE CARIBBEAN

7

The Social Museum

Museums are products of their social context, and it is proper that they should be so. It is, however, dangerous to assume that a place is guaranteed for museums in the society of the future. If we accept that their purpose is to be of service to society, then it is vital they be responsive to their social environment in order to remain relevant to changing social needs and goals.
George F. MacDonald (1992: 158; original emphasis)

MacDonald eloquently points out the risk for social museums – their mortality – while at the same time underlining the main ways in which their existence can be safeguarded. The social museum needs to continuously reevaluate itself in order to ensure that it is responsive to its environment and remains relevant as the needs and goals of its communities change. Any museum that places a community at the core of its mission and the heart of its organization needs to make sure that it keeps changing along with that community. Yet, MacDonald's words should not be seen as an impossible challenge for all museums to constantly be in flux. In actuality, it provides comfort in assuring that not all museums have to be fixated on permanence and long-term missions, but that there is room for ephemeral museums to play out their role in the present without a demand for longevity. The landscape of the social museum leaves space for many different types of institutions to exist: some ephemerally, some permanent and ever-changing, but all embedded in their societies.

The core focus of this research has been to uncover the practices and the processes by which museums in the Caribbean are working to connect more closely to the various communities they serve. Whether deliberately or unintentionally, and in differing degrees of success, museums that employ community engagement aim to become more *social* museums. Certainly, all museums are 'social' to some extent. However, the question is to which degree they strive for and succeed in fulfilling the role of an outspokenly social actor.

Building on the results presented in the previous three chapters, this chapter engages in an overarching discussion of Caribbean museums as social museums. This discussion focuses on some of the most noteworthy observations and interpretations made during the course of this research. As such, it aims to answer the research question: "how do community engagement practices and processes affect the role of Caribbean museums in relation to Caribbean society?" (see *Research Questions and Objectives*, page 18). This broad discussion of the social museum in the Caribbean takes place on both macro and micro levels by switching between regional and local perspectives and highlights both Caribbean characteristics and individual particularities. The chapter divides the discussion into three parts, each in turn approached from three different angles.

The first part focuses on the Caribbean museum scene as a whole by comparing grassroots museums with governmental museums. Firstly, it explores what the location of grassroots vs. governmental museums reveals about which communities these museums are choosing to engage with. Primarily, this discussion contrasts museums located in capital cities with those outside. Secondly, the discussion shifts to examine the differences between grassroots and governmental museums when it comes to the dynamism of the institutions and their ability to change their exhibitions and respond to (changing) societal needs. Oftentimes, dynamism is aided by political and financial independence. Thirdly, the comparison between grassroots and governmental museums is concluded by critically reconsidering the 'problem' of sustainability and introducing the notion of the ephemeral museum. Predominantly a macro level discussion, this first part of the chapter aims to highlight characteristics of Caribbean museums in order to broaden the global museological debate and to shift its typical focus to a grassroots perspective.

The second part is similarly concerned with the Caribbean museum scene as a whole, but zooms in to focus particularly on the various participatory practices employed throughout the region. Firstly, it considers how Caribbean museums are applying multi-vocality through narratives and other participatory practices as a means to target specific communities. This phenomenon is set in relation to the wide diversity of communities present in the region and considers how such multi-vocality supports identity construction, inclusivity, but also exclusion. Secondly, a closer look is taken at which types of museums, such as archaeology museums or natural history museums, engage in which kinds of participatory practices. Here, we unpack why certain museums use certain participatory practices and what this means for their potential to be social museums. Thirdly, participatory practices throughout the Caribbean region are divided by the four main linguistic areas (Dutch, English, French, and Spanish) in order to identify whether museums in each geopolitical sub-region employ participatory practices differently. The underlying hypothesis is that the different histories of these linguistic areas have left a colonial legacy in terms of their museums which may have resulted in distinct 'participatory styles.' As a regional discussion interspersed with local examples, this second part of the chapter aims to critically assess how participatory practices are employed in the region, how this impacts identity formation, and whether differences within the region can be explained by museum type or linguistic area. It is important here to note that the employment of any participatory practice by a museum does not necessarily indicate any measure of impact – practices may be employed unsuccessfully, or at least may be perceived to be unsuccessful by communities.

The third part of the discussion is zoomed in the furthest to assess the processes of community engagement in the Caribbean. Centered largely on the two in depth case studies undertaken in the course of this research, the discussion is mostly at micro level. Although it has implications for the wider Caribbean region, the conclusions drawn in this part cannot directly be transposed to other museums, communities, or islands and countries. Nonetheless, valuable lessons can be learned from these case studies about the complex process of engaging with communities. Firstly, this part assesses the issue of representativity and how community engagement can be a struggle when participants are not (deemed) representative. Secondly, it explores the essential investment of time, resources, and effort. Often underestimated, community engagement processes need significant investments of time in order to build the necessary amount of trust and mutual understanding for fruitful engagement. Finally, the discussion considers the negotiation process involved in the sharing of power between museums and communities. If either party wants less or more power, conflict can ensue. Conflict may also result from misunderstandings or incompatibilities when it comes to representativity and investment.

As a whole, the chapter presents both macro and micro level perspectives relating to Caribbean museums and their participatory practices and community engagement processes. The reader should take note that although the chapter intends to provide a comprehensive view of museums in the Caribbean region and add to the global museological discourse, neither the data nor their interpretations can be considered all-inclusive.

Grassroots and Governmental Museums

Within the Caribbean, the creation of grassroots museums is a highly noticeable participatory practice, albeit one that has not received much academic attention. As elsewhere in the world, governmental museums such as national museums tend to take center stage in museological and political discussions and inquiries. Certainly, as institutions that (partly) depend on public funding and therefore demand public scrutiny, some of this attention is justified. However, in the act of defining and studying museums, governmental institutions have been given too big a role, perhaps due to their history as instruments of nationalism or as a result of their colonial legacies. As such, museological debates and collections of best practices are missing out on examples of other types of museums, such as grassroots museums, which are set up and run by individuals, communities, or non-governmental organizations. Grassroots museums exist around the world, but are often overlooked or dismissed in museological literature, for instance by applying terms such as 'museum-like'[178] or 'amateur museums.' Although they have been receiving more scholarly attention (*e.g.* Candlin 2016), still greater emphasis can be placed on their characteristics and modes of operation.

Locations

In order to investigate the differences between grassroots and governmental museums in the Caribbean, it is informative to look at the locations of these museums. Upon dividing museums in these two categories of ownership on geographical maps of the region, it became apparent that there are noticeable differences in the placement of these museums (see figures 44-46). Namely, governmental museums are predominantly located in capital cities whereas grassroots museums can mostly be found elsewhere.

---

178 The term 'museum-like' has also been used to indicate those institutions that have deliberately chosen *not* to call themselves museums out of protest, for instance North American Indigenous institutions (Cooper 2008: 138).

On the map, this is most clearly seen in the larger countries or islands (*e.g.* Jamaica, Dominican Republic, Puerto Rico, Guadeloupe, Trinidad), due to the fact that the layout is more visible here and relatively more museums were present and/or visited. In these places, governmental museums are strongly clustered in the capital cities. Grassroots museums, although a few can be found in these capitals as well, are mostly located in other parts of the country.

Some more detailed observations of this phenomenon can be made. Governmental museums which are located outside of the capital cities can have been created with outreach as a deliberate intention – such as the *National Museum West* and the *National Gallery West* in Montego Bay, Jamaica, which are each branches of the corresponding national institution located in Kingston. In the Dominican Republic and Puerto Rico, governmental museums outside of the capital cities are archaeological museums: opened on or next to an archaeological site, the reasons for their non-capital locations are practical. In the Lesser Antilles, we can take a closer look at Dominica and Martinique, which both have mostly governmental museums. In Dominica, due to being (parts of) forts or national parks, several are located outside of the capital city again for practical reasons, whereas the *Kalinago Barana Auté* in the Kalinago Territory is a governmentally owned grassroots initiative (see Chapter 5). Somewhat similarly in Martinique, although many museums were created as grassroots initiatives, several have been passed on to governmental ownership for their continued sustainability and are now managed through the regional government.[179] Thus, a wide range of museums in terms of type, content, location, and related communities are all represented as governmentally owned. Grassroots museums can be found in capital cities, but largely elsewhere. Their appearance is particularly striking on islands where there are no governmental museums, such as Anguilla, Grenada, or Carriacou.

The explanations for the prevalence of governmental museums in capital cities are largely (historically) political. Financially and politically tied to cultural or other ministries, many governmental museums are (part of) national museums, trusts, and parks and thus carry national responsibility for the preservation and exhibition of heritage. Capital cities often being both heavily populated by nationals and frequently visited by tourists, placing museums in these locations allows for them to reach both local and tourist audiences and fulfill their nationally mandated missions. In addition, collections research or conservation can be supported by other public institutions such as universities or libraries. Nonetheless, the existence of grassroots museums elsewhere shows that there is a demand for and support of museum institutions by communities beyond the capital cities. Some of these museums were created to fill perceived gaps in the collections of governmental museums, for instance by preserving rural heritages (*e.g. Rome Museum*, Grenada).[180] Others are intended to reach out to communities inadequately represented in governmental museums, such as cultural (minority) communities (*e.g. Charles Town Maroon Museum*, Jamaica),[181]

---

179 Conversation with curator at *Musée Régional d'Histoire et d'Ethnographie* (Fort-de-France, Martinique, 16 March 2015).

180 Conversation with founder of *Rome Museum* (Walker, Grenada, 18 July 2014).

181 Conversation with relative of founder of *Charles Town Maroon Museum* (Charles Town, Jamaica, 26 July 2014).

or local communities unable to travel to and access museums in the capital (*e.g. Museo Profesor Tremols*, Dominican Republic).[182]

Thus, the creation of grassroots museums is a striking example of community engagement revealed through the location of these museums. Covering topics that are of interest to (local, cultural) communities, representing their narratives and histories, and providing access to heritage in other locations, these museums are deliberately working to fill gaps left by governmental museums and reach audiences who might otherwise be left out. These individuals and communities are stepping in to create museums where governmental museums are perceived to have fallen short. In closing, it can be reiterated that both the audiences and roles of grassroots and governmental museums are dissimilar. Although they may overlap, they position themselves differently in relation to Caribbean society, with governmental museums fulfilling national mandates and frequently adopting wide community engagement practices targeting many communities, and with grassroots museums reaching out to local communities, minority communities, or those not adequately catered to by governmental institutions. Collectively, they have shifted the role of Caribbean museums in relation to society by engaging with multiple layers and levels of contemporary Caribbean communities.

Dynamism

The political context of governmental museums as opposed to the more independent status of grassroots museums also has implications for their flexibility and dynamism, or their capacity to quickly respond to changing societal needs. In part, the limited dynamism of governmental museums is due to their bureaucracy, which not only demands governmental assessment and adherence to national policies, but also may result in slow decision-making processes. Elections and political changes often lead to the development of new policies which museums are then tasked to implement. However, by the time policy planning has concluded, new elections may be around the corner, allegiances swap over, and any planned changes are put to a halt.[183] Governments may change even twice within the same year, effectively halting any museum progress due to rapid changes in course.[184] Governmental museum staff can become frustrated with these political dependencies and the resulting stagnation. As an example, in one case the simple suggestion of creating a walkway – through grass which was frequently muddy and not accessible to wheelchairs or strollers – had been on hold for 9 years.[185]

For the other part, the limited dynamism of governmental museums is the result of their dependency on public funding. In some places with tight governmental budgets, funding for museums is similarly limited. The government of Jamaica, which is struggling with heavy debt-to-GDP ratios, has procured international loans and developed financial agreements which also place their spending under international restrictions and scrutiny. This has direct consequences for governmental museums, for example

---

182 Conversation with founder of *Museo Profesor Tremols* (Laguna Salada, Dominican Republic, 21 January 2015).

183 Conversation with guide at *Centro Indigena Caguana* (Utuado, Puerto Rico, 29 January 2015).

184 Conversation with curator at *National Museum & Art Gallery of Trinidad & Tobago* (Port of Spain, Trinidad, 6 January 2015).

185 Conversation with guide at *Centro Indigena Caguana* (Utuado, Puerto Rico, 29 January 2015).

by suspending the hiring of new staff.[186] Even when financially capable, governments may be reluctant to fund governmental museums, particularly those which have been perceived as stagnating, as they do not observe the museum having enough impact.[187] Museum staff expressed similar sentiments throughout the region that culture seems to come last in government spending. As noted in Puerto Rico, Caribbean culture "is lived by the people, but not preserved by the government."[188]

This is somewhat ironic, particularly considering the increasing investments in tourism and tourist development. To name a recent example, this has led to a public conflict in St. Lucia between the government and the Saint Lucia National Trust in 2017[189] (Seon 2017). Seen by many as a punishment of the Trust for opposing the construction of a dolphin park and their criticism of a Chinese-sponsored multibillion-dollar development project, the government of St. Lucia cut the entire subvention of the Trust to $0 for the 2017-2018 budget. The Prime Minister stated that this cut was not due to any conflict, but rather the result of a tight governmental budget in which every cent has to be justified and that government had decided no longer to pay for the recurrent expenses of the Trust. The opposition party has been vocal in opposing this cut, describing the decision as "vindictive" (Seon 2017). The Trust released a statement reaffirming their achievements since 1972 and future plans for the conservation and protection of St. Lucia's natural and cultural heritage, calling the decision "an unprecedented, unjustified and exceedingly unfortunate measure" (Saint Lucia National Trust 2017a: 3). As a direct result of this financial cut, the Saint Lucia National Trust had to announce the immediate closure of the *Walcott Place* museum which had only just been completed and opened to the public in 2016 (Saint Lucia National Trust 2017b; see figure 57). This example highlights the dependency of governmental museums and the immediate effect that a change in government or funding might have on such institutions.

As a final point relating to the funding of governmental museums: although they may benefit from public funding, they may be restricted (partially or entirely) from accessing private funds. Particularly concerning corporate sponsorship, governmental museums may not be allowed to accept such funds as they need to remain 'neutral' institutions. Governments may need to maintain their independence from private corporations as far as to disallow sponsorship of or even donations to governmental museums (*e.g. Museum of Parliament & National Heroes Gallery*, Barbados).[190]

The situation for grassroots museums is vastly different, both organizationally and financially. Run by individuals, communities, or non-governmental organizations, they do not operate as governmental institutions. However, their relationships to government may take many different forms. On one end of the spectrum are museums which are fully autonomous and are managed on every level by individuals

---

186 Conversation with archaeologist at *Jamaica National Heritage Trust* (Kingston, Jamaica, 23 July 2014).

187 Conversation with director of *Museo del Hombre Dominicano* (Santo Domingo, Dominican Republic, 16 January 2015).

188 Conversation with archaeologist at *Museo de Historia, Antropología y Arte* (San Juan, Puerto Rico, 28 January 2015).

189 Conversation with accountant at *St. Lucia National Trust* (via Skype, 4 May 2017).

190 Conversation with facilities coordinator at *Museum of Parliament & National Heroes Gallery* (Bridgetown, Barbados, 15 October 2015).

Figure 57: Walcott Place, St. Lucia, while under construction in October 2015.

in private capacities. On the other end of the spectrum are museums whose owners, staff, or board may contain individuals who are (also) politically active. Some of these grassroots museums may have complicated organizational structures while others lie in the hands of a sole individual. In practice, most grassroots museums enjoy greater independence than governmental museums, giving them opportunities to more easily implement new ideas and more rapidly respond to community needs. Thus, many of these museums tend to be quite dynamic in the sense that they are continuously developing their exhibitions, their facilities, and their programs. Even if in some cases the exhibition galleries might appear to be static on the whole, in reality new objects and new information may be added on a regular basis without the need to change everything at once.

Financially, grassroots museums may at first appear to be disadvantaged as opposed to governmental museums, as they do not directly receive public funding. However, as the previous paragraphs showed, public funding can also come with particular restrictions and disadvantages. Although the running costs of grassroots museums are generally not governmentally financed, they still may receive recurring or incidental governmental support. For instance, grassroots museums may be located in buildings, monuments, or parks which are governmentally owned or rented. Grassroots museums may also apply for governmental funding for specific projects or events, such as new developments or programs. In these cases, funding will be sought on the basis of grants and other funding parties, such as private or corporate funders, may also be approached. Generally, such governmental funding will only be accepted if it is not contingent on political interference in the museum's functioning.

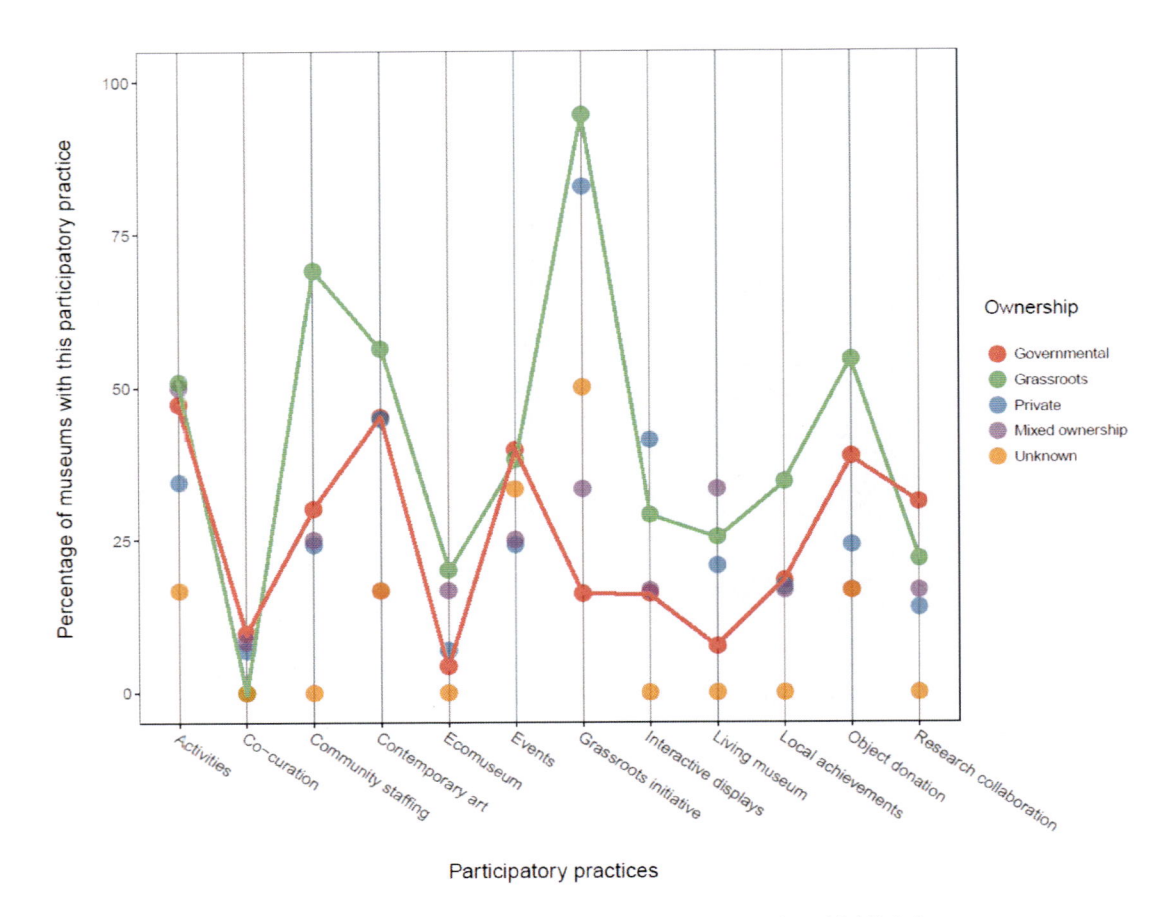

Figure 58: Percentage of museums which have any of the participatory practices, highlighting governmental museums vs. grassroots museums.

In fact, grassroots museums may also have deliberate missions to remain fully financially independent. *Casa Pueblo* in Puerto Rico refuses to accept any donations from governments or organizations.[191]

The organizational and financial differences between governmental museums and grassroots museums and their resulting differences in dynamism can be seen in the types of participatory practices which these two categories of museums employ and also in the frequency and speed at which they are able to alter or implement such practices. To begin with a closer look at the participatory practices of governmental museums, on first glance it is apparent that governmental museums employ relatively fewer participatory practices across the board (see figure 58). Upon closer inspection, we can see that governmental museums are rarely grassroots initiatives, which is to be expected as most of them were governmentally founded. Perhaps more surprising is that they less frequently exhibit local achievements, possibly due to their mission to appeal to a wide audience and therefore refrain from celebrating individual achievements. In addition, the ecomuseum concept (see *Ecomuseums*, page 73) is rarely

---

191 Conversation with founder of *Casa Pueblo* (Adjuntas, Puerto Rico, 29 January 2015).

THE SOCIAL MUSEUM IN THE CARIBBEAN

adopted by governmental museums, probably also due to the ecomuseum's inherent focus on a particular community and its needs. Also noticeable is that governmental museums relatively contain fewer interactive displays, which could be a result of funding (either the amount of funding or the restrictions on what funds can be used for). Instead, governmental museums direct their community engagement endeavors towards a few specific participatory practices. Often unable to overhaul exhibitions on a regular basis, governmental museums respond to changing societal needs by implementing and changing activities and events. These practices which engage with communities during the museum visit, as opposed to being part of the organization of the museum or the collecting and exhibiting processes, are more temporary and flexible. Of particular note is governmental museums' frequent collaboration with others (such as universities) in terms of research. Possibly due to their governmental ties, they more often engage in collections research or public research, exhibiting those results within the museum.

On the other hand, grassroots museums are overall and relatively more participatory. Expectedly, this is most dominantly seen in the practices which relate to the foundation and organization of the museum, such as the categories 'grassroots initiative,' 'ecomuseum,' and 'community staffing.' Relatively high degrees of participation can also been seen in practices relating to collection and exhibition processes, such as the exhibition of work by contemporary artists. Grassroots museums also more frequently exhibit, or at least more transparently credit in their exhibitions, objects donated by the public. Equally many grassroots museums engage their communities through activities and events as governmental museums. In actuality, there are only two categories in which grassroots museums relatively less frequently employ participatory practices: research collaboration and co-curation. The former may be due to them having fewer ties to governmental research institutes. The latter is due to the definition of co-curation as being exhibitions created as a collaboration between a museum and community members (see *Co-curation*, page 92). As grassroots museums are run by community members, in effect the process of the creation of their exhibitions is not in the same way a collaboration between 'outsiders' and 'insiders' and thus this category has been left blank for these museums.

In summary, the differences in dependencies of organization and funding of governmental museums vs. grassroots museums has distinct implications on the dynamism of these institutions and their ability to adapt to changing needs of Caribbean societies. This is visible in the different participatory practices employed by these two categories of museums, whereby governmental museums predominantly engage with their communities temporarily through activities and events, unlike grassroots museums which engage with their communities throughout all aspects of their work. Thus, the participatory practices employed across the board by grassroots museums allow them to respond to community needs in a plurality of ways: whether there is a desire for different staffing or a request to exhibit newly donated objects. Governmental museums often find themselves in less flexible situations, thereby directing their community engagement efforts towards activities and events that take contemporary needs into account.

Sustainability

A demand for sustainability particularly plagues grassroots museums, many of which have been accused of not being sustainable. In some cases, this perceived problem of sustainability is due to a lack of consistent sources of funding or of long-term plans. For the most part, however, the problem is placed with the staffing of these museums, particularly those with only a handful or a single member of staff. The arguments in any of these cases are easily made. Grassroots museums that function on the basis of ad hoc funding may at any moment run into financial trouble, leading them to closure, with the future of their collections uncertain. Similarly, if such a museum does not have meticulous long-term plans, specifically for the conservation and preservation of the collections, objects may deteriorate irreparably and, in the absence of comprehensive catalogues, knowledge of the collections may be lost. Of course, the previous section has shown that the sustainability of governmental museums cannot be guaranteed either.

Nonetheless, it is the sustainability of the 'human resources' of these museums that is seen as the most problematic. Particularly for grassroots museums run by individuals, what will happen to their collections and their museum when they pass away? Certainly, accessibility can already be an issue with these museums if their owner is temporarily unavailable to open the museum – like when *Sur la Trace des Arawaks* in St. Martin was closed during the maternity leave of the owner in 2014. Naturally, the death of the owner places the museum in great uncertainty. Questions arise over the inheritance of the collection and whether any friends or family members are willing to take over the museum. The *Whaling Museum*, known first as *Athneal's Private Petit Museum*, was founded by local harpooner Athneal Ollivierre on the island of Bequia. Upon his death in 2000, the museum passed to his closest friend and nephew Harold Corea, who was also a whaler and had been an actor in, or at least heard, all of the stories of the collection. Following Mr. Corea's subsequent death, the future of the collection became uncertain. At the time of visiting (2015) it had been moved to the *Boat Museum* in Bequia and efforts were underway to find a volunteer to keep the museum open.

If no relatives or community members are interested in preserving the collections or keeping the museum open, other solutions may be sought. As mentioned in the opening of this chapter, several grassroots museums in Martinique have changed ownership and been passed on to the government to assure their long-term sustainability. For instance, *La Maison de la Canne* was created in 1987 by a foundation who wished to preserve the rapidly disappearing sugar cane heritage on the island. In light of the aging of the foundation's members and in order to ensure its accessibility and sustainability, the museum was donated to the regional government.[192] In the case of *Museo Profesor Tremols* in the Dominican Republic, it is the local community who has taken an interest in the future of the museum and its collections. Plans were being developed in 2015 to catalogue the collections and the community suggested moving (parts of) the collections to a new purpose-built building. The underlying idea was that such a move would improve the accessibility of these collections – which are now

---

192 Conversation with curator at *Musée Régional d'Histoire et d'Ethnographie* (Fort-de-France, Martinique, 16 March 2015).

Figure 59: The objects in The Old House, St. Martin, became vibrant through the narratives of the founder and in dialogue with visitors.

located in the home of the owner – and ensure the longevity of the museum which the community deems highly valuable. In yet again other cases, collections may be sold or auctioned off and the museum simply closed.

Thus it is particularly the lifespan of people which is primarily noted as the 'problem' for the sustainability of grassroots museums. Therefore, the 'solution' is mainly proposed in terms of cataloguing collections, changing the museum's ownership, or moving the collections. However, I would argue that it is in fact not only impossible to preserve these individually-owned grassroots museums, but perhaps even undesirable. The reason being that the owners and founders of these museums are their essence; in their absence the main value or purpose of the museum may vanish.

To illustrate this argument with an example, the late Pierre Beauperthuy of *The Old House* in St. Martin – who was tragically murdered in 2015 in the home which was also his museum – had been essential to animating his collections. Known around the island and to many visitors as an extraordinary storyteller, it was his memories, his narratives, and his life that formed the essence of the museum. Without him, his museum could have been mistaken for an indoor garage sale: a house full of furniture and objects, stacked on top of each other, some items on the floor, everything covered in dust (see figure 59). Framed sepia photographs are placed on chairs, mothballs are on the bed under a mosquito net, and the display cases filled in 1999 have since been covered by so many new objects that their original contents are difficult to see. While this image may be a visitor's first impression, it does not convey the essence of the museum and it is certainly not the image with which the visitor will have left. Mr. Beauperthuy welcomed every visitor personally and inquired where you are from, adjusting his narrative to topics that might be of relevance to you. He would enthusiastically plunge into the history of the house, his childhood home, and his family tree, tracing his lineage to Pierre Auguste Beauperthuy who had been sent to St. Martin in 1843 by Napoleon III to set up salt works.[193] As he guided you through the small rooms of his home, the objects gained depth and meaning through his narrative. He opened drawers and showed hidden items, letting you touch certain things, inviting you into their hidden meanings. By the end, you are left in awe of Mr. Beauperthuy's life, his extraordinary experiences, and his stories. Before leaving, he would ask you to sign his guestbook as he has asked every visitor, including members of royal families – "perhaps one day, you will be famous too!" he laughed.

During the course of the visit, it becomes apparent that the museum is a valuable part of local heritage. In truth, despite reports of Mr. Beauperthuy's collection having been the reason for the armed robberies, it is the founder himself, rather than his collection, who is the most valuable part of the museum. How could one attempt to preserve a museum whose essence lies not in its objects but in its owner? A museum that is animated, which comes alive, thanks to the narratives of its creator and his or her dialogue with the visitor? Certainly, one could collect an oral history of the owner, preserving video or audio footage of a guided tour of the museum (see *Grassroots Initiatives*, page 68). Or, one could catalogue the collections and try to recreate the museum, possibly in a different location. But in any of these cases, the essential value and purpose of the museum would change to such a degree that perhaps it cannot be considered the same museum.

It is these considerations of the 'problem' of sustainability for grassroots museums that have led me to critically reconsider the role of museums in the Caribbean – and elsewhere. Traditionally, since the formal modern development of museums as extensions of the nation state, their purpose was heavily focused on longevity, permanence, and the conservation of heritage for future generations. Although museums certainly have very significant roles to play in the present and for contemporary societies, their long-term purpose is automatically assumed and in some cases prioritized. These museums have vast collections in storages, of which only a small percentage is permanently on display, with other objects temporarily gaining exposure. In the ICOM definition of the museum, the term 'permanent institution' is prominent, advocating for sustainability as a priority.

Yet, perhaps sustainability does not need to be a priority for all museums: perhaps there are those, such as grassroots museums founded by individuals, whose purpose and role lies almost exclusively in the present. I propose calling them 'ephemeral museums' to signify their relatively short-lived existence in a single form. This is certainly not to say that their collections are worthless for the future and should not be preserved. Rather, that the museum as an animated entity, comprised of the landscape, collections, owner, and narratives, ceases to be when one of these parts is lost. The museum as it was has played its part and thinking it can be preserved intact would be missing the point. While one could preserve parts of the ephemeral museum, such as the collections or the museum building, the result would be a new museum, with a new purpose and a new societal role. Ephemeral museums may be particularly suited to engage with communities who might otherwise feel disassociated from the more

---

193 Conversation with founder of *The Old House* (Quartier D'Orleans, St. Martin, 2 February 2014).

traditional museum concept. In comparing governmental museums and grassroots museums, their temporality should be reconsidered, implying differences in their societal roles which can work complementarily. Specifically for grassroots museums, the need for sustainability can be critically examined and in the case of each museum one can consider whether it has fulfilled its societal role or whether continuation of parts of it in a different form is desirable. As such, governmental museums and grassroots museums may have different roles to play in contemporary society and for future societies.

Participatory Practices

The diversity of the Caribbean and her people draws frequent attention and is often mentioned as one of the particular characteristics of the region – including in this research. Thus one of the first aims of this research was to see whether the diversity of Caribbean communities was reflected in Caribbean museums and their participatory practices. In this section, the discussion will keep a regional perspective but will focus on regional trends in the adoption and adaptation of participatory practices, rather than the broad comparison made in the previous section between grassroots museums and governmental museums. It should be reiterated, though, that the noted presence of a participatory practice in any given museum does not necessarily imply its success or its impact.

Multi-vocality

Multi-vocality – the inclusion or presence of multiple voices – has been debated within museological literature for a number of decades. Particularly related to community engagement literature, and part of the landscape of the New Museology, multi-vocal exhibitions are often advocated as a way for museums to step away from authoritative, master narratives and showcase how histories and heritages are complex and multi-faceted. The goal of such multi-vocal exhibitions is to 'impartially' present multiple perspectives, to allow visitors to make their own interpretations, and to include multiple communities or audiences within the museum narrative.

Such multi-vocal exhibitions can also be found in the Caribbean, where the voices of multiple communities can be 'heard' within the same museum. Quite literally showcasing the voices of multiple local communities within one museum, is the exhibition *Nos communes d'hier à aujourd'hui* [Our municipalities from yesterday to today] at the *Ecomusée CreoleArt* in Guadeloupe. This exhibition consists of a long row of 32 identical wooden cabinets, each of which corresponds to one of the municipalities of Guadeloupe. Each municipality was contacted to fill their cabinet with information and items characteristic or important to them and to decorate and design the inside of the cabinet as they wished. Thus, outwardly identical, the cabinets are all unique. Some municipalities have created their cabinet with school groups or local historical societies, in other cases a local mayor has taken a leading position, yet others have sent objects and asked the museum to arrange them on their behalf. Many cabinets contain short histories of the municipality with photographs, objects, or local products, and encourage people to come and visit. Although perhaps not as literal, other examples of multi-vocal exhibitions can be found in which the main narrative is complemented by the stories of local community members or in which academic specialists such as volcanologists, archaeologists, biologists, or others are quoted.

There is also the possibility of museums with single narratives to encourage the inclusion or indeed intervention of other voices. Although certainly not 'objective,' the main panel texts in the *Musée Schoelcher* in Guadeloupe are written as a rather linear narrative by an anonymous curatorial voice. This narrative, quite chronologically, tells the tale of Victor Schoelcher, the founder of the museum's collection: from his family life and his collection of plaster casts of famous marble statues, to his travels around the world, and concluding with his political activities towards the abolition of slavery in France. Opened in 1887, the museum's core collection remains the same, although its displays, objects on loan, and narratives have been changed. It is particularly Schoelcher's involvement in the French abolition of slavery that the museum's staff has identified as a topic demanding exploration from multiple perspectives. Thus, at the time of visiting (March 2015), the main museum exhibitions were subject to an intervention by Guy Gabon. Her contemporary art exhibition, *Carte Blanche*,[194] consisted of multiple artworks, each grappling with the legacies and traces of slavery, the slave trade, and colonization, as well as with the fragility of these traces due to the threat of forgetfulness (panel texts, Musée Schoelcher). As most of her artworks were made in situ, they are also inspired by her conversations with museum visitors (Virassamy 2015). In addition, the museum is part of the UNESCO supported *Route de l'Esclave*, which visitors can follow throughout Guadeloupe. The sites on this route are marked with special panels and the route as a whole is complemented by a booklet, as well as a series of short YouTube films. Thus, while the museum's panels tell one narrative, this voice is complemented by that of the UNESCO slave route project and by annual artistic interventions.

Multi-vocal exhibitions may also contain the voices of multiple persons from the same community. As communities are not homogeneous, museums may struggle to represent a community within their exhibition. One example, already mentioned in a previous chapter (see *Co-curation*, page 92), was the co-curated temporary exhibition *Rastafari* held at the *National Museum Jamaica*. This exhibition contained two sets of panel texts, one written by curators and one written by Rastafari in their own words and tone. Besides the existence of two clear perspectives, visible to the visitor in the form of these panel texts, additional narratives were told by the Rastafari who volunteered as exhibition guides. The Rastafari community had disagreed on numerous occasions throughout the exhibition-making process, due to their diverse perspectives and opinions. Some community guides preferred the Rastafari panels, while others used the curatorial panels as part of their own narrative during their tours.

While there are many Caribbean examples of multi-vocal museums – museums which exhibit voices from multiple communities, or multiple voices from one community, or otherwise complement the museum narrative with external interventions – many of these are not aimed to present strongly conflicting perspectives. Rather than presenting contentious perspectives and encouraging the visitor to pick a side in the

---

194 *Carte Blanche* is an annual exhibition grant created and funded by *Musée Schoelcher*. Since 2010, each year a different local artist is granted *carte blanche* to engage the permanent exhibition of the museum in a temporary intervention.

debate, most of these multi-vocal exhibitions seem intent to make people feel included rather than risk them feeling confronted.

In addition to these examples, one could interpret multi-vocality to include those museums which present single narratives of communities who have otherwise been underrepresented or misrepresented in (national) museum narratives. Elsewhere, such museums have been criticized for their *lack* of multi-vocality and their espousing of single narratives without gratifying alternative viewpoints (*e.g.* the *Museum of Free Derry* in Northern Ireland, Crooke 2011b: 34). However, this criticism has been contested by Fiona Candlin who states that while these museums may be presenting their narratives from a single perspective, unlike traditional master narratives they are often transparently partisan and do not pretend to be objective (Candlin 2016: 88-91). In fact, where communities or heritages have been traditionally not represented, underrepresented, or misrepresented, such museums which tell these 'alternative' narratives, may in fact be supporting multi-vocality in the wider museum sphere. What's more, if these museums had attempted to develop their exhibits from a balanced, multi-perspective approach, they could risk perpetuating oppression.

Multi-vocality by presenting these kinds of 'alternative' histories in Caribbean museums is most commonly the result of grassroots initiatives. Many of these museums have been created purposefully to preserve and/or present heritages and histories that are not (aptly) included in other (national) museums. In some cases, the mission of the museum might be to improve the visibility of a minority community or to alter a dominant narrative. For example, while most museums in Jamaica – particularly the national museums – explain how maroon communities resulted from the co-habitation of escaped enslaved Africans with Amerindian groups concealed in the interior, staff at the *Charles Town Maroon Museum* emphasize that their ancestry does not include Amerindians although they did learn many things from them.[195] Such narratives may be important for visitors and staff alike in affirming identities and sharing information which they have not readily been able to access elsewhere. Particularly for communities who have been underrepresented in the past, such knowledge may be important to community members for positioning themselves in relation to others. As one visitor wrote elsewhere in Jamaica, "next time someone drop a racist remark I can drop some facts on them" (guest book entry, National Museum West, July 2015).

Some museums which present 'alternative' histories may have more outspoken political intentions, for instance to advocate for increased rights for their community or to seek justice for past crimes. An example of a highly contested and political 'alternative' narrative is told at the *Museo Memorial de la Resistencia Dominicana*, Dominican Republic. With a mission to promote awareness of the struggles of Dominicans during the dictatorship of Rafael Trujillo (assassinated in 1961), the museum tells a highly contested history which was hushed for many decades (De Peña Díaz 2013). The museum complex includes former torture cells and its exhibitions speak openly of murder and genocide, such as the massacres of Haitians. The museum takes a strong position as a human rights advocate and memorializes the victims of the dictatorship, encouraging visitors to provide information about friends or family members who were affected.

---

195 Conversation with relative of founder of *Charles Town Maroon Museum* (Charles Town, Jamaica, 26 July 2014).

Figure 60: The multilingual displays of Museo Tula, Curaçao, begin at the museum entrance.

Considering such a history which was politically suppressed for many decades, it seems hardly surprising that the museum cannot be neutral in its retelling of these histories. Although it presents multiple voices through its extensive panel texts and other media which contain detailed research, the museum does not actively encourage alternative or opposing viewpoints. Nonetheless, this should not be grounds to criticize the museum as lacking multi-vocality. Indeed, such a museum "assists in the process of creating multiple perspectives because it supplants and challenges existing unilateral accounts" (Candlin 2016: 90).

Beyond the content of the narratives which are told in panel texts or tours, their form, *i.e.* the languages used, can also support multi-vocality. These languages may reveal which communities are targeted by the museum. Some museums may 'speak' only in one language, focusing on a local or tourist language. Others may be bi- or multi-lingual, varying in their panel texts, guides, or audio tours. Some museum displays may be in local or creole languages, highlighting the close ties to a local community. In Curaçao, the *Savonet Museum*'s panels can be read in all three official languages, Papiamentu, Dutch, and English, plus also in Spanish. The island has a very high degree of bilingualism, with many people able to converse in two or even more languages, although Papiamentu is most widely spoken as a first language. Other museums on the island reveal their narrower intended audiences through the languages used. The *Curacao Maritime Museum,* aimed primarily at (Dutch and other) tourists, has panels only in Dutch and English. On the other hand, *Museo Tula,* whose mission is to represent the local Afro-Caribbean community, has panels in Papiamentu with some of them accompanied by English translations (see figure 60). Certain colonial documents related to slavery are presented in the original Dutch. As a final Curaçaoan example, the *Octagon Museum* about the history of Simón Bolívar has bilingual panel texts in English and Spanish, as the museum is frequently visited by Venezuelans.

Beyond narratives, museums may support multi-vocality through the use of additional participatory practices, such as the exhibition of donated objects from members of communities, the development of a diverse range of activities, or by supporting local artists in exhibiting their work and their contemporary critiques of society. Certainly, grassroots initiatives and community staffing are fundamental participatory practices which can support multi-vocality throughout much of the museum's work. In addition, multi-vocality can also be achieved when museum displays are activated strongly through dialogues between staff and visitors. In these cases, visitors "play an active part in establishing the exhibition narrative" (Candlin 2016: 45), temporarily adding their voices to those of the museum. This type of multi-vocality will be different with each visit.

As a final note, although Caribbean museums can be multi-vocal in a multitude of manners and to varying degrees, they are not per se *inclusive*. Certain museums may so strongly advocate specific community voices, that other (opposing) voices may be unquestionably excluded. In other cases, dissident voices may be present but only peripherally so. Nonetheless, from a regional perspective, many Caribbean museums have adopted multi-vocality in their narratives and other aspects of their work and thus Caribbean museums as a whole can engage with more parts of Caribbean society. Although certain communities may be excluded from certain museums, taken on the whole the Caribbean museum sphere has become more multi-vocal and more inclusive, not least due to its many grassroots initiatives.

Museum Types

Here we will look in more detail at which types of museums employ which participatory practices by highlighting a few expected as well as some unexpected examples. All museums studied in the course of the regional museum survey were divided into seven museum types (see *Regional Museum Survey*, page 49). These categories are: archaeology, art, built heritage (*e.g.* forts), history, mixed content (for those museums which have more than one focus), nature/science, and popular culture (*e.g.* film, music, food). In charting the relative frequencies of the participatory practices employed by museums of each type, for instance how many percent of art museums engage in co-curation, some trends can be visualized (see figure 50). This visual representation can be assessed in more detail as to why certain museums types are participatory in certain ways.

To begin with a few correlations that were expected due to fieldwork observations or which make sense due to the definitions of the categories. For instance, of all visited museums of the 'art' type, 100% of them employ the participatory practice 'contemporary art' by collecting and/or exhibiting these kinds of artworks. Based on the definitions of the 'museum type' categories and the participatory practices, this was to be expected, although it is still interesting to see that even art museums with largely historical art collections engage with contemporary artists. Another observation made during fieldwork can also be supported by this data visualization, namely that popular culture museums are predominantly (in 75% of the cases) the result of grassroots initiatives. It seems that even if governmentally created museums include popular culture, it does not typify the institution as a whole. Museums which focus on rum, cacao, cigars, sports, music, or films are mostly private or grassroots museums.

Trends can also be discerned which reveal certain types of museums to be generally 'more participatory' while others are 'less participatory' (see figure 61). In this image, lines have been drawn to highlight the relative percentage of participatory practices employed by built heritage museums and by mixed content museums. Overall, built heritage museums very rarely adopt participatory practices, with the exception of being 'living museums.' This type of museum consists mainly of tangible heritage sites, such as forts, religious buildings, ruins, or historic city centers. While some of these sites may contain or be connected to exhibition spaces with objects on display, many of them only provide information on panels or in the form of audio tours. It is primarily the structures themselves – the church, the fort, the houses – which are on display to the public. Thus, in many ways, it makes sense that these types of museums or heritage sites do not have donated objects on display (since they rarely have objects on display at all). However, built heritage museums could strive to pursue more engagement with communities through activities, events, or interactive displays, for instance. Built heritage museums do engage with communities in a particular way that is more rare for other museums types, namely as living museums. Historic city centers are prime examples as they are literally being lived in: visitors to such a site might easily approach residents and engage in dialogue with them while owners or managers of this type of built heritage need to be in regular contact with residents.

On the other end of the spectrum, when seen over all the participatory practices, mixed content museums are quite participatory. It is difficult to make generalizations about this type of museum, as the museums are so diverse: from small house-museums to large, national institutions. Nonetheless, these museums are characterized by their relatively frequent inclusion of participatory practices and this may in part be due to their diversity in collections and content. For instance, some of these museums have chosen to add contemporary artworks to their displays, even if the remainder of their collections are not specifically focused on art. Many mixed content museums engage in activities and events, possibly to explore their diverse collections with different audiences or to bring the different aspects of the museum into public view. However, they more rarely engage in research collaborations with, for instance, universities or other institutions. Perhaps due to the diverse nature of their collections, these mixed content museum might not be able to dedicate their staff to researching only a segment of these collections. These museums also have a large amount of donated objects on display and in fact in some cases these donations may actually be the reason for the museum's broad focus. The *Musée du Rhum: Musée Universel* in Guadeloupe is a quintessential example. Located at the distillery Reimonenq, the museum was opened in 1990 as a rum museum and expanded with an additional gallery containing reconstructed distillery equipment in 1992. Following the donation of entomologist Fortuné Chalumeau's extensive collections of specimens, the museum added an impressive insect gallery. Similar expansions were made in 1997 with the addition of a gallery on local trades and crafts as well as a model ship gallery. As a result, the 'museum of rum' became a 'universal museum' in name as well as in focus.

We have seen that built heritage museums are generally low in their employment of participatory practices, whereas mixed content museums are overall highly

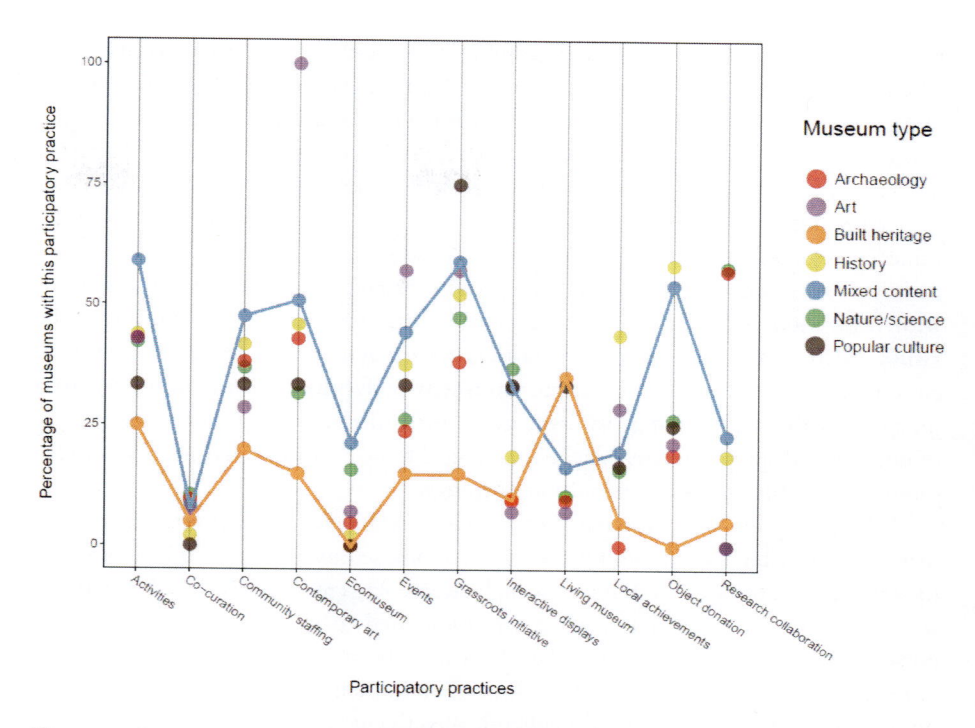

Figure 61: Percentage of museums which have any of the participatory practices, high-lighting built heritage museums vs. mixed content museums.

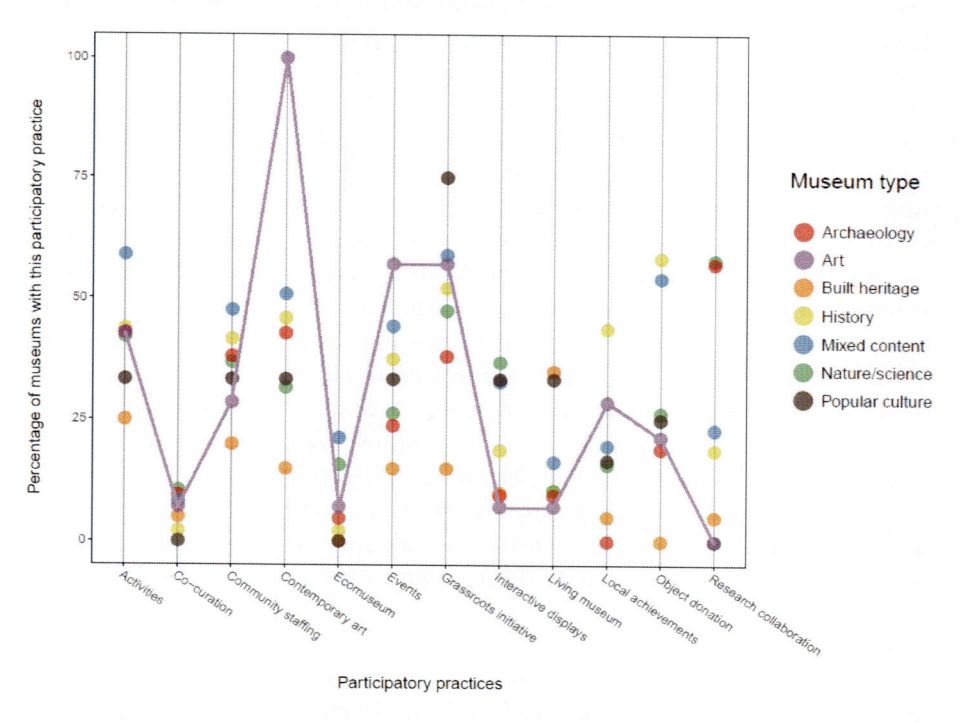

Figure 62: Percentage of museums which have any of the participatory practices, high-lighting art museums.

participatory. Other museum types seem to have very specific participatory styles whereby they employ certain practices heavily and others exceedingly rarely. A closer look at art museums and archaeology museums highlights this specificity of participatory practices. Art museums reveal a preference for certain types of participatory practices, even when disregarding the obviously high presence of 'contemporary art' (see figure 62). For instance, many art museums host events and they exhibit local achievements, primarily by celebrating the lives and works of local artists. However, art museums very rarely contain interactive displays or engage in research collaborations with institutions – at least, such collaborations are not transparently visible to the visitor. Such preferences for specific participatory practices may reveal differences in curatorial practices. Curators in art museums may prefer their galleries to be free from interactive displays, directing visitors to enjoy the collections in specific ways. Instead of interactive displays, visitors may be encouraged to take part in activities or return for events such as fundraisers or exhibition openings.

Archaeology museums also have very specific preferences for their use of participatory practices which are quite different from art museums (see figure 63). Unlike art museums, archaeology museums to a high degree engage in research collaborations with institutions, the results of which are showcased to visitors. Many archaeology museums rely on past or ongoing archaeological fieldwork and research for the creation of their collections and to update the information in their panels. While some of these museums conduct archaeological fieldwork directly, others are in close contact with universities, national trusts, or commercial archaeological companies. Many archaeology museums also exhibit contemporary art, which might seem surprising at first. However, if one considers the frequent presence of illustrations, sculptures, dioramas, and other artworks which are added to archaeology museums to visualize past cultures, the use of this participatory practice makes sense. Yet, archaeology museums more rarely organize events and strikingly few contain interactive displays. The latter may be partially explained as a matter of funding and the prioritization of funds, with the majority of archaeology museums (62%) being governmental institutions.

In sum, the prevalence of participatory practices differs based on the type of museum, such that it is more likely to find interactive displays in a nature/science museum than in an art museum, or that community members have the opportunity to attend events at most art museums but only at a small amount of built heritage museums. Certain museum types, such as mixed content museums, are relatively highly participatory with regards to all practices, while others, like built heritage museums, are much less participatory. In other cases the museum's type, and thus its collections and the curatorial culture of its staff, lead to distinctly specific participatory styles in which some practices occur frequently and others are largely disregarded. Naturally, museums can always (re-)consider whether such a focus is suitable depending on their collections, resources, mission, and the communities they wish to engage with.

Linguistic Differences

Using a similar relative representation of the data, participatory styles can also be identified, albeit tentatively, when dividing the museums' participatory practices into the four linguistic areas of the Dutch, English, French and Spanish Caribbean (see figure 52). As mentioned in Chapter 2, these linguistic areas delineate geopolitical

THE SOCIAL MUSEUM IN THE CARIBBEAN

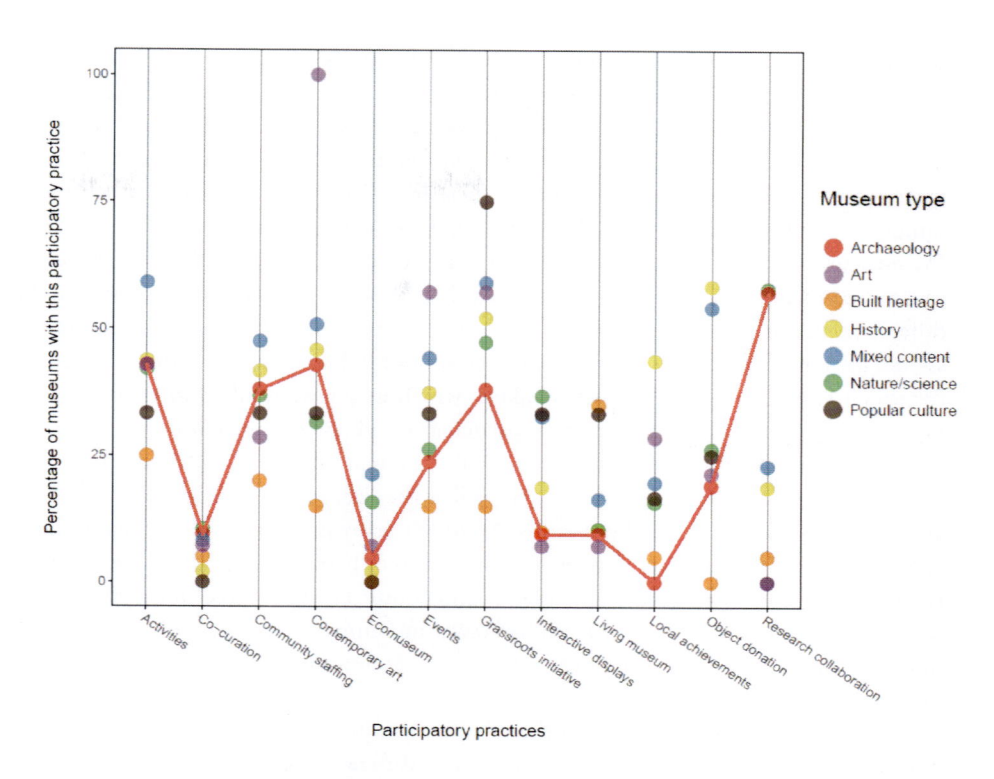

Figure 63: Percentage of museums which have any of the participatory practices, highlighting archaeology museums.

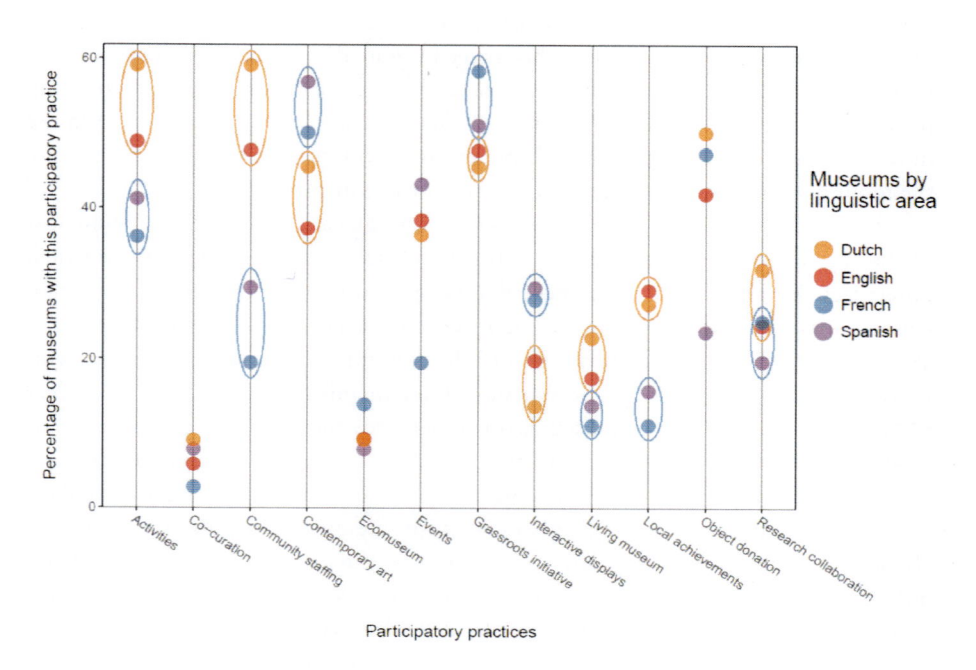

Figure 64: Percentage of museums which have any of the participatory practices, highlighting pairs of Dutch-English museums vs. French-Spanish museums.

sub-regions which can reveal colonial legacies in all aspects, including in museums. A separation of the data by linguistic area shows, for instance, the percentage of museums in the Spanish-speaking Caribbean which have interactive displays. It should be emphasized that the figure represents relative frequencies of these practices, in order to better compare the museums according to these four linguistic areas. In actuality, the sample is overrepresented by English (86 museums or 44%) and Spanish museums (51 museums or 26%), whereas the French (36 museums or 19%) and Dutch museums (22 museums or 11%) are underrepresented. It is possible that due to these absolute differences in museums per linguistic area the relative results can be biased. Similarly, it should be remembered that this data might be subject to bias due to my language skills (of which French and Spanish were weakest) which may have resulted in erroneously not recognizing the presence of certain participatory practices. Beyond these possible biases, the participatory style was certainly also influenced by the different types of museums visited in each linguistic area, as well as the sizes of the countries and islands and their respective amount of museums. Although many museums were visited in the Spanish-speaking Caribbean, these were confined to only two places – the Dominican Republic and Puerto Rico. Multiple islands and countries were visited in the English-speaking Caribbean, but most of them had fewer museums on average. This, of course, can affect the roles of these museums, as well as the communities they engage with and the participatory practices they employ.

Nonetheless, even when keeping these biases in mind, it is certainly interesting to note that this representation of the data shows a difference in participatory practices per linguistic area. In particular, one could very tentatively speak of a Dutch-English participatory style and a French-Spanish participatory style, as the dots symbolizing the participatory practices of museums per linguistic area mostly occur together in these two pairs (see figure 64). To look at this image in more detail, it appears that relatively more Dutch and English museums organize activities, have community staff, are living museums, celebrate local achievements, and engage in research collaborations. On the other hand, more French and Spanish museums are exhibiting contemporary art, are the result of grassroots initiatives, and have interactive displays.

The remaining four participatory practices do not clearly show these same linguistic pairing. Co-curation and ecomuseums are both relatively rare practices, for which differences in presence might be more due to opportunity rather than for any other reason. Although, the slightly higher occurrence of ecomuseums in French-speaking areas might be due to the French origin of the concept and a greater familiarity with it. The final two categories that do not show these linguistic pairings, both have clear outliers: relatively few French museums organize events and relatively few Spanish museums exhibit object donations. These two outliers are interesting points for discussion. Possibly the former might be because some of the French museums are managed collectively through the regional government and events are organized collectively – it may also simply be a lack of transparent information on the presence of events. The latter outlier may be due to cultural, curatorial, historical, or legal differences. Perhaps these museums have such extensive collections as a result of colonial legacies that they do not encourage object donations – or maybe donated objects are not always marked as such in the exhibition space for curatorial purposes. Apart from these four categories, the remainder seem to show patterns of participatory styles.

What might be the reasons for linguistic pairs of participatory styles? Could more French and Spanish museums include contemporary art in their exhibitions simply because more French and Spanish art museums were visited? No, an equal amount of 8% of museums visited in the English, French, and Spanish-speaking areas were typified as art museums, with none categorized as such in the Dutch-speaking Caribbean.[196] Yet, 37-57% of all museums included contemporary artworks in their exhibitions or collections. Thus the answer must be more complex than a simple correlation with the amount of museums of a certain type visited and might be influenced by cultural differences, perhaps in the amount of support given to contemporary artists.

Similarly we may wonder why French and Spanish museums more often have interactive displays. An initial hypothesis might be that it is due to differences in funding, particularly in the funding necessary for digital interactive displays. Certainly, relatively many of the Spanish museums are private institutions which may have more access to funds. However, the category of interactive displays also contains many non-digital forms of interactivity such as experimentation, demonstration, or tasting, none of which necessarily depend on heavy funding. Thus, this difference may well also be caused by curatorial or cultural differences.

In the case of the prevalence of local achievements being included in Dutch and English museums, this seems most likely to be the result of a different relationship between museums and communities, with relatively more Dutch (36%) and English (33%) museums having grassroots ownership. The difference might also be amplified by cultural differences which direct the extent to which local individuals are celebrated publicly.

In sum, although there are many caveats to be made, and possible sampling or researcher biases, a tentative hypothesis can be suggested that different participatory styles exist depending on the museum's location in the Dutch-, English-, French- or Spanish-speaking Caribbean. Although more research is needed to support this interpretation and to uncover the underlying reasons for these differences, they could partially be due to diverse colonial legacies, curatorial training, museological traditions, cultural specificities, or directed by the particular communities museums are attempting to engage. As a result of these distinct participatory styles, the role of Caribbean museums in Caribbean societies might similarly differ in each of the four linguistic areas, with both the styles and roles more closely comparative between Dutch-English museums and French-Spanish museums.

Community Engagement Processes

The previous sections of this chapter have taken a regional perspective on characteristics of Caribbean museums and their participatory practices. In this final section, the discussion zooms in to a micro level in order to more closely consider the dynamics of community engagement processes. Whereas it is one thing to observe which participatory practices are employed by a museum, it requires a different approach to grasp the underlying dynamics that are involved in the conception, development, implementation, and evaluation of community engagement projects. Such an understanding

---

196 Of course, 'mixed content' or other categories of museum types also contain art, but this analysis refers to those museums which were categorized as 'art' museums.

of dynamics tends to take longer, as multiple parties are involved over a period of time, constantly influencing the course of the process. These sections concerning the processes of community engagement will focus on the two case studies undertaken in the course of this research: the *Kalinago Barana Autê* in Dominica and the *Bengal to Barbados* exhibition project at the *Barbados Historical Museum & Society*.

Representativity

Both case studies were similar in the sense that the communities in question were relatively small (both consisting of roughly 3000 persons) and form a minority group within the overall population of their respective countries.[197] One might think that with such relatively small communities their representation would not be particularly difficult. At a first glance it seems possible to identify these communities, pick a few 'key' members, and invite them as representatives to work on a community engagement project, such as a new museum or exhibition. In fact, the representativity of communities, even in the case of communities of such relatively small sizes, is considerably more complicated and prone to lead to conflict if not well handled. Representativity needs to be carefully considered as heritage is often important to all members of the community and thus any heritage project needs to ensure that it is of benefit (whether tangibly or intangibly) to the community as a whole rather than only for a select few.

The *Kalinago Barana Autê* (KBA) is a museum located in Dominica's Kalinago Territory which was conceived initially by the community but then funded and developed by the government (see Chapter 5). It is currently owned by the government, although it is managed and operated locally. The initial creation of the museum, although proposed by members of the community, was largely undertaken by non-community members. The proposal was developed by the Ministry of Tourism and the project was completed primarily through private tender – to the disappointment of many community members who argue to this day that they would have never constructed it like that. With the appointment of a manager from the community in 2002, much of the responsibility for the KBA shifted to the community, who have been in charge of all day-to-day operations of the museum since its opening in 2006.

The Kalinago community can be represented through a number of groups. Politically, primarily on a local level, the chief and council represent the Territory, although there are some issues with their degree of independence in this regard. On a national political level, the Ministry for Kalinago Affairs works to represent the community. Culturally, the community knows several groups of representatives, such as the Karina Cultural Group or the Kalinago Dancers. None of these groups of representatives alone would be suitably representative of the Kalinago community as a whole in relation to the KBA. The existence of the KBA affects and impacts the lives of community members in too many different ways: *e.g.* for the preservation of heritage, as a community gathering place, as a tourism attraction, as an economic resource, for employment, for the sale of products and produce, for education, and for leisure. Thus, the personal interests of

---

197 Just about 4% of the population of Dominica is considered to be Kalinago according to the community's population estimates, slightly less per the most recent census. Just over 1% of the population of Barbados forms part of the local East Indian community according to the census (see Chapter 5 and Chapter 6 for detailed data).

some representatives might not align with, or even be detrimental to, those of other community members.

To find a balance, it was clear that no single or handful of community representatives would be sufficient for the operation of the KBA. Instead, what seems to work better, is to have a wide network of representatives who are connected to the museum through various relationships – from those working as guides, to the volunteer dancers who come in for bigger tour groups, the nearby baker who sends down freshly baked cassava bread, the crafts persons who work on the site, or the many community members who grow vetiver to thatch the buildings when maintenance is needed. This web of representatives can be frequently engaged in discussions about the museum and updated about new plans or changes. Through the familial lines of the community, word tends to travel quickly and by engaging such a wide web, the community is able to be represented more aptly and more frequently. To balance all these representatives and to maintain this web of relationships, a manager or core staff team is critical. In the past, the position of manager of the KBA led to some conflict within the community, with individuals expressing envy of the person who was lucky enough to benefit from the museum directly through employment while most other community members benefit indirectly or in other (less tangible) ways – or indeed insist they do not benefit at all. With the new management team appointed in 2016, hopefully some of these concerns have been mitigated as now multiple people – representing different interests and families – are employed in the managerial team.

The *Bengal to Barbados* exhibition project was initiated in 2015 by a member of the local East Indian community and author of a book on the 100 year history of this community in Barbados (Nakhuda 2013; see Chapter 6). The *Barbados Museum & Historical Society* (BMHS) was asked to partner with the community, co-curate the exhibition, and to host it within the museum. The exhibition was initially due to open in the summer of 2016, but was delayed as more time was needed for its development. Although the museum was keen to place as much responsibility and decision-making power with members of the East Indian community, they in turn preferred relying on the expertise of the museum staff.

As a community, the Barbadian East Indian community is noticeably fragmented. Originating largely from five different strands of migration, most of the community is split into two pillars: Gujarati-Muslims and Sindhi-Hindus. Yet, even such a split does not reflect the heterogeneity of the community. Depending on religion, profession, age, and gender, the status of community members differs vastly – both within the community and within Barbadian society as a whole. Recognizing this heterogeneity, an Exhibition Planning Committee was formed to contain individuals from different parts of the community, hoping to be able to address the ideas, heritages, and concerns of the wider community in this manner. At the start of the project, the Exhibition Planning Committee met monthly at the museum. Unfortunately, several committee members were regularly unable to attend these meetings during working hours, thereby not being able to represent their (part of the) community at all. Even when present, not all committee members were able to make themselves heard. As the project progressed, the committee realized that even its members would not be able to represent the diversity of their community.

Noting representativity as a main point of concern which affected all aspects of the exhibition – who it was for, what the narrative would say, which objects would be exhibited, what events would surround it, where it would end up after closing – the committee looked for solutions. The pace of the co-curation project was reduced to provide time to enable more community members to be involved (discussed in more detail below). Alongside the Exhibition Planning Committee meetings at the museum, which had set agendas to monitor the project's progress, larger community meetings were proposed. Focused on a theme (*e.g.* exhibition content) these meetings are to be held in community gathering places in evenings or weekends, open for all interested community members to discuss their ideas and provide feedback on the exhibition plan. The idea was that each event could be held at a different meeting place, thereby possibly attracting different segments of the community. The committee proposed that these wider community meetings could also be used to decide on events to be held alongside the exhibition and other participatory elements. Although these changes were not implemented until after my fieldwork, they will help to increase the representativity of the exhibition creation process. Unfortunately, any assessment of impact of these changes was not yet possible. As a final suggestion, the representativity of the Exhibition Planning Committee could be improved by museum staff meeting with community members individually to discuss plans. This could support the involvement of community members who felt that others were monopolizing the committee meetings, barring them from being able to participate fully.

In summary, although both case studies were related to relatively small communities, representativity was no simple matter in either case. A few community representatives, with their own personal interests, are not able to sufficiently represent the community as a whole, leading to other community members not benefitting from the heritage project. In the case of the KBA, a wide web of community members are tied to the museum through different relationships and with different interests – they are involved frequently in the museum, communicating outwards to other community members and inwards to the management team. Thus, more people have a stake in the museum and can notice its benefits. At the BMHS, the representativity of the East Indian community within the Exhibition Planning Committee was low. By planning meetings with larger groups of community members, on their own terms and at their own venues, more people could be involved in the exhibition project, improving its visibility and its value. What seems to have worked elsewhere in the region in the development of new museums, is the consultation and collaboration with a wide range of stakeholders. Although now closed due to unfortunate circumstances noted earlier in this chapter, *Walcott Place* in St. Lucia was developed in conversation with international literary communities, local artists, neighborhood residents, as well as social services and cultural organizations.[198]

Particularly in the Caribbean, with its diversity of communities and heterogeneous societies, representativity is a key issue in community engagement processes and one which requires significant effort to ensure a wide representation of the communities concerned. This is crucial as heritage projects such as museums and exhibitions may affect a community in terms of identity, political influence, rights, recognition,

---

198 Conversation with Attaché to the Prime Minister of St. Lucia (Castries, St. Lucia, 21 October 2015).

THE SOCIAL MUSEUM IN THE CARIBBEAN

resources, education, or sustainability. In the case of misrepresentation, communities may suffer from museums or exhibitions intended to benefit them. By improving the representativity of community engagement processes, Caribbean museums have the opportunity to be of greater benefit to their communities and Caribbean society.

Investment

Continuing the focus on the process of community engagement, this part is directed at the investment – of time, effort, resources, dedication – needed to carry out such a project most successfully. Insights are again drawn from the two case studies. Community engagement projects can run into various risks if the necessity to deeply invest in them is underestimated or neglected. For instance, community engagement projects may need to adjust the expected outcomes of the project halfway through when it turns out that they cannot be achieved after all. A particularly common limitation for museums is the time pressure to produce exhibitions, events, or programs. Under this pressure, community engagement projects might be pushed to make deadlines, hindering the organic development of the project, and finally cutting short any longer-term outcomes in favor of immediate goals.

Investment is needed throughout all stages of the project. The *Bengal to Barbados* exhibition project undertaken by the *Barbados Museum & Historical Society* (BMHS) and the East Indian community in Barbados showcased the early stages of a community engagement project. Here, the investment of time was particularly crucial in order for the museum staff and East Indian community to gain a better understanding of each other. During the first few months of the project, it became clear that both parties had underestimated the time needed for this and thus the timeframe of the project was significantly extended (by nearly two years) in order to adapt. Time was needed for BMHS staff to understand the complexity of the East Indian community, to identify a group of representatives, to collaborate with a wide range of community members, to learn the community's history, and to grasp the expertise and skills of its members. At the same time, the (representatives of the) East Indian community needed to invest time to understand the BMHS as an institution, its history and its staff, as well as the particular expertise and skills it could contribute to the project.

This investment of time at the beginning of a community engagement project is crucial to fully appreciate what respective parties can contribute throughout the process and what their aims or anticipated outcomes are. It became clear that for the East Indian community members invested in the exhibition project, the exhibition was just one step in a longer process. For instance, they envisioned the exhibition to lead to the creation of a community museum, which could be built around the objects selected for the exhibition.[199] While this East Indian museum was being built, the exhibition could travel to different community centers and locations. It would be one step in gaining exposure for the community as part of Barbadian society, helping them to raise awareness of their history and heritages. Of secondary importance was the opportunity to celebrate their own heritage as a community. It should be remembered here that the East Indian community members surveyed in the course of this case study were deeply divided on the importance of the exhibition project. Thus, this long-term view was

---

199 Meeting with Exhibition Planning Committee (Bridgetown, Barbados, 21 March 2016).

characteristic for those who were already supportive of the exhibition's importance, whereas others who felt that the exhibition itself was not so important also did not envision it to grow into a longer process of community building.

The BMHS had different aims with the exhibition project, as they did not initially envision their own involvement to extend far beyond the closing date of the exhibition. In the original plan, the exhibition would be open to the public for three months, after which its materials would be returned to the community. Following the closing of the exhibition, a few more events or public programs would be planned around different religious feast days until the end of the year. The aim was primarily educational for the wider Barbadian society in order to "dispel myths."[200] For the BMHS as an institution, the intended outcome was to test run a co-curation project and to see "how open we can be."[201]

Clearly, the East Indian community members and BMHS staff brought different views of the aims of the exhibition project to the table. However, these differences were not immediately apparent until time was invested into the project, building trust and respect between all participants, enabling them to speak more openly of their goals. It became clear that the initial aims of both needed to be reconsidered and adjusted, developing collective outcomes to work towards. The duration of the project was greatly extended, allowing representativity to be improved and also supporting longer-term goals. A longer project time was beneficial for the East Indian community members involved, assisting their aspirations to improve the position of their community in Barbadian society. It was also intended to advocate for the benefits of the exhibition project within the East Indian community to hopefully gain wider support of the project within the community itself. BMHS staff needed to adjust their expectations of the exhibition project and its place within their exhibition schedule due to the extended duration, challenging them to let go of their 'curatorial rigor' and work more flexibly. This enabled them to place the exhibition project in different terms and to consider it as a step in the development of a longer relationship. Following on this first investment of time, it also became clear that BMHS staff would have to take up a bigger role in the exhibition project, as the East Indian community preferred to defer to their museological expertise in more matters than had previously been anticipated. Thus, the museum needed to invest more resources and staff hours than had originally been planned. All in all, the scope of the project had been underestimated and the aims of the participants were not fully understood. Therefore, more time, effort, and resources had to be committed to this community engagement process and adjustments were made to ensure that the process would be fruitful to all participants.

Reevaluation was also needed in the case of the *Kalinago Barana Autê* (KBA) in Dominica, which presents a case study of a later stage of a community engagement process. With the first ideas for the museum surfacing in the Kalinago community in the 1970s, the project had already been on-going for a long time before the museum finally opened in 2006. Even after its opening to the public, plans needed to be adjusted as the community engagement process continued to develop. These readjustments of investment were related to the changing relationship of ownership of the KBA between

200 Meeting with deputy director of *Barbados Museum & History Society* (via Skype, 7 February 2016).
201 Meeting with deputy director of *Barbados Museum & History Society* (via Skype, 7 February 2016).

the Kalinago community and the government of Dominica through its Ministry of Tourism. In the early stages of the project, when the KBA was a concept in the minds of Kalinago community members, it was only a community project. Involvement of the Ministry of Tourism came later, when the necessary financial investment could not be made due to the communal land ownership of the Kalinago which limits financial loans. In essence, the need for financial investment transformed the grassroots museum project into a community engagement project. This change led to adjustments in all aspects of the project, with the Kalinago community investing time and resources into planning the museum, providing materials for its construction, and expanding the production of crafts for sale. The Ministry of Tourism invested time and resources in project planning, commercial tender of the museum site, and the construction of an access road. During this period of the planning and construction of the KBA, owner-ship over the project had shifted away from the Kalinago community to be shared with the government of Dominica. This shifted back a bit when a community member was appointed manager of the museum, enabling the community to reinvest itself through the day-to-day operation of the museum.

Since the opening of the KBA, the government of Dominica has noted that it wishes to place ownership of the museum with the Kalinago community, once certain criteria have been met.[202] These criteria are related to the financial viability of the KBA, as well as to the sustainability of its management and ownership. So far, the government has maintained that it cannot confer ownership of the KBA to the Kalinago community and has moved up the date for such a change several times. The Kalinago community itself is divided on the matter of ownership of the KBA, some adamant that it must be community owned, while others have pointed out that community ownership might be (financially) detrimental to the KBA. In the interim, the government and the Kalinago community have renegotiated their relationship multiple times, alongside reevaluations of the project and adjustments.

The current stage of the KBA community engagement process shows the need for a transparency of investment and of benefits received. As transparency has been some-what lacking, participants in the community engagement process are misinformed of the investments made, and the benefits received, by the government and the Kalinago community respectively. Some Kalinago community members assume that government financially benefits from the KBA and would prefer any financial surplus to remain in the community. On the other hand, the manager of the KBA asserts that the KBA breaks even most months, or is in fact supported by government in times of financial shortfall due to high maintenance costs or lower revenues.[203] Both the government (as owners) and the Kalinago community (as managers) could improve their transparency in this regard. For instance, government could be better informed of the investments made by the community in maintaining the site and the benefits for the community in terms of the KBA as a social gathering place, a cultural hub, and a financial resource. On the other hand, the Kalinago community could be notified of the investments of the government in terms of financial and infrastructural support, as well the benefits of the KBA for the state as an educational resource and a guardian of cultural heritage.

---

202 Interview with manager of *Kalinago Barana Autê* (Kalinago Territory, Dominica, 15 August 2015).
203 Interview with manager of *Kalinago Barana Autê* (Kalinago Territory, Dominica, 15 August 2015).

As the community engagement process continues and reevaluations cause changes in investment, transparency remains crucial.

In sum, throughout all stages of a community engagement process, participants need to invest their time, effort, resources, and dedication in order to continue to work towards collective outcomes. In the beginning, the investment of time is crucial for parties to identify representatives and for participants to gain mutual understanding and build trust, thereby being able to share their respective aspirations for the project. Time is also needed to possibly expand the duration of the project in order to develop a long term relationship that continues to be beneficial after initial project aims have been achieved or to develop follow-up projects. As the community engagement process continues, it is necessary to keep reevaluating it, readjusting the investments made, and renegotiating the relationship of the participants. At all stages, transparency is crucial in order to support these investments and any resulting benefits. By investing deeply into community engagement processes, Caribbean museums can develop long-lasting relationships with communities, deepening their commitment to Caribbean societies, anchoring their institution within their society, and supporting communities in achieving communal goals.

Negotiation & Conflict

Community engagement processes benefit from greater representativity and deep investment. In discussing these two topics, it was already apparent that a (perceived) lack of either can result in tensions between participants. Such tensions need to be negotiated carefully in order to avoid them leading to conflict. This final section looks more closely at this need for negotiation and the potential for conflict by again revisiting the two case studies. In doing so, one should keep in mind the issues related to representativity and investment, although the focus here will lie on additional potential sources of friction, such as a power imbalance, a lack of valuation of expertise, or uneven access. It will highlight a few examples from the two case studies which reveal the presence or risk of such friction, and how this was then negotiated or whether it led to any conflict.

In both case studies, one can identify differences in power – political, economic, influential – between the government (or the governmental institution) on the one hand and a relatively small local community on the other hand. This is not to judge the existence of these power differences, but it is important to be aware of them in order to assess how power is balanced, shifted, or countered in the course of community engagement processes (*cf.* Perkin 2010). Certainly, the risk is that if power is extremely unbalanced, exploitation or manipulation of participants may occur instead of collaboration (Boast 2011; Clifford 1997).

In the case of the *Bengal to Barbados* exhibition project, the *Barbados Museum & Historical Society* (BMHS) set out on the project with the intention to defer significant decision-making power to the East Indian community. Although BMHS staff asked the representatives of the East Indian community to decide on many specific details of the exhibition project – *e.g.* objects, themes, texts, events, and programs – most of the underlying, foundational decisions were made by the BMHS staff directly. These foundational matters – such as the exhibition time and duration, the venue, the available space for the exhibition, the time available for programs and events, as well as the usable resources – are core decisions which narrow down any further options and are thus essential for the decision-making process as a whole. For instance, deciding on the venue had direct implications as to how many objects could fit into this space, whether audio-visual content could be shown, and whether it would be in a location that was relevant and accessible to the East Indian community. Whereas BMHS staff wanted to place most of the decision-making power with the representatives of the East Indian community, they did not seem to have deeply considered the implications of the fact that they were making these foundational decisions. This certainly could have been a source of friction and possibly led to conflict in any community engagement project. However, in this case, representatives of the East Indian community communicated clearly at an early stage that they wanted *less* decision-making power, and in fact asked BMHS staff to shift the power balance *more* towards the institution. Thus, most decisions were negotiated collectively in order to agree on who would be in charge of which aspect of it – *e.g.* BMHS staff would write the panel texts and the representatives of the East Indian community would decide on their topics beforehand and review them afterwards. Through this continual negotiation, the power balance was constantly checked and adjusted, ultimately reducing the risk of conflict.

Besides a power imbalance, there is also a risk of conflict when devaluing the expertise and knowledge contributed by participants in a community engagement project. In all collaborations, participants bring a different set of skills and knowledge to the table in order to achieve common goals. This may lead to friction or conflict if participants feel that their expertise or knowledge is not valued, and that therefore their voices are not being heard and their contributions disregarded. Such a devaluation of expertise and knowledge is a common source of contention in community engagement processes, when participants are purposefully invited in, but later feel that they have only been involved in a tokenistic manner (*e.g.* Fouseki 2010; Fouseki & Smith 2013; Lagerkvist 2006).

In the case of the *Kalinago Barana Autê* (KBA) in Dominica, a devaluation of Kalinago expertise and knowledge during the construction of the museum became a long-term source of friction. The original construction of the museum buildings had been tendered and thus the site was not built by the Kalinago, but by people from outside the community. Although the museum plan was designed to resemble traditional Kalinago dwellings through the use of traditional materials and designs, Kalinago expertise was not consulted for the collection of these materials nor for the actual construction. Several community members noted that the wood for the buildings had not been harvested at the right time, making it weaker and more prone to deterioration, requiring frequent, costly maintenance. Kalinago community members had unique expertise which would have been useful (even essential) for the construction of the KBA. Unfortunately, this expertise had been overlooked at the time resulting in this simmering conflict. Remaining a point of friction over the years, during this research the story was brought up as a bad example multiple times. However, it was generally raised constructively, as an example of how things had gone wrong in the past with the KBA and why it was important now to carefully consider the construction of the site and its maintenance for future sustainability. Such discussions were possible in part because the balance of power had shifted in the interim through the appointment of the local management team. This shift has resulted in the Kalinago community having more influence on the operation of the site and its maintenance, thus giving them a stronger voice in the matter and logically placing greater value on their own expertise. The end result of this changed balance of power was thus also a change in the valuation of the knowledge of the community, thereby reducing the extent to which the past construction of the museum could remain a source of contemporary conflict.

Finally, conflict may be the result of uneven access to the community engagement process. Such uneven access may be due to physical or other practical barriers, for instance because of the working times, language used, or meeting locations. Perhaps more problematically, uneven access may also be the result of underlying social barriers, such as discrimination. In many cases, participants may be unaware that others are experiencing inaccessibility, especially if this is due to social barriers. This may be a particularly shocking discovery to community engagement participants when they are operating under the assumption that they are doing everything they can to be accessible and non-discriminatory (Lagerkvist 2006).

Representatives of the East Indian community in Barbados experienced practical barriers keeping them from fully participating in the *Bengal to Barbados* exhibition project as the Exhibition Planning Committee meetings were held in meeting rooms at the BMHS on weekdays, during regular working hours. Community representatives had to choose to go out of their way to the museum, as well as find ways in which to compensate for missing work hours. Not all were in the position to be able to do so. Certainly, this problem was discussed among the Exhibition Planning Committee – but only with those present. Although alternatives were suggested, BMHS staff could not work on the project outside of working hours, so ultimately the time stayed the same and while ideas were entertained of changing the location for some of the meetings, these had not yet been implemented.

Social barriers were problematic for a number of reasons, some of which had to do with internal tensions within the East Indian community, others with the position of the community within Barbadian society. BMHS staff was weary early on of the gender imbalance within the Exhibition Planning Committee and felt that women were not only underrepresented but largely silent during meetings in the presence of men.[204] BMHS staff felt that East Indian women were positioned in an inferior role within the East Indian community and, thus, tried to work deliberately towards their inclusion. However, the idea that the East Indian community is repressive to women was countered by Haajima Degia who opposed these victimizing stereotypes, instead arguing that the Gujarati-Muslim's "diasporic identity was to be created and shaped by women" (Degia 2016). In fact, she argued that women play and played a vital role within the East Indian community, working in the household, agriculture, and business, although their actual contributions are often only modestly revealed to outsiders. Through the process of migration, "traditional gender roles which in the homeland had occurred [...] had not been maintained here in Barbados" (Degia 2016). These statements called attention to the fact that BMHS staff had been operating under the assumption of prejudices, which were more informed by stereotypical thoughts of Muslim women in general, than related to actual insight into the Barbadian East Indian community. Thus, whereas BMHS staff felt that they were being particularly

---

204 Meeting with deputy director of *Barbados Museum & History Society* (via Skype, 7 February 2016).

inclusive to East Indian women and improving their access to the community engagement process, their positive discrimination was seen very differently by women within the community. These women noted that staff was perpetuating stereotypical prejudices and consequently felt misunderstood, increasing their effort needed to access the community engagement process. By attending Haajima Degia's lecture *A History of Gujarati-Muslim Migration to Barbados* (Degia 2016), Kevin Farmer of the BMHS was able to adjust his perceptions and begin renegotiating how to successfully improve accessibility for East Indian women, based on their needs.

Power balance, valuation of expertise, and accessibility are all aspects of the community engagement process which need to be negotiated and renegotiated continuously. In many cases, these issues can be intertwined as these examples have shown: a power imbalance may lead to a devaluation of expertise, thereby promulgating uneven access and so on. If poorly negotiated, any or all of these issues may become sources of friction and lead to conflict, resulting in the community engagement process to fail for (some of) its participants. As community engagement is a long-term process, negotiation needs to be continuous. The chance of successful negotiation is improved by better representation of the communities involved and a deep investment of time, resources, and effort. By engaging in community engagement processes, Caribbean museums have had to shift their role in relation to Caribbean society. Museums and their staff can no longer present themselves as a neutral party or arbiter, but rather have to enter into negotiations as subjective entities and individuals. This embeds museums into society as more social, subjective institutions, a change which is supported by the wide-spread presence of grassroots museums in the region.

Summary

Museums throughout the Caribbean are adopting and adapting participatory practices and community engagement processes to connect more deeply to the various communities which they serve or which they are a part of. Highly deliberately or largely unintentionally, these museums are positioning themselves as ever more social museums, aiming to directly benefit society through their work. How have these community engagement practices and processes *actually* affected the role of Caribbean museums in Caribbean society? This chapter formed an overarching discussion around this question, focusing on some of the most noteworthy observations and interpretations made in the course of this research.

Starting on a macro level, it explored the regional museum scene by looking at the different roles that governmental museums and grassroots museums can play. Revealing how governmental and grassroots museums are often physically located in different places – *i.e.* capital cities vs. elsewhere – it showcased how both kinds of museums function complementarily not only in terms of content but also to reach different audiences. Whereas governmental museums often have national mandates and reach out to a wide range of communities, grassroots museums may target particular communities that are otherwise left out or underrepresented. Collectively, they are able to engage with multiple layers of society. In terms of the dynamism of these museums, or their ability to flexibly adapt to changing societal needs, there are clear differences depending on funding and organization. With governmental museums being politically dependent and often experiencing funding restrictions, their community engagement practices are typically temporary: *e.g.* activities or events. Grassroots museums, however, enjoy greater independence even if they may seem financially disadvantaged. In these museums, community engagement practices occur more frequently and across all aspects of the museum's work. While both kinds of museums are able to respond to changing societal needs, governmental museums have a more transient role in this sense, as their core aspects (*e.g.* organization, exhibitions, staff) change more slowly. In terms of sustainability, governmental museums generally have long-term missions and aim to ensure their value for many future generations. Of course, in practice, these museums may also encounter political or financial difficulties, possibly leading to closure. Particularly with individually-owned grassroots museums, their lack of sustainability is often raised as a 'problem'. Here, I have argued instead that these 'ephemeral museums' have a role to play in the present, rather than in the future. These museums and their collections are activated by their founder or owner, who gives them meaning. Once this agency is lost, the museum ceases to be in its current shape, possibly able to reform into a new museum. Together, governmental museums and such ephemeral museums play out strong social roles for present-day communities as well as future generations. In general, the locations, dynamism, and sustainability of governmental museums and grassroots museums differ, but complementarily work to engage with different parts of Caribbean society.

Zooming in to investigate Caribbean museums more individually, the participatory practices employed throughout the region were discussed. The practice of multi-vocality was examined by looking at several ways in which a museum can incorporate multiple voices. For instance, through exhibitions with voices from multiple communities, voices of different members of the same community, or by inviting an intervention into the museum space. In these cases, the goal is just to include many voices, not necessarily to encourage debate or present conflicting views. Another approach is to present histories which are not, or cannot, be told in mainstream museums. These histories may present views that are not shared elsewhere or political opinions which may not (be able to) receive national support. While Caribbean museums may not always be inclusive, the use of multi-vocality in various ways has made them more inclusive overall to a wider range of communities. Also, the participatory practices employed in the Caribbean depend on the type of museum. Some museum types, such as those with mixed content, are highly participatory when looking across the board at all participatory practices. Others, such as those in the category of built heritage, very rarely engage in participatory practices of any kind. Yet again, other museum types have a clear style whereby certain participatory practices are preferred over others – *e.g.* archaeology museums often engage in research collaborations, but rarely host events or have interactive displays. These participatory differences depend on the museum's collections, setting, staff, and so on. Ultimately, museums of different types are engaging with communities in different ways, fulfilling different social roles. Beyond the type of museum, there also appears to be a difference in participatory style between museums in the Dutch- and English-speaking Caribbean, and those in the French- and Spanish-speaking Caribbean. Although more research is needed to support this hypothesis, it may well be that colonial legacies, cultural differences, curatorial training, or museological traditions have resulted in distinct differences in participatory styles. If so, the social role of museums will also differ depending on linguistic areas.

Finally, on a micro level, the discussion veered to the process of community engagement by exploring the two case studies undertaken in the course of this research. Representativity was a key issue in these community engagement processes, even in the case of relatively small, local communities. Through significant effort, a wide range of participants should be involved in or tied to the community engagement project in order to cover differing perspectives and expertise. If representativity is not sufficiently sought, the project might head into serious problems and participants may feel exploited. An investment of time, effort, and resources is needed throughout all stages of the project in order to identify representatives, build trust, develop mutual understanding, and construct a deep relationship. Only with such a deep investment can a community engagement project hope to work towards collective goals for the longer-term. Any such project needs to be constantly reevaluated and adjusted as the process continues, coupled with a transparency of investments made and benefits received. By investing in such processes, Caribbean museums anchor themselves within society through long-term relationships. Conflict may arise from various sources, including a lack of representativity or investment, which are often interrelated. Thus, negotiation is constantly needed to ensure there is no imbalance of power, lack of valuation of expertise, or uneven access to the process. Such negotiations are certainly improved by better representativity and deeper investment into the process. Within these negotiations, museums must take on subjective roles as participants, rather than of neutral arbitration, thus placing themselves also into society as more subjective entities.

Although Caribbean museums can still do more to improve their community engagement practices and processes, and particularly to investigate their societal *impact*, it is clear that they have changed their societal role. The existence of both governmental and grassroots museums throughout the region has enabled Caribbean museums to target more layers of society, to respond in different ways to changing needs, and to work for both present-day communities and future generations. Through adopting different participatory practices, Caribbean museums are able to represent more layers of society and to engage with communities uniquely, depending on the museum's type and the linguistic area it is in. Caribbean museums differ in their societal role depending on their content and place, as this influences the participatory practices they employ. Finally, through community engagement processes, Caribbean museums have developed more ties to individual members of Caribbean society, and ensured that their institutions are anchored deeply into society for the long-term, acting as subjective participants within it.

8

Conclusions

No museum is an island.
Stephen E. Weil (1983: 103)

Initially presented as a keynote address in 1980, Weil stressed this viewpoint that museums exist in a network of interdependence as opposed to isolation. Concerned with the support museums could give each other, as well as the bad influence they might have on each other in worse cases, his argument was that museums have to connect in order to survive and thrive. Considering the profoundly societal roles of museums today, this statement has taken on an added dimension and perhaps become even more true. Museums are not only dependent on other museums, but exist solely within a community of people, an integral part of the complex organism that is society. In the Caribbean, this system of museums existing within participatory relationships is pronounced. However, one might argue that Weil's original metaphor was flawed by equating islands with isolation: in the Caribbean, since pre-colonial times, sea-scapes have closely linked the islands and mainland together. Indeed, speaking from a Caribbean perspective, Édouard Glissant put forth a similar notion of the museum as consisting of a network of interrelationships, of a collection of worlds. However, he proposed this idea through a different island-related metaphor:

I imagine the museum as an archipelago.
Édouard Glissant (Glissant & Obrist 2012: 5)

For this particular research into community engagement, it was useful to combine aspects of these two metaphors in order to consider Caribbean museums as a mosaic. At the start of this research project, I had never been to the Caribbean and only had a vague, stereotypical image in my mind's eye of what a Caribbean museum might look like. Now, after four years of research and many museum visits, the picture has become both clearer and more complex. There is no single quintessential Caribbean museum, just as there is no quintessential Caribbean country or island. The Caribbean as a region can be viewed as a patchwork in which a diversity of islands and countries are interwoven to form a complex whole. In the same way, Caribbean museums can be seen as a multi-faceted mosaic. Each museum has its own unique characteristics and qualities. Yet, at the same time, any given museum is also like a number of other museums in some way – the collection's history might be similar to *A*, its location similar to *B*, its visitors to *C*, and so on. Just as some tiles in a mosaic might be similar in color, size, or shape. Attempting another metaphor, perhaps we could speak of a Caribbean museological set of ingredients, from which each museum has made its own unique dish. In the course of this research and fieldwork, the image of the 'Social Museum in the Caribbean' has been slowly simmering.

The Social Museum in the Caribbean

Having determined that there is no quintessential Caribbean museum, it is time to reveal this mosaic image of the social museum in the Caribbean. Caribbean museums are able to take on a myriad of societal roles and reach out to different levels of society and diverse audiences. They are able to do so because the Caribbean museum landscape consists of a wide range of museums types, which have different ownership structures, unique museum settings, and improvise in adopting a range of participatory practices in order to connect to a multiplicity of related communities. Thus, the diversity of contemporary Caribbean society is actively reflected in the region's museumscape. Indeed, Caribbean museums are embedding themselves purposefully as subjective actors in their societies through community engagement processes. Particularly grassroots museums take on strong societal roles by reaching out to communities and engaging with histories, heritages, and themes that otherwise may be (or are) excluded. Some of these grassroots museums, ephemeral museums, have singular roles to play in the present and cannot be sustained in the same form for the future. Without glossing over the difficulties that Caribbean museums face – *e.g.* financial insecurity, limited regional training opportunities for staff, natural disasters, colonial pressures, political conflict – they are resilient institutions. They work dynamically and flexibly, driven by passion and creativity, and are significantly valuable participants in Caribbean society. The mosaic of the Caribbean museumscape has three defining characteristics: diverse, grassroots, and dynamic.

Experiencing the social museum in the Caribbean has led to a confrontation of the definition of what a museum is or can be. It has broadened my understanding of the meaning of the term in order to encompass a wide collection of phenomena, each aimed at disclosing and sharing some kind of heritage with the public. This research has also reinforced my conviction that museums are not a product of the elite, nor are they a resource reserved for the select few. When one is willing to recognize the different forms the museum can take, it becomes apparent that people everywhere in the world – no matter their circumstances – need museums, create museums, and visit museums.

Recommendations

In the wake of this study, which provides a first regional insight into the community engagement practices and processes of Caribbean museums, the opportunities for further research, collaboration, and engagement have only increased. For those working in or with Caribbean museums, it is hoped that this dissertation can be a source of inspiration. While many contemporary Caribbean museums apply community engagement practices, examples from other museums in the region can provide support to keep reaching out to communities. Caribbean museums, despite their differences, are often faced with similar problems or settings. Thus, it is immensely valuable for Caribbean museologists to continue building a regional contact network, exchanging expertise and sharing their collective capabilities. Regional organizations, such as the Museums Association of the Caribbean, are key to providing a place for these exchanges. Through consolidation efforts, museums in the Caribbean can work together to strengthen their societal roles even further.

For those wishing to research museums or collections in the Caribbean, this research may provide a starting point or present opportunities for case studies. Many of the museums researched in the course of this project have never been studied in greater detail and there are also ample opportunities for regional or thematic museological studies. For instance, the hypothesis that museums' participatory styles are related to their linguistic area and thus are the result of colonial legacies. As another example, ephemeral museums would be a valuable focus for further research. In addition, the impact of community engagement practices and processes would benefit from assessment.

Finally, for those working in or with museums anywhere in the world, museological research warrants expansion by shifting the focus from national museums or major institutions to grassroots museums and ephemeral museums. More effort could be made to engage in museological research in all geographical regions of the world and to understand the value of museums based on the needs of their particular, related communities. All of this research would require a broadening of the understanding of the term museum and of the field of museology. Caribbean museums can inspire institutions around the world thanks to their creativity, flexibility, resiliency, wide engagement, deep dedication, passion, and patience. No museum is an island; the global museumscape is an archipelago of interconnected institutions, embedded into their communities, benefitting greatly from an exchange of expertise.

Acknowledgements

I am grateful to many for their assistance and support in the completion of this research.

Firstly, I am indebted to my supervisors. Willem Willems encouraged me to greatly expand my research throughout the region and to dedicate myself to fieldwork. Thank you for trusting me to work independently, but for checking in every Thursday. Following Willem's passing, Corinne Hofman took over supervision and was greatly helpful in expanding my contact network and providing feedback on the manuscript. To Mariana Françozo, thank you for *getting* my research, strategizing along the way, providing perfect feedback, and for your mentorship. There are a million ways in which you have guided me, from academic support to safeguarding my wellbeing. Suffice it to say, after many fieldwork adventures shared, I am the luckiest.

I would like to thank the members of the reading committee whose careful reviews and thoughtful comments greatly improved this manuscript. Thank you also to Tina Solos for the diligent proofreading under tight deadlines.

Secondly, this dissertation owes much to collaborations and conversations with colleagues. Mereke van Garderen, thank you for your computer science intervention and the fruitful visualization collaboration. To my office buddies, Eldris Con Aguilar and Eloise Stancioff for working together, travelling together, panicking together, and helping each other. There is no bond like sharing a LIAT flight. Many thanks to Maria Patricia Ordoñez, *paranymph* extraordinaire, museum buddy, and bringer of excellent chocolate. Thank you Rosalie Hans for sharing your expertise in African community museums. To the PhD community, you have been a monumental support.

Thank you to everyone in the NEXUS1492, HERA-CARIB and ISLAND-NETWORKS research groups as well as the heritage department for collaborations and expertise: Alice, Amanda, Amy, André, Andrzej, Andy, Angus Martin, Angus Mol, Arie, Arlene, Becki, Catarina, Corinne, Daniel, Eduardo, Eldris, Eloise, Emma, Esther, Floris, Gareth, Habiba, Hannes, Hayley, Isabella, Jan, Jana, Janne, Jaime, Jason, Jay, Jimmy, Jorge, Julijan, Katarina, Kirsten, Laura, Lewis, Lou, Maaike, Mariana, Marlena, Marlieke, Menno, Mereke, Monique, Pauline, Patrick, Roberto, Ryan, Samantha, Sjoerd, Sony, Termeh, Tibisay, Till, Tom, Uditha, Ulrik, Viviana, Willem, Wouter. Especially thanks to those who guided me on my fieldwork or shared in museum visits. To Maribel and Ilone, thank you for the constant support.

My sincere gratitude to all of those who have supported me in the Caribbean. Board members and members of the Museums Association of the Caribbean, I thank you for inviting me into such a dynamic network of driven and inspiring museum lovers and artists. Museum staff at all 195 museums visited, thank you for providing invaluable information. In Dominica, I could not have completed the case study without the assistance of Cozier Frederick, Kevin Dangleben, Patsy Thomas, Lennox Honychurch, the chief and council, and all survey participants. In Barbados, I am especially grateful to Kevin Farmer, Alissandra Cummins, Kaye Hall, Natalie McGuire, Haajima Degia, Sabir Nakhuda, Suleiman Bulbulia, and all survey participants. Kevin, thank you for all the thought-provoking conversations on our drives.

Always, I remain thankful to my friends and my family. To my museum girls for enjoying culture together all over the globe, and for visiting me in between. To Krijn for designing the cover and to the rest of the VALUE family for keeping it playful and for always inventing cool new projects. All my nerds for their welcome distractions and excellent banter. My extended family for always being proud of my progress, and for visiting me in St. Maarten for the happiest occasion. To my parents for inspiring me, for finding this PhD opportunity in the first place, and for always encouraging me to keep going, even if that means gluing my shoes along the way. Most of all, to Vincent who married me in the field and made sure I took every opportunity to make the most of my research, I am eternally grateful.

Little by little, one goes a long way

References

Allaire, Louis. 2013. Ethnohistory of the Caribs. In William F. Keegan, Corinne L. Hofman & Reniel Rodríguez Ramos (eds) *The Oxford Handbook of Caribbean Archaeology* (97-108). Oxford: Oxford University Press.

Ambrose, Timothy & Paine, Crispin. 2012. *Museum Basics*. London & New York: Routledge.

Anderson, Benedict. [1983] 2006. *Imagined Communities: Reflections on the Origin and Spread of Nationalism*. London & New York: Verso.

Ariese-Vandemeulebroucke, Csilla E. 2018. Engaging Youth Audiences in Caribbean Museums. *Caribbean Museums* 2-3: 6-23.

Arjona, Marta; Brinkley, Francis Kay; Camargo-Moro, Fernanda de; Ebanks, Roderick C.; Espinoza, Manuel; Lacouture, Felipe; Lumbreras, Luis G.; Magalhaes, Aloisio & Mostny, Grete. 1982. Museum Development and Cultural Policy: Aims, Prospects and Challenges. *Museum* 34.2: 72-82.

Arnold, Ken. 2015. From Caring to Creating: Curators Change Their Spots. In Conal McCarthy (ed.) *The International Handbooks of Museum Studies: Museum Practice* (317-339). Malden, Oxford & Chichester: John Wiley & Sons.

Arnstein, Sherry R. 1969. A Ladder of Citizen Participation. *Journal of the American Institute of Planners* 35.4: 216-224.

Barbados Statistical Service. 2013. *2010 Population and Housing Census: Volume 1*. Available at: http://www.barstats.gov.bb/files/documents/PHC_2010_Census_Volume_1.pdf (Accessed: 18 July 2016).

Barnes, Eric. 2008. Mexico's National Program of Community Museums: Local Patrimonies in a Multicultural Mexico. *Museum History Journal* 1.2: 209-233.

Bather, Francis A. & Sheppard, Thomas. 1934. The Museums of the British West Indies. *Journal of the Barbados Museum and Historical Society* 1.4.

Belk, Russell W. 1994. Collectors and Collecting. In Susan M. Pearce (ed.) *Interpreting Objects and Collections* (317-326). London & New York: Routledge.

Bennett, Tony. 1988. The Exhibitionary Complex. *New Formations* 4.1: 73-102.

Bennett, Tony. 1995. *The Birth of the Museum: History, Theory, Practice*. London: Routledge.

Bérard, Benoît. 2008. La Mission Archéologique Française en Dominique. *Les Nouvelles de l'Archéologie* 111-112: 95-100.

Bérard, Benoît. 2013. L'Occupation Saladoïde Ancienne de la Dominique, vers une Nouvelle Définition des Territoires Culturels Précolombiens. In Benoît Bérard (ed.) *Martinique, Terre Amérindienne: Une Approche Pluridisciplinaire* (235-245). Leiden: Sidestone Press.

Bérard, Benoît; Billard, Jean-Yves; L'Etang, Thierry; Lalubie, Guillaume; Nicolizas, Constantino; Ramstein, Bruno & Slayton, Emma. 2016. Technologie du Fait Maritime chez les Kalinago des Petites Antilles aux XVIe et XVIIe Siècles. *Journal de la Société des Américanistes* 102.1: 129-158.

Bernard, H. Russell. 2006. *Research Methods in Anthropology: Qualitative and Quantitative Approaches.* Lanham, New York, Toronto & Oxford: Altamira.

Black, Graham. 2015. Developing Audiences for the Twenty-First-Century Museum. In Conal McCarthy (ed.) *The International Handbooks of Museum Studies: Museum Practice* (123-151). Malden, Oxford & Chichester: John Wiley & Sons.

Boast, Robin. 2011. Neocolonial Collaboration: Museum as Contact Zone Revisited. *Museum Anthropology* 34.1: 56-70.

Boomert, Arie. 1986. The Cayo Complex of St. Vincent: Ethnohistorical and Archaeological Aspects of the Island-Carib Problem. *Antropológica* 66: 3-68.

Boomert, Arie. 2000. *Trinidad, Tobago and the Lower Orinoco Interaction Sphere: An Archaeological/Ethnohistorical Study.* PhD dissertation, Leiden University.

Boomert, Arie. 2009. Una Etapa en la Colonización Precolombina del Caribe. Paper presented at the *XV Congreso AHILA: El Mundo Precolonial y sus Transformaciones a Partir del Contacto con los Europeos*, AHILA: Leiden (46-57).

Boomert, Arie. 2014. The Caribbean Islands. In Colin Renfrew & Paul Bahn (eds) *The Cambridge World Prehistory* (1217-1234). Cambridge: Cambridge University Press.

Borromeo, Federico. [1625] 2010. *Sacred Painting – Museum.* Translated and edited by Kenneth S. Rothwell, introduction and notes by Pamela M. Jones. Cambridge: Harvard University Press.

Boucher, Philip P. 1992. *Cannibal Encounters: Europeans and Island Caribs, 1492-1763.* Baltimore & London: The John Hopkins University Press.

Boylan, Patrick J. (ed.) 2004. *Running a Museum: A Practical Handbook.* Paris: ICOM.

Breton, Raymond. [1665] 1892. *Dictionaire Caraibe-Français.* Reprinted by Jules Platzmann. Leipzig: Teubner.

Breton, Raymond. [1666] 1900. *Dictionaire Français-Caraibe.* Reprinted by Jules Platzmann. Leipzig: Teubner.

Breton, Raymond. [1667] 1877. *Grammaire Caraibe: Suivie du Catéchisme Caraibe.* Republished by Lucien Adam & Ch. Leclerc. Paris: Maissonneuve.

Bright, Alistair J. 2011. *Blood Is Thicker Than Water: Amerindian Intra- and Inter-insular Relationships and Social Organization in the Pre-colonial Windward Islands.* Leiden: Sidestone Press.

Brinkley, Frances Kay. 1982. The Eastern Caribbean: A Museum on Every Island. *Museum* 34.2: 127-129.

Broekhoven, Laura N.K. van; Buijs, Cunera C.M. & Hovens, Pieter (eds). 2010. *Sharing Knowledge and Cultural Heritage: First Nations of the Americas.* Leiden: Sidestone Press.

Brookes, Hazel. 2008. How Caribbean Museums are Dealing with Diversity. Paper presented at the *2008 CAM Triennial: Museums & Diversity: Museums in Pluralistic Societies*, CAM: Georgetown. Available at: http://www.maltwood.uvic.ca/cam/activities/past_conferences/1999conf/BrookesCAM.pdf (Accessed: 22 October 2014).

Burón Díaz, Manuel. 2012. Los Museos Comunitarios Mexicanos en el Proceso de Renovación Museológica. *Revista de Indias* 72.254: 177-212.

Butler, Shelley R. 2015. Reflexive Museology: Lost and Found. In Andrea Witcomb & Kylie Message (eds) *The International Handbooks of Museum Studies: Museum Theory* (159-182). Malden, Oxford & Chichester: John Wiley & Sons.

Callaghan, Richard T. 2013. Archaeological Views of Caribbean Seafaring. In William F. Keegan, Corinne L. Hofman & Reniel Rodríguez Ramos (eds) *The Oxford Handbook of Caribbean Archaeology* (283-295). Oxford: Oxford University Press.

Callender, Allison. 2015. Accessibility of Museums in Barbados. *The International Journal of the Inclusive Museum* 7.1: 17-27.

Campbell, David. 2008. Democratic Norms to Deliberative Forms: Managing Tools and Tradeoffs in Community-based Civic Engagement. *Public Administration and Management* 15.1: 305-341.

Candlin, Fiona. 2016. *Micromuseology: An Analysis of Small Independent Museums.* London & New York: Bloomsbury.

Caribbean Community Secretariat. 1979. *Workshop on Museums, Monuments and Historic Sites, Kingston, Jamaica, 1978.* Kingston: Caribbean Community Secretariat.

Carib Reserve Act, Chapter 25:90, 1978. Commonwealth of Dominica. Available at: http://www.dominica.gov.dm/laws/chapters/chap25-90.pdf (Accessed: 22 January 2016).

Carib Reserve (Amendment) Act 2015. Commonwealth of Dominica. Roseau: Government Printery. Available at: http://www.dominica.gov.dm/laws/2015/Carib%20Reserve%20(Amendment)%20Act,%202015.pdf (Accessed: 22 January 2016).

Christopher, Anthony J. 2013. The Commonwealth Censuses: Partial Insights into Issues of Identity. *Commonwealth & Comparative Politics* 51.3: 326-342.

Clavir, Miriam. 2002. *Preserving What is Valued: Museums, Conservation and First Nations.* Vancouver: UBC Press.

Clifford, James. 1997. *Routes: Travel and Translation in the Late Twentieth Century.* Cambridge: Harvard University Press.

Cole, Sarah A. 2014. Moments of Change: A "Bottom Up" Push towards a More Inclusive Museum. *Museums & Social Issues* 9.1: 56-59.

Collomb, Gérard & Renard, Yves. 1982. On Marie-Galante (Guadeloupe): A Community and Its Ecomuseum. *Museum* 34.2: 109-113.

Commonwealth of Dominica, Central Statistical Office. 2011. *2011 Population and Housing Census.* Available at: http://www.dominica.gov.dm/cms/files/2011_census_report.pdf (Accessed: 19 January 2016).

Con Aguilar, Eldris; Álvarez, Arlene; Frederick, Cozier & Hofman, Corinne L. 2017. Teaching Indigenous History and Heritage – Reviving the Past in the Present: Caribbean Experiences from the Dominican Republic and Dominica. *Creative Education* 8: 333-346.

Cooper, Karen Coody. 2008. *Spirited Encounters: American Indians Protest Museum Policies and Practices.* Lanham & Plymouth: AltaMira Press.

Cooper, Karen Coody & Sandoval, Nicolasa I. 2006. *Living Homes for Cultural Expression: North American Native Perspectives on Creating Community Museums.* Washington D.C. & New York: Smithsonian Institution & National Museum of the American Indian.

Corbey, Raymond. 1993. Ethnographic Showcases, 1870-1930. *Cultural Anthropology* 8.3: 338-369.

Crooke, Elizabeth. 2007. *Museums and Community: Ideas, Issues and Challenges.* London: Routledge.

Crooke, Elizabeth. 2008. An Exploration of the Connections among Museums, Community and Heritage. In Brian J. Graham & Peter Howard (eds) *The Ashgate Research Companion to Heritage and Identity* (415-424). Aldershot: Ashgate.

Crooke, Elizabeth. 2011a. Museums and Community. In Sharon Macdonald (ed.) *A Companion to Museum Studies* (170-185). Malden & Oxford: Wiley – Blackwell.

Crooke, Elizabeth. 2011b. The Politics of Community Heritage: Motivations, Authority and Control. In Emma Waterton & Steve Watson (eds) *Heritage and Community Engagement: Collaboration or Contestation?* (24-37). Abingdon & New York: Routledge.

Crooke, Elizabeth. 2015. The "Active" Museum: How Concern with Community Transformed the Museum. In Conal McCarthy (ed.) *The International Handbooks of Museum Studies: Museum Practice* (481-502). Malden, Oxford & Chichester: John Wiley & Sons.

Cummins, Alissandra. 1992. Exhibiting Culture: Museums and National Identity in the Caribbean. *Caribbean Quarterly* 38.2: 33-53.

Cummins, Alissandra. 1994. The 'Caribbeanization' of the West Indies: The Museum's Role in the Development of National Identity. In Flora Kaplan (ed.) *Museums and the Making of Ourselves: The Role of Objects in National Identity* (192-221). Leicester: Leicester University Press.

Cummins, Alissandra. 1998. Confronting Colonialism: The First 60 Years at the BMHS. *Journal of the Barbados Museum and Historical Society* 42: 1-35.

Cummins, Alissandra. 2004. Caribbean Museums and National Identity. *History Workshop Journal* 58: 224-245.

Cummins, Alissandra. 2012. Memory, Museums and the Making of Meaning: A Caribbean Perspective. In Michelle L. Stefano, Peter Davis & Gerard Corsane (eds) *Safeguarding Intangible Cultural Heritage* (23-32). Woodbridge: Boydell Press.

Cummins, Alissandra. 2013. Natural History = National History: Early Origins and Organizing Principles of Museums in the English-speaking Caribbean. In Alissandra Cummins, Kevin Farmer & Roslyn Russell (eds) *Plantation to Nation: Caribbean Museums and National Identity* (11-46). Chicago & Melbourne: Common Ground Publishers.

Cummins, Alissandra. 2017. *Why Caribbean Museums Matter – History as an Act of Consciousness: The Origins of the Museums Association of the Caribbean and the State of Caribbean Museums.* [Keynote Lecture: 24 October, Museums Association of the Caribbean Annual General Meeting and Conference – Beyond Boundaries: Transcending Geographies, Disciplines, and Identities, Miami].

THE SOCIAL MUSEUM IN THE CARIBBEAN

Cummins, Alissandra; Farmer, Kevin & Russell, Roslyn (eds). 2013. *Plantation to Nation: Caribbean Museums and National Identity.* Chicago & Melbourne: Common Ground Publishers.

Davidson, Lee. 2015. Visitor Studies: Toward a Culture of Reflective Practice and Critical Museology for the Visitor-Centered Museum. In Conal McCarthy (ed.) *The International Handbooks of Museum Studies: Museum Practice* (503-527). Malden, Oxford & Chichester: John Wiley & Sons.

Davis, Peter. 2008. New Museologies and the Ecomuseum. In Brian J. Graham & Peter Howard (eds) *The Ashgate Research Companion to Heritage and Identity* (397-414). Aldershot: Ashgate.

De Carli, Georgina. 2004. Vigencia de la Nueva Museología en América Latina: Conceptos y Modelos. *Revista ABRA* 24.33: 55-75.

Degia, Haajima. 2007. *Ethnic Minority Dominance in a Small-island-developing-state and the Implications for Development: The Case of Barbados.* Master's thesis, Ohio University. Available at: https://etd.ohiolink.edu/rws_etd/document/get/ohiou1180899906/inline (Accessed: 8 August 2016).

Degia, Haajima. 2014. *Ethnic Identity Creation of Gujaratis.* PhD dissertation, University of the West Indies.

Degia, Haajima. 2016. *A History of Gujarati-Muslim Migration to Barbados.* [Lecture: 11 March, University of the West Indies: Department of History and Philosophy – Special History Forum, Cave Hill].

Delatour, Patrick. 1984. *Monuments and Sites in the Caribbean.* Paris: UNESCO.

De Peña Díaz, Luisa. 2013. The Memorial Museum of the Dominican Resistance: Its Composition and Role in Society. In Alissandra Cummins, Kevin Farmer & Roslyn Russell (eds) *Plantation to Nation: Caribbean Museums and National Identity* (195-204). Chicago & Melbourne: Common Ground Publishers.

Derrida, Jacques. [1967] 1976. *Of Grammatology.* Translated by Gayatri Chakravorty Spivak. Baltimore & London: The John Hopkins University Press.

Devenish, David C. 1985. Barbados Museum: Reminiscences of a Contract Appointment. *Newsletter (Museum Ethnographers Group)* 19: 58-67.

Dommelen, Peter van. 2010. Colonial Matters: Material Culture and Postcolonial Theory in Colonial Situations. In Chris Tilley, Webb Keane, Susanne Küchler, Mike Rowlands & Patricia Spyer (eds) *Handbook of Material Culture* (104-124). London, Thousand Oaks, New Delhi & Singapore: Sage Publications.

Farmer, Kevin. 2013. New Museums on the Block: Creation of Identity in the Post-Independence Caribbean. In Alissandra Cummins, Kevin Farmer & Roslyn Russell (eds) *Plantation to Nation: Caribbean Museums and National Identity* (169-177). Chicago & Melbourne: Common Ground Publishers.

Felfe, Robert. 2005. Collections and the Surface of the Image: Pictorial Strategies in Early-Modern *Wunderkammern.* In Helmar Schramm, Ludger Schwarte & Jan Lazardzig (eds) *Collection, Laboratory, Theater: Scenes of Knowledge in the 17th Century* (228-265). Berlin: Walter de Gruyter.

Findlen, Paula. 1989. The Museum: Its Classical Etymology and Renaissance Genealogy. *Journal of the History of Collections* 1.1: 59-78.

Findlen, Paula. 1994. *Possessing Nature: Museums, Collecting, and Scientific Culture in Early Modern Italy.* Berkeley, Los Angeles & London: University of California Press.

Fisher, Linford D. 2014. "Dangerous Designes": The 1676 Barbados Act to Prohibit New England Indian Slave Importation. *The William and Mary Quarterly* 71.1: 99-124.

Fitzpatrick, Scott M. 2011. Verification of an Archaic Age Occupation on Barbados, Southern Lesser Antilles. *Radiocarbon* 53.4: 595-604.

Fleming, David. 2012. Human Rights Museums: An Overview. *Curator: The Museum Journal* 55.3: 251-256.

Forte, Maximilian C. (ed.) 2006. *Indigenous Resurgence in the Contemporary Caribbean: Amerindian Survival and Revival.* New York: Peter Long.

Foucault, Michel. [1969] 1972. *The Archaeology of Knowledge: And the Discourse on Language.* Translated by A.M. Sheridan Smith. New York: Pantheon Books.

Foucault, Michel. [1975] 1977. *Discipline and Punish: The Birth of the Prison.* Translated by Alan Sheridan. New York: Pantheon Books.

Fouseki, Kalliopi. 2010. 'Community Voices, Curatorial Choices': Community Consultation for the *1807* Exhibitions. *Museum and Society* 8.3: 180-192.

Fouseki, Kalliopi & Smith, Laurajane. 2013. Community Consultation in the Museum: The 2007 Bicentenary of Britain's Abolition of the Slave Trade. In Viv Golding & Wayne Modest (eds) *Museums and Communities: Curators, Collections and Collaboration* (232-245). London & New York: Bloomsbury.

Françozo, Mariana & Broekhoven, Laura van. 2017. Dossiê "Patrimônio indígena e coleções etnográficas." *Boletim do Museu Paraense Emílio Goeldi* 12.3: 709-711.

Françozo, Mariana & Strecker, Amy. 2017. Caribbean Collections in European Museums and the Question of Returns. *International Journal of Cultural Property* 24.4: 451-477.

Frederick, Faustulus & Shepherd, Elizabeth. 1971. *In Our Carib Indian Village.* New York: Lothrop, Lee & Shepard Company.

Fuller, Nancy J. 1992. The Museum as a Vehicle for Community Empowerment: The Ak-Chin Indian Community Ecomuseum Project. In Ivan Karp, Christine Mullen Kreamer & Steven D. Lavine (eds) *Museums and Communities: The Politics of Public Culture* (327-365). Washington: Smithsonian Institute.

Gable, Eric. 2013. The City, Race, and the Creation of a Common History at the Virginia Historical Society. In Viv Golding & Wayne Modest (eds) *Museums and Communities: Curators, Collections and Collaboration* (32-47). London & New York: Bloomsbury.

Galla, Amareswar. 2005. Cultural Diversity in Ecomuseum Development in Viet Nam. *Museum International* 57.3: 101-109.

Galla, Amareswar. 2008. The First Voice in Heritage Conservation. *International Journal of Intangible Heritage* 3: 10-25.

García Perdigón, Jorge Rolando. 2014. La Labor Museológica de la Revolución Cubana y el Proceso de Transformación en la Proyección Social de los Museos en Cuba. *Intervención* 5.9: 65-75.

Garderen, Mereke van. 2018. *Pictures of the Past: Visualizations and Visual Analysis in Archaeological Context.* PhD dissertation, University of Konstanz.

Garderen, Mereke van; Pampel, Barbara & Brandes, Ulrik. 2016. A Labeling Problem for Symbol Maps of Archaeological Sites. In Yifan Hu & Martin Nöllenburg (eds) *Graph Drawing and Network Visualization: 24th International Symposium, GD 2016, Athens, Greece, September 19-21, 2016, Revised Selected Papers* (605-607). Cham: Springer.

Garderen, Mereke van; Pampel, Barbara; Nocaj, Arlind & Brandes, Ulrik. 2017. Minimum-Displacement Overlap Removal for Geo-referenced Data Visualization. *Computer Graphics Forum* 36.3: 423-433.

Gilette, Arthur. 2000. Carnival, Cricket and Culture: Museum Life in Antigua and Barbuda. *Museum International* 52.2: 45-49.

Glissant, Édouard & Obrist, Hans Ulrich. 2012. Édouard Glissant & Hans Ulrich Obrist. Series: 100 Notes – 100 Thoughts / 100 Notizen – 100 Gedanken #038. Germany: Hatje Cantz Verlag.

Golding, Viv. 2013. Collaborative Museums: Curators, Communities, Collections. In Viv Golding & Wayne Modest (eds) *Museums and Communities: Curators, Collections and Collaboration* (13-31). London & New York: Bloomsbury.

Golding, Viv & Modest, Wayne (eds). 2013. *Museums and Communities: Curators, Collections and Collaboration.* London & New York: Bloomsbury.

Gosden, Christopher. 1999. *Anthropology and Archaeology: A Changing Relationship.* London & New York: Routledge.

Government of the Republic of Trinidad and Tobago, Central Statistical Office. 2012. *Trinidad and Tobago 2011 Population and Housing Census: Demographic Report.* Port of Spain: The Central Statistical Office. Available at: https://guardian.co.tt/sites/default/files/story/2011_DemographicReport.pdf (Accessed: 8 August 2016).

Gurian, Elaine Heumann. 1999. What is the Object of this Exercise? A Meandering Exploration of the Many Meanings of Objects in Museums. *Daedalus* 128.3: 163-183.

Hall, Stuart (ed.) [1997] 2010. *Representation: Cultural Representations and Signifying Practices.* London, Thousand Oaks & New Delhi: Sage Publications.

Hanoomansingh, Peter. 1996. Beyond Profit and Capital: A Study of the Sindhis and Gujaratis of Barbados. In Rhoda E. Reddock (ed.) *Ethnic Minorities in Caribbean Society* (273-342). Trinidad and Tobago: Institute of Social and Economic Studies (ISER), University of the West Indies.

Haslip-Viera, Gabriel. 2013. *Race, Identity and Indigenous Politics: Puerto Rican Neo-Taínos in the Diaspora and the Island.* New York: Latino Studies Press.

Henry-Wilson, Maxine. 2003. *Culture in the Future of the Caribbean Community* [Lecture: 24-26 April, Distinguished Lecture Series Commemorating the Thirtieth Anniversary of the Caribbean Community, Paramaribo]. Available at: https://caricom.org/communications/view/culture-in-the-future-of-the-caribbean-community-by-hon-maxine-henry-wilson-minister-of-education-youth-and-culture-jamaica (Accessed: 4 June 2014).

Hoelscher, Steven. 2011. Heritage. In Sharon Macdonald (ed.) *A Companion to Museum Studies* (198-218). Malden & Oxford: Wiley – Blackwell.

Hofman, Corinne L. 2013. The Post-Saladoid in the Lesser Antilles (A.D. 600/800-1492). In William F. Keegan, Corinne L. Hofman & Reniel Rodríguez Ramos (eds) *The Oxford Handbook of Caribbean Archaeology* (205-220). New York: Oxford University Press.

Hofman, Corinne L. & Carlin, Eithne B. 2010. The Ever-dynamic Caribbean: Exploring New Approaches to Unraveling Social Networks in the Pre-Colonial and Early Colonial Periods. In Eithne B. Carlin & Simon van de Kerke (eds) *Linguistics and Archaeology in the Americas: The Historization of Language and Society* (107-122). Boston: Brill.

Hofman, Corinne L. & Hoogland, Menno L.P. 2012. Caribbean Encounters: Rescue Excavations at the Early Colonial Island Carib Site of Argyle, St. Vincent. *Analecta Praehistorica Leidensia* 43/44: 63-76.

Hofman, Corinne L. & Hoogland, Menno L.P. 2015. Beautiful Tropical Islands in the Caribbean Sea: Human Responses to Floods and Droughts and the Indigenous Archaeological Heritage of the Caribbean. In Willem J.H. Willems & Henk P.J. van Schaik (eds) *Water & Heritage: Material, Conceptual and Spiritual Connections* (99-119). Leiden: Sidestone Press.

Hofman, Corinne; Mol, Angus; Hoogland, Menno & Valcárcel Rojas, Roberto. 2014. *Stage of Encounters: Migration, Mobility and Interaction in the Pre-Colonial and Early Colonial Caribbean*. World Archaeology 46.4: 590-609.

Honychurch, Lennox. [1975] 1995. *The Dominica Story: A History of the Island*. London & Basingstoke: Macmillan Education.

Honychurch. Lennox. [1997] 2000. *Carib to Creole: A History of Contact and Culture Exchange*. Roseau: The Dominica Institute. D. Phil thesis, University of Oxford.

Honychurch, Lennox. 2016. *Not One of the 'Down Islands': Landscape and Ecology*. [Lecture: 15 March, Barbados Museum and Historical Society Lecture Series – Becoming Bajan: The Evolution of Barbadian Identity, Bridgetown].

ICOM. 1946. *ICOM Constitution.*

ICOM. 1951. *ICOM Statutes.*

ICOM. 1961. *ICOM Statutes*

ICOM. 1974. *ICOM Statutes.*

ICOM. 1989. *ICOM Statutes.*

ICOM. 2007. *ICOM Statutes.*

ICOM. 2017. *ICOM Code of Ethics for Museums*. Paris: ICOM.

Inniss, Tara. 2012. Heritage and Communities in a Small Island Developing State: Historic Bridgetown and its Garrison, Barbados. In Amareswar Galla (ed.) *World Heritage: Benefits Beyond Borders* (69-81). Paris & Cambridge: UNESCO & Cambridge University Press.

Jayaram, N. 2003. The Politics of 'Cultural Renaissance' Among Indo-Trinidadians. In Bhikhu Parekh, Gurharpal Singh & Steven Vertovec (eds) *Culture and Economy in the Indian Diaspora* (123-141). London & New York: Routledge.

Karp, Ivan. 1992. Introduction: Museums and Communities: The Politics of Public Culture. In Ivan Karp, Christine Mullen Kreamer & Steven D. Lavine (eds) *Museums and Communities: The Politics of Public Culture* (1-17). Washington: Smithsonian Institute.

Karp, Ivan & Lavine, Steven D. (eds). 1991. *Exhibiting Cultures: The Poetics and Politics of Museum Display*. Washington & London: Smithsonian Institution Press.

Karp, Ivan; Mullen Kreamer, Christine & Lavine, Steven D. (eds). 1992. *Museums and Communities: The Politics of Public Culture*. Washington: Smithsonian Institute.

Kavanagh, Gaynor. 1994. Visiting and Evaluating Museums. In Gaynor Kavanagh (ed.) *Museum Provision and Professionalism* (90-94). London & New York: Routledge.

Keegan, William F. & Hofman, Corinne L. 2017. *The Caribbean before Columbus*. New York: Oxford University Press.

Kelly, Lynda. 2006. Measuring the Impact of Museums on their Communities: The Role of the 21st Century Museum. Paper presented at the *2006 INTERCOM Symposium: New Roles and Missions of Museums*, ICOM – INTERCOM: Taipei. Available at: http://www.intercom.museum/documents/1-2Kelly.pdf (Accessed: 22 October 2014).

Kreps, Christina. 2011a. Changing the Rules of the Road: Post-colonialism and the New Ethics of Museum Anthropology. In Janet Marstine (ed.) *The Routledge Companion to Museum Ethics: Redefining Ethics for the Twenty-First-Century Museum* (70-84). Abingdon & New York: Routledge.

Kreps, Christina. 2011b. Non-Western Models of Museums and Curation in Crosscultural Perspective. In Sharon Macdonald (ed.) *A Companion to Museum Studies* (457-472). Malden & Oxford: Wiley-Blackwell.

Lagerkvist, Cajsa. 2006. Empowerment and Anger: Learning How to Share Ownership of the Museum. *Museum and Society* 4.2: 52-68.

Laguer Díaz, Carmen A. 2013. The Construction of an Identity and the Politics of Remembering. In William F. Keegan, Corinne L. Hofman & Reniel Rodríguez Ramos (eds) *The Oxford Handbook of Caribbean Archaeology* (557-567). Oxford: Oxford University Press.

Lavine, Steven D. 1992. Audience, Ownership, and Authority: Designing Relations between Museums and Communities. In Ivan Karp, Christine Mullen Kreamer & Steven D. Lavine (eds) *Museums and Communities: The Politics of Public Culture* (137-157). Washington: Smithsonian Institute.

Lee, Maria A. 2015. Curating the Nation: The Politics of Recognition in a Bahamian National Museum. *The International Journal of Bahamian Studies* 21.1: 91-107.

Lemieux & Schultz. 1973. *Report on CCA/Canadian National Museums Survey*. Unpublished report of the Caribbean Conservation Association.

Lenik, Stephan. 2012. Carib as a Colonial Category: Comparing Ethnohistoric and Archaeological Evidence from Dominica, West Indies. *Ethnohistory* 59.1: 79-107.

Lidchi, Henrietta. [1997] 2010. The Poetics and the Politics of Exhibiting Other Cultures. In Stuart Hall (ed.) *Representation: Cultural Representations and Signifying Practices* (151-222). London, Thousand Oaks & New Delhi: Sage Publications.

Linares, José. 2013. The History and Evolution of Cuban Museums. In Alissandra Cummins, Kevin Farmer & Roslyn Russell (eds) *Plantation to Nation: Caribbean Museums and National Identity* (57-67). Chicago & Melbourne: Common Ground Publishers.

MacDonald, George F. 1992. Change and Challenge: Museums in the Information Society. In Ivan Karp, Christine Mullen Kreamer & Steven D. Lavine (eds) *Museums and Communities: The Politics of Public Culture* (158-181). Washington: Smithsonian Institute.

Maréchal, Jean-Philippe. 1998. For an Island Museology in the Caribbean. *Museum International* 50.3: 44-50.

Markovits, Claude. 2000. *The Global World of Indian Merchants, 1750-1947: Traders of Sind from Bukhara to Panama*. Cambridge: Cambridge University Press.

Martin, John Angus. 2013. *Island Caribs and French Settlers in Grenada: 1498-1763*. Grenada: Grenada National Museum Press.

Masson, Georgina. 1972. Italian Flower Collectors' Gardens in Seventeenth Century Italy. In David R. Coffin (ed.) *The Italian Garden* (63-80). Washington D.C.: Dumbarton Oaks.

McLean, Fiona. 2008. Museums and the Representation of Identity. In Brian Graham & Peter Howard (eds) *The Ashgate Research Companion to Heritage and Identity* (284-298). Aldershot & Burlington: Ashgate Publishing.

Modest, Wayne. 2010. *Museums, Slavery and the Caribbean Exhibitionary Complex: Toward a Museology of Displacement.* PhD dissertation, University of the West Indies.

Modest, Wayne. 2012. We Have Always Been Modern: Museums, Collections, and Modernity in the Caribbean. *Museum Anthropology* 35.1: 85-96.

Monahan, Patrick. 2017. In Battered Puerto Rico, an Art Museum Full of Treasures Is Open for Business. *Vanity Fair* [Online], 6 October. Available at: https://www.van ityfair.com/style/2017/10/puerto-rico-art-museum (Accessed: 9 October 2017).

Mullen Kreamer, Christine. 1992. Defining Communities Through Exhibiting and Collecting. In Ivan Karp, Christine Mullen Kreamer & Steven D. Lavine (eds) *Museums and Communities: The Politics of Public Culture* (367-381). Washington: Smithsonian Institute.

Murphy, Bernice L. 2004. The Definition of the Museum: From Specialist Reference to Social Recognition and Service. *ICOM News* 2004.2: 3.

Museums Association of the Caribbean. 2011a. *Museum Directory for the Dutch-speaking Caribbean.* Unpublished directory by the Museums Association of the Caribbean.

Museums Association of the Caribbean. 2011b. *Museum Directory for the English-speaking Caribbean.* Unpublished directory by the Museums Association of the Caribbean.

Museums Association of the Caribbean. 2011c. *Museum Directory for the French-speaking Caribbean.* Unpublished directory by the Museums Association of the Caribbean.

Museums Association of the Caribbean. 2011d. *Museum Directory for the Spanish-speaking Caribbean.* Unpublished directory by the Museums Association of the Caribbean.

Nakhuda, Sabir. 2013. *Bengal to Barbados: A 100 Year History of East Indians in Barbados.* Barbados: Sabir Nakhuda.

Nederveen Pieterse, Jan. 2005. Multiculturalism and Museums: Discourse About Others in the Age of Globalization. In Gerard Corsane (ed.) *Heritage, Museums and Galleries – An Introductory Reader* (163-183). London & New York: Routledge.

Nettleford, Rex. 2003. *The Caribbean's Creative Diversity: The Defining Point of the Region's History* [Lecture: 21 March, Distinguished Lecture Series Commemorating the Thirtieth Anniversary of the Caribbean Community, Paramaribo]. Available at: http://www.caricom.org/jsp/speeches/30anniversary_lecture_2_nettleford.jsp (Accessed: 4 June 2014).

Nettleford, Rex. 2004. Ideology, Identity, Culture. In Bridget Brereton (ed.) *General History of the Caribbean: Volume V – The Caribbean in the Twentieth Century* (537-558). Paris & London: UNESCO & Macmillan Caribbean.

Nettleford, Rex. 2008. Respect and Understanding: Engaging Creative Diversity, the Caribbean Experience. Paper presented at the *2008 CAM Triennial: Museums & Diversity: Museums in Pluralistic Societies*, CAM: Georgetown. Available at: http://www.maltwood.uvic.ca/cam/activities/past_conferences/1999conf/CAM%20 Nettleford%20Scan.pdf (Accessed: 22 October 2014).

NEXUS1492. 2013. *Ethics Code: Full Ethical Review ERC*. Unpublished document by NEXUS1492.

Nicks, Trudy. 2003. Introduction. In Laura Peers & Alison K. Brown (eds) *Museums and Source Communities: A Routledge Reader* (19-27). London & New York: Routledge.

Office of the Registrar General India. 2001. *Census of India 2001*. New Delhi: Office of the Registrar General.

Ohmer, Mary. 2010. How Theory and Research Inform Citizen Participation in Poor Communities: The Ecological Perspective and Theories on Self- and Collective Efficacy and Sense of Community. *Journal of Human Behavior in the Social Environment* 20.1: 1-19.

Oliver, José R. 1998. *El Centro Ceremonial de Caguana, Puerto Rico: Simbolismo Iconográfico, Cosmovisión y el Poderío Caciquil Taíno de Boriquén*. Oxford: Archaeopress.

Onciul, Bryony. 2013. Community Engagement, Curatorial Practice, and Museum Ethos in Alberta, Canada. In Viv Golding & Wayne Modest (eds) *Museums and Communities: Curators, Collections and Collaboration* (79-97). London & New York: Bloomsbury.

Peers, Laura & Brown, Alison K. 2003a. Introduction. In Laura Peers & Alison K. Brown (eds) *Museums and Source Communities: A Routledge Reader* (1-16). London & New York: Routledge.

Peers, Laura & Brown, Alison K. (eds). 2003b. *Museums and Source Communities: A Routledge Reader*. London & New York: Routledge.

Perkin, Corinne. 2010. Beyond the Rhetoric: Negotiating the Politics and Realising the Potential of Community-driven Heritage Engagement. *International Journal of Heritage Studies* 16.1-2: 107-122.

Phillips, Ruth B. 2003. Introduction. In Laura Peers & Alison K. Brown (eds) *Museums and Source Communities: A Routledge Reader* (155-170). London & New York: Routledge.

Podgorny, Irina. 2013. Travelling Museums and Itinerant Collections in Nineteenth-Century Latin America. *Museum History Journal* 6.2: 127-146.

Pratt, Mary Louise. 1991. The Arts of the Contact Zone. *Profession* 91: 33-40.

Premdas, Ralph R. 2002. Self-Determination and Sovereignty in the Caribbean: Migration, Transnational Identities, and Deterritorialisation of the State. In Ramesh Ramsaran (ed.) *Caribbean Survival and the Global Challenge* (49-64). Kingston: Ian Randle Publishers.

Pyburn, K. Anne. n.d. *Anne Pyburn's Principles of Community Engagement for Archaeologists*. Unpublished. Available at: http://www.academia.edu/5129190/Anne_Pyburns_Principles_of_Community_Engagement_for_Archaeologists (Accessed: 22 October 2014).

Pyburn, K. Anne. 2008. Public Archaeology, Indiana Jones, and Honesty. *Archaeologies: Journal of the World Archaeological Congress* 4.2: 201-204.

Quiccheberg, Samuel. [1565] 2013. *The First Treatise on Museums: Samuel Quiccheberg's Inscriptiones 1565*. Edited by Mark A. Meadow, translated by Bruce Robertson & Mark A. Meadow. Los Angeles: Getty Research Institute.

Ramtahal, Kumaree. 2013. Opening Doors to Our Cultural Heritage: The Indian Caribbean Museum of Trinidad and Tobago. In Nerea A. Llamas (ed.) *Preserving Memory: Documenting and Archiving Latin American Human Rights. Papers of the Fifty-Sixth Annual Meeting of the Seminar on the Acquisition of Latin American Library Materials* (120-132). New Orleans: SALALM.

Ridge, Mia. 2013. From Tagging to Theorizing: Deepening Engagement with Cultural Heritage through Crowdsourcing. *Curator* 56.4: 435-450.

Rivera, Rodolfo & Soto Soria, Alfonso. 1982. *Report of the Mission to Costa Rica, the Dominican Republic and the OAS English-speaking Member States in the Caribbean Area.* Unpublished report of the Organisation of the American States.

Ronan, Kristine. 2014. Native Empowerment, the New Museology, and the National Museum of the American Indian. *Museum & Society* 12.1: 132-147.

Rouse, Irving. 1992. *The Taínos: Rise and Decline of the People Who Greeted Columbus.* New Haven: Yale University Press.

Russell, Ian. 2010. Heritage, Identities, and Roots: A Critique of Arborescent Models of Heritage and Identity. In George S. Smith, Phyllis Mauch Messenger & Hilary A. Soderland (eds) *Heritage Values in Contemporary Society* (29-41). Walnut Creek: Left Coast Press.

Russell, Roslyn. 2013. Framing Identity, Encouraging Diversity: Recent Museum Developments in Barbados. In Alissandra Cummins, Kevin Farmer & Roslyn Russell (eds) *Plantation to Nation: Caribbean Museums and National Identity* (179-194). Chicago & Melbourne: Common Ground Publishers.

Said, Edward W. [1978] 2003. *Orientalism.* London: Penguin Group.

Saint Lucia National Trust. 2017a. *Proposed Elimination of Government's Annual Contribution to the Saint Lucia National Trust for the 2017-18 Financial Year.* Press Release, 24 April. Available at: https://slunatrust.org/assets/content/documents/PR_on_ProposedZeroSubventionApr2017.pdf (Accessed: 14 June 2017).

Saint Lucia National Trust. 2017b. *Closure of Walcott Place.* Press Release, 31 May. Available at: https://slunatrust.org/assets/content/documents/Press_Release_Closure_of_Walcott_Place.pdf (Accessed: 14 June 2017).

Sandell, Richard. 1998. Museums as Agents of Social Inclusion. *Museum Management and Curatorship* 17.4: 401-418.

Sandell, Richard. 2003. Social Inclusion, the Museum and the Dynamics of Sectoral Change. *Museums and Society* 1.1: 45-62.

Sandell, Richard. 2012. Museums as Agents of Social Inclusion. In Bettina Messias Carbonell (ed.) *Museum Studies: An Anthology of Contexts* (562-574). Malden, Oxford & Chichester: Blackwell Publishing.

Sands of Time Consultancy. 2011. *Caribbean Museums: Survey 2011 – Final Report.* Unpublished report by the Museums Association of the Caribbean.

Sauvage, Alexandra. 2010. To Be or Not To Be Colonial: Museums Facing Their Exhibitions. *Culturales* VI.12: 97-116.

Scott, Carol A. 2006. Museums: Impact and Value. *Cultural Trends* 15.1: 45-75.

Scott, Carol A. 2009. Exploring the Evidence Base for Museum Value. *Museum Management and Curatorship* 24.3: 195-212.

Scott, Carol A. 2015. Museum Measurement: Questions of Value. In Conal McCarthy (ed.) *The International Handbooks of Museum Studies: Museum Practice* (97-122). Malden, Oxford & Chichester: John Wiley & Sons.

Seon, Ernie. 2017. Prime Minister Chastanet Confirms Cut in Subvention to St. Lucia National Trust. *Pride News* [Online], 25 April. Available at: http://pridenews.ca/2017/04/25/prime-minister-chastanet-confirms-cut-subvention-st-lucia-national-trust/ (Accessed: 14 June 2017).

Shafie, Termeh; Schoch, David; Mans, Jimmy; Hofman, Corinne L. & Brandes, Ulrik. 2017. Hypergraph Representations: A Study of Carib Attacks on Colonial Forces, 1509-1700. *Journal of Historical Network Research* 1.1: 52-70.

Shearn, Isaac. 2014. *Pre-Columbian Regional Community Integration in Dominica, West Indies*. PhD dissertation, University of Florida.

Siegel, Peter E. 2013. Caribbean Archaeology in Historical Perspective. In William F. Keegan, Corinne L. Hofman & Reniel Rodríguez Ramos (eds) *The Oxford Handbook of Caribbean Archaeology* (21-46). Oxford: Oxford University Press.

Silverman, Lois H. 2010. *The Social Work of Museums*. London & New York: Routledge.

Simon, Nina. 2010. *The Participatory Museum*. Santa Cruz: Museum 2.0.

Simon, Nina. 2014. Where's the Community in the Crowd? Framing and the Wall Street Journal's "Everybody's a Curator." *Museum 2.0* [Online], 5 November. Available at: http://museumtwo.blogspot.nl/2014/11/wheres-community-in-crowd-framing-and.html (Accessed: 1 August 2017).

Simon, Nina. 2016. *The Art of Relevance*. Santa Cruz: Museum 2.0.

Singleton, Raymond. 1978. *CARICOM Museum Report*. Unpublished report of CARICOM.

Skerrit, Roosevelt. 2015. *"Keeping It Real"… in the Community! An Opportunity for the General Public to Interact with the Cabinet of Ministers on the 2015/2016 National Budget*. Speech held: 13 August 2015, Salybia Primary School. Recording available at: https://www.youtube.com/watch?v=1EwdNmzcuqI (Accessed: 19 January 2016).

Smith, Kelvin. 2006. Placing the Carib Model Village: The Carib Territory and Dominican Tourism. In Maximilian C. Forte (ed.) *Indigenous Resurgence in the Contemporary Caribbean: Amerindian Survival and Revival* (71-87). New York: Peter Long.

Smith, Laurajane. 2015. Theorizing Museum and Heritage Visiting. In Andrea Witcomb & Kylie Message (eds) *The International Handbooks of Museum Studies: Museum Theory* (459-484). Malden, Oxford & Chichester: John Wiley & Sons.

Smith, Laurajane & Waterton, Emma. 2009. *Heritage, Communities and Archaeology*. London: Duckworth.

Solomon, Sheila. 1979. *Framework for Cultural Development in the Caribbean* [Alt. *Mission Report on an Identification Mission in Cultural Development in the Caribbean*]. Paris: UNESCO.

Stapley-Brown, Victoria. 2017. Puerto Rico's Museums on the Mend. *The Art Newspaper* [Online], 4 October. Available at: https://www.theartnewspaper.com/news/puerto-ricos-museums-on-the-mend (Accessed: 9 October 2017).

Svensson, Anna. 2017. *A Utopian Quest for Universal Knowledge: Diachronic Histories of Botanical Collections between the Sixteenth Century and the Present*. Stockholm: KTH Royal Institute of Technology.

Taylor, Douglas & Hoff, Berend. 1980. The Linguistic Repertory of the Island-Carib in the Seventeenth Century: The Men's Language – A Carib Pidgin? *International Journal of American Linguistics* 46.4: 301-312.

Tilley, Christopher. 1994. *A Phenomenology of Landscape: Places, Paths, and Monuments.* Oxford: Berg.

Tlili, Anwar. 2008. Behind the Policy Mantra of the Inclusive Museum: Receptions of Social Exclusion and Inclusion in Museums and Science Centres. *Cultural Sociology* 2.1: 123-147.

Towle, Ed L. & Tyson, George F. 1979. *Towards a Planning Strategy for the Management of Historical/Cultural Resources Critical to Development in the Lesser Antilles.* Island Resources Foundation.

Varine, Hugues de. 2006. Ecomuseology and Sustainable Development. *Museums & Social Issues* 1.2: 225-232.

Varutti, Marzia. 2013. Learning to Share Knowledge: Collaborative Projects in Taiwan. In Viv Golding & Wayne Modest (eds) *Museums and Communities: Curators, Collections and Collaboration* (59-78). London & New York: Bloomsbury.

Vergo, Peter. 1991. *The New Museology.* London: Reaktion.

Virassamy, Estelle. 2015. Guy Gabon au Musée Schoelcher. *France-Antilles* [Online], 21 February. Available at: http://www.guadeloupe.franceantilles.fr/loisirs/sortir/guy-gabon-au-musee-schoelcher-309580.php (Accessed: 19 June 2017).

VSNU. 2004. *The Netherlands Code of Conduct for Scientific Practice: Principles of Good Scientific Teaching and Research.* Amsterdam: VSNU.

Walcott, Derek. 1992. *Nobel Lecture: The Antilles – Fragments of Epic Memory.* Speech held: 7 December 1992, Stockholm. Recording available at: https://www.nobelprize.org/mediaplayer/index.php?id=1503 (Accessed: 16 November 2017).

Waterton, Emma; Smith, Laurajane & Campbell, Gary. 2006. The Utility of Discourse Analysis to Heritage Studies: The Burra Charter and Social Inclusion. *International Journal of Heritage Studies* 12.4: 339-355.

Watson, Sheila (ed.) 2007. *Museums and Their Communities.* London & New York: Routledge.

Weil, Stephen E. 1983. *Beauty and the Beasts: On Museums, Art, the Law, and the Market.* Washington D.C.: Smithsonian Institution Press.

Whiting, John S. 1983. *Museum Focussed Heritage in the English-speaking Caribbean.* Paris: UNESCO.

Williams, Tammy Ronique. 2012. Tourism as a Neo-colonial Phenomenon: Examining the Works of Pattullo & Mullings. *Caribbean Quilt* 2: 191-200.

Zea de Uribe, Gloria. 1982. Recent Advances in Colombian Museology. *Museum* 34.2: 124-126.

List of Figures

Cover   *The Social Museum in the Caribbean.*

Photographs by Csilla Ariese-Vandemeulebroucke and design by Krijn Boom.

1.   *Musée Schoelcher, Guadeloupe, was opened to the public in 1887.*

Photograph by Csilla Ariese-Vandemeulebroucke.

2.   *The artworks of Museo Bellapart, Dominican Republic, are accessed through a Honda dealership.*

Photograph by Csilla Ariese-Vandemeulebroucke.

3.   *Map of the islands and countries in the Caribbean where fieldwork was conducted.*

Image by Csilla Ariese-Vandemeulebroucke. Map by D-Maps, ©D-Maps2017 Central America: States.

4.   *Fields from the database constructed for the regional museum survey, with clarifications.*

Image and database by Csilla Ariese-Vandemeulebroucke.

5.   *Matrix of the participatory practices per museum, colored by museum type. The museums are sorted by type and then from most to least participatory practices.*

Image by Mereke van Garderen & Csilla Ariese-Vandemeulebroucke.

6.   *Presenting and discussing survey results, 2016. Left: Kalinago Barana Autê. Right: Barbados Museum & Historical Society.*

Photographs by Chouboutouiba Cozier Frederick (left) and Kevin Farmer (right).

7.   *A display case made from a jukebox showcases geological collections at Museo Profesor Tremols, Dominican Republic.*

Photograph by Csilla Ariese-Vandemeulebroucke.

8.   *Ecomusée de Marie-Galante: Habitation Murat, Marie-Galante, consists of an extended museum landscape.*

Photograph by Csilla Ariese-Vandemeulebroucke.

9. *When diving in the Underwater Sculpture Park, Grenada, visitors participate in protecting the reef.*

Photograph by Csilla Ariese-Vandemeulebroucke.

10. *The site at Centro Indígena Caguana, Puerto Rico, was first excavated in 1915 and opened to the public in 1965. Archaeological investigations continue to contribute objects and information to the exhibitions.*

Photograph by Csilla Ariese-Vandemeulebroucke.

11. *The maroons' resistance to slavery is also shown on the outside of the asafu yard of the Charles Town Maroon Museum, Jamaica.*

Photograph by Csilla Ariese-Vandemeulebroucke.

12. *Mind's Eye: The Visionary World of Miss Lassie, Grand Cayman, is dedicated to the preservation of the home and other artworks of Gladwyn K. Bush.*

Photograph by Csilla Ariese-Vandemeulebroucke.

13. *Interactive displays in the human body gallery at the Museo Infantil Trampolín, Dominican Republic.*

Photograph by Csilla Ariese-Vandemeulebroucke.

14. *Entry to the Kalinago Barana Autê, Dominica.*

Photograph by Csilla Ariese-Vandemeulebroucke.

15. *Dominica. Left: satellite image. Right: map with a terrain view showing elevations.*

Map data ©2016 Google.

16. *Surveyor John Byres' map of Dominica, 1776.*

Map by John Byres.

Plan of the Island of Dominica Laid Down by Actual Survey under the Direction of the Honorable the Commissioners for the Sale of Lands in the Ceded Islands. London: S. Hooper. Repository: Library of Congress, Geography and Map Division, Washington D.C. (Catalog#74690599).

17. *Plans for the design of the 'Carib Cultural Village,' 1987.*

Plan by Lennox Honychurch (2000: 219, fig. 14.1).

18. *Map of the Kalinago Barana Autê, posted near the entrance.*

Photograph by Csilla Ariese-Vandemeulebroucke.

19. *The Kalinago Territory cricket tournament was a wonderful event for hanging out with the community and also offered opportunities for conducting surveys.*

Photograph by Csilla Ariese-Vandemeulebroucke.

20. *Gender and age distributions of survey respondents in Dominica.*

Image by Csilla Ariese-Vandemeulebroucke.

21. *Respondents' visitation percentage and number of visits to the Kalinago Barana Autê.*

Image by Csilla Ariese-Vandemeulebroucke.

Appendix

Index: Caribbean Museums Database

This is an index of the museums included in the regional museum survey and thus in the Caribbean Museums Database. The full Caribbean Museums Database, which contains the complete entries of all of these museums, totaling 600 pages, is accessible online as a resource accompanying this dissertation.

Anguilla
Heritage Collection Museum

Aruba
Aruba Aloe N.V. Factory & Museum
Fort Zoutman Historical Museum
National Archaeological Museum Aruba
San Nicolas Community Museum

Barbados
Barbados Museum & Historical Society
George Washington House
Historic Bridgetown and its Garrison
Mount Gay Visitor Centre
Museum of Parliament & National Heroes Gallery
Nidhe Israel Synagogue & Museum
The Exchange

Belize
Abandoned Sugar Mill (Lamanai)
Government House (House of Culture)
Lamanai Archaeological Reserve
Luba Garifuna Cultural Museum
Museum of Belize
Traveller's Liquor Heritage Centre

Bequia
Bequia Maritime Museum
Bequia Tourism Association Information Bureau
Whaling Museum & Boat Museum

Carriacou
Carriacou Museum

Curaçao
Curaçao Maritime Museum
Fortchurch & Protestant Cultural Historical Museum
Het Curacaosche Museum
Jewish Cultural Historical Museum
Kas di Pal'i Maishi
Kura Hulanda Museum
Museo Tula
National Archaeological Anthropological Memory Management
Octagon Museum
Postmuseum
Savonet Museum
Tele Museum
Yotin Kortá: The Money Museum

Dominica
Cabrits National Park: Fort Shirley
Kalinago Barana Autê
Morne Trois Pitons National Park: Emerald Pool
The Dominica Museum
The Old Mill Cultural Centre & Historic Site
Touna Kalinago Heritage Village

Dominican Republic
Amber World
Calle El Conde
Casa Museo General Gregorio Luperón
Catedral Primada de América
Centro Cultural de las Telecomunicaciones
Centro León
Chocomuseo
Colonial City of Santo Domingo
Finca la Protectora
La Aurora Cigar World
Larimar Museo Dominicano
Museo Arqueológico Regional Altos de Chavón
Museo Bellapart
Museo Casa de Tostado

Museo de Ambar (Amber Art Gallery)
Museo de Arte Moderno
Museo de Arte Taino
Museo de la Altagracia
Museo de las Casas Reales
Museo del Hombre Dominicano
Museo del Ron y la Caña
Museo Fortaleza de Santo Domingo: Fortaleza Ozama
Museo Infantil Trampolín
Museo La Isabela: Parque Nacional
Museo Memorial de la Resistencia Dominicana
Museo Mundo de Ambar (Amber World Museum)
Museo Nacional de Historia Natural
Museo Nacional de Historia y Geografía
Museo Naval de las Atarazanas Reales
Museo Profesor Tremols
Museo Sacro La Vega
Museo Virreinal Alcázar de Colón
Panteón de la Patria
Parque Nacional Histórico La Vega Vieja
Quinta Dominica
Sala de Arte Pre-Hispánico: Fundación García Arévalo
Santo Cerro: Nuestra Señora de las Mercedes

French Guiana
Bagne de Saint-Laurent-du-Maroni
Centre Spatial Guyanais
Musée de l'Île Royale

Grand Cayman
Cayman Islands National Museum
Cayman Turtle Centre
Mind's Eye: The Visionary World of Miss Lassie
National Gallery of the Cayman Islands
Pedro St. James National Historic Site
The Mission House

Grenada
Belmont Estate
Grenada National Museum
La Sagesse Natural Works
Rome Museum
The Priory
Underwater Sculpture Park
West Indies Cricket Heritage Centre
Westerhall Estate

Guadeloupe
Domaine de Séverin
Ecomusée CreoleArt (Ecomuseum of Guadeloupe)
La Route de l'Esclave
Musée Départemental Edgar Clerc
Musée du Rhum: Musée Universel
Musée l'Herminier
Musée Municipal Saint-John Perse
Musée Schoelcher

Jamaica
African-Caribbean Institute of Jamaica
Bank of Jamaica Money Museum
Bob Marley Museum
Charles Town Maroon Museum
Coyaba Gardens & Museum
Devon House Mansion
Firefly House
Fort Charles & Museum
Jamaica Music Museum
Jamaica National Heritage Trust
Jamaican Military Museum and Library
Liberty Hall
National Gallery of Jamaica
National Gallery West
National Museum Jamaica
National Museum West
Natural History Museum of Jamaica
New Seville (Seville Great House)
Shaare Shalom Jamaican Jewish Heritage Centre
Sunshine Palace & Taíno Museum
University of the West Indies Geology Museum
University of the West Indies Museum
White Marl Taíno Museum
Zabai Tabai Taíno Indian Museum

Marie-Galante
Ecomusée de Marie-Galante: Habitation Murat
Marie-Galante Kreol West Indies
Musée Art & Tradition: Poupées Matrones

Martinique
Bibliothèque Schoelcher
Centre de Découverte des Sciences de la Terre
Centre d'Interprétation Paul Gauguin
Distillerie Depaz

Ecomusée de Martinique
Espace Muséal Aimé Césaire: Hôtel de Ville
Fort Saint-Louis
La Maison de la Canne
La Savane des Esclaves
L'Église du Fort
L'Étang des Salines
Maison du Bambou: Martinique Recycl'Art
Maison Régional des Volcans
Musée Départemental d'Archéologie et de Préhistoire
Musée du Père Pinchon
Musée Régional d'Histoire et d'Ethnographie
Musée Volcanologique Franck A. Perret
Rocher du Tombeau des Caraïbes

Puerto Rico
Casa Pueblo
Castillo San Cristóbal
Castillo San Felipe del Morro
Centro Ceremonial Indígena de Tibes
Centro Indígena Caguana
Corralón de San José [prev. Museo del Indio]
Galería Botello
Galería Nacional
Instituto de Cultura Puertorriqueña
Museo Casa Blanca
Museo de Historia, Antropología y Arte
Museo de las Américas
Museo del Mar
Museo de San Juan

St. Barthélemy
The Wall House Museum

St. Lucia
Fond Doux Estate
Luigi St Omer's Murals in Anse la Raye
Morne Fortune: Apostles Battery & The Powder Magazine
Pigeon Island National Landmark
Pitons Management Area *incl.* Sulphur Springs
St. Lucia National Museum
Walcott Place

St. Maarten
St. Maarten National Heritage Foundation Museum
Yoda Guy Movie Exhibit

St. Martin
Fort St. Louis
Sur la Trace des Arawaks
The Old House

St. Vincent
Argyle International Airport: Heritage Village
Heritage Museum & Science Center
Kalinago Tribe
National Public Library
St. Vincent and the Grenadines National Trust
St. Vincent Botanic Gardens: Curator's House

Suriname
Christiaankondre & Langemankondre
Historic Inner City of Paramaribo
Moiwana Monument

Tobago
Fort King George
Tobago Museum

Trinidad
Central Bank Money Museum
Cleaverwoods Recreational Park
Indian Caribbean Museum of Trinidad & Tobago
Museum of the City of Port of Spain
Museum of the Trinidad & Tobago Police Service
National Museum & Art Gallery of Trinidad & Tobago
Santa Rosa First Peoples Community Museum
Temple in the Sea: Sewdass Sadhu Shiv Mandir
The Red House

Questionnaire: Kalinago Barana Autê

[Date: .... 2015]

1) Have you ever visited the Kalinago Barana Autê?   ☐ Yes   ☐ No
--> If yes, how often have you been to the Kalinago Barana Autê?   ☐ 1-2 times
                           ☐ 3-5 times
                           ☐ More than 5 times

--> If no, why have you not visited the Kalinago Barana Autê?
....

2) If yes, why have you visited the Kalinago Barana Autê?
☐ For enjoyment   ☐ As a performer or artist   ☐ To learn about my heritage
☐ For an event   ☐ As a tour guide   ☐ To build or maintain the site
☐ As staff   ☐ To sell crafts/souvenirs
☐ Other: ....

3) Please characterize the Kalinago Barana Autê in three **positive** keywords:
The Kalinago Barana Aute is .... ; .... and ....

4) Please characterize the Kalinago Barana Autê in three **negative** keywords:
The Kalinago Barana Aute is .... ; .... and ....

5) Do you feel that the Kalinago Barana Autê is important for your community?
☐ Not at all   ☐ A little   ☐ Neutral   ☐ A lot ☐ Extremely
Please explain: ....

6) Do you feel that the Kalinago Barana Autê benefits your community?
☐ Not at all   ☐ A little   ☐ Neutral   ☐ A lot ☐ Extremely
Please explain: ....

7) Is there anything you would like to see changed about the Kalinago Barana Autê?
☐ The activities   ☐ The buildings   ☐ The entry fee   ☐ The narrative/story
☐ The objects   ☐ The staff   ☐ The tour   ☐ The visitors
☐ Nothing   ☐ Other: ....
Please elaborate: ....

8) Please indicate your age:
☐ Under 15   ☐ 15-24   ☐ 25-34   ☐ 35-44
☐ 45-54   ☐ 55-64   ☐ 65+

9) Please indicate your gender:
☐ Female   ☐ Male   ☐ Prefer not to say

10) Finally, if you would like to share more about this topic in an interview, please write down your name and phone number:
....

Thank you for your time!

Questionnaire Results: Kalinago Barana Autê

Q 1.1 Have you ever visited the KBA?	
Yes	144
No	6

Q 1.2 If yes, how often have you been to the KBA?	
1-2 times	21
3-5 times	17
More than 5 times	106

Q 1.3 If no, why have you not visited the KBA?	
No specific reason	3
I just don't want to go there	1
Too difficult to go down	1
I just pass through	1

Q 2 Why have you visited the KBA?	
For enjoyment	90
For an event	29
As staff	4
As a performer or artist	5
As a tour guide	5
To sell crafts/souvenirs	8
To learn about my heritage	16
To build or maintain the site	5

[Q 2.9] Top 3 'other' purposes:	
Sea/river/to bathe	20
Business/meetings	12
Taking visiting friends & family	9

Q 2.9 'Other':	
Sea/river/to bathe	20
Relaxation	3
Part of a hike	2
To explore	1
Roasting breadfruit	1
Collecting fruits	1
Business/meetings	12
Workshops	6
School trip	4
Tours or tourist transport	3
Training guides	1
Bring food to the staff	1
Set up cassava baking	1
Looking at a job	1
Bringing homestay visitors	1
Taking visiting friends or family	9
My friend or relative works there	4
Birthday party	2
Graduation	2
Historical activity	1
Socializing	1
Session with elders & visitors from Martinique	1
Opening event	1
My land is close by	5
"It's my place, I go anytime I want"	1
"Because I am a Kalinago, I belong there"	1

Q 3 Please characterize the KBA in three positive keywords:	
Beautiful	36
Attractive	18
Wonderful view	11
Beautiful place/site	7
Pretty	4
Scenic	4
Picture-perfect	2
Sightseeing	2
Lots to see	2
Picturesque	1
Lovely scenery	1

THE SOCIAL MUSEUM IN THE CARIBBEAN

Q 3 Please characterize the KBA in three positive keywords (continued):	
Bright	1
Gorgeous	1
Cultural	19
Historic(al)	10
Traditional	9
Educational	4
Local	3
Indigenous	2
Preserving	2
(Reflects) our heritage	2
Good information	1
Antique	1
Local bread	1
Ancestors	1
Carib people	1
Cassava	1
Identity	1
Help visitors dance the music	1
Informative	1
Heritage site	1
See our past	1
Learn different crafts	1
Good idea of the Carib people	1
Carib	1
Authentic	1
Different language	1
Crafts are good	1
Historical significance	1
Conserved	1
Carib music	1
Delicious meals	1
Social	1
Unique	17
Different	2
Icon	1
Special	1
Experience	1
Notable	1
Popular	1
Paramount destination	1
Showcase	1
Nice (place)	10
Exciting	8

Q 3 Please characterize the KBA in three positive keywords (continued):	
Interesting	8
Important	7
Good	7
Good place	4
Excellent	3
Amazing	3
Breathtaking	3
Wonderful	3
Fun	2
Lovely	1
Magnificent	1
Awesome	1
Incredible	1
Sophisticated	1
Inspirational	1
Excitement	1
Relaxing	10
Peaceful	9
Quiet	9
Comfortable	2
Refreshing	2
Wellness	1
Leisure	1
Stress-free	1
Private	1
Nice ambiance	1
Secluded	1
Meditating	1
Tourist attraction/touristic	9
Entertainment	2
Enjoying	2
Nice visit	1
Tourists should visit	1
Lots of visitors off-season	1
Slow when the cruise ships are over	1
Visitors visit	1
Private tours	1
Camp	1
Good for visitors	1
Natural	9
Cool	7
Good location	5
Waterfall	3

Q 3 Please characterize the KBA in three positive keywords (continued):	
Cool breeze	2
Spacious	2
Adventurous	2
Valley	1
Nice shades	1
Nice environment	1
The water	1
Fresh air	1
Big	1
Nice place to explore	1
Pool	1
Friendly staff	4
Welcoming	2
Inviting	1
Visitor friendly	1
All guests are welcome	1
Hospitable	1
Loving	1
Accessible	1
Unity	1
Clean	4
Tidy	1
Well kept	1
Neat	1
Pristine	1
Employment	3
Development	3
Income	1
Improvement	1
Cash	1
Earning	1
Vendors	1
Venue	1
Good investment	1
Valuable	1
Economic	1
Helps us	1
Enhances the reserve	1
Good workshops	1
New	1

[Q 3] Top 5 positive keywords:	
Beautiful	36
Cultural	19
Attractive	18
Unique	17
Wonderful view	11

[Q 4] Top 4 negative keywords:	
[No negative keywords]	107
Needs (some) improvement	7
Underdeveloped	3
Poor management	3

Q 4 Please characterize the KBA in three negative keywords:	
[No negative keywords]	107
Needs (some) improvement	7
Underdeveloped	3
Better job with the upkeep	1
Outdated	1
Archaic	1
Doesn't match expectations	1
Not enough (people expect more)	1
Limited	1
Incomplete	1
Underutilized	1
Too small	1
Depreciating	1
Could be more prevalent	1
Poor management	3
Disorganized	2
Unprofessional	1
Irregular	1
Work schedule	1
Lack of communication	1
Management and workers need togetherness	1
Doesn't work according to business plan	1
No janitorial services	1
Lack of marketing manager	1
Staffing	1
More trained employees	1
Uninformative	2

Q 4 Please characterize the KBA in three negative keywords (continued):	
Lacks information	1
Lacks culture	1
More pictures	1
Lacks authenticity	1
The cassava	1
More localized	1
Doesn't portray real significance	1
Steep	2
Too far	2
Too far down	2
Tiring walk	1
Poor lighting	2
River crossing dangerous/difficult	2
Dangerous	1
Poorly landscaped	1
Environmental problems	1
Not enough self-managed	1
More funds for local management	1
Government interference	1
Government runs it	1
More local involvement	1
Doesn't make enough money	1
Expensive (for visitors)	1
Slow as season closes	1
More excitement	1

Q 5.1 Do you feel that the KBA is important for your community?	
Not at all	0
A little	0
Neutral	4
A lot	81
Extremely	65

Q 5.2 Please explain: [People may give multiple reasons]	
Our culture, our history, ancestors, preservation, reidentify the Caribs	49
Attracts tourists, brings people in (to the territory), teaches others about the Kalinago, exchange	45
Income, employment	32
Fun, relaxing, events, meetings	18
[No answer or no explanation]	18
[Other answers] confidence, display talents, puts community on the map, unique thing to see, could be better	7

Q 6.1 Do you feel that the KBA benefits your community?	
Not at all	5
A little	32
Neutral	34
A lot	71
Extremely	8

Q 6.2 Please explain: [People may give multiple reasons]	
[No answer], I don't really know	35
Earning, employment, economically, crafts, dancers	32
Some people benefit, only those working there	22
Not much benefit, not really, to an extent, some way	19
Draws tourists, brings in visitors	18
Everyone benefits, yes it does	13
More could benefit, doesn't meet expectations	8
Culturally, preservation	7

Q 7 Is there anything you would like to see changed about the KBA?	
The activities	19
The objects	7
The buildings	24
The staff	25
The entry fee	4
The tour	3
The narrative/story	9
The visitors	5
Nothing	45
Other	60

Q 7.10 'Other': [People may give multiple reasons]	
More advertising and publicity	13
Improve the trails and access roads	12
More local, traditional foods and drinks	7
Improvement overall	6
Stronger bond with the community, more collaboration	4
Herbal and vegetable garden	3
Better access to the ocean, better bathing	2
More employment	2
Local management	2
Better signs to the facility	2
Create a living experience	2
More flowers	1
More production	1
Realistic visitor expectations	1
More vendors for big tours	1
Implement business plan	1
A zoo with parrots and peacocks	1
Bring in water by pipe line	1
More authenticity	1
Indigenous music	1
An organized craft association	1
Needs to be completed	1
A bus system for access	1
More traditional – less modernized	1
Wheelchair access	1
Improve washrooms	1
Improve the bridge over the river	1
More tours directly from the cruise ships	1
People living onsite in traditional clothes	1
Open in the evenings	1
Only natural souvenirs	1
Enlarge it	1
More attractive	1

Q 7.11 Please elaborate [People may give multiple reasons]	
Activities	19
More or different activities	8
Cultural activities	2
Indigenous activities	2
Bird watching	1
Live shows	1
Educational meetings	1
Objects	7
More objects, more traditional objects	5
Cultural presentation	1
Personal items of (past) chiefs	1
Buildings	24
Remodeling, restructuring, maintenance, or improvement	11
More houses, more local	5
Cabins for overnight stays	4
More things to visit	2
Modern materials (*e.g.* shingles) to reduce maintenance	2
More traditional	1
Staff	25
Staff in traditional clothes	4
More young people involved/employed	3
More staff	3
More local control	3
Better management, different management style	3
Employ marketing staff	1
Employ janitorial staff	1
High salary for staff	1
Meetings with all staff	1
More community involvement	1
Faster payment of services (*e.g.* vetiver vendors)	1
More hygienic with the cassava	1
More multilingual staff	1
More hospitality	1
Entry fee	4
Too high	2
Should be free for all Kalinago (also from other islands)	1
Tour	3
In more languages	1
Narrative/story	9

THE SOCIAL MUSEUM IN THE CARIBBEAN

Q 7.11 Please elaborate [People may give multiple reasons] (continued)	
More informative plaques at places (self-guided)	2
More information, more history, more images	2
More aspects of the Kalinago	1
More about past chiefs	1
Visitors	**5**
More visitors	5

Q 8 Age	
Under 15	10
15-24	37
25-34	26
35-44	24
45-54	25
55-64	18
65+	10

Q 9 Gender	
Female	74
Male	76

Table 3: Results of all surveys in Dominica (n = 150).

Questionnaire: Bengal to Barbados

[Date: ……….……………………… 2016]

1) Are you involved in the *Bengal to Barbados* Exhibition project? ☐ Yes ☐ No

--> If *no*, why are you not involved in the project?

……

--> If *yes*, how are you involved?

……

--> If *yes*, do you feel that your voice is being heard? ☐ Yes ☐ Sometimes ☐ No

Please explain: ……………………………………………………………………………………………

2) Do you feel that this exhibition is important for your community?

☐ Not at all ☐ A little ☐ Neutral ☐ A lot ☐ Extremely

Please explain: ……………………………………………………………………………………………

3) What do you hope the exhibition will achieve? (pick up to three aims)

☐ Awareness ☐ Cultural celebration ☐ Dispel myths
☐ Education ☐ Empowerment ☐ Enjoyment
☐ Recognition ☐ Pride ☐ Stronger community
☐ Tolerance ☐ Understanding ☐ Unity
☐ Other: ………………………………………………………………………………………

4) Do you think the exhibition will benefit your community?

☐ Not at all ☐ A little ☐ Neutral ☐ A lot ☐ Extremely

Please explain: ……………………………………………………………………………………………

5) Please say three *positive* things about the exhibition project:

The project is ……………………………… ; …………………………… and ……………………………

6) Please say three *negative* things about the exhibition project:

The project is ……………………………… ; …………………………… and ……………………………

7) Which communities do you consider yourself a part of?

☐ Barbadian ☐ Caribbean ☐ East-Indian
☐ Christian ☐ Hindu ☐ Muslim
☐ None ☐ Other(s): …………………………………………………………………

8) Please indicate your age:

☐ Under 15 ☐ 15-24 ☐ 25-34 ☐ 35-44 ☐ 45-54
☐ 55-64 ☐ 65+

9) Please indicate your gender:

☐ Female ☐ Male ☐ Prefer not to say

10) Finally, if you would like to share more about this project in an interview, please contact the researcher, Csilla [EMAIL] or write down your phone number:

Thank you for your time!

Questionnaire Results: Bengal to Barbados

Q 1.1 Are you involved in the BTB Exhibition project?

Yes	12
No	39

Q 1.2 If no, why are you not involved in the project?

[No explanation given]	15
Did not know/was not aware of the project	13
Was not asked	6
Not aware how to be involved	2
I would like to be involved	1
No knowledge on the topic	1
I am involved in other projects at the museum	1

Q 1.3 If yes, how are you involved?

Am on the committee	3
Researcher	2
Moving artefacts	2
General assistance	1
Planner	1
Culinary aspects	1
Activities & preparation	1
[No explanation given]	1

Q 1.4 If yes, do you feel that your voice is being heard?

Yes	7
Sometimes	2
No	2

Q 1.5 Please explain

Yes, only recently got involved & could contribute more	1
Yes, get to give input	1
Yes, told of plans & asked for opinion	1
Yes, offer suggestions that are taken into consideration	1
Yes, able to put forward many ideas & suggestions	1
Yes, consultation happens among the Muslim committee	1
Yes [no explanation]	1
Sometimes [no explanation]	2
No, certain individuals tend to monopolise the discussion during committee meetings	1
No [no explanation]	1

Q 2.1 Do you feel that this exhibition is important for your community?

Not at all	0
A little	16
Neutral	7
A lot	13
Extremely	14

Q 2.2 Please explain:

[No explanation]	24
Educate public about East-Indian culture & customs	5
General awareness/knowledge	4
Educate about important contributions made	4
Educate about migration history	3
Not sure	3
Education will lead to cultural tolerance	1
Such information is currently lacking	1
It is always important to highlight the history of a people	1
Time for recognition	1
Our heritage is being lost	1
Clear up misconceptions	1
Unique, first of its kind	1
Some will be interested	1
Diverse representation of narratives is important	1

[Q 2.1 + Q 7] Respondents who rated importance as "A little" or "Neutral"	23	
Barbadian	10	43%
Caribbean	6	26%
East-Indian	5	22%
Christian	1	4%
Hindu	14	61%
Muslim	6	26%

[Q 2.1 + Q 7] Respondents who rated importance as "A lot" or "Extremely"	27	
Barbadian	21	78%
Caribbean	10	37%
East-Indian	10	37%
Christian	1	4%
Hindu	4	15%
Muslim	18	67%
Afro-Caribbean	1	4%

Q 3 What do you hope the exhibition will achieve? (Pick up to three aims)		
Awareness	38	76%
Cultural celebration	20	40%
Dispel myths	16	32%
Education	29	58%
Empowerment	2	4%
Enjoyment	9	18%
Recognition	14	28%
Pride	15	30%
Stronger community	18	36%
Tolerance	15	30%
Understanding	24	48%
Unity	15	30%
[Other]	2	4%

Q 3.13 'Other':	
Appreciation & gratitude	1
More diverse museum audience	1

[Q 3] Total amount of responses	217
[Q 3] Average responses per respondent	4.3

Q 4.1 Do you think the exhibition will benefit your community?	
Not at all	0
A little	13
Neutral	13
A lot	12
Extremely	11

Q 4.2 Please explain:	
[No explanation]	29
Will educate/make the Barbadian public more aware	5
Not sure how it will benefit	3
Increase the awareness of the younger generation	2
Dispel myths	2
Baja public will be more tolerant of the Indian community	1
Will educate about migration history	1
Stimulate curiosity	1
Content will benefit the community	1
Preserve our history	1
Depends on if the exhibit can be easily understood	1
Marketing will be needed to maximise impact	1
Greater understanding of diverse Barbadian narratives	1

Q 5 Please say three positive things about the exhibition project	
[No positive words]	23
Education(al)	13
Awareness	7
Informative	5
Understanding	1
Culturally enlightening	1
Cultural	1
Interesting	7
Great idea	3
Good	2
Fun	2
Positive reaction	2
Exciting	1
Entertaining	1
Inspirational	1
Looking forward to it	1
Not attempted before	3
Innovative	2
Unique	1
Long awaited. Long overdue	2
Needed	2
Timely	2
Important	2
Beneficial to all	1
Beneficial to Indian	1
Dispel myths	1
Stimulate cultural diversity	1
Unity	1
Recognition of the community	1
Interaction	1
Well planned	1

[Q 5] Top 3 positive keywords:	
Education(al)	13
Awareness	7
Interesting	7

Q 6 Please say three negative things about the exhibition project	
[No negative words]	41
Biased	2
One-sided	1
Based on men's views	1
Monopolised by two members of the Indian group	1
2 men want to do everything	1
Long-overdue	2
Exclusive	1
Private	1
Unknown by many	1
Most people are not involved	1
Narrow	1

[Q 6] Top 2 negative keywords:	
Biased	2
Long-overdue	2

Q 7 Which communities do you consider yourself a part of?	
Barbadian	32
Caribbean	17
East-Indian	15
Christian	3
Hindu	18
Muslim	24
None	0
[Others]: Afro-Caribbean	1

[Q 7 + Q 8] Communities of respondents aged under 35	27	
Barbadian	18	67%
Caribbean	11	41%
East-Indian	9	33%

[Q 7 + Q 8] Communities of respondents aged 35+	24	
Barbadian	14	58%
Caribbean	6	25%
East-Indian	6	25%

Q 8 Age	
Under 15	1
15-24	13
25-34	13
35-44	9
45-54	7
55-64	4
65+	4

Q 9 Gender	
Female	30
Male	21

Table 4: Results of all surveys in Barbados (n = 51).

Q 1.1 Are you involved in the BTB Exhibition project?	
Yes	10
No	34

Q 1.2 If no, why are you not involved in the project?	
[No explanation given]	15
Did not know/was not aware of the project	11
Was not asked	4
Not aware how to be involved	2
I would like to be involved	1
No knowledge on the topic	1

Q 1.3 If yes, how are you involved?	
Am on the committee	3
Moving artefacts	2
General assistance	1
Planner	1
Culinary aspects	1
Activities & preparation	1
[No explanation given]	1

Q 1.4 If yes, do you feel that your voice is being heard?	
Yes	6
Sometimes	2
No	2

Q 1.5 Please explain	
Yes, get to give input	1
Yes, told of plans & asked for opinion	1
Yes, offer suggestions that are taken into consideration	1
Yes, able to put forward many ideas & suggestions	1
Yes, consultation happens among the Muslim committee	1
Yes [no explanation]	1
Sometimes [no explanation]	2
No, certain individuals tend to mono-polise the discussion during committee meetings	1
No [no explanation]	1

Q 2.1 Do you feel that this exhibition is important for your community?	
Not at all	0
A little	15
Neutral	6
A lot	11
Extremely	12

Q 2.2 Please explain:	
[No explanation]	24
Educate public about East-Indian culture & customs	4
General awareness/knowledge	3
Educate about important contributions made	3
Educate about migration history	3
Not sure	2
It is always important to highlight the history of a people	1
Time for recognition	1
Our heritage is being lost	1
Clear up misconceptions	1
Unique, first of its kind	1
Some will be interested	1

[Q 2.1 + Q7] Respondents who rated importance as "A little" or "Neutral"	21	
Barbadian	9	43%
Caribbean	5	24%
East-Indian	5	24%
Christian	1	5%
Hindu	14	67%
Muslim	6	29%

[Q 2.1 + Q7] Respondents who rated importance as "A lot" or "Extremely"	23	
Barbadian	17	74%
Caribbean	8	35%
East-Indian	10	43%
Christian	0	0%
Hindu	4	17%
Muslim	18	78%

Q 3 What do you hope the exhibition will achieve? (Pick up to three aims)		
Awareness	31	70%
Cultural celebration	17	39%
Dispel myths	12	27%
Education	23	52%
Empowerment	1	2%
Enjoyment	7	16%
Recognition	10	23%
Pride	14	32%
Stronger community	13	30%
Tolerance	11	25%
Understanding	18	41%
Unity	10	23%
[Other]	0	0%

[Q3] Total amount of responses	167

[Q3] Average responses per respondent	3.8

Q 4.1 Do you think the exhibition will benefit your community?	
Not at all	0
A little	12
Neutral	12
A lot	11
Extremely	9

Q 4.2 Please explain:	
[No explanation]	29
Will educate/make the Barbadian public more aware	4
Not sure how it will benefit	3
Increase the awareness of the younger generation	2
Dispel myths	2
Baja public will be more tolerant of the Indian community	1
Will educate about migration history	1
Preserve our history	1
Depends on if the exhibit can be easily understood	1

Q 5 Please say three positive things about the exhibition project	
[No positive words]	20
Education(al)	11
Awareness	5
Informative	5
Understanding	1
Culturally enlightening	1
Cultural	1
Interesting	6
Great idea	3
Good	2
Fun	2
Positive reaction	2
Exciting	1
Entertaining	1
Inspirational	1
Looking forward to it	1
Not attempted before	3
Innovative	2
Unique	1
Long awaited. Long overdue	2
Needed	2
Timely	2
Important	2
Beneficial to all	1
Beneficial to Indian	1
Unity	1
Recognition of the community	1
Well planned	1

[Q 5] Top 3 positive keywords:	
Education(al)	11
Interesting	6
Awareness	Informative	5

THE SOCIAL MUSEUM IN THE CARIBBEAN

Q 6 Please say three negative things about the exhibition project	
[No negative words]	34
Biased	2
One-sided	1
Based on men's views	1
Monopolised by two members of the Indian group	1
2 men want to do everything	1
Long-overdue	2
Exclusive	1
Private	1
Unknown by many	1
Most people are not involved	1
Narrow	1

Q 8 Age	
Under 15	1
15-24	12
25-34	11
35-44	7
45-54	7
55-64	3
65+	3

Q 9 Gender	
Female	24
Male	20

[Q 6] Top 2 negative keywords:	
Biased	2
Long-overdue	2

Q 7 Which communities do you consider yourself a part of?	
Barbadian	26
Caribbean	13
East-Indian	15
Christian	1
Hindu	18
Muslim	24
None	0
[Others]	0

[Q 7 + Q 8] Communities of respondents aged under 35	24	
Barbadian	15	63%
Caribbean	10	42%
East-Indian	9	38%

[Q 7 + Q 8] Communities of respondents aged 35+	20	
Barbadian	11	55%
Caribbean	3	15%
East-Indian	6	30%

Table 5: Results of the surveys in Barbados with East Indian community members (n = 44).

Q 1.1 Are you involved in the BTB Exhibition project?	
Yes	2
No	5

Q 1.2 If no, why are you not involved in the project?	
Did not know/was not aware of the project	2
Was not asked	2
I am involved in other projects at the museum	1

Q 1.3 If yes, how are you involved?	
Researcher	2

Q 1.4 If yes, do you feel that your voice is being heard?	
Yes	1
Sometimes	0
No	0

Q 1.5 Please explain	
Yes, only recently got involved & could contribute more	1

Q 2.1 Do you feel that this exhibition is important for your community?	
Not at all	0
A little	1
Neutral	1
A lot	2
Extremely	2

Q 2.2 Please explain:	
Educate public about East-Indian culture & customs	1
General awareness/knowledge	1
Educate about important contributions made	1
Not sure	1
Education will lead to cultural tolerance	1
Such information is currently lacking	1
Diverse representation of narratives is important	1

[Q 2.1 + Q7] Respondents who rated importance as "A little" or "Neutral"	2	
Barbadian	1	50%
Caribbean	1	50%
East-Indian	0	0%
Christian	0	0%
Hindu	0	0%
Muslim	0	0%

[Q 2.1 + Q7] Respondents who rated importance as "A lot" or "Extremely"	4	
Barbadian	4	100%
Caribbean	2	50%
East-Indian	0	0%
Christian	1	25%
Hindu	0	0%
Muslim	0	0%
Afro-Caribbean	1	25%

Q 3 What do you hope the exhibition will achieve? (Pick up to three aims)		
Awareness	7	100%
Cultural celebration	3	43%
Dispel myths	4	57%
Education	6	86%
Empowerment	1	14%
Enjoyment	2	29%
Recognition	4	57%
Pride	1	14%
Stronger community	5	71%
Tolerance	4	57%
Understanding	6	86%
Unity	5	71%
[Other]	2	29%

Q 3.13 'Other':	
Appreciation & gratitude	1
More diverse museum audience	1

[Q3] Total amount of responses	50
[Q3] Average responses per respondent	7.1

THE SOCIAL MUSEUM IN THE CARIBBEAN

Q 4.1 Do you think the exhibition will benefit your community?	
Not at all	0
A little	1
Neutral	1
A lot	1
Extremely	2

Q 4.2 Please explain:	
Will educate/make the Barbadian public more aware	1
Stimulate curiosity	1
Content will benefit the community	1
Marketing will be needed to maximise impact	1
Greater understanding of diverse Barbadian narratives	1

Q 5 Please say three positive things about the exhibition project	
[No positive words]	3
Education(al)	2
Awareness	2
Interesting	1
Dispel myths	1
Stimulate cultural diversity	1
Interaction	1

[Q 5] Top 2 positive keywords:	
Education(al)	2
Awareness	2

Q 6 Please say three negative things about the exhibition project	
[No negative words]	7

Q 7 Which communities do you consider yourself a part of?	
Barbadian	6
Caribbean	4
East-Indian	0
Christian	2
Hindu	0
Muslim	0
None	0
[Others]: Afro-Caribbean	1

[Q 7 + Q 8] Communities of respondents aged under 35	3	
Barbadian	3	100%
Caribbean	1	33%
East-Indian	0	0%

[Q 7 + Q 8] Communities of respondents aged 35+	4	
Barbadian	3	75%
Caribbean	3	75%
East-Indian	0	0%

Q 8 Age	
Under 15	0
15-24	1
25-34	2
35-44	2
45-54	0
55-64	1
65+	1

Q 9 Gender	
Female	6
Male	1

Table 6: Results of the surveys in Barbados with Barbados Museum & Historical Society staff members (n = 7).

Summary in English

The Social Museum in the Caribbean as a Mosaic

In the opening chapter of this dissertation, the research project is framed; the outer edges of the mosaic are determined. In that introduction, a brief history of museums in the Caribbean is outlined and previous museological research in the Caribbean is reviewed, noting the niches into which this research project could expand and add new insights. A foundational understanding of museums within the region and their colonial histories is provided by the seminal work of Alissandra Cummins (1992; 1994; 1998; 2004; 2012; 2013) and expanded by the research of other museologists working in and on the Caribbean (*e.g.* Farmer 2013; Maréchal 1998; Modest 2012). The focal point of the dissertation is placed on the topic of community engagement in museums as a way to investigate the roles museums are taking on in contemporary society. In the absence of previous region-wide studies into community engagement, Caribbean museums provide a unique opportunity for novel research. The premise of studying community engagement in Caribbean museums is promising, particularly due to the fact that the region is characterized by such a diversity of communities. The chapter ends by presenting the research questions underpinning the dissertation and provides an outline of the dissertation as a whole.

The second chapter develops the theoretical frameworks which are at the core of the research project; the style of the mosaic is selected and the underlying image is sketched. Theoretically, the dissertation is positioned firmly within a contemporary continuation of the New Museology, which focuses strongly on the societal roles of museums. Thus, museological research and practices within the framework of the New Museology are critically considered in the form of a discussion of the works of some of the relevant authors in the field. Definitions of 'community' and 'community engagement' (*e.g.* Crooke 2008; Crooke 2011a; Watson 2007) are dissected, with attention to both the possibility of inclusion and the risk of exclusion. The variety of participatory practices which museums may adopt in their desire to engage with communities are exemplified through the work of Nina Simon (2010; 2016). Following on from these practices, the impact or outcomes of community engagement processes need critical evaluation and consideration, taking inspiration from studies conducted primarily in Europe and North America (*e.g.* Fouseki 2010; Fouseki & Smith 2013; Fuller 1992; Lagerkvist 2006; Onciul 2013; Ronan 2014; Smith 2015). The discussion is expanded into new territories by considering museums in other geographical regions of the world (*e.g.* Kreps 2011b; Varutti 2013) and by shifting the discussion beyond major established institutions towards so-called 'micromuseums' (Candlin 2016). The necessity to include grassroots museums in the scope of this research is underpinned by a critical consideration of the definition of the term 'museum' and the development of a broad working definition to be of relevance in the Caribbean.

Building on this theoretical framework, the third chapter discloses the methodology of the research, the selection of tools needed to make the mosaic. Essentially, the research undertaken in the course of this project can be divided into two parts: a macro level regional museum survey of participatory practices and localized, micro level case studies of community engagement processes. For the regional museum survey, fieldwork was conducted in 25 different islands/countries, resulting in visits to 195 museums. This fieldwork relied primarily on museological techniques for museum visitation and documentation, as well as anthropological methods for engaging with community members and museum staff. In the course of this fieldwork, data was collected in the form of photographs, maps, flyers, catalogues, informal interviews, and extensive field notes. A Caribbean Museums Database was designed specifically for this data, which is made available online, and categories were developed for 'museum types,' 'museum ownership,' and 'participatory practices.' Afterwards, this data was visualized and analyzed through a computer science collaboration, allowing for the creation of maps, figures, matrices, and charts. For the localized case studies, fieldwork was conducted over a longer period of time focusing on two places: the *Kalinago Barana Autê* in Dominica and the *Bengal to Barbados* exhibition project at the *Barbados Museum & Historical Society* in Barbados. This case study fieldwork also relied on a combination of museological techniques and anthropological methods, with more emphasis placed on the latter through the use of participant observation, surveys, and interviews. In the course of these two case studies, data was collected in the form of paper-based surveys (150 and 51 respectively), interviews, lectures, literature, and field notes. The survey data was coded, visualized into charts, and analyzed in combination with the other contextual data.

The fourth chapter presents the results of the regional museum survey, particularly the participatory practices employed by these museums; the tiles are placed into the mosaic and the image is filled out. Twelve participatory practices are identified which are organized into three groups: those which lie at the heart of the organization of the museum (*e.g.* if the museum is an ecomuseum or has community staffing), those which are involved in exhibition making (*e.g.* exhibiting donated objects or contemporary artwork), and finally the participation which occurs during museum visitation (such as activities and events). Each of these practices is described or defined, coupled with ample examples from museums visited throughout the region. The chapter showcases how participatory practices are present at (nearly) every museum, but also that they are adopted and adapted in a wide diversity of ways.

The fifth chapter focuses on the case study conducted in the Kalinago Territory, Dominica, at the *Kalinago Barana Autê* (KBA); details are added to the mosaic. The chapter begins by placing the museum in its historical and cultural context, sketching the history of the Kalinago community and the process of the creation of the museum. This information provides the frame to explore the ongoing community engagement process of the development and running of the museum, based on the perceptions of the Kalinago community. The KBA was a community initiative, but was developed and funded by the government of Dominica. It is currently still owned by the government, but is managed and operated by the community. The Kalinago community is generally positive about the intrinsic value of the KBA, using it frequently for recreation and social gatherings, and note the importance of the museum for outside visitors. The community is more divided when it comes to the instrumental value of the museum, being positive about its educational and cultural value, but conflicted over its financial impact and its role as a source of employment. Part of this contention may be due to the status of the community engagement process currently – namely, that the museum is not (yet) owned by the Kalinago. A lack of transparency may also be part of the problem, as many community members who do not directly benefit from employment or income do not necessarily consider other (intrinsic or instrumental) values for themselves and others. Certainly, there is potential for the museum and its community engagement process to be further improved. However, the frequent use of the site along with the generally positive evaluation by the community show that it has already been a valuable community engagement project.

In a similar vein, the sixth chapter is concerned with the case study conducted at the *Barbados Museum & Historical Society* (BMHS), Barbados, about the *Bengal to Barbados* exhibition. The chapter begins by exploring the history of the East Indian community in Barbados and its five strands of migration in order to understand the complex composition of the community today. Contextually, the history of the BMHS is also included, as well as a discussion of the museum's current direction and aims. Within this setting, the first stages of the co-curation project are explored as they are perceived by both members of the East Indian community and the museum staff. BMHS staff is largely positive about the exhibition concept and rates the exhibition as highly important, particularly for educational reasons for Barbadian society. The East Indian community is considerably more divided, with some rating the exhibition as highly important and others as largely unimportant. Differences can be seen along gender and generational lines, as well as between the two main pillars of the community: Gujarati-Muslims and Sindhi-Hindus. Mindful of these issues, efforts were made early on to improve the representativity of those involved in the exhibition project and to create more awareness of the exhibition within the East Indian community. Coupled with negotiation, transparency of the aims and outcomes of the project was needed and significantly more time was invested in order to understand the participants involved, build mutual trust, and develop a working balance of power.

The seventh chapter presents a discussion of the research as a whole, developing a number of interpretations by combining the macro level and micro level results together; patterns are identified in the completed mosaic. Although community engagement practices and processes – and particularly research into their impact – can still be expanded and improved, Caribbean museums have certainly been working to alter their role in contemporary society. The strong presence of grassroots museums alongside governmental museums ensures that a wide range of communities can be targeted, that museums can respond dynamically and flexibly in different ways, and that they can take on present-day as well as future mandates. By adopting diverse participatory practices, Caribbean museums can be both widely representative and engage with communities in unique ways, depending also on the museum's type and the linguistic area it is located in. By working through community engagement processes, Caribbean museums have connected directly to more members of their communities, anchoring themselves more squarely and subjectively into society.

Finally, in the eighth chapter, the image of the social museum in the Caribbean is revealed: not as a single, quintessential museum but rather as a complex and dynamic mosaic. The Caribbean museum landscape, consisting of a wide range of museum types which are able to take on a multitude of societal roles, can reach out to different levels of society and diverse audiences. It actively reflects the diversity of contemporary Caribbean society and is characterized in particular by grassroots initiatives. By recognizing the museum as a phenomenon that can take on many different shapes and sizes, its value for a myriad of communities becomes apparent.

Summary in Dutch

Het Sociale Museum in de Caraïben: Grassroots erfgoedinitiatieven en publieksparticipatie

Een mozaïek is het enige beeld dat recht kan doen aan de musea in de Caraïben. Zij zijn even divers en veelzijdig als de vele gemeenschappen die de kern vormen van hun organisaties en het hart van hun missies. Deze uitgesproken *sociale* musea passen participatiemethodes toe en verwikkelen zich in publieksparticipatie processen om zich nog sterker te verankeren in hedendaagse Caribische gemeenschappen. Dit proefschrift presenteert een mozaïek van 195 Caribische musea en de resultaten van een uniek onderzoeksproject.

In het inleidende hoofdstuk van dit proefschrift wordt het onderzoeksproject ingekaderd; de buitenranden van het mozaïek worden bepaald. In die inleiding wordt een korte geschiedenis van musea in de Caraïben geschetst samen met een beschrijving van eerder museologisch onderzoek in de regio. Hierbij wordt getoond in welke niche dit onderzoek past om nieuwe inzichten te creëren. Fundamentele kennis van musea in de regio en met name hun koloniale geschiedenis wordt verkregen aan de hand van het elementaire werk van Alissandra Cummins (1992; 1994; 1998; 2004; 2012; 2013) en verder uitgebreid met het onderzoek van andere museologen die werken in of met de Caraïben (bijv. Farmer 2013; Maréchal 1998; Modest 2012). De focus van het proefschrift wordt vervolgens gelegd op het thema publieksparticipatie in musea om te kunnen onderzoeken welke rol musea spelen in de hedendaagse samenleving. Bij gebrek aan eerdere regionale studies over publieksparticipatie bieden Caribische musea een uitermate unieke mogelijkheid voor baanbrekend onderzoek. Het uitgangspunt om publieksparticipatie in Caribische musea te bestuderen is met name veelbelovend dankzij het feit dat de regio zich kenmerkt door zo'n veelzijdigheid van gemeenschappen. Het inleidende hoofdstuk sluit af met het uiteenzetten van de onderzoeksvragen die aan de basis van dit proefschrift liggen en biedt tevens een overzicht van het gehele proefschrift.

Het tweede hoofdstuk ontwikkelt het theoretische raamwerk dat aan de kern ligt van het onderzoeksproject; de stijl van het mozaïek wordt gekozen en de onderliggende afbeelding geschetst. Theoretisch staat het proefschrift stevig in de huidige voortzetting van de *New Museology* (Nieuwe Museologie), welke zich vooral richt op de maatschappelijke rol van musea. Een kritische uiteenzetting van museologisch onderzoek en methodes binnen de *New Museology* wordt gepresenteerd aan de hand van het werk van een aantal relevante auteurs in het vakgebied. De definities van '*community*' (gemeenschap) en 'community engagement' (publieksparticipatie) (bijv. Crooke 2008; Crooke 2011a; Watson 2007) worden geanalyseerd, met aandacht voor zowel de mogelijkheden tot inclusie als het risico van uitsluiting. Het werk van Nina Simon (2010; 2016) illustreert de diversiteit aan participatiemethodes welke musea kunnen toepassen om het publiek te betrekken bij hun werkzaamheden. Na deze uiteenzetting van methodes volgt een kritische evaluatie van de gevolgen of uitkomsten van publieksparticipatie processen, met name aan de hand van studies uit Europa en Noord-Amerika (bijv. Fouseki 2010; Fouseki & Smith 2013; Fuller 1992; Lagerkvist 2006; Onciul 2013; Ronan 2014; Smith 2015). Deze discussie wordt uitgebreid naar nieuw terrein door ook musea in andere regio's van de wereld te betrekken (bijv. Kreps 2011b; Varutti 2013) en door het gesprek te verplaatsen van de grote gevestigde instellingen naar zogeheten 'micromuseums' (Candlin 2016). De noodzaak om *grassroots* musea op te nemen in dit onderzoek wordt ondersteund door een kritische beschouwing van de term 'museum' en de ontwikkeling van een bredere definitie die relevant was tijdens veldwerk in de Caraïben.

Verder bouwend op dit theoretische raamwerk beschrijft het derde hoofdstuk de methodologie van het onderzoek, ofwel de selectie van gereedschappen die nodig zijn om het mozaïek te leggen. In grote lijnen kan het onderzoek van dit proefschrift verdeeld worden in twee delen: op macroniveau een regionaal overzicht van musea en participatiemethodes en op microniveau lokale casestudies van publieksparticipatie processen. Voor het regionale overzicht van musea werd veldwerk uitgevoerd in 25 verschillende (ei)landen, met bezoeken aan 195 musea. Dit veldwerk maakte vooral gebruik van museologische technieken voor museumbezoek en documentatie, maar baseerde zich ook op antropologische methodes voor interacties met leden van de gemeenschap en museumpersoneel. In de loop van dit veldwerk werden data verzameld in de vorm van foto's, kaarten, folders, catalogi, informele interviews en uitgebreide notities. Een 'Caribbean Museums Database' werd speciaal voor deze data ontworpen en is online beschikbaar gesteld. Ook werden er categorieën bepaald voor 'museumsoort' (*types*), 'museumeigendom' (*ownership*) en 'participatiemethodes' (*participatory practices*). Dankzij de toepassing van informatica werden de data hierna geanalyseerd en gevisualiseerd, waardoor kaarten, figuren, matrices en grafieken konden worden gemaakt. Voor de lokale casestudies werd over een langere periode veldwerk verricht, waarbij de focus lag op twee plaatsen: de *Kalinago Barana Autê* op Dominica en het *Bengal to Barbados* tentoonstellingsproject in het *Barbados Museum & Historical Society* op Barbados. Dit casestudie veldwerk berustte ook op een combinatie van museologische technieken en antropologische methodes, waarbij de nadruk lag op het laatste door het gebruik van participerende observatie, enquêtes en interviews. In de loop van deze twee casestudies werden data verzameld in de vorm van papieren enquêtes (respectievelijk 150 en 51), interviews, lezingen, literatuur en notities. De data van de enquêtes werden manueel gecodeerd, gevisualiseerd in grafieken en samen met andere contextuele data geanalyseerd.

Het vierde hoofdstuk presenteert de resultaten van het regionale overzicht van musea en met name de participatiemethodes die deze musea toepassen; de stenen worden in het mozaïek geplaatst en de afbeelding gevuld. Twaalf participatiemethodes worden geïdentificeerd en zijn vervolgens verdeeld in drie groepen: zij die aan de kern van de organisatie van een museum liggen (bijv. als het een ecomuseum betreft of als personeel ook lid is van de gemeenschap), zij die betrokken zijn bij het maken van tentoonstellingen (bijv. het tentoonstellen van gedoneerde voorwerpen of de aanwezigheid van hedendaagse kunst), en tenslotte de participatie die tijdens het museumbezoek plaatsvindt (zoals activiteiten en evenementen). Elk van deze participatiemethodes wordt beschreven of gedefinieerd en vervolgens geïllustreerd aan de hand van diverse voorbeelden van musea uit het gehele Caribische gebied. Het hoofdstuk laat zien dat participatiemethodes in (bijna) elk museum aanwezig zijn, maar ook dat ze op zeer verschillende manieren worden toegepast en aangepast.

Het vijfde hoofdstuk richt zich op de casestudie die uitgevoerd werd in de Kalinago Territory, Dominica, bij de *Kalinago Barana Autê* (KBA); details worden toegevoegd aan het mozaïek. Het hoofdstuk begint door het museum in haar historische en culturele context te plaatsen door middel van een overzicht van de geschiedenis van de Kalinago gemeenschap en de oprichting van het museum. Deze informatie biedt een beginpunt om het publieksparticipatie proces rondom de oprichting en het beheer van het museum te verkennen, gebaseerd op de percepties van de Kalinago. De KBA was een initiatief van de gemeenschap, maar werd uiteindelijk ontwikkeld en gefinancierd door de overheid van Dominica. Momenteel ligt het eigendom nog altijd in handen van de overheid terwijl het beheerd en bestuurd wordt door de gemeenschap. De Kalinago gemeenschap is over het algemeen positief wat betreft de intrinsieke waarde van de KBA, gebruiken het regelmatig zelf voor recreatie en sociale gelegenheden en noemen ook het belang van het museum voor bezoekers van buitenaf. De gemeenschap is echter minder overtuigd van de instrumentele waarde van het museum, waarbij ze wel positief zijn over haar educatieve en culturele waarde, maar verdeeld zijn over de financiële impact en de rol van het museum als bron van werkgelegenheid. Een deel van deze tegenstrijdigheid kan te wijten zijn aan de huidige status van het publieksparticipatie proces – namelijk, dat het museum (nog) geen eigendom is van de Kalinago. Een gebrek aan transparantie kan ook een deel van het probleem zijn, aangezien leden van de gemeenschap die niet rechtstreeks profiteren van een baan of inkomen, niet altijd andere (intrinsieke of instrumentele) waarden voor zichzelf of anderen herkennen en meenemen in hun overwegingen. Natuurlijk zijn er mogelijkheden om het museum en haar publieksparticipatie proces verder te verbeteren. Echter laat het frequente gebruik van het museum en de over het algemeen positieve beoordeling door de gemeenschap zien dat het nu al een waardevol publieksparticipatie project is.

Op een vergelijkbare manier gaat het zesde hoofdstuk over de casestudie die uitgevoerd werd bij het *Barbados Museum & Historical Society* (BMHS), Barbados, over de *Bengal to Barbados* tentoonstelling. Het hoofdstuk begint met de geschiedenis van de Indiase gemeenschap in Barbados en haar vijf migratiestromen om de complexe compositie van de huidige gemeenschap te kunnen doorgronden. In het belang van de context wordt ook de geschiedenis van het BMHS opgenomen, samen met een discussie van de huidige missie en doelstellingen van het museum. Tegen deze achtergrond worden de eerste fases van het co-curatieproject verkend, gezien zowel vanuit het oogpunt van de leden van de Indiase gemeenschap als die van het museumpersoneel. Het BMHS personeel is voornamelijk positief over het tentoonstellingsconcept en beoordeelt de tentoonstelling als zeer belangrijk, met name ter educatie van de gehele Barbadiaanse samenleving. De Indiase gemeenschap is aanzienlijk meer verdeeld, waarbij sommigen de tentoonstelling als zeer belangrijk beoordelen en anderen als tamelijk onbelangrijk. Verschillen zijn zichtbaar tussen de seksen en generaties, maar ook tussen de twee voornaamste pijlers van de gemeenschap: de Gujarati-moslims en de Sindhi-hindoes. Met aandacht voor deze kwesties werd al van het begin af aan ingezet om de representativiteit van de deelnemers aan het tentoonstellingsproject te verbeteren en om meer bekendheid van de tentoonstelling te creëren binnen de Indiase gemeenschap. Naast onderhandelingen was het noodzakelijk om transparant te zijn over het doel en de verwachte uitkomsten van het project en derhalve werd er meer tijd geïnvesteerd om de betrokkenen beter te leren kennen, om wederzijds vertrouwen op te bouwen en om een werkende machtsbalans te ontwikkelen.

Het zevende hoofdstuk presenteert de discussie van het gehele onderzoek, waarbij verschillende interpretaties ontwikkeld kunnen worden door het samenbrengen van de resultaten van de macro- en microniveaus; patronen worden herkend in het voltooide mozaïek. Alhoewel participatiemethodes en publieksparticipatie processen – en vooral studies naar hun impact – nog altijd uitgebreid en verbeterd kunnen worden, hebben Caribische musea zeker gewerkt aan het aanpassen van hun rol in de hedendaagse samenleving. De sterke aanwezigheid van *grassroots* musea naast overheidsmusea zorgt ervoor dat een grote diversiteit aan gemeenschappen kan worden betrokken, dat musea op verschillende wijzen dynamisch en flexibel kunnen reageren en dat ze zowel hedendaagse als toekomstgerichte mandaten kunnen hebben. Door de toepassing van verscheidene participatiemethodes kunnen Caribische musea zowel breed representatief zijn als zich op unieke manieren engageren met gemeenschappen, afhankelijk ook van het soort museum en de geopolitieke subregio waarin zij zich bevindt. Dankzij het werken met publieksparticipatie processen hebben Caribische musea rechtstreeks contact met meer leden van hun gemeenschappen, waardoor zij zich ook sterker en subjectiever verankeren in de samenleving.

Tenslotte wordt in het achtste hoofdstuk het beeld van het sociale museum in de Caraïben onthuld: niet als een enkel, typerend museum, maar eerder als een complex en dynamisch mozaïek. Het Caribische museumlandschap, bestaande uit een breed scala van museumsoorten die een verscheidenheid aan sociale rollen kunnen aannemen, kan meerdere niveaus van de samenleving en verschillende publieksgroepen bereiken. Het weerspiegelt actief de diversiteit van de hedendaagse Caribische samenleving en kenmerkt zich met name door *grassroots* initiatieven. Door het erkennen van het museum als een fenomeen dat vele verschillende vormen en maten kan aannemen wordt haar waarde voor een veelzijdigheid aan gemeenschappen duidelijk.

Curriculum Vitae

Csilla Esther Ariese was born in Amsterdam on 26 November 1987. She was selected for the first edition of Leiden University's PRE-University College (2004-2006), which she successfully completed alongside her secondary education at the Vossius Gymnasium in Amsterdam (*cum laude*, 2000-2006). She began her studies in geo-archaeology at the Free University in Amsterdam, before moving to Sweden where she obtained a BA degree *with distinction* in archaeology from Gothenburg University (2008-2010). Her thesis, *A Twisted Truth* (2010), was a comparative archaeological and historical study of the 17th century shipwreck *Batavia*. Afterwards, she obtained a MSc degree *with distinction* in international museum studies, also at Gothenburg University (2010-2012). In *A Series of Firsts* (2012), she critically investigated the representations of the Dutch East India Company (VOC) and its 'discoveries' as shown in Australian and Dutch museums.

As part of her studies, she was project leader for the *Gender Matters* exhibition (2011) which was set across three museums: Göteborgs Naturhistoriska Museum, Göteborgs Stadsmuseum, and Sjöfartsmuseet Akvariet Göteborg. Within the framework of internships, she worked at the Néprajzi Múzeum in Budapest, Hungary, and the Western Australian Museum Shipwreck Galleries in Fremantle, Australia. Additionally, she was a work experience volunteer at the Amsterdam Museum. On a freelance basis, she researches and translates VOC archival documents.

In 2013, she obtained a four-year PhD position at Leiden University's Faculty of Archaeology, within the ERC-Synergy project *NEXUS1492: New World Encounters in a Globalising World*. This publication is the result of her PhD research, for which she conducted fieldwork in 25 different islands and countries throughout the Caribbean, visiting 195 museums. During this time, Csilla participated in teaching activities for several MA courses at the faculty, as teaching assistant, thesis supervisor, and instructor, most frequently for Critical Museology. In 2015 she was elected Secretary to the Board of the Museums Association of the Caribbean. In the same year, she co-founded the VALUE project – for research and outreach on the past, heritage, and video games – which was formalized two years later as the VALUE Foundation. In 2018 she was offered a postdoctoral research position at Leiden University within the NEXUS1492 project. In this position, she is now developing a publication to provide a comprehensive overview of Amerindian archaeological collections currently held in European museums.

Csilla's authored and edited publications reflect her wide range of interests. *Engaging Youth Audiences in Caribbean Museums* (2018) and *How Caribbean Museums Contribute to a More Sustainable Society* (2017) resulted from her PhD research. *The Interactive Past* (2017), *From the Stone Age to the Information Age* (2017), and *Video Games in Archaeology* (2016) are all thanks to her involvement in VALUE. Lastly, her internship in Fremantle provided the opportunity to write *Databases of the People aboard the VOC Ships Batavia (1629) & Zeewijk (1727)* (2012), of which a revised edition appeared as *Australia's Earliest European Graves* (2016). In all of Csilla's endeavors her aim is to engage people with stories of the past.